An Introduction to Assembly Language Programming and Computer Architecture

An Introduction to Assembly Language Programming and Computer Architecture

Joe Carthy
Department of Computer Science
University College Dublin

INTERNATIONAL THOMSON COMPUTER PRESS
I Ⓣ P An International Thomson Publishing Company

London • Bonn • Boston • Johannesburg • Madrid • Melbourne • Mexico City • New York • Paris
Singapore • Tokyo • Toronto • Albany, NY • Belmont, CA • Cincinnati, OH • Detroit, MI

An Introduction Assembly Language Programming and computer Architecture

British Library Cataloguing-in-Publication Data
A catalogue record for this book is available from the British Library

Library of Congress Cataloguing-in-Publication Data
A catalog record for this book is available from the Library of Congress

---

First printed 1996 and reprinted 1996, 1997, 1998 and 1999
Reprinted 2000 and 2001 by Thomson Learning

Commissioning Editor: Samantha Whittaker

Typeset in the UK by Tradespools Ltd
Printed in the UK by the Alden Group, Oxford

ISBN 1-85032-129-9

Thomson Learning
Berkshire House
High Holborn
London WC1V 7AA
UK

http://www.thomsonlearning.co.uk

Imprint of Thomson Learning

Dedicated to
my parents

Michael and Elizabeth Carthy

John Kelly
(1940–1995)

Two roads diverged in a wood, and I –
I took the one less travelled by,
And that has made all the difference.

Robert Frost

Table of Contents

Preface

This text is about two separate but related topics: assembly language programming and computer architecture. The text is based on a course for first-year computer science students given at University College Dublin (UCD). There are many fairly comprehensive texts dealing with either assembly language programming or computer architecture, but few actually cover both areas. I believe there is a need to treat both areas in an introductory textbook. It is not possible to study computer architecture in any depth without some knowledge of assembly language programming. Indeed, one of the reasons for studying assembly language programming is to gain an insight into how computers actually work, which naturally leads to a study of their architecture. Assembly language programming is difficult and many texts assume that the reader is already an experienced programmer. I believe it is possible to introduce a relative programming novice to assembly language programming. With this in mind, the first chapter of this text introduces and reviews basic programming concepts, using the C language for illustration purposes. The reader is then introduced to assembly language programming. Having mastered some fundamental assembly language programming concepts, the reader is well prepared to tackle the second part of the text, which aims to introduce the field of computer architecture to the beginner.

The assembly language of the world's most popular microprocessor family, the Intel 8086 family, is presented. In addition, M68000 assembly language programming is also briefly described. I believe that the best way to learn how to program is to write many small programs. This text presents many examples, which are included on the accompanying disk. The reader is encouraged to run these programs and to experiment with them. There are sufficient exercises to test the reader's understanding of the material and solutions are presented to a number of the exercises.

Once assembly language programming has been presented in Part I, Part II of the text goes on to describe the architecture of computers in simple language, explaining the technical jargon that newcomers to computing find so difficult and confusing. However, this discussion does not concern itself with the electronic details of computers, no more than a book on housing design would discuss the details of how bricks and nails are manufactured! A practical approach to the computer architecture is adopted with a view to giving the reader a good high-level understanding of this aspect of computing. The text presents case studies of state-of-the-art microprocessors such as Intel's Pentium and IBM/Motorola's PowerPC and also the well known Intel 8086 and Motorola 68000 families of microprocessors.

Structure

As already mentioned, the text is divided into two parts. Part I concentrates on assembly language programming and consists of four chapters. Chapter 1 is an informal introduction to programming using the C language. Chapter 2 introduces basic 8086 assembly language programming concepts. Chapters 3 and 4 describe 8086 programming in some detail, while Appendix C introduces M68000 assembly language programming.

Part II of the text concentrates on computer architecture and also consists of four chapters. Chapter 5 describes the hardware and software that make up a typical computer system. Chapter 6 introduces the basic concepts of computer architecture from the perspective of executing programs. Chapter 7 continues the discussion of computer architecture by looking at mechanisms (cache memory, pipelining and so on) that enhance the basic architecture presented in Chapter 6. Chapter 8 presents case studies of well known microprocessors: Intel's 8086 family (including the Pentium), Motorola's 68000 family, IBM/ Motorola's PowerPC and Digital's Alpha microprocessor.

Appendix A describes the units of measurement used in computing. Appendix B deals with information representation in a computing system, covering such topics as two's complement numbers and ASCII codes. Appendix C introduces M68000 programming. Appendix D describes how 8086 instructions are encoded in machine code. Appendix E outlines solutions to selected exercises presented in the earlier parts of the text. Finally, Appendix F explains what is included on the sample program disk.

The book need not, and probably should not, be read in the chapter order. The reader with little background in computing might begin with Chapter 5 to gain an overview of computer systems, before tackling the material in Part I. Appendix B dealing with information representation should, if necessary, be consulted during the reading of Chapters 2 to 4. A reader with high-level language programming experience need only review some of the final examples of Chapter 1 (since they are used as the basis for examples in later chapters).

Who should read this book?

The simple answer is anyone who is interested in understanding either assembly language programming or computer architecture. It is suitable for first-year computer science or engineering students taking degree or diploma-level courses. It is also suitable for computer enthusiasts wishing to advance their knowledge and programming skills.

Joe Carthy
November 1994

(E-mail: carthy@ccvax.ucd.ie)

Acknowledgements

There are many I wish to thank, for helping me along the way, so that I was in a position to write this book. The most precious gift that anyone can give is that of their time. A number of people and especially my family and friends have given me that gift in abundance.

First, I thank my late parents, Michael and Elizabeth Carthy. I owe them everything and I dedicate this book to their memory.

I wish to thank Rhona in a very special way for an indispensable contribution of time, energy, enthusiasm and support, as well as for proof-reading this (exciting!) material. Thanks to Beth and Sam for being there to keep us sane! These few words are very inadequate to express my gratitude.

I wish to thank my family for being a family! Special thanks are due to my sisters Mary and Ann (and their husbands Seamus and George!) for looking after me for many years. Thanks to Des and Mairead, Dec and Kay, John and Ann, Bernard and Niamh, Michael and Jean and Gerry and Carmel. I also must mention some junior family members: Julie, Sarah, James, Paul, Alan, Beth and Donnacha; Colin, Aoife, Elizabeth and George; Des, David, Shane and Elizabeth; Anita, Patrick, Richard and Patricia; Michael, John, Siobhan, Kieran and Claire; Brian, Conor and Sean; Emma, Michael and Elaine.

I am also grateful to Rhona's family for their support. Thanks to Maisie, Jack, Helen, Lainey and Fr. Seamus.

John Kelly was my guide and mentor, not only in this venture, but in so many different ways down through the years. Always a source of help and wisdom, he was most importantly my true and dear friend.

I wish to thank my colleagues in the Department of Computer Science at UCD for their support and kindness down through the years. I owe special thanks to Professor Frank Anderson for his ongoing support and encouragement. Thanks also to Professor John Dean for his friendship, support and advice. This text would not have been possible without the use of the department's resources. Indeed, thanks to all in UCD for providing such an excellent work environment.

I also wish to thank Professor Keith van Rijsbergen (University of Glasgow) for his patient help and guidance, which has proved invaluable to me.

I thank John Dunnion who, as well as being a loyal friend, frequently rescues me from technical problems.

Thanks to another friend, Tom Wade, for words of VAX wisdom! Thanks also to Brendan Byrne and Bernard Reardon for many insights into the world of computing. I wish to thank Patricia Geoghegan for looking after all of us in the computer science department.

I owe Damian Dalton a special acknowledgement for his very direct contribution to this text. Damian clarified many hardware mysteries for me (I accept responsibility for any errors!) and I would have had great difficulty in completing this work without his unstinting help and friendship.

I wish to thank Ann Marie for testing the programs and checking the text. Thanks too to Rotan, Duncan, Eamonn, Philip and Robert for their help and assistance.

I wish to thank Samantha Whittaker of ITP for her interest and encouragement. This book would not have materialized but for Samantha's prompting! Thanks also to Jonathan Simpson and David Penfold for all of their help.

I wish to mention a special place. Tubberduff has been and always will be dear to me. May God always smile upon it and those who live there.

Finally, I thank God, for everything!

'I can do all things through Christ who strengthens me'
(Paul's Letter to the Phillipians, Chapter 4, verse 13)

Part I
Introduction to Assembly Language Programming

- Chapter 1

  Computer programming: an informal introduction

- Chapter 2

  Assembly language concepts

- Chapter 3

  8086 assembly language programming

- Chapter 4

  8086 programming continued

1

Computer programming: an informal introduction

This chapter provides an informal introduction to computer programming and introduces the beginner to some fundamental programming concepts such as: input/output, variables and control flow. The C programming language is used to illustrate these concepts. C was chosen because of its widespread popularity and use as a programming language. Readers familiar with programming may skip this chapter, but if you are unfamiliar with the syntax of C, it is worth acquainting yourself with it, as the assembly language programs used in later chapters will be first presented in C. However, you should not be overly concerned with the details of the C language as C is only being used as a vehicle to illustrate programming concepts. There are many textbooks available for those interested in the C language but this is not one of them!

1.1 Overview

One point about programming must be clarified immediately: *Anyone can learn to program computers.* This statement may or may not surprise you. Many people have misconceptions about what skills you need to write computer programs, for example, whether you need to be logical or mathematical or interested in electronics? Our contention is, as already stated, that anyone can learn to program. However, you must be willing to spend some time studying and practising. The same applies to acquiring any skill, such as driving a car, learning to swim, learning to play poker and so on. You can view programming as a skill acquired from study, training and practice. In order to learn how to program you will sooner or later have to use a computer. Learning to use the computer is *a separate and independent* skill. In fact, strange as it may seem, you need to know very little about using computers in order to program them! At the minimum, you need to know how to switch on the computer, enter your program and have it executed. This can be mastered in about an hour! The important point is that using a computer is a separate skill to programming one. When you have problems, in your early days of programming, try to identify whether they have to do with *using* the computer or with your programming ability.

There are two aspects to programming that have to be mastered. One concerns *problem solving* and the other concerns the *programming language* that is to be used. You have to learn how to solve problems – this is the core of programming. However, you also have to learn a programming language in which to express your problem solution so that it can be implemented on a computer. Again, these are two separate skills. You must try not to confuse them. It is difficult, however, to explain one without reference to the other. In summary, the would-be programmer must acquire three skills:

- computing skills – how to switch on and use a computer
- problem-solving skills
- programming language skills.

1.1.1 Computing skills

These are the easiest to acquire and you most likely have them already. For the purposes of this text you need to know how to start your computer system and how to use a word processor (or editor) to enter your programs and save them. Finally, you need to be able to access a program called an assembler and a program called a linker and be able to use them so as to have your program executed.

1.1.2 Problem solving

Computer programming is about *problem solving*. Every computer program solves some particular problem, even programs to play games. It is impossible to write a computer program unless you *understand* the problem you are being asked to solve. In programming, *you*, not the computer, solve the problem. A computer program describes to the computer *what* it has to do and *how* it is to be done. *You* give the computer instructions in the form of a program, telling it what to do and how to do it. The set of instructions required to solve a problem is a **computer program**. It is also the solution to the problem because, when the computer follows these instructions, it will produce the *answer*, that is, the required results (assuming the program is correct). The term **algorithm** is used to describe the set of steps that solve a problem. An algorithm may be expressed in English or in a formal computer language, whereas a computer program must be expressed in a programming language. In programming, we first develop an algorithm for the problem at hand and then we translate this algorithm to a computer program so that it can be executed on a computer.

Sometimes we make mistakes in telling the computer what to do. We overlook part of the problem or do not understand what to do. In these cases, the computer program will not produce the 'right answer'. It is, however, still solving a problem; it is simply *not* the problem we wanted to solve. For this reason it is important to thoroughly check that your programs do indeed solve the problem you intended. It is important to note that this *testing* does not *prove* that the programs are correct, it shows that they are correct for the *tests used*. Program correctness is a major area in computer programming and is not addressed in this text.

An important principle concerning problem solving is that we can, and should, solve problems *independently of any programming language*. Only when we have solved a problem should we consider the programming language. Beginners find this hard to understand, but it is worth repeating: we do not need a programming language to solve problems. Of course, when it comes to actually implementing our solution and testing it, then we must use a programming language. We distinguish two phases in programming: the **problem solving phase** (**analysis** phase, **design** phase) and the **implementation phase.** It is very important to distinguish between these phases and keep the two separate. Beginners (and others!) continually make the mistake of rushing into the implementation without fully considering the problem to be solved. The seriousness of this mistake is not too obvious when we write short programs of a few dozen lines of code. We can easily scrap our ideas and start again. However, in large programs consisting of hundreds or thousands of lines of code, taking months to design and implement, such an error can be extremely costly, because it is very time-consuming to correct.

1.1.3 Problem-solving techniques

Given a problem to solve, where do we start? One important principle here is to 'divide and conquer'. In problem-solving terms this means taking your problem and dividing it into sub-problems. Then you tackle each one of these separately. If necessary, divide the sub-problems into further sub-problems. Continue this process of dividing into sub-problems and tackling each one separately until you can write the solution to each sub-problem. When you have solved all your sub-problems then you have, in effect, solved your initial problem. This technique is used in many aspects of problem solving. For example, if you have to decorate an entire house (a large problem), you typically divide the job into tasks to decorate the individual rooms. Taking each room, you create separate tasks of decorating the walls, ceilings and floors. When you have finished all of these smaller tasks, the whole house will have been decorated and the initial large problem solved. This same approach when applied to programming is called **top down programming** and is one of a number of programming techniques.

Another useful technique, which may be used in conjunction with the above, is to write down all of the **input** your program is going to work on. Then write down the **output** you expect the program to produce. Solving the problem then becomes a question of transforming or **processing** the input to produce the output. In order to write computer programs you must learn to instruct the computer how to perform input, processing and output operations. You must learn the instructions that correspond to these operations. These instructions are given to the computer in the form of a computer program which is written in a programming language.

1.2 Programming languages

Just as people use English, French, or German as languages to talk to each other, you must use a language to program a computer. There are many programming languages which can be used, including C, Pascal, COBOL, Ada, Fortran, LISP, Prolog, RPG II, ALGOL and BASIC. These are called **high-level** languages because they are problem oriented, that is, they are designed to help you solve problems. This means that they have facilities that make it easier to implement the solution to problems than so called **low-level** languages. There are also many low-level languages or **assembly languages** such as 8086 assembly language and **M68000** assembly language. In this text we describe 8086 assembly language programming (Appendix C introduces M68000 assembly language programming). It is more difficult to implement the solution to a problem in a low-level language.

Most programmers will, typically, be working with one language at any one time, although they may be familiar with several. It is important to note again that a knowledge of programming *techniques* is independent of any programming language. Armed with such a knowledge and a knowledge of one programming language, it is quite straightforward to learn another language. Put another way, *the first programming language you learn will be the most difficult.* It should be pointed out that the experience of learning a second or third language will serve you well in gaining a better understanding of programming.

One of the reasons for the variety of languages is that some languages are designed for particular kinds of problem. For example, **COBOL** is used in *commercial problem solving*, for example in accounting and banking; **Fortran** is oriented towards scientific and engineering problems; **C**, a relative newcomer, is quite versatile and is used in various applications from graphics to database management systems. Assembly languages are used where efficiency is extremely important or where other languages cannot be used because certain operations, which cannot be carried out using a high level language, can be carried out using assembly language.

As we noted earlier, a given problem can be solved *independently* of a programming language. You then have the choice of which language to use. Almost all languages will allow you to do the job but some make it easier by providing facilities that are useful for the particular task at hand. Often, the decision as to which language to use is easy – if you only know one language, you have no choice! Similarly, if your employer only wants COBOL programs, then you must program in COBOL. Ideally, you should choose the language with the facilities best suited for the problem at hand.

1.2.1 Language structure

All languages have a **grammar**. This is a set of rules about what constitutes a valid sentence in the language. A grammar helps people to communicate with each other. However, people can still understand each other when they make grammatical mistakes. For example, if I write: 'I am going to town and I will *bought* some things', you know that I have made a mistake and should have written *buy*, but you understand what I meant. This is a fundamental way in which computers, obeying the instructions in a program, *differ* from people. Basically, computers do not understand instructions, they simply carry them out. They must be given instructions that specify *exactly* what they have to do. If you make a mistake entering an instruction, a computer will not understand the instruction and it will display an **error** message. This message means that there is a mistake in your instructions – often a spelling error or a missing bracket or quotation mark. In a programming language, just as in English, you must always have the correct number of quotation marks and brackets. Left brackets such as (, { and [are called **opening brackets**. The quotation marks at the start of a phrase: " (double) and ' (single) are called **opening quotes**. Right brackets such as `)` , `}` and `]` are called **closing brackets** and quotation marks at the end of a phrase **closing quotes.** A simple rule is that for every opening bracket or quotation mark you must have a corresponding closing bracket or quotation mark.

Example 1.1

Matching brackets and quotes:

```
"Hello"
( a > 10 )
'x'
a[10]
```

The errors caused by misspellings or incorrect punctuation are called **syntax errors**. Each programming language has its own syntax. When you make a syntax error you may get an unhelpful message from the computer such as: `line 23 syntax error` which tells you that there is an error on line 23. You must figure out what is wrong. In fact, the error may be on a previous line, such as 21 or 22! The computer only detected that there was an error when it reached line 23.

What to do when an error occurs

When a syntax error occurs, you must work out what mistakes you have made. This means checking the statements of your program and seeing where the syntax is incorrect. You then **edit** your program using a word processor (or text editor) to correct the mistake. When you have corrected your program, it can be translated into machine language and executed. To **execute** or to **run** a program means that the computer carries out the instructions making up the program. This is just the same as starting a word processor or spreadsheet. They too are programs which you run and are no different from the programs you write. To a computer, all programs are the same, that is, they are all sets of instructions telling the computer what to do.

Statements

When people communicate in English or any language, they use sentences to convey information. When you write down a sentence in English you have a period, or full stop, at the end. This tells us where the sentence finishes. Without it, it would be difficult to read English text. You could call the period a **sentence terminator**, that is, it indicates the end of a sentence. Similarly, when you write programs you also use sentences to communicate with the computer. In programs, sentences are called **statements**. They also have a terminator. Different languages use different terminators. The C and Pascal languages use the semicolon '`;`' as the statement terminator. If you leave out the semicolon at the end of a statement, the computer will not know where one statement finishes and the next begins. This is a common syntax error. By convention, we write statements one per line as it makes them easier to read, but in C or Pascal we can write a number of statements on the same line, provided that each one is terminated by a semicolon.

1.2.2 Machine code.

Computers are primitive machines which only process instructions and data that are in binary form, that is, made up of 1s and 0s (See Appendix B). They cannot directly process instructions written in programming languages such as Pascal, C or 8086 assembly language. The language understood by a computer is called **machine code**. The first computer programs were written in machine code. Writing programs in machine code is a difficult and error-prone task. Better languages, which could be more easily understood by people, were developed as computing advanced. The first of these were the **assembly languages.** Then followed languages such as Fortran and COBOL. Remember that the machine can still only process machine code. So, in order to allow us to write programs in assembly language or C or COBOL (which *we* can more easily understand), these programs must be **translated** into the computer's machine code. This translation is carried out by computer programs called **translators**. There are different types of translators such as **assemblers** and **compilers.** Compilers take programs written in high-level languages, such as Fortran, C and COBOL, and translate them to machine code. They also check for syntax errors before producing the machine-code translation. If a translator discovers a syntax error, it displays an error message (as mentioned earlier). The translator will only produce a machine-code program if there are no syntax errors. The machine-code program is usually called an **executable** program. Assemblers are translators that are used for assembly languages such as 8086 or M68000 assembly language. Every type of computer will have its own specific compilers and assemblers.

1.2.3 Summary

Programming involves:

- solving problems;
- expressing this solution in a computer language in the form of a program;
- translating this program into machine language;
- executing and testing the program.

1.3 The C programming language

A C program is made up of a group of statements. Each one is terminated by a semicolon. These statements allow us to control the computer. Using them, we can display information on the screen, read information from the keyboard, store information on disk and retrieve it, and process information in a variety of ways. In this section we will study the statements that arise in writing programs. We can classify them as follows: I/O (input/output) statements, variable declaration statements, variable manipulation statements (for example, to do arithmetic) and conditional statements. We also look at the use of sub-programs, which enable to us to break large programs into meaningful units. Associated with the different types of statement is a set of special words called **reserved words (keywords)**. Every programming language has its own set of reserved words. These words have a special meaning in the language and can only be used for particular purposes. The following are some of the reserved words of the C language that will be used in this text: `int`, `float`, `char`, `if` and `while`. All program code and variable names will be printed using `typewriter face` in this text.

1.3.1 I/O statements: output

Output is the term used to describe information that the processor sends to peripheral devices, for example to display results on a screen or to store information in a disk file. One of the commonest forms of output is that of displaying a message on your screen. In C, we use `printf()` to display output on the screen. The following `printf()` statement will display the message `My name is Beth. This is my first program` on the screen:

```
printf ( "My name is Beth. This is my first program" );
```

This is a single C program statement. In order to have it executed, it must be part of a complete program. The complete C program to display the message is:

```
main()
{
  printf ( "My name is Beth. This is my first program" );
}
```

All C programs start with `main()` followed by an opening brace '`{`' and finish with a closing brace '`}`'. You may have as many statements as you wish between the braces. The braces are used to group a collection of statements together. Such a group is called a **compound** statement. A single statement is called a **simple** statement. A compound statement is treated as if it was a simple statement and may be used anywhere that a simple statement may be used. This is a very important feature of C (and any language providing compound statements, such as Pascal). Early versions of Fortran and BASIC do not provide compound statements and, as a result, it is more difficult to write programs in these languages.

1.3.2 I/O statements: input and variables

Input is the term used to describe the transfer of information from peripheral devices to the processor, for example, input may come from the keyboard or from a disk file. Before we describe input statements, let us consider where to store the information that is read in. We must arrange to store the input so that it can be processed. This introduces the concept of **variables**. A variable may be viewed as a container for a value. This solves our input problem. We input the data into a variable, but how do we identify this variable and distinguish it from other variables? The solution is simple, we give each variable a unique **name**, which we use to identify it. The statements:

```
char colour[80];
int age ;
```

define variables called `colour` and `age`. They tell the computer the names of the variables and what kind of information they will contain. In this case, `colour` will hold characters (up to 80 of them), while `age` will contain an integer (whole number). We call such statements **declarations**. We use the term **type** to describe the kind of information that may be stored in a variable, so that the variable `age` is of type integer. In C and Pascal, variables must be declared before they can be used. A common error is to omit the declaration of a variable. This error results in a syntax error message when we attempt to use the undeclared variable. Misspelling the variable name is another form of this error since the misspelled variable name will be treated as an undeclared variable. We can use any names we wish for variables with the exceptions of the reserved words mentioned earlier. It is a good idea to choose **meaningful** names for variables because it makes programs easier to understand.

Example 1.2

Consider a program to prompt users to enter their favourite colour. The program reads this colour and displays a message followed by the colour entered by the user. The program may be written in C as follows:

```
/* colour.c: program to prompt for colour and display a
message
Author: Joe Carthy
Date: 01/01/95                    */

main()
{
    char colour[80];      /* Variable to hold colour */

    printf("Enter your favourite colour: ");
    gets (colour);      /* Read colour from keyboard */
    printf("Yuk ! I hate %s", colour );
  }
```

If we execute the program the following appears on the screen (the bolded text is that entered by the user – we will use this convention throughout the text):

```
Enter your favourite colour: blue
Yuk ! I hate blue
```

The first statement in the program declares a variable called `colour`. Its type is that of a list of characters (also referred to as a **string**). The `printf()` statement is used to display the message which prompts for input. The statement `gets (colour);` reads text from the keyboard, for example the word `blue` may be entered and it places the text in the variable `colour`. The statement `printf("Yuk ! I hate %s", colour );` instructs the computer to display the message `Yuk ! I hate blue` on the screen. Note that `%s` does not appear on the screen, it has been replaced by the value of the variable `colour`, *blue* in this example. It is the method used to tell `printf()` to display the value of a variable. The name of the variable follows the message. The `%s` indicates to `printf()` that the variable contains text so that `printf()` can display it appropriately. We use `%d` to display integers and `%f` to display real numbers (numbers with a decimal point such as 3.14).

We often represent a computer's memory as a list of boxes or containers. A variable, as we have said, may be regarded as a container or a box in memory. Pictorially, we can represent the `colour` variable as a location in memory (in fact it occupies 80 locations in memory) as in Figure 1.1.

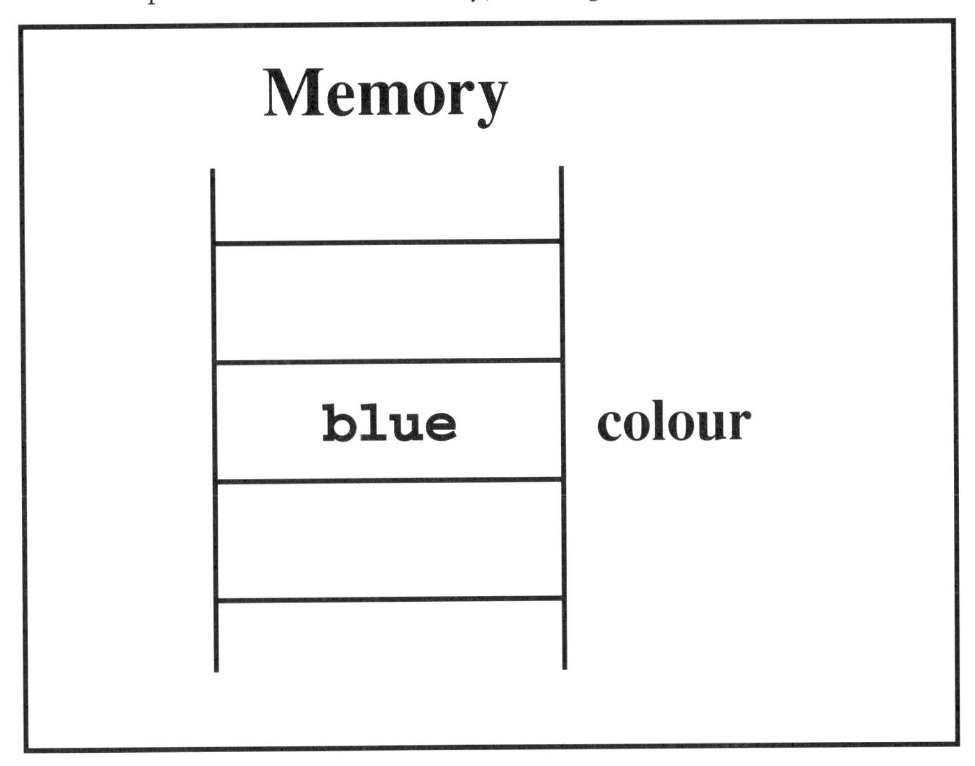

Figure 1.1 Memory variable colour.

We can use `gets()` to give values to **string** variables and `printf()` to display the value contained in *any* variable. We use the expression **'the value of a variable'** to mean **'the value contained in a variable'**. We take the phrase 'the value of `colour` is blue' to mean 'the value contained in the variable called `colour` is blue'. We will use the shorter form from now on.

From the above examples, we see that `printf()` has the ability to display messages enclosed in quotation marks. (Such a message is called a **string constant** as it will never change. A string constant is always enclosed in double quotes (") in the C programming language. Single quotes are used to specify a single character i.e. a character constant.) In addition, `printf()` can also display the values of variables. For example:

```
printf ( "What's your favourite colour" );
```

displays the string constant, inside the quotation marks on the screen, while

```
printf ( "%s", colour );
```

displays the value of the variable `colour`, which in this example is a string, that is, a list of characters. Make sure you understand the difference between:

```
printf( "colour" );
```

and

```
printf( "%s", colour );
```

In the first case, a string constant is displayed, so the word *colour* appears on the screen. In the second case, the value of a variable called `colour` is displayed which could be anything, for example the word *blue* or whatever value the user has given the variable, say *red, pink and orange*. There is nothing to prevent you storing more than one word in a string variable.

Comments

The text between `/*` and `*/` is called a **comment** and is ignored by the computer. The compiler, which translates the C program to machine code, ignores comments, which are intended as documentation to help explain, to someone reading the program, how the program works. Comments are an important component of programs. When you read your programs, some weeks or months after writing them, you may find them difficult to understand if you have not included comments to explain what you were doing. They are even more important if someone else will have to read your programs, for example your tutor who is going to grade them! It is useful to give, as the first comment in any program, the name of the file containing the program, the author's name and the date on which the program was written, as shown in Example 1.2.

1.3.3 More about variables: assignment statement

In Example 1.2 we saw that we can directly input a value into a variable. There is also another way to give variables a value. It is called **assignment**. It allows us to give a value to the variable directly in a program without input. We may give the variable a constant value or compute a value based on the values of other variables. For example, suppose we have a variable called `feet`, to which we wish to give the value 12. In C we write:

```
feet = 12 ;
```

This can be read as 'feet is **assigned** the value 12' or 'feet **becomes** 12'. Of course, we could use any value instead of 12. Other examples of assigning values to variables might be:

```
feet = 130;
ins = 10;
metres = 4;
```

We assume that the above variables have already been declared as either integers or reals (called **floats** in C). The following statement would declare the variables as floats (which means that they store real numbers):

```
float feet, ins, metres;
```

Alternatively they could have been declared as **integers** (which means that they must store whole numbers):

```
int feet, ins, metres;
```

Note that we can declare a number of variables in a single declaration. The variable names are separated by a comma, the omission of which is another common syntax error.

Example 1.3

Consider a program to convert feet to inches. A simple (and fairly useless) C program to do this is given below. This is version 1 of the program, other versions are developed as we proceed through the chapter.

```
/* convert.c: converts feet to inches. Version 1.
Author: Joe Carthy
Date: 01/01/95                    */

main()
{
  int feet, inches ;

  feet = 10;
  inches = feet * 12 ;
  printf("The number of inches is %d \n", inches ) ;
}
```

Executing this program produces as output:

```
The number of inches is 120
```

Pictorially, after execution of the second assignment statement, the variables in memory may be visualized as in Figure 1.2. Here we use the value of one variable (`feet`) to compute the value of another variable (`inches`).

Other examples of such an assignment are:

```
pints = gallons * 8;
cms = (km * 100000) + (m * 1000);
```

where the values of variables on the right hand side are used to compute the values assigned to the variables on the left hand side of the assignment.

Note: The character `\n` (called newline) is used in the `printf()` statement in Example 1.3 to cause the next output to go onto a new line. This character can appear anywhere in a string. The following `printf()` statements illustrate the use of `\n`:

```
printf("\n This message appears on a new line followed by a
blank line \n\n");
printf("three\nfour\nfive\n") ;
```

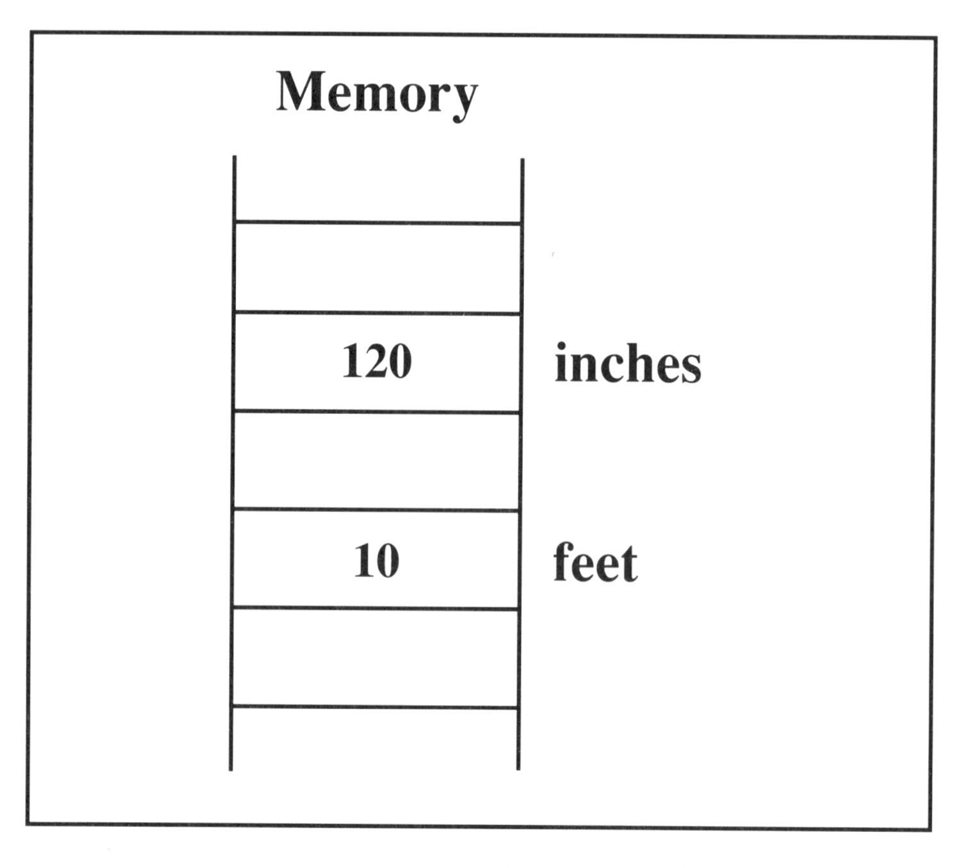

Figure 1.2 Memory variables: feet and inches.

They would produce as output:

```
This message appears on a new line followed by a blank line

three
four
five
```

The program to convert feet to inches, as presented in Example 1.3, is very limited in that it always produces the same answer. It always converts the same quantity of feet (10) to inches. A more useful version would prompt the user to enter the number of feet to be converted and display the appropriate result.

Example 1.4

Converting feet to inches, version 2:

```
/* convert2.c: convert feet to inches. Version 2
Author: Joe Carthy
Date: 01/01/95                  */
```

```
main()
{
  int feet, inches ;
  printf("Enter quantity of feet: ");

  scanf("%d", &feet ) ;
  inches = feet * 12 ;
  printf('The number of inches is %d\n', inches ) ;
}
```

Executing this program produces as output:

```
Enter quantity of feet: 4
The number of inches is 48
```

The statement `scanf( "%d", &feet );` reads a whole number from the keyboard into the variable `feet`. The `&` character is vital and `scanf()` will not function properly without it. Yes, it has a messy look to it, but (unfortunately!) in the C programming language, this is one of the common methods for reading numbers. The `%d` tells `scanf()` to read a whole number; `%f` is used to read a real number; `%c` to read a character and `%s` to read a string (which may not contain a space or tab character; in other words, it reads a single word).

Example 1.5

As another example of the use of I/O and variables consider a simple calculator program. This program prompts for two numbers, adds them and displays the sum:

```
/* calc.c: calculator program
Author: Joe Carthy
Date: 01/01/95                    */

main()
{
  int num1, num2, sum;

  printf('Enter first number: ');
  scanf('%d', &num1 );
  printf('Enter second number: ');
  scanf('%d', &num2 );

  sum = num1 + num2 ;

  printf('The sum of %d and %d is %d \n', num1, num2, sum);
}
```

Executing this program produces as output:

```
Enter first number: 14
Enter second number: 10
The sum of 14 and 10 is 24
```

Note that in this program we illustrate that a single `printf()` can display the value of a number of variables, in this case the values of three variables.

Arrays

We encountered arrays already in Example 1.2 where `colour` was declared as a list or array of characters. An array is a named list of items, such as characters or integers. It is an example of what is called a **data structure**. To declare an array we specify its name, its type and the number of elements in the list, for example `char colour[80]` or `int months[12]`, the first of which is a list of 80 characters called `colour`; the second is a list of 12 integers called `months`.

To access an element of an array, we use its position in the list, that is, its **index** or **subscript**, so that `colour[0]` refers to the first element in the `colour` array, `months[10]` refers to the `11`th element in the `months` array. The C language specifies that arrays begin with subscript `0`. While this may seem unnatural, it is quite common in computing to count from 0. For example, locations in memory are numbered (addressed) from 0 upwards. It is important to note that the subscripts for `colour`, as defined above, range from 0 to 79 and not to 80; similarly the subscripts for `months` range from `0` to `11` and not up to `12`. So, for any array in C, the elements go from 0 to `size -1` where `size` is the number of array elements specified in the declaration of the array. This still gives us `size` elements in the array. It is a common error to attempt to access an array element that does not exist. For example, many beginners attempt to use the element `months[12]`, which will usually cause the program to crash, often with an esoteric error message such as 'bus error' or 'segmentation fault'. If you get either of these messages it generally means that you have an array subscripting error. Such an error is sometimes described as 'array subscript out of bounds' error.

Records

Another data structure of importance in programming is the **record** (called a **structure** in C). It is a collection of variables, treated as a unit. You are no doubt familiar with records such as personnel records and bank account records. A personnel record might include a name, address, age and department information. It is convenient to keep this information as a unit for each employee. In C such a record might be declared as:

```
struct personnel
{
  char name[60];
  char address[80];
  int age;
  char department[20];
}
```

In essence we have defined a *new type* for variables called `personnel`. Variables of type `personnel` can be declared as:

```
struct personnel person, person1;
```

Thus person is a variable of type personnel. The parts that make up the record are called **fields** and are accessed by giving the variable name, followed by a period, followed by the field name, for example person.name, person.age, person.address. The fields may be treated as normal variables; the fact that they are part of a record does not alter the way you operate on them. Records are convenient because an entire record may be written to a file (or read from a file) in a single operation.

1.3.4 Symbolic constants

In Example 1.4 the number 12 (number of inches in a foot) is a constant. It will never change when we run the program. In mathematics, we often give constants a name such as **pi**, rather than writing down the actual value. This idea is also used in programming. We can give each constant a symbolic name like a variable name. We then use this name in our code instead of the actual value. The two main advantages of using constants are first that they make programs easier to read and understand. Second, if you need to change the value of a constant, you have only to change one statement in your code, where you give the constant value its name (where the constant is **defined**). Each language which provides the facility to define constants has its own syntax for doing so. As a convention, we use uppercase letters for the names of constants so that we can distinguish them from variable names. In C, we use a directive called #define to define a constant. A **directive** is a command to the language translator (in this case the C preprocessor). The #define directive allows us to define names for constant values. Before the C compiler is invoked to translate the program to machine code, the C preprocessor replaces each occurrence of the constant name by the actual value. Constants are defined at the start of the program before main().

As an example, consider the following statement to compute sales tax at a rate of 12%:

```
tax = total_price * 0.12 ;
```

If we compute the sales tax in a number of places in our program, then the constant 0.12 will occur in a number of places. If the sales tax changes at some future point to 14%, we must search through the program and replace all occurrences of 0.12 by 0.14. By using a symbolic constant, we can make this much easier. The constant would be defined once at the start of the program as follows:

```
#define   SALES_TAX   0.12
```

and it can be used in any subsequent statement as follows:

```
tax = total_price * SALES_TAX ;
```

From the above code, you can see how easy it is to change the program to take account of a change in the tax rate. You simply change the value of the constant in the `#define` directive. In each statement where the constant appears, it will be replaced by the correct value. It is very important to note that constants are not variables. They take on one value and maintain it for ever; hence their name.

It is also important to note that C is a **case-sensitive language.** This means that it distinguishes between upper- and lower-case letters. Keywords (such as `if, while, int, float` etc.) must be entered in lower case. Variables with names having the same spelling but in a different case are treated as *different* variables. So the names `Feet`, `FEET`, `feet` and `fEeT` represent different variables from the C language's point of view. This gives rise to many syntax errors for beginners. As a convention, many C programmers spell variable names in lower-case letters. Upper-case letters are usually used for constants. This allows you to distinguish easily between constants and variables when reading a program. This is only a convention or **style** of programming. A good programming style enhances the readability of programs. Programmers usually develop their own individual styles. The important point is to be consistent; for example, if you use upper-case letters for constants, then make sure you do so for all constants in your program.

Fundamental principles:

- Variables have a name and type which are specified in the variable declaration.
- Variables store values generated by either an assignment or an input statement.

These two principles are fundamental to writing computer programs.

1.3.5 Summary

So far we have written a number of useful programs and you should now be familiar with two basic concepts: **input/output (I/O)** and the use of variables. A feature of the programs presented so far is that the statements are executed sequentially (one after the other). No statements have been repeated or skipped. We now go on to look at conditional statements, which allow us to alter the order (called the **flow of control**) in which statements are executed.

Exercises

1.1 Write a program to prompt the user to enter a name. The program should read the name and display 'Hello' followed by the name, for example `Hello Sam`.

1.2 Write a program to convert metres to centimetres.

1.3 Modify the calculator program to do subtraction instead of addition.

1.4 Conditional statements

People are used to making decisions. For example, consider the following sentences:

- If I get hungry, then I will eat my lunch.
- If it gets cold, then I will wear my coat.

These two sentences are called **conditional sentences.** Such sentences have two parts: a **condition** ('If I get hungry', 'If it gets cold') and an **action** ('I will eat my lunch', 'I will wear my coat'). The action will be only be carried out *if* the condition is satisfied. To test if the condition is satisfied we can rephrase the condition as a question with a *yes* or *no* answer. In the case of the first sentence, the condition may be rephrased as 'Am I hungry ?' If the answer to the question is *yes*, then the action will be carried out (the lunch gets eaten!), otherwise the action is not carried out. We say the **condition is true** (**evaluates** to true) in the case of a *yes* answer. We say the **condition is false** (evaluates to false) in the case of a *no* answer. Only when the condition is true will we carry out the action. This is part of how we handle decisions on a daily basis.

In programming, we have exactly the same concept. We have **conditional statements.** They operate exactly as described above. One of the most fundamental of these is known as the `if-then` statement. This statement allows us to test a condition and carry out an action if the condition is true. In C, the keyword `if` is used for such a statement and there is **no** `then` keyword. As an example, we could modify the program to convert feet to inches to test if the value of feet is positive (greater than 0) before converting it to inches. We could write the program as follows, noting that a condition in C is **always** enclosed in parentheses `( )`.

Example 1.6

Converting feet to inches, version 3:

```
/* convert3.c: convert feet to inches. Version 3
Author: Joe Carthy
Date: 01/01/95                    */
main()
{
  int inches, feet ;
  printf("Enter quantity of feet: ");
  scanf("%d", &feet ) ;

  if ( feet > 0 )     /* is feet > 0 ? */
  {
    inches = feet * 12 ;
    printf("%d feet = %d inches \n", feet, inches);
  }

  if ( feet <= 0 )     /* is feet < 0 ? */
  {
    printf("Please enter a positive value for feet \n");
    printf("You entered %d \n", feet);
  }
}
```

Executing this program with -42 as input produces as output:

```
Enter quantity of feet: -42
Please enter a positive value for feet
You entered -42
```

The first `if` statement tests if the value of `feet` is greater than `0`. If this is the case then the conversion is carried out and the result displayed. Otherwise, if the value of `feet` is not greater than `0`, this does not happen, that is, the action statements are skipped. The second `if` statement tests if `feet` is less than or equal to `0`. If this is the case, then the message to enter a positive value is displayed. If this is not the case, the `printf()` is skipped and the program terminates. In this particular example, only one of the conditions can evaluate to true since they are mutually exclusive; `feet` cannot be greater than `0` and, at the same time, be less than or equal to `0`. Because this type of situation arises very frequently in programming, that is, we wish to carry out some statements when a condition is true and other statements when the same condition is false, a special form of the `if-then` statement is provided called the `if-then-else` statement (we omit the `then` keyword in C). We rewrite the above program to illustrate its usage.

Example 1.7

Converting feet to inches, version 4:

```
/* convert4.c: convert feet to inches. Version 4
Author: Joe Carthy
Date: 01/01/95                    */

main()
{
  int inches, feet ;
  printf("Enter quantity of feet: ");
  scanf("%d", &feet ) ;

  if ( feet > 0 )
  {
    inches = feet * 12 ;
    printf("%d feet = %d inches \n", feet, inches);
  }
  else
  {
    printf("Please enter a positive value for feet \n");
    printf("You entered %d \n", feet);
  }
}
```

This program performs exactly the same function as that in Example 1.6. However, it is more efficient in that only one condition has to be evaluated, whereas in Example 1.6 two conditions have to be evaluated.

There are only six types of condition that can arise when comparing two values. They can be tested for equality (are they the same?), inequality (are they different?); is one greater than the other?; is one less than the other?; is one greater than or equal to the other?; and finally is one less than or equal to the other? The following illustrates how to write the various conditions to compare the variable `feet` to the value 0 in C:

`( feet == 0 )`	is `feet` equal to 0?
`( feet != 0 )`	is `feet` not equal to 0?
`( feet > 0 )`	is `feet` greater than 0?
`( feet < 0 )`	is `feet` less than 0?
`( feet >= 0 )`	is `feet` greater than or equal to 0?
`( feet <= 0 )`	is `feet` less than or equal to 0?

Technically, the symbols `==`, `!=` (or <>), `<`, `>`, `<=` and `>=`, are called **relational operators**, since they are concerned with the relationship between values. We call a condition (say `feet < 0`) a **Boolean expression**. This simply means that there are only two possible values (**true** or **false**) which the condition can yield. The term **expression** is widely used in programming. Informally it means something that yields a value. We are familiar with arithmetic expressions such as 2+2 which evaluates to 4. A Boolean expression is one which evaluates to either true or false. Examples of expressions include constants (`0`, `100`, `"a"`), variables (`feet`, `inches`) and arithmetic expressions (`feet * 12`, `4/8`). The right-hand side of an assignment statement is always an expression.

Example 1.8

As another example, let us modify the calculator program (Example 1.5) to handle either subtraction or addition. The user is prompted for the first number, then for a plus or minus character to indicate the operation to be carried out and finally for the second number. The program calculates and displays the appropriate result:

```
/* calc2.c: calculator program. Version 2
Author: Joe Carthy
Date: 01/01/95                    */

main()
{
  int num1, num2, sum;
  char operation, dummy ;

  printf("Enter first number: ");
  scanf("%d", &num1 );
  printf("Enter operation (+ or -): ");
  scanf("%c%c%c",&dummy, &operation, &dummy);
  printf("Enter second number: ");
  scanf("%d", &num2 );
```

```
    if ( operation == "+" )
    {
      sum = num1 + num2 ;
      printf("The sum of %d and %d is %d \n", num1, num2, sum);
    }

    if ( operation == "-" )
    {
      sum = num1 - num2 ;
      printf("Subtracting %d from %d equals %d \n", num2,
      num1, sum);
    }
}
```

Executing this program produces as output:

```
Enter first number: 9
Enter operation (+ or -): -
Enter second number: 4
Subtracting 4 and 9 equals 5
```

The statement `scanf("%c%c%c", &dummy, &operation, &dummy);` is messy! The reason for reading three characters is that the Return character (`"\n"`) must be entered before `scanf()` reads the first number entered. However, `scanf()` leaves the Return character available for input, so that the next `scanf()` will read it as its first character, so we must arrange to read this Return character, in the second `scanf()`. Then we read the operation to be carried out, here a + or - character, which also must be followed by a Return character. This Return character will also be left available for input, so we remove it as well, so that it does not interfere with the entry of the second number. Characters entered at the keyboard are stored in an area of memory called an **input buffer**. Sub-programs to read characters remove them from this buffer. The problem with `scanf()` is that it does not remove the `"\n"` automatically. Figure 1.3 illustrates the input buffer (as if no characters had been removed) for the characters entered in the above example. While this level of detail is confusing, it highlights a common problem that can arise when using `scanf()` to read characters and numbers in C programs.

Fundamental principles:

- A condition can only evaluate to true or false.
- The action associated with a condition is carried out only if the condition is true.

Tip: To evaluate a condition, simply re-phrase it as a question. The answer is *yes* for true and *no* for false.

1.4.1 Summary

Conditions are basically comparisons. We compare two values and, based on the comparison (whether it is true or false), we take a certain course of action.

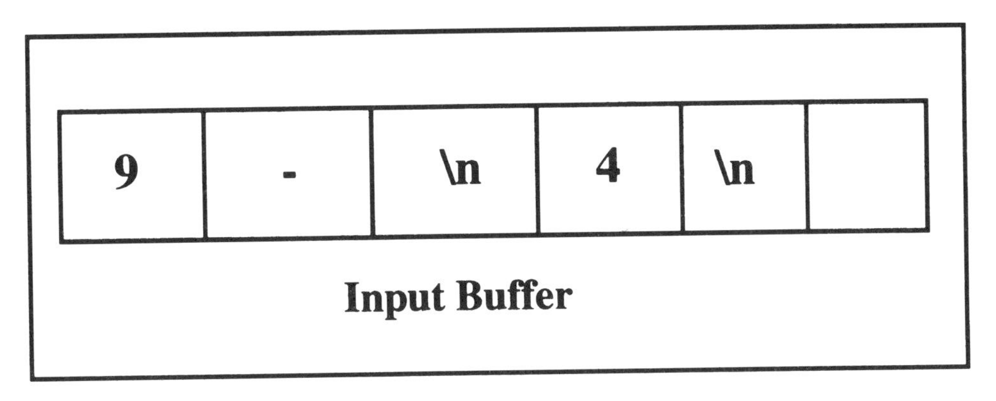

Figure 1.3 Keyboard input buffer containing characters entered for Example 1.3.

Conditional statements allow you to alter the control flow in a program. They are thus called **control structures**. There are two basic types of control structure in programming. The `if` and `if else` statements are called **selection** control structures. They allow you to select an alternative action, that is, you make a decision as to what to do next. The other type of control structure is the **loop** (also called the **iteration** control structure). A loop allows you repeatedly to execute a statement. This is the subject of the next section.

Exercises

1.4 Modify the calculator program to handle multiplication and division as well as addition and subtraction.

1.5 Write a program to read two different numbers and display which is the larger and which is the smaller of them.

1.6 Write a program to simulate a cash register for a single purchase. The program should read the unit cost (real number) of an item and the numbers of items purchased. The program should display the total cost for the items. If the unit cost is greater than 1000, the program should display an error message. [Hint: %f should be used in `scanf()` and `printf()` to handle real numbers.]

1.5 Loops: repeating parts of a program

So far, all of our programs have carried out one major task, such as converting a single quantity of feet to inches. Frequently, we wish to repeat such a calculation. Say we have 30 values for feet, which we wish to convert to inches. We would have to run the program described earlier 30 times to achieve the desired result. Instead, we would like to be able to repeat part of the program 30 times, that is, allow the program to repeat, 30 times, the process of reading a value to be converted and displaying the result. Programming languages provide such a facility. It is another fundamental programming concept which must be mastered. It is called **looping** (or **iteration**).

1.5.1 The `while` loop

There are a number of looping techniques but basically all program looping can be performed using one particular looping construct called a `while` loop (the other mechanisms are provided for convenience). Loops are another form of conditional statement. In the case of a loop, we use the condition to decide whether to repeat a statement or not. We repeat the statement based on the evaluation of the condition in a similar fashion to carrying out the action part of an `if` statement. The action part of a loop is referred to as the **loop body**. This may be a simple or compound statement. The loop body is executed only if the condition evaluates to true; the condition is then re-evaluated to test if it is still true. If it is true, we repeat execution of the loop body and test the condition again. This process continues until the condition evaluates to false.

In certain situations, the condition will never evaluate to false and the loop will continue to execute endlessly. Such a loop (usually the result of a programming error!) is called an **endless** or **infinite** loop. An endless loop may be terminated by interrupting the program or switching off the computer, both of which terminate the program as well. A combination of keys is pressed to interrupt a program such as pressing the control key and the C key simultaneously (denoted by Ctrl/C). The operating system detects the interrupt and terminates the program.

Example 1.9

Modify the calculator program of Example 1.5 to sum ten pairs of numbers. In other words, we wish to read in the two numbers to be summed, calculate the sum and display the result, ten times, by running the program once. We use a `while` loop to repeat the necessary statements:

```
/* calc3.c: calculator program. Version 3
Author: Joe Carthy
Date: 01/01/95                    */

main()
{
  int count, sum, num1, num2;

  count = 0;
  while ( count < 10 )
  {                   /* Loop Body */
    printf("Enter first number: ");
    scanf("%d", &num1 );
    printf("Enter second number: ");
    scanf("%d", &num2 );

    sum = num1 + num2 ;

    printf("The sum of %d and %d is %d \n", num1, num2, sum);
    count = count + 1 ;      /* Guarantees loop halts */
  }
```

```
  printf("Calculator program terminated\n");
}
```

Executing this program produces as output:

```
Enter first number: 4
Enter second number: 6
The sum of 4 and 6 is 10
Enter first number: 20
Enter second number: 30
The sum of 20 and 30 is 50
Enter first number: 65
  .........
  .........
Calculator program terminated
```

The `while` statement tests the condition `(count < 10)` and if it evaluates to true, the statements in the loop body are executed and the condition is re-evaluated. If the condition is false we simply skip the action specified by the loop body; in this example we execute the final `printf()` statement and the program terminates.

Each time we execute the loop body (go around the loop) we process one pair of numbers and add 1 to `count`. The variable `count` is used in this example to control how many times we execute the loop body. So after going around ten times, `count` will have the value `10`. Each time you go around the loop the condition is tested. You only execute the loop body if the result is true. So when `count` has value `10`, we leave the loop (the loop **terminates**), that is, we go to the next statement after the loop body if there is one. What would happen if we omitted the statement

```
count = count + 1 ;
```

from the loop body? This is a very common error to make when using loops. If we omit the statement to increment `count`, the loop will never terminate as `count` will always be less than `10`. Such an error is a **logical** or **runtime** error. These differ from syntax errors because the program can be executed but produces incorrect results. For this reason, they are a more serious error than syntax errors. It is very difficult to ensure that there are no logical errors in large programs. Thorough testing of programs may increase our confidence that a program is correct, but such testing on its own can never establish the correctness of a program. It is important to bear this fact in mind and it is worth while investigating the area of program correctness.

Example 1.10

Write a program to sum the integers 1 to 99 (calculate the sum of 1+2+3+...+99) and display the result:

```
/* sum.c: calculate 1+2+3+.....+99
Author: Joe Carthy
Date: 01/01/95                  */
main()
{
  int i, sum ;
  sum = 0 ;
  i = 1 ;

  whilc ( i <= 99 )
  {
    sum = sum + i ;
    i = i + 1 ;
  }

  printf("Summation is : \n", sum) ;
}
```

Executing this program produces as output:

```
Summation is : 4950
```

The loop body is executed only if the condition `(i <= 99)` evaluates to true. Since we have **initialized** `i` to `1` (the first value assigned to a variable is called the **initial** value) the condition evaluates to true and the loop body is executed. In the loop body, a running total for `sum` is calculated by adding the value of `i` to `sum`, that is, `sum` is assigned the value `sum + i`. The variable `i` is then increased by 1. We then test the condition again. The variable `i` now has the value 2 and the condition `(i <= 99)` remains true, so we execute the loop body assigning `sum` the value 3 (1+2) and increasing `i` to 3. Next time around the loop `sum` becomes 6 (3+3) and `i` becomes 4. We test the condition again and continue in this manner until `i` eventually reaches the value 100. When we test the condition, in this case, it evaluates to false (`i` is greater than `99`) and so the loop body is not executed. Instead we continue at the first statement after the loop body, the `printf()` statement.

Note: If a condition evaluates to false the first time it is tested then the loop body will not be executed.

Variable initialization

In the last two examples it is crucial that the variables `count` and `i` are initialized to appropriate values for the loop to operate correctly. As a general programming principle, all variables should be initialized to appropriate values, usually at the beginning of a program. If you do not initialize a variable, you cannot be sure what value it may contain (sometimes `0` for numbers). A program may not run correctly if you use the value of an uninitialized variable based on the assumption that it contains something sensible like 0.

How many iterations?

Frequently, we will not know in advance how many times to repeat a loop, so that we cannot use the `while` loop in the manner presented in Examples 1.9 and 1.10. In Example 1.11 we rewrite the calculator program to continue calculating for as long as the user requires. The user may wish to sum one pair of numbers or 100 pairs. The user indicates if they wish to finish by entering 0 as the first number. This type of loop is sometime referred to as a **non-deterministic** loop, as you do not know in advance how many times it will be repeated.

Example 1.11

Sum pairs of numbers until 0 entered:

```
/* calc4.c: sums until the user enters 0 as the first number.
Version 4.
Author: Joe Carthy
Date: 01/01/95                    */

main()
{
  int num1, num2, sum;

  num1 = -1;        /* Any non-zero value will do */

  printf("To exit: enter 0 as value for first number \n");
  while ( num1 != 0 )
  {               /* Loop Body */
    printf("Enter first number: ");
    scanf("%d", &num1 );
    if ( num1 != 0 )          /* 0 means we are finished */
    {
      printf("Enter second number: ");
      scanf("%d", &num2 );

      sum = num1 + num2 ;

      printf("The sum of %d and %d is %d
\n",num1,num2,sum);
    }
  }

  printf("Calculator program terminated\n");
}
```

In this example, we continue to execute the loop body as long as the user enters a non-zero value for `num1`. The loop body will always be executed once in *this* example. *Why?* Because the loop condition will always be true when the program begins execution, since num1 is defined to be -1. As an exercise, you should rewrite the above program so that the user is prompted for input before the loop body is executed.

1.5.2 Debugging with loops

If you have difficulty understanding loops, it is a good idea when you implement any of the above programs to put a printf() statement in the loop body, so that you can see how often the loop is repeated. For example, statements such as the following could be used in the examples presented earlier:

```
  printf("count = ", count);  /* feet conversion program
*/
  printf("sum = ", sum);  /* sequence summation program
*/
```

This is also a useful debugging technique. **Debugging** is the term used for finding and correcting errors (**bugs**) in your program. By placing printf() statements in your code, you can **trace** the execution of your program, inspecting the values of variables and checking if loops are executed the correct number of times. A printf() in the action part of an if statement allows you to verify that the action was indeed carried out. When your program is working correctly, these printf() statements are removed.

There are programs called **debuggers** which allow you to execute your programs in an editor-like environment. They allow you to stop your program at any statement you wish (called a **break point**) and display the values of variables. You may even change the value of a variable and resume the execution of your program. They are very useful tools for programmers. Programming is often carried out in an integrated environment which allows you to edit, compile, run and debug programs. Borland's TurboC and Microsoft's QuickC are examples of such environments.

1.5.3 Nested loops

A loop may contain, as part of its loop body, any statement including another loop (called an inner loop or **nested loop**). The nested loop may in turn contain a loop as part of its loop body and so on.

Example 1.12

Write a program to display 10 lines so that there is one star ('*') on line 1, two stars on line 2, three stars on line 3 and so on. The output should appear as follows:

```
*
**
***
****
.......
```

The program is:

```
/* triangle.c: displays triangle composed of *'s
Author: Joe Carthy
Date: 01/01/95                          */

main()
{
  int stars, lines ;

  lines = 1;
  while (lines <= 10)        /* outer loop */
  {
    stars = 1 ;
    while (stars <= lines)      /* inner loop: displays * on
                each line */
    {
      printf("*");
      stars = stars + 1;
    }
    printf("\n");            /* start a new line */
    lines = lines + 1;
  }
}
```

The inner loop displays the correct number of * characters on each line. The outer loop controls the number of lines displayed.

1.5.4 *The* `for` *loop*

There is another form of loop construct called the `for` loop. It is used when we know the number of times we wish to repeat the loop body. In a high-level language it is written in a form similar to:

```
for i := 1 to 60 do       /* this is NOT C code */
{
  /* loop body statements */
  }
```

This loop specifies that the statements in the loop body are to be repeated 60 times. The variable `i` is called the **loop counter** and is automatically incremented by 1 during each iteration of the loop body in a `for` loop. Any variable may be used as a loop counter. The C syntax of the `for` loop above is somewhat messy:

```
for ( i = 1; i <= 60; i = i + i; )
{
  /* loop body */
}
```

The `for` loop does not provide extra power. We can achieve the same effect, as we have seen in our earlier examples, with a `while` loop. The `for` loop is a convenient notation that is useful in certain cases to make programs easy to read.

Exercises

1.7 Modify the feet conversion program to cater for the conversion of five values.

1.8 Modify the feet conversion program to allow users to process as many values as they wish. The program should ask the user to enter `"y"` to continue. See Example 1.8 as regards reading characters and numbers.

1.9 Write a program to read ten integers, sum them and calculate the average. The program should display the sum and the average.

1.10 Write a program to allow you to enter as many numbers as you wish. The program should sum the numbers and calculate the average. You may use `0` as the value used to indicate that you are finished entering numbers. Such a value is called a **sentinel**.

1.5.5 The `goto` Statement

As mentioned before, conditional statements allow you to alter the flow of control in a program so as to take alternative actions or repeat actions. We refer to `if` and `while` statements as control structures, which allow you to define, in a clear manner, the flow of control in your program. The `goto` statement is another statement that allows you to alter control flow. It allows you to branch **unconditionally** to another statement in your program. A **label** is used to identify the statement to which to branch.

Example 1.13

Write a program using `goto` statements to sum the integers 1 to 10:

```
/* goto.c: sample program using goto statement
Author: Joe Carthy
Date: 01/01/95                    */

main()
{
  int i, sum ;

    i = 1 ;
    sum = 0 ;
```

```
start:  if ( i > 10)        /* start labels this statement */
          {
          goto finish ;     /* transfer control to finish */
          }
          sum = sum + i ;
          i = i + 1 ;
          goto start ;        /* transfer control to start */


finish:  printf("Sum = %d\n", sum);
}
```

The goto statements in the above code implement a loop to sum the integers. The label start (any name may be used) is defined once and is followed by a colon (:). It may be used in any number of goto statements where the colon will be omitted. Since the first goto statement is in the action part of an if statement, it will only be executed when the condition (i > 10) is true. The second goto statement will transfer control to the statement labelled start each time it is executed.

The goto statement should only be used if absolutely necessary, which in high-level language programs is quite rare. This is because the use of the goto statement can make a program very difficult to read and to reason about. The usual conditional statements should be used if at all possible. There is a form of programming called **structured programming**, which, among other things, advocates using well defined control structures. The goto statement has a poor reputation among advocates of structured programming, some of whom believe it should never be used. On some occasions, its use can improve the clarity of a program and a balanced approach to using the goto statement should be adopted.

The reason for discussing the goto statement is that in assembly language programming, instructions similar to goto are the only ones available for implementing control structures such as while loops and if-then structures. Assembly language does not provide high-level control structures. This is one of the reasons why assembly language programs can be difficult to read.

It is also worth noting, at this point, that in high-level languages the use of compound statements (groups of statements treated as if they were a single statement) is fundamental to the clarity of conditional statements. Consider the two code fragments in Example 1.14, which carry out the same function, one using compound statements and the other not using them:

Example 1.14

Implementing a code fragment with and without compound statements.

```
/* Using compound statements */
```

```
    if ( feet > 0 )
    {
      inches = feet * 12 ;
      printf("%d feet = %d inches \n", feet, inches);
    }
    else
    {
      printf("Please enter a positive value for feet \n");
      printf("You entered %d \n", feet);
    }

  /* An implementation without using compound statements */

    if ( feet > 0 )
      goto then1 ;

      printf("Please enter a positive value for feet \n");
      printf("You entered %d \n", feet);
      goto endif ;

  then1:  inches = feet * 12 ;
      printf("%d feet = %d inches \n", feet, inches);
  endif:
```

The second code fragment is considerably more difficult to understand and is obviously to be avoided if possible. In languages without compound statements, such as Fortran and BASIC (or at least their early versions), we have no choice but to use `goto` statements. Similarly, in assembly language programming this type of solution is the only one possible. Assembly language does not provide compound statements and high-level control structures are not provided *directly*. Thus, in order to implement conditional statements in assembly language, we use unconditional jump (equivalent to `goto`) instructions, conditional jump instructions (similar to the `if` and `goto` combination used in Example 1.14) and labels to specify where to transfer control to.

1.6 Sub-programs

Sub-programs (sub-routines) allow us break our programs into smaller more manageable units. They are fundamental to the development of programs longer than a few dozen statements. A sub-program is simply a facility for giving a name to a group of statements (i.e. a compound statement). A sub-program that returns a value is called a **function**. A sub-program that is not a function and does not return a value is called a **procedure**. The C language only supports functions. Sub-programs are defined once but can be invoked (used, called) as often as desired. We have already used sub-programs extensively. The statements used for I/O, such as `printf()`, `gets()` and `scanf()`, are all examples of sub-program usage. These sub-programs have been defined elsewhere so that we do not have to define them in our programs. They are part of a sub-program library that is available when programming in

C. So, when we use printf() in a program, we are **calling a sub-program** named printf(). We also called the gets() and scanf() sub-programs in the examples presented earlier.

Sub-programs make our programming task easier for two main reasons. First, they allow us to reuse the same group of statements many times by referring to them by name rather than repeating the code. From the previous examples, it can be seen that sub-programs such as printf() and scanf() are used very frequently. Secondly they make our programs easier to read and understand. This is because the name of the sub-program usually describes the purpose of the statements making up the sub-program. Consequently, a sensible name should be chosen for the sub-program.

Sub-programs are defined in the same way as main(), which is a sub-program, albeit a special one because program execution begins by calling main(). Variables may be declared inside sub-programs and are said to be **local** variables, that is, they can only be accessed inside the sub-program in which they are declared.

In order to pass information to sub-programs we may use **parameters**. These are the values inside the parentheses when the sub-program is called. For example, take the statement

```
printf("%d feet = %d inches \n", feet, inches);
```

In this case, the printf() sub-program is passed three parameters: a string and two variables. A string is always passed as the first parameter to printf() and it specifies what is to be printed. In the sub-program definition, the parameters must be declared so that the sub-program can determine the kind of parameters that will be passed. This declaration can use any names for the parameters, which are called **dummy** parameters. When we invoke the sub-program, we pass **actual** parameters to it. The values of the actual parameters are processed by the sub-program. We do not have to pass parameters to a sub-program. As an example, we define a sub-program called newline() which outputs the "\n" character as follows.

Example 1.15

Defining a sub-progam called newline() which takes no parameters:

```
newline()     /* No parameters required */
{
  printf ("\n");
}
```

This sub-program requires no parameters. Such a sub-program will always carry out the same task. Parameters allow us to vary the task a sub-program carries out. You may define as many sub-programs as you wish. Usually the code of the.sub-programs is included in the same file as the main() program and may either precede or follow the main() program. Usually sub-programs follow the main() program.

Example 1.16

Complete the program that defines and calls a sub-program called `newline()`:

```
/* call.c: calls the sub-program newline().*/
Author: Joe Carthy
Date: 01/01/95                    */

main()
{
  printf("this program calls the newline() sub-program");
  newline();
  printf("this appears on a separate line \n");
}

newline()     /* Output a newline */
{
  printf ("\n");
}
```

This program produces as output:

```
this program calls the newline() sub-program
this appears on a separate line
```

It is possible to store sub-programs in separate files to the one used for the main program. For example, the sub-programs `gets()`, `scanf()`, `printf()` and so on are stored in a file referred to as a **sub-program library** or simply **library**. There is nothing special about a library. It is merely a file containing only sub-programs. To use any of the sub-programs in your main program, the library must be **linked** to the main program file. The library containing `printf()`, `scanf()` and other I/O sub-programs is automatically linked to your main program. If you create your own libraries (which is a good idea) then you have to use some form of **link** command to carry out this linking. The details vary from system to system but will be available in your language manual or from the on-line help facility provided with your language translator.

1.7 Character I/O

In our discussion of C programming, we have used `printf()` to display strings and numbers and `scanf()` to input numbers. In this section we wish to consider character I/O, how to input single characters and display single characters. We will then show that we can perform more complicated I/O (for example, read in strings and numbers) using character I/O. The reason for doing this is that in assembly language programming, character I/O is sometimes the *only* I/O facility available.

1.7.1 Library I/O sub-programs

The C language provides library functions for character I/O. One such sub-program is called `getchar()`. It reads a single character. It is used as follows:

```
c = getchar() ;
```

A character is read in from the keyboard (by default) and is assigned to the variable `c` (or any variable of your choice). A similar function called `putchar()` is provided to display a character on the screen (by default). It is used as follows:

```
putchar( c );              /* display character in c */
putchar('\n');             /* display newline character */
```

Once we know how to perform character I/O, we can use our programming skills to do more complex I/O such as reading and displaying strings and numbers. Numbers and strings are simply sequences of characters and for I/O purposes they are manipulated as individual characters. In other words, a string is read from the keyboard one character at a time. The fact that we use a sub-program such as `gets()` to read strings does not alter this. The `gets()` sub-program simply hides from us that it reads the characters one at a time. In this section, we will describe how to write our own sub-programs, like `gets()`, for carrying out I/O operations. As an example, we rewrite the program to read and display a colour (from Example 1.2) using `getchar()` to read the colour entered. The program prompts the user to enter a colour. Using `getchar()`, it reads the characters entered terminating when the Return key (`'\n'` in C) is pressed. We do not store the `'\n'` in the variable `colour`; instead we store the `'\0'` character as the last character of the string. (`'\0'` is called the null character and corresponds to the ASCII NUL character, which has ASCII code 0. ASCII codes are described in Appendix B.)

The `'\0'` character is always used in C to indicate the end of a string. This allows you to write sub-programs to process strings of any length. You simply process the string, character by character, until you reach the `'\0'` character. This is exactly what a sub-program such as `printf()` does. It continues processing the characters in the string passed to it, until the `'\0'` character is reached, in which case it terminates. It is important when writing C programs to be aware of the importance of the `'\0'` character to terminate strings and to allow space for it when defining the length of a string. We will adopt the same convention in our assembly language programs.

Example 1.17

This program prompts the user to enter a colour, reads the colour entered and displays it. The code to read a string using character input consists of a loop to continue reading characters until `'\n'` is encountered.

```
/* colour2.c: program to prompt for colour and display it.
Version 2
Author: Joe Carthy
Date: 01/01/95                    */
main()
{
  char colour[80];
  int i;          /* array index for colour */

  printf("Enter a colour:");
  i = 0;

  colour[i] = getchar() ;      /* read character and store it
in colour */

  while ( colour[i] != '\n' )   /* repeat until \n
encountered */
  {
    i = i + 1;        /* increment index for next element */
    colour[i] = getchar();   /* read next character */
  }
  colour[i] = '\0';      /* terminate the string in C fashion
*/

  printf("You entered %s \n" colour);
}
```

This program produces as output:

```
Enter a colour: orange
You entered orange
```

The first character entered by the user is stored in `colour[0]`. The variable `i` is used to index the `colour` string, so that successive characters are stored in successive elements of `colour`. Each time around the loop, the character entered is tested to check if it is the `'\n'` character. When the user enters the Return character, the `'\n'` character is assigned to the `i`th element of the `colour` array and the loop terminates. After the loop finishes, the program overwrites the `'\n'` character with the `'\0'` character, so as to terminate the string according to the C string handling convention.

We can display strings using a character output sub-program in the same manner as we can read them using a character input sub-program. In Example 1.18, using the `putchar()` sub-program, we modify the above program to display the colour entered. In this case, we display the string one character at a time. Since strings are terminated by the `'\0'` character in C, we stop displaying characters when we encounter `'\0'`.

Example 1.18

As for Example 1.17, except that we use `putchar()` for displaying the colour entered.

```
/* colour3.c: program to prompt for colour and display it.
version 3
Author: Joe Carthy
Date: 01/01/95                    */

main()
{
  char colour[80];
  int i;

  printf("Enter a colour:");
  i = 0;

  colour[i] = getchar() ;   /* read character and store it
in colour */

  while ( colour[i] != '\n' )     /* repeat until \n
encountered */
  {
    i = i + 1;        /* increment index for next element */
    colour[i] = getchar();   /* read next character */
  }
  colour[i] = '\0';      /* terminate the string in C fashion
*/

  printf("You entered: ");

  /* Now display the string using putchar() */
  i = 0;
  while ( colour[i] != '\0' )     /* repeat until '\0' */
  {
    putchar(colour[i]) ;     /* display character */
    i = i + 1;          /* next element
  }
  putchar('\n');
}
```

This program reads the colour entered as explained earlier. It then uses the `putchar` sub-program to display the characters, stored in the `colour` array, one at a time. It produces as output:

```
Enter a colour: pink
You entered: pink
```

1.7.2 String I/O sub-programs

Now that we know how to read and display strings using character I/O functions, we can write useful sub-programs to read and display any string. We now define two such sub-programs based on the last example. The first is called `get_str()`. It reads a string, terminated by `'\n'` (Return), from the keyboard into the string variable which is passed as a parameter. It terminates the string variable with the `'\0'` character, as is the convention in C . The second sub-program is called `put_str()`. It displays the value of a string variable, passed as a parameter, on the screen. The string passed to `put_str()` must be terminated with the `'\0'` character.

Example 1.19

Definitions of `get_str()` and `put_str()` sub-programs:

```
get_str( str )     /* Read a string terminated by \n and
store it in the parameter passed, terminated by \0 */
char str[];        /* Parameter definition: */
{
  int i;           /* to index elements of string */
  i = 0;           /* arrays always start at 0 */

  str[i] = getchar() ;     /* read first character */
  while ( str[i] != '\n' ) /* finished ? */
  {
    i = i + 1;       /* i indexes next free element */
    str[i] = getchar();
  }
  str[i] = '\0';           /* terminate with \0, overwriting \n
*/
}

put_str(str)          /* display string parameter */
char str[]
{
  int i;
  i = 0;
  while ( str[i]!= '\0' )  /* finished ? */
  {
    putchar( str[i] ) ;  /* display element i */
    i = i + 1;
  }
}
```

Example 1.20

The following is the program from Example 1.18 to read and display a colour. The `main()` function calls the two sub-programs defined above to perform its task:

```
/* colour4.c: program to prompt for colour and display a
message. Version 4
Author: Joe Carthy
Date: 01/01/95                    */

main()
{
  char colour[80];

  put_str("Enter a colour:");
  get_str( colour ) ;
  put_str("You entered:");
  put_str( colour ) ;
  put_str("\n");
}
```

Executing this programs produces as output:

```
Enter a colour: red blue and orange !!
You entered: red blue and orange !!
```

In this program, the variable `colour` is passed as a parameter to the sub-programs `get_str()` and `put_str()`. It is called an **actual** parameter because it is the variable that the sub-programs actually access. We can pass any string variable to these sub-programs, regardless of its length, provided that it is terminated by the `'\0'` character.

We can see from this example that we can build useful sub-programs from simple I/O functions to carry out more complex I/O. This idea is very useful in assembly language programming because once we learn to read and display single characters we can develop sub-programs like those above to perform more complex I/O. The development of such sub-programs is also a useful method of illustrating the various programming concepts discussed in this chapter.

1.7.3 Handling numbers using character I/O

Reading numbers

When information is entered at the keyboard, it is read character by character by sub-programs such as `getchar()` and `gets()`. If we take this a step further, these sub-programs read the ASCII codes of the characters entered and store them appropriately. Appendix B describes how information is represented in a computer system, including the use of ASCII codes to represent characters. All information is stored in binary form in a computer system. It is important to distinguish between the representation of characters and numbers. For example, the character `'2'` is represented by ASCII code 50 (`0011 0010` in binary). This code is used if we wish to display the character `'2'` on the screen. The number 2 is represented as a pure binary number (`0000 0010`), which is used if we want to do arithmetic with the number 2. Thus, the number 32 is represented by the binary number `0010 0000` in a single byte, but to display this number, we must display the characters '3' and '2', which are represented by the ASCII codes 0011 0011 and 0011 0010. If we wish to read numbers for arithmetic purposes, then we must convert the ASCII codes of the digits entered to their numeric equivalents. In general, we use the following formula to convert the ASCII code of any digit to its numeric equivalent:

```
number = ASCII code - '0' /* '0'= 48, (ASCII code for '0').
*/
```

However, we are not finished yet. This conversion only works with single digit numbers. If we enter a multi-digit number such as 368, then we have more work to do: we must convert the character '3' to 3 and multiply it by 100, convert '6' to 6 and multiply by 10, convert '8' to 8 and finally add the three resulting numbers to get the number 368.

Example 1.21

The following sub-program, getn(), performs the required processing and returns the number required. This version deals with positive numbers only. It assumes that only digits are entered and that the number is terminated by '\n'. In this example, because getn() is returning a value, in the definition of getn(), we specify the type of value to be returned, in this case an integer. This is the purpose of the keyword int before the function name. (In fact, technically, we should do this with all function declarations in C and in ANSI C we are forced to do so. The C code used in this text is based on the original specification of the C language, as described by Kernighan & Ritchie. An ANSI standard for C was developed in the 1980s and it included a number of changes to the language.)

```
int getn()      /* read positive number and return it */
{
  int digit, n;
  n = 0 ;
  c = getchar();          /* read first character */
  if ( c != '\n' )
  {
    digit = c - '0' ;     /* convert character to number */
    n = digit ;       /* store number in n */
    c = getchar();        /* get next digit */
    while ( c != '\n' )     /* finished ? */
    {
      digit = c - '0' ;  /* convert character c to number */
      n = (n * 10) + digit ; /* compute new value for n */
      c = getchar();       /* get next digit */
    }
  }
  return ( n ) ;
}
```

The `return` statement is the mechanism used by a C function to return a value, allowing us to write:

```
num = getn();
```

which will assign the variable `num`, the value entered at the keyboard.

Example 1.22

To handle negative numbers, the above sub-program is modified as outlined below. We assume that a negative number is entered so as to begin with `'-'`, followed immediately by the digits making up the number and that the number entered is terminated by `'\n'`.

```
int getn()  /* version 2: reads a signed number and returns
it */
{
  int sign, digit, n;
  n = 0 ;
  sign = 1 ;          /* assume number is positive */

  c = getchar();        /* read first character */
  if ( c == '-' )       /* negative number ? */
  {
    sign = -1;         /* record its sign */
    c = getchar() ;     /* get next digit */
  }

  if ( c != '\n' )
  {
    digit = c - '0' ;       /* convert character to number */
    n = digit ;          /* store number in n */
    c = getchar();        /* get next digit */
    while ( c != '\n' )     /* finished ? */
    {
      digit = c - '0' ;     /* convert c to number */
      n = (n * 10) + digit ; /* compute new value for n */
      c = getchar();      /* get next digit */
    }
  }

  return ( n * sign ) ;       /* return -n if sign == -1
               otherwise return +n */
}
```

We are now in a position to write the calculator program from Example 1.5 using the `getn()` and `put_str()` sub-programs that we have developed.

Example 1.23

This program prompts for two numbers, adds them and displays the sum:

```
/* calc5.c: calculator program version 5
Author: Joe Carthy
Date: 01/01/95                    */

main()
{
  int num1, num2;

  put__str("Enter first number: ");
  num1 = getn();
  put__str("Enter second number: ");
  num2 = getn();

  sum = num1 + num2 ;

  printf("The sum of %d and %d is %d \n", num1, num2, sum);
}
```

Executing this program produces as output:

```
Enter first number: 14
Enter second number: 10
The sum of 14 and 10 is 24
```

As can be seen, we still had to use `printf()` because we have not developed a sub-program for displaying numbers.

Displaying numbers

Displaying a number is similar to reading one in that we must display it as a sequence of single characters using ASCII codes. This means that we must decompose a number into its constituent digits, convert each digit to its equivalent ASCII code and display the digits in the correct order. The conversion from a single digit number to its equivalent ASCII code is carried out by the formula:

```
ascii = digit + '0'    /* '0' = 48 (ASCII code of 0) */
```

Consider a number such as 327. In order to display the digits one at a time, we decompose the number so that we first display the `'3'`, followed by the `'2'` and finally the `'7'`. So, given a number, we first display the left-most digit and then the remaining digits from the left. However, it is awkward to generate the digits in this order. It is easier to compute the right-most digit. We do this by dividing the number by 10 and taking the remainder. C provides a modulus operator, `%`, which returns the remainder, so that `327%10` returns `7`. It is also important to note that C carries out integer division when dividing integers, that is, the fractional part of the result is ignored, so that `327/10` returns `32`.

We can use these two operations to generate the digits making up a number. Table 1.1 illustrates the process of decomposing the number 58217 into its component digits: With this technique, the most significant digit of a number will be the last to be computed. We display the computed digits in reverse order when using this technique to generate the digits making up a number. To do so, we repeat the process of dividing the number by `10`, storing the remainder in the appropriate element of an array, until the result of the division by `10` is `0`. This means that we store the least significant digit in element `0` of the array, the next digit in element `1` and so on, so that the digits making up the number are stored in the array in the opposite order to that in which we wish to display them. To display the digits, we display the last digit stored in the array, then we display the second-last digit in the array and we continue in this manner until we reach element `0` of the array. If the number to be displayed is negative, we first display a "-" sign, then convert the number to a positive one and proceed to display it as outlined above.

Table 1.1 Decomposing the number into its component digits.

Number	Number/10	Number%10 (remainder)
58217	5821	7
5821	582	1
582	58	2
58	5	8
5	0	5

Example 1.24

The following is a sub-program called `putn()`, which displays a number. An array called `numstr` is used to store the ASCII codes of the digits. The number to be displayed is passed as a parameter.

```
putn( number )        /* displays a signed number */
int number
{
  int i, div, rem, numstr[13] ;



  if ( number < 0 )       /* number is negative */
  {
    putchar('-') ;      /* display sign */
    number = -number ;   /* convert to positive */
  }

  i = 0 ;          /* store characters from numstr[0 ] */

  div = number / 10;      /* div is result of division */
  rem = number % 10;      /* rem is remainder */
```

```
    while ( div != 0 )
    {
      numstr[i] = rem + '0';    /*convert to ASCII, store in
      numstr[i] */
      i = i + 1 ;       /* i is index of next free element */
      number = div;     /* new number is old one / 10 */
      div := number / 10;
      rem = number % 10;
    }

    numstr[i] = rem + '0' ;   /* last digit */

    while ( i >= 0 )     /* display characters numstr[i] to
    numstr[0] */
    {
      putchar( numstr[i] );
      i = i - 1;
    }
  }
```

The `putn()` sub-program firsts tests if the number is negative. If it is, it displays a `'-'` sign and converts the number to its positive form. It then breaks the number into its component digits, storing their ASCII equivalents in the array `numstr`. Finally, it displays the characters in `numstr` from the last element to element `0`. Now that we have a sub-program to display a number, we are in a position to write the complete calculator program (of Example 1.5) using the sub-programs defined above based on character I/O.

Example 1.25

Calculator program using `getn()`, `put__str()` and `putn()` sub-programs:

```
/* calc6.c: calculator program version 6
Author: Joe Carthy
Date: 01/01/95                    */

main()
{
  int num1, num2, sum;

  put__str("Enter first number: ");
  num1 = getn();
  put__str("Enter second number: ");
  num2 = getn();

  sum = num1 + num2 ;
```

```
    put_str("The sum of ");
    putn( num1 );
    put_str(" and " );
    putn( num2 );
    put_str(" is " );
    putn( sum );
    putchar("\n");
}
```

Because put_str() can only display one string and putn() can only display one number, we need seven statements to replace the single call to the printf() sub-program used in Example 1.5!

Note: It is not suggested that you should use put_str() or get_str() instead of printf() or scanf() and the other C library functions when writing C programs. They are provided to illustrate how sub-programs like printf() and scanf() can be programmed once you know how to perform character I/O. In assembly language programming, as mentioned before, you may only have access to facilities for carrying out character I/O. In that eventuality, you can build up your own library of complex I/O sub-programs based on those facilities, in the same manner as put_str(), putn(), get_str() and getn() were developed. This is the approach used in this text and the assembly language versions of these sub-programs are developed in later chapters. The development of these sub-programs is also a useful method of obtaining assembly language programming experience.

Exercises

1.11 Rewrite the feet conversion program to use the sub-programs getn(), putn() and put_str() defined above.

1.12 Write modified versions of putn() and put_str() called putn_nl() and put_str_nl() which generate a newline after displaying their output.

1.13 Write and test a sub-program called revout(str) which takes a string as a parameter and displays it in reverse order.

1.14 Write and test a sub-program called reverse(instr,outstr) which takes the first string parameter, reverses it and passes it out via the second parameter.

1.15 Rewrite putn() to use the reverse() sub-program from Exercise 1.14.

1.16 Write a program to read a string and display a message indicating if the string is a palindrome, that is, it is spelled the same backwards as forwards, for example abba.

1.8 Summary

In this chapter we have briefly surveyed the major concepts involved in programming and looked at their implementation in the C programming language. Concepts such as I/O, variables, control flow and sub-programs are fundamental and must be understood. In the following chapters we will describe how these programming concepts are implemented in assembly language programs. At this point, it is important that you have grasped the concepts described and have not become bogged down in the details of the C programming language. The C language was used as a vehicle to explain programming concepts and is useful, in this text, in so far as it serves that purpose.

1.9 Reading list

1.9.1 Programming

Anderson, R.B. (1979) *Proving Programs Correct*, John Wiley, New York.
Bornat, R. (1987) *Programming from First Principles*, Prentice Hall, London.
Bronson, G. and Menconi, S. (1991) *A First Book of C*, West Publishing Co., St. Paul, MN.
Dahl, O.-J., Dijkstra E.W. and Hoare, C.A.R. (1972) *Structured Programming*, Academic Press, London.
Goldschlager, L. and Lister A. (1988) *Computer Science, a Modern Introduction*, Prentice Hall, London.
Gries, D. (1981) *The Science of Programming*, Springer Verlag, New York.
Grogono, P. and Nelson, S.H. (1982) *Problem Solving and Computer Programming*, Addison Wesley, Reading, MA.
Kelly, A. and Pohl, I (1992) *C by Dissection*, Benjamin Cummings, Menlo Park, CA.
Kernighan, B.W. and Ritchie D.M. (1978) *The C Programming Language*, Prentice Hall, Englewood Cliffs, NJ.
Miller, L.H. and Quilici, A.E. (1993) *Joy of C*, John Wiley, New York.
Plum, T. (1983) *Learning to Program in C*, Prentice Hall, Englewood Cliffs, NJ.

1.9.2 Using computers

Colantonio, E.S. (1989) *Computers and Applications*, D.C. Heath and Company, Lexington, MA.
Sumner, M. (1988) *Computers, Concepts and Uses*, Prentice Hall, Reading, MA.
Stern, N. and Stren R.A. (1993) *Computing in the Information Age*, John Wiley & Sons, Chichester.

2

Assembly language concepts

We have already looked at fundamental programming concepts such as I/O, variables, data structures and conditional statements in the C programming language. In the following chapters we describe how these concepts are implemented in assembly language. It is important to understand a programming concept before undertaking its implementation in assembly language. This chapter is an overview of some concepts required for assembly language programming. First, we look briefly at the idea of assembly language programming. Then we describe a processor model that is relevant for this type of programming. Finally, we describe some basic programming mechanisms that arise in assembly language programming.

2.1 Assembly language programming

Most computer programs are written in high-level languages such as C, COBOL, Fortran, Ada and PASCAL. The advantage of using high-level languages is that it is easier to understand, write and maintain programs written in such languages. Each language provides facilities for allowing you to solve a problem without worrying about the underlying computer hardware. Programs written in these languages are translated (**compiled**) to machine code by programs called **compilers**. Assembly language is a **low-level** language. It is translated to machine code by an **assembler** program. The programmer must be familiar with some details of the hardware to write assembly language programs. Assembly language programs are made up of primitive operations called **instructions**. A task which requires a single statement in a high-level language may require a dozen assembly language instructions.

A very important feature of high-level languages is their relative **portability**. Given a program in C, PASCAL or any high-level language, we can move (**port**) the high-level language program (source program) to another machine, where it can be compiled and executed (provided there is a compiler available). Usually, no major changes will be required to the programs and they are said to be **portable**. Low-level language programs, assembly language and machine code programs are *not* portable. Programs written in a low-level language must be rewritten completely if they are to be moved to a different type of machine. The following question naturally arises: *why use low-level languages?* There are a number of reasons for the use of low-level languages. First, you have access to primitive operations, not usually provided in high-level languages, such as those used for bit manipulation operations. You also have access to CPU (central processing unit) registers and interrupt handling facilities, which again cannot, usually, be accessed directly from a high-level language. If you are writing **systems software** (like the programs that make up the operating system) then such low-level facilities are sometimes required. Small parts of an operating system are programmed in assembly language, although most operating systems software is programmed in a high-level language such as C.

Second, programs written in a low-level language are usually more efficient in that they run faster and occupy less memory space than high-level language programs that have been translated to machine code. An experienced programmer can produce more efficient machine code than a compiler (assembly language instructions are translated directly to their machine code equivalents). However, with the increasing processing power (in terms of both CPU speed and memory capacity) of modern computers, this second reason for using low-level languages is becoming less important. The software used in 'games machines' is often programmed in assembly language to give the required performance as these machines typically have small amounts of memory and may not have very powerful processors.

Finally, and perhaps most importantly, in order to *understand more fully* how computers operate, it is essential to study the architecture of computers and basic assembly language programming.

To summarize, low-level language programs are difficult and slow to construct, debug and maintain. They are inherently non-portable. Thus, they are only used when absolutely necessary. High-level language programs are easier to construct, debug and maintain. They are also, usually, portable. In addition, some high-level languages provide low-level facilities. C, for example, provides a set of bit manipulation operators. Systems programs, which formerly would have been programmed in assembly language, are now being written in languages such as C.

2.2 Hardware model for assembly language programming

Assembly language programming requires some knowledge of the architecture of the machine to be used. Figure 2.1 illustrates the machine components that are of immediate interest to the programmer from an assembly language programming point of view. These are the processor (in particular its registers) and the memory.

2.2.1 The processor

From a programming perspective we do not have to concern ourselves with details of the processor or the system buses (see Part II). The buses are used to connect the CPU to the other devices, such as memory, keyboard and screen and internally in the microprocessor to connect registers to the processor. Registers are a vital part of the microprocessor unit because *all* data manipulation takes place in registers. A register is simply a storage location. Data stored in a register is immediately available to the processor for manipulation. This means that it is much faster to access data in a register than it

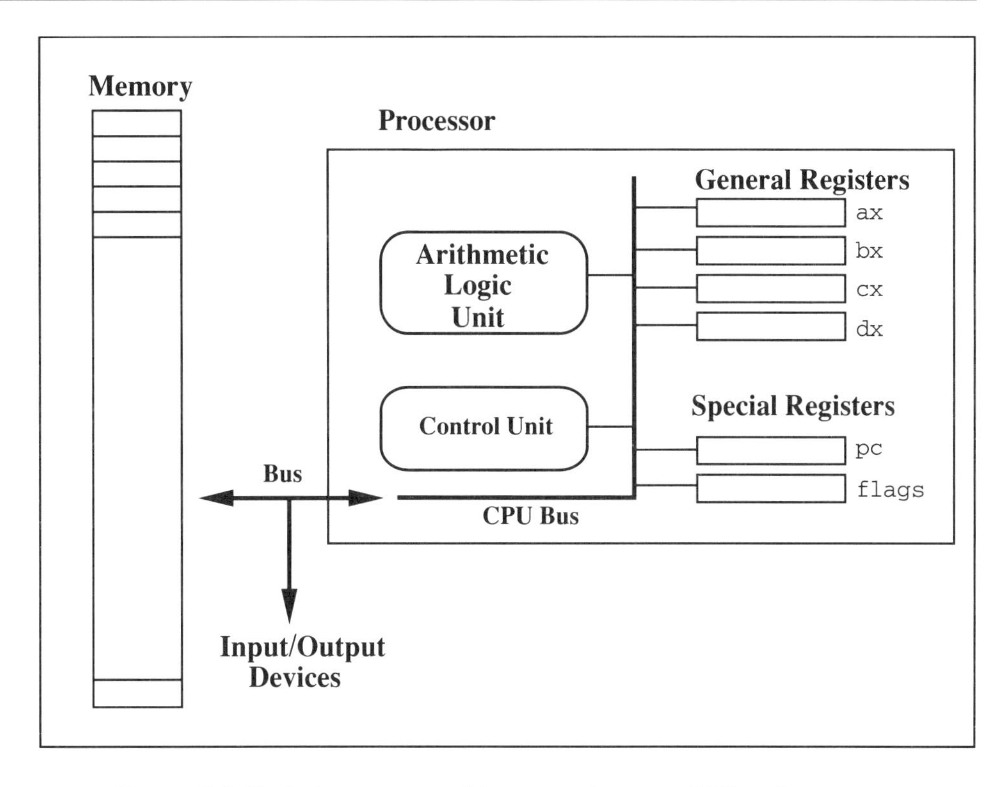

Figure 2.1 Typical computer architecture using some 8086 register names.

is to access data in a memory location. The actual number of registers varies from machine to machine but is always very small when compared to the number of memory locations available. Typically, the greater the number of registers, the more powerful the machine. The size of a register is also very important. Basic microprocessors use 4-bit registers, that is, each register can only hold 4 bits; these have been followed by machines using 8-bit registers, 16-bit registers, 32-bit registers and 64-bit registers. The 8086 uses 16-bit registers but it is a member of a family of microprocessors (80286, 80386, 80486, sometimes abbreviated to 80*x*86), the later members of which use 32-bit registers. The M68000 is also a member of a family of microprocessors (M68020, M68030, M68040, sometimes abbreviated to M680*x*0) all of which use 32-bit registers.

From Figure 2.1, we can see that registers fall into two classes: **general** (purpose) registers and **special** (purpose) registers. General registers are those available to the programmer for general programming purposes. Special registers are those which the processor uses for its own specific purposes. There are always at least two, and usually three, special registers: the **program counter** (**pc**), the **status** register (also called the **flags** or the **condition codes register**) and optionally, the **stack pointer** (**sp**) register.

The program counter contains the address in memory of the next instruction to be executed by the processor. This register controls the sequence in which instructions are carried out. Instructions which alter the flow of control (for example for selection and loops) modify the program counter.

The status register is a collection of bits used to record the status that results from executing certain instructions, such as the arithmetic instructions. The individual bits are referred to as **flags**. A flag can only take on the values 0 or 1 since it is a single bit. We say a flag is **set** if it has the value 1. For example, one of the flags is called the **zero** flag or **Z**-flag. It is set when the result of an arithmetic operation is 0. We say a flag is clear if it has the value 0. The Z-flag is clear when the result of an operation is non-zero. We will see the importance of the status register later when we look at how conditional statements are implemented in assembly language.

The stack pointer is used in manipulating an area of memory referred to as the **stack.** The stack is used in the implementation of sub-programs in assembly language. It is also used as a place for storing information temporarily.

The **arithmetic logic unit (ALU)** performs the actual processing of information, while the **control unit** controls the execution of instructions. The operation of these components does not impinge on the programmer, but is fundamental to understanding how information is processed. They are described in more detail in Part II.

2.2.2 Memory

Memory consists of thousands or millions of cells. Each cell can hold an 8-bit number or a **byte**. Memory cells are numbered starting at zero, up to some maximum value, typically in the range 1 to 32 million upwards. The programmer must understand that a program is stored in memory, as are variables used in the program. In addition, in assembly language, variables may be stored in registers. In this text, variables stored in memory are called memory variables to distinguish them from variables stored in registers. Memory locations are used to hold data to be processed and the results of processing. Data stored in memory must be transferred to a register before it can be processed. While the delay in carrying out this transfer is small in human terms (20 to 100 nanoseconds, 20 to 100 billionths of a second!), it can be significant in computing terms when perhaps millions of items of data have to be transferred.

An extensive discussion of hardware is provided in Part II where we are concerned with understanding *how* programs are actually executed.

2.3 Programming concepts

While the examples used in this and the following chapters are based on 8086 assembly language, the principles apply to assembly language programming in general. (Appendix C introduces the M68000 assembly language.) We do not examine the 8086 instructions in detail at this point; instead we use them to illustrate concepts that arise in assembly language programming. This allows us to concentrate in the following chapters on the specific details of assembly language programming.

2.3.1 *Variables in assembly language*

In C programs, we declare variables before using them; for example, the statements `char c; int i;` declare variables called `c` and `i`. In assembly language we have a choice as to how we implement variables. We can use variable names as in C, whereby the variables are stored in memory or we may use a register to act as a variable. A register's name is *always fixed*, so that ax and bx are 8086 register names, while d0 and d1 are M68000 register names. You cannot use your own name for a register, whereas with a memory variable you must supply a name yourself. Since there are usually a small number of registers available for your use, you are restricted in the number of variables that can be implemented using registers. You may use as many memory variables as you wish. The 8086 uses 16-bit registers, four of which are called ax, bx, cx and dx. We will sometimes use these registers to act as variables in the examples that follow.

As in C, memory variables must be declared before they can be used. Unlike C, we do not specify a variable type in the declaration in assembly language. Instead we declare the name and **size** of the variable, the latter being the number of bytes the variable will occupy. We may also specify an initial value. A **directive** (a command to the assembler) is used to define variables. In 8086 assembly language, the directive **db** defines a byte-sized variable; **dw** defines a word-sized variable (16 bits) and **dd** defines a double-word (long word, 32 bits) variable. A C variable of type int may be implemented using a size of 16 or 32 bits, that is, dw or dd is used. A C variable of type char, which is used to store a single character, is implemented using the db directive.

Example 2.1

Sample variable declarations. The ? means that the value of the variable is undefined, so the variable will have as its value whatever happens to be in memory when the program is executed. In other words, a variable always has some value whether or not the programmer assigns it one. If a variable is left undefined then it may have any value. On some machines such variables will have the value 0 but this should not be assumed to be the case.

```
reply     db     'y'
prompt    db     'Enter your favourite colour: ', 0
colour    db     80 dup(?)
i         db     20
k         db     ?
num       dw     4000
large     dd     80000
```

In Example 2.1, reply is defined as a character variable, which is initialized to 'y'. The variable prompt is defined as a string, terminated by the Null character. The definition of the variable colour demonstrates how to declare an array of characters of size 80, which contains undefined values. The purpose of dup is to tell the assembler to duplicate or repeat the data definition directive a specific number of times, in this case 80 dup specifies that 80 bytes of storage are to be set aside since dup is used with the db directive. The (?) with the dup means that storage allocated by the directive is uninitialized or undefined. Variables i and k are byte sized variables, where i is initialized to 20 and k is left undefined. The variable num is a 16-bit variable, initialized to 4000 and the variable large is a 32-bit variable, initialized to 80000.

2.3.2 *Assembly language instructions*

An assembly language program is made up of a sequence of **instructions**. A typical instruction carries out a single operation, for example a single assignment or a single arithmetic operation. Example 2.2 illustrates the use of a number of instructions. Note that in 8086 assembly language the ';' character introduces a comment and it is not a statement terminator, as in the C language. No visible terminator character is required in assembly language, as only one instruction is allowed on a line, so that the end of line is the terminator. For an entire line comment, the semicolon must be the first character on the line as follows:

```
; This is a comment and ';' is the first character on the line
```

Comments, as noted in Chapter 1, are an important documentation aid and are especially useful in assembly language programs which are difficult to understand at the best of times. In many of our assembly language programs we use a comment, after an instruction, which describes how the instruction might be carried out in C.

Example 2.2

Implement the following C code fragment in assembly language:

C code:

```
int i, j, k;

i = 1;
i = i + 4;
j = 2;
k = i + j;
```

Assembly language:

```
i   dw   ?    ; variable definition
j   dw   ?
k   dw   ?

mov i, 1      ; i = 1
add i, 4      ; i = i + 4
mov j, 2      ; j = 2
mov ax, j     ; ax = j
add ax, i     ; ax = ax + i
mov k, ax     ; k = ax
```

The variables `i`, `j`, `k` have to be declared separately in an assembly language program. We use word-size declarations (but in this example byte sizes would have been adequate). Assignment in assembly language is carried out by some form of 'move' (or 'load') instruction. The `mov i, 1` instruction is an example; it reads as 'move the value 1 into the variable i'. Note that the 8086 mov instruction is spelled without an 'e'. The arithmetic instructions such as the add and sub instructions also carry out assignment. The instruction add i, 4 adds 4 to the value of i and stores the result in i. Similarly, sub j, 2 subtracts 2 from the value of j and stores the result in j.

The instructions in Example 2.2 operate on two values which we call **operands.** The variables i, j, k and the constants 1, 4 and 2 are all examples of operands. The first operand in an 8086 instruction is called the **destination** operand as it is the one **modified** by the instruction. It must always be a variable (register or memory variable). The second operand in an 8086 instruction is called the **source** operand. It provides the 'source' of the data with which to modify the destination operand. The source operand may be a variable or a constant and remains unchanged after an instruction. (Note: M68000 instructions use the first operand as the source operand and the second operand as the destination.)

An important rule for 8086 assembly language programming is that the source and destination operands may *not* both be memory variables in the same instruction. This is the reason for implementing the C statement

```
k = i + j
```

as

```
mov ax, j       ; ax = j
add ax, i       ; ax = ax + i
mov k, ax       ; k = i + j
```

We *cannot* write:

```
add k, i        ; This is ILLEGAL !!!!
```

because of the rule prohibiting the use of two memory variables in an instruction. This rule does not apply to all microprocessors and the M68000, for example, allows instructions with two memory variables as operands.

As can be seen from the above example, to achieve the same result, more instructions are required in assembly language than in a high-level language. The term **statement** is used to describe the unit of execution in a high-level language program, while the term **instruction** is used in assembly language programming. A high-level language statement is usually implemented by several assembly language instructions.

Example 2.3

Write the following C statement in assembly language:

```
sum = result1 + result2 + result3;
```

Assembly language:

```
mov   ax, result1       ; ax = result1
add   ax, result2       ; ax = ax + result2
add   ax, result3       ; ax = ax + result3
mov   sum, ax           ; sum = ax
```

This example again illustrates that a single high-level language statement may have to be implemented by several assembly language instructions. We assign register ax (or any register) the value stored in result1. The first add instruction adds the value in result2 to that in ax, storing the result in ax. The second add instruction adds result3 to ax, again storing the result in ax. Finally we store the total in the variable sum.

Example 2.4

Store the character 'A' in register bx.

```
mov    bx, 'A'          ; bx = 'A' ;
```

The character 'A' is represented by the ASCII code 01000001 in binary. The assembler automatically translates character constants such as 'A' to their ASCII codes, so we do not need to know the ASCII codes of printable characters. We simply write them as character constants, as in C. If we wish, we have the option of specifying the ASCII code of a character, using a decimal, hexadecimal or even a binary number. So we could write any of the following instructions to store 'A' in register bx:

```
mov    bx, 65D
mov    bx, 41H
mov    bx, 01000001B
```

This is represented in Figure 2.2. Since bx is a 16-bit register and the ASCII code only requires 7 bits, the number stored in bx is padded on the left hand side with zeros to make up 16 bits.

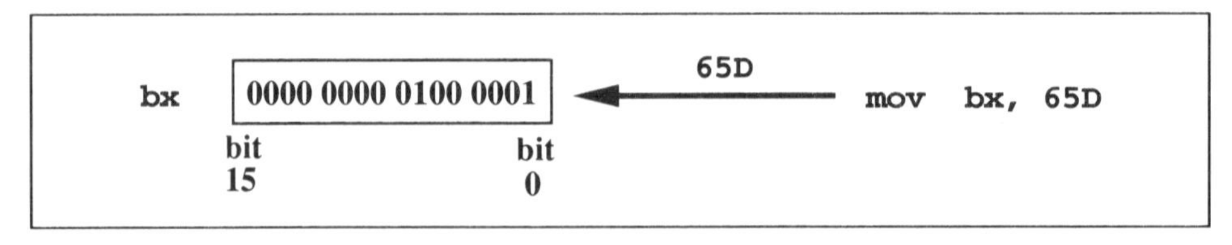

Figure 2.2 Register bx after executing the mov bx, 65D instruction. The effect is to overwrite the bx register with 65D as a 16-bit number.

The D in 65D specifies a decimal number, the B in 01000001B specifies a binary number and the H in 41H specifies a hexadecimal number (base 16, see Appendix B). The same ASCII code is used in the three versions; it is simply represented in different number bases. When using a printable character in an instruction, enclosing the character in single quotes (for example, 'A') is the most readable way of referring to it. However, you have to use the ASCII code for non-printable **control** characters such as Carriage Return (ASCII `13D`) and Linefeed (ASCII `10D`). In this text we use the term Return to refer to the Carriage Return character. Control characters are output like any other character, the difference being in their effect on the output device. Bel (ASCII `7D`), for example, causes the computer's speaker to beep when it is output. The Return character causes the cursor (or print head) to go back to the start of the current line and the Linefeed character causes the cursor (or print head) to go on to the next line. By outputting these two characters one after the other, we cause output to appear on a new line and achieve the same effect as that achieved by displaying the `'\n'` character in C programs.

Notation

Assembly language instructions (for the assemblers used in this text) may be written in either upper case, lower case or mixed case, so that `MOV, mov, Mov` are all acceptable. Many assembly language books only use upper-case letters for instructions because *some* assemblers specify that instructions must be written in upper case. I prefer, when possible, to use lower-case letters for instructions as I find them easier to enter and read. You should use which ever notation you find appropriate, the important point being to use the same style consistently.

2.3.3 Constants in assembly language

In C programs we use the `#define` directive to define symbolic constants. In assembly language we have a similar facility. The `equ` directive is used by a number of assembly languages to define a constant. An assembly language directive is a command to the assembler program. Unlike instructions (for example, `mov, add`), which are translated to their machine code equivalents for execution by the processor, directives are carried out by the assembler. The general form for defining a constant is

```
CONSTANT_NAME          equ  definition
```

Example 2.5

Define constants with names `CR, LF` and `BEL` for the control characters Return (ASCII `13D`), Linefeed (ASCII `10D`) and Bel (ASCII `7D`):

```
CR      equ     13D
LF      equ     10D
BEL     equ     7D
```

These constants may now be used anywhere in your program, instead of writing the ASCII code directly. This makes the program easier to read. The assembler, before translating your program to machine code, simply replaces each occurrence of a constant by its definition, just as if you entered its definition. Constants are often written in upper case so as to distinguish them from variable names, but this is merely a convention. You may use whatever case you prefer for constants, but again you should use the same style consistently.

Program layout: indentation

When writing a program, we format each line so that there is space for a label at the left hand side, whether we use one or not. It is also a good idea to enter programs so that operands and comments are laid out consistently in columns. The use of the **tab** key makes this very easy. This use of **indentation** makes programs easier to read and is strongly recommended. You should adopt the practice of laying out your programs neatly. This also applies to programs written in high-level languages.

2.3.4 Input and output (I/O) in assembly language

In our discussion of programming in Chapter 1, we saw that I/O is a fundamental part of programming. Thus, we need to look at how to carry out I/O in assembly language. Each processor provides instructions for carrying out I/O with the devices that are attached to it, for example the keyboard and screen. Low-level I/O is quite complicated and, unless we are programming an I/O device, we can usually avoid the details of low-level I/O. One of the important functions of an operating system (MS-DOS in this case) is to provide a range of services (in the form of sub-programs) such as I/O and others that can be used by programmers. The operating system allows programmers to carry out I/O without having to worry about I/O device details. If we are to use the operating system to perform I/O, we must have a means to call the operating system I/O sub-program. In addition, we must be able to specify what kind of I/O operation we wish to carry out. We may wish to read a character from the keyboard, to display a character on the screen or to do disk I/O. The `int` instruction is used by the 8086 to access operating system services. For example, the two instructions

```
mov     ax, 01H
int     21H
```

will cause the operating system to read a character from the keyboard and store it in the `ax` register. The number `21H` tells the operating system that we wish to access one of its many I/O sub-programs. The operating system uses the number in the `ax` register to determine which of its I/O sub-programs we wish to invoke, `01H` indicating that it is the 'read character from keyboard' sub-program. So, in order to access any operating system sub-program, we must know what number to use with the `int` instruction. In addition, we may have to pass another number in the `ax` (or some other) register providing details of what we wish the operating system to do for us. We describe I/O in more detail in Chapter 3, while Chapter 5 describes operating systems in more detail.

2.3.5 Terminating a program

When a program has finished executing, it terminates and the operating system takes control so that we can carry out our next task. This happens automatically when we write high-level language programs. In assembly language, we must explicitly terminate our programs and return control to the operating system. This is carried out in the same fashion as carrying out an I/O operation, so we use the `int` instruction as follows:

```
mov    ax, 4c00h
int    21h
```

These two instructions cause an 8086 program to terminate and return control to the operating system.

2.3.6 *Sub-programs*

The use of sub-programs was described in Chapter 1. They provide the facility of giving a name to a group of statements. For example, the instructions to compute `ax = bx + cx` could be written as a sub-program with the name `add_regs` (or whatever name you choose). Then to do this calculation you call the `add_regs` sub-program. As in a high-level language, the sub-program must be defined (once) and may be called as often as required.

Example 2.6

Calling the sub-program `add_regs`:

```
mov     cx, 10                       ; cx = 10
mov     bx, 15                       ; bx = 15
                   call add_regs     ; carries out ax = bx + cx
mov     sum, ax                      ; sum = ax
```

The **call** instruction invokes the sub-program, that is, it transfers control to the sub-program. The sub-program carries out its task and when finished execution resumes at the instruction following the `call` instruction, the `mov sum, ax` instruction in our example.

Example 2.7

Defining the `add_regs` sub-program:

```
add_regs:                ; Adds cx to bx and returns result
                         ; in ax
          mov ax, 0      ; ax = 0
          add ax, bx     ; ax = ax + bx
          add ax, cx     ; ax = ax + cx
          ret            ; ax will contain bx + cx
```

We use a **label** to name a sub-program; for example, `add_regs` in the above code fragment is a label. It 'labels' a particular instruction of your program, in this case the instruction where execution of the sub-program begins. We use a label when we wish to refer to a particular instruction or memory variable in a program. Labels for instructions are terminated by a colon (:) when they are defined. The colon is omitted when they are used as in the `call` instruction above. Labels are a fundamental feature of assembly language programs. They are required for loops and selection statements and not just for sub-programs. In general, they are used when we wish to transfer control to another part of a program – they identify the place to which control is to be transferred. The `ret` instruction is used to terminate a sub-program and arrange for execution to resume at the next instruction following the `call` instruction. We say **control** (point of execution) is returned to the instruction following the `call` instruction. The operation of the `call` and `ret` instructions is described further in Section 2.4.

A major difference between assembly language sub-programs and those of C (or any high-level language) is in the mechanism for passing parameters. In C, we simply enclose the parameters in parentheses after the name of the sub-program as in the following two examples:

```
printf("what's your favourite colour");
get_str( colour ) ;
```

The same mechanism for passing parameters is not available in assembly language. One method of passing a parameter to a sub-program in assembly language is to store the parameter value in a specified register. The sub-program then accesses the value in that register. This is the method we used to communicate with the operating system earlier, where we used the `ax` register to pass some information to the operating system sub-program. This method of parameter passing makes it more difficult to read assembly language programs. However, you should always remember that C programs (or those of any language) have to be translated to machine code, which is the binary form of assembly language. Therefore, anything that can be carried out in C can, by definition, be carried out in assembly language. High-level languages are designed to make programming easier. Facilities such as compound statements and parameter passing are provided for that purpose. Assembly language is much more primitive than a high-level language, but more powerful in that you have complete freedom to choose the instructions that best implement a particular program. The high-level parameter-passing mechanism of C must be implemented using the techniques available to the assembly language programmer. There are other methods of passing parameters to sub-programs and these are described later.

2.3.7 *Conditional statements*

The essence of a conditional statement is the evaluation of a condition to true or false and taking appropriate action according to the result. Thus there are two operations to be carried out:

- evaluate the condition; for example, is `ax` equal to `bx`, and
- transfer control to the appropriate point depending on the evaluation of the condition.

In assembly language, these two operations are carried out by separate instructions, so that a conditional statement will be implemented by two assembly language instructions (in general). The first instruction will evaluate the condition and the second will transfer control, depending on the result of the evaluation. When a condition is evaluated, its result is stored in the **status** register, where various flags are used to record the result. This is how the instruction to transfer control can test whether the condition evaluated to true or false.

Example 2.8

Compare two variables stored in registers ax and bx. If they are equal, then add 10 to ax and subtract 10 from bx. If they are not equal then add 2 to ax and subtract 2 from bx.

C version (assume i stands for ax and j stands for bx):

```
if ( i == j )
{
    i = i + 10 ;
    j = j - 10 ;
}
else
{
    i = i + 2 ;
    j = j - 2 ;
}
```

Assembly language:

```
          cmp   ax, bx        ; compare ax and bx
          je    eq_lab        ; if ax == bx goto
                              ;eq_lab
          add   ax, 2         ; else (ax not equal to
                              ;bx) ax = ax + 2
          sub   bx, 2         ; bx = bx -2
          jmp   endif         ; goto endif
eq_lab:
          add   ax, 10        ; ax = ax + 10
          sub   bx, 10        ; bx = bx - 10
endif:
```

The cmp instruction compares operands in assembly language. It stores the result of the comparison in the status register, so that certain flags of the register are set to 1 or 0 according to the result of the comparison. The 8086 je instruction is one of a number of **conditional jump** (branch) instructions that are used to transfer control to another part of your program. The je instruction means 'jump if equal', that is, if the result of the comparison is that the items compared are equal. The je instruction tests the status register to check the result of the comparison. If the result is that the operands are the same, then the je instruction transfers control (jumps) to the instruction at eq_lab. The jmp instruction is an **unconditional** jump instruction. It is the equivalent of the goto statement of C. It always transfers control to the point specified by the label. Because of the primitive nature of assembly language instructions, we use a combination of conditional and unconditional jump instructions to implement the selection (`if-then`) and looping statements of high-level languages. Note the similarity of the above example and the C code fragment using `goto` of Example 1.14 in Chapter 1, where the importance of compound statements was illustrated.

There are other conditional jump instructions for testing the other conditions that arise, such as inequality, less than, greater than and so on. They all operate in the same fashion. They test the flags in the status register and jump if the appropriate flags are set. (This is why the status register is also called the **condition codes** register.) Before using one of these conditional jump instructions, the flags must be set. This is usually done by a **compare** instruction, but a number of other instructions also set flags in the status register. They include the arithmetic instructions such as `add` and `sub`. For example, if the result of an instruction is `0`, then a flag in the status register called the **Z**-flag (zero flag) is set to `1`. This is the flag that the `je` instruction tests. In fact the `je` instruction has another name, it is also called `jz` (jump if zero). The `jne` instruction tests for inequality and it is also called the `jnz` (jump if not zero) instruction.

Example 2.8 was concerned with the implementation of the `if-then` statement in assembly language. Loops are implemented in a similar fashion, as illustrated in Example 2.9.

Example 2.9

The following code fragment is a loop to sum the integers 1 to 20.

C version:

```
i = 1;                          /* loop counter */
sum = 0;
while ( i != 21 )
{
        sum = sum + i;
        i = i + 1;
}
     /* sum now contains the result */
```

Assembly language:

```
            mov   sum, 0
            mov   cx, 1        ; loop counter
while1:     cmp   cx, 21
            je    finished
                  add  sum, cx        ; sum = sum + cx
                  inc  cx             ; cx = cx + 1
            jmp   while1
finished:                      ; sum now contains the result
```

As for selection, we use a combination of unconditional and conditional jump instructions to implement the loop control structure. The value of `cx` is compared with `21` and if it equals `21`, the `je` instruction transfers control to `finished`. Otherwise a running total is accumulated in `sum`, `cx` is incremented by 1 and the `jmp` instruction transfers control to `while1`, that is, it loops back to `while1`. The process is then repeated until `cx` reaches `21`. The `inc` instruction:

```
inc   cx
```

carries out the same operation as

```
add   cx, 1
```

but is a more efficient instruction. We will discuss instruction efficiency later. There is a similar instruction called `dec` to subtract 1 (decrement) from a variable.

One of the issues that arises in representing numbers (see Appendix B) is that we need to take care to handle unsigned and signed numbers appropriately. When comparing numbers for equality or inequality, the sign does not matter, as the bit patterns representing the numbers are either identical (they are equal) or they are not. In assessing if one number is greater than (or less than and so on) another number, then the sign does matter. The reason for this is that different representations are used for signed and unsigned numbers. For example, the bit pattern `1111 1111` represents –1 if interpreted as a two's complement number (signed number), while it represents the number 255 if interpreted as an unsigned number. Thus, an instruction to compare one number with another must be aware of which interpretation is intended, whether the numbers are signed or unsigned. In assembly language, to make this distinction, we use **separate** instructions for signed and unsigned numbers. For example, the instruction `jg` (jump if greater than) is used to test if one signed number is greater than another signed number. The instruction `ja` (jump if above) is used to test if an unsigned number is greater than another unsigned number. It is the responsibility of the assembly language programmer to use the appropriate instruction, depending on whether signed or unsigned numbers are being used.

All processors use a status register in a similar fashion to that indicated above. It may be used for other purposes, such as recording the occurrence of overflow (the result of an operation is too big or small to fit in a register). For the moment, you only need to understand its function in conditional jump instructions.

Exercises

2.1 Translate the following C code fragment to assembly language (a) using C like variables and (b) using registers to do the assignments:

```
int i, k ,d;
char c;
char colour[80];

i = 10 ;
k = i + 4;

c = '5';
d = c - '0'     /* convert it to a number */
```

2.2 Write a code fragment to sum the sequence 2, 4, 6, 8, ..., 18, 20, 22, 24. The result should be stored in a variable called `sum`.

2.3 Translate the following C code fragment to assembly language. It tests if the variable `c` contains a digit in character form and converts it to its numeric form if it does. (It could be written much more elegantly in C!)

```
        if ( c < '0' )          /* c is not a digit */
             goto fin ;
        if ( c > '9' )          /* c is not a digit */
             goto fin ;
        d = c - '0' ;           /* c must be a digit so
                                   we convert it to a number */
fin:
```

2.3.8 Indirect addressing

In Example 2.1, we saw how to declare strings, that is, arrays of characters. Given that we have defined a string variable **message** as `message db 'Hello',0`, an important feature is that the characters *are stored in consecutive memory locations*. If the `'H'` is in location `1024`, then `'e'` will be in location `1025`, `'l'` will be in location `1026` and so on. A technique known as **indirect addressing** may be used to access the elements of the array. Indirect addressing allows us to store the address of a location in a register and use this register to access the value stored at that location. This means that we can store the address of the string in a register and access the first character of the string via the register. If we increment the register contents by 1, we can access the next character of the string. By continuing to increment the register, we can access each character of the string, in turn, processing it as we see fit.

Figure 2.3 illustrates how indirect addressing operates, using register `bx` to contain the address of a string `"Hello"` in memory. Here, register `bx` has the value `1024`, which is the address of the first character in the string. Another way of phrasing this is to say that `bx` **points** to the first character in the string. In 8086 assembly language we denote this by enclosing `bx` in square brackets: `[bx]`, which reads as the value **pointed to** by `bx`, which means *the contents of the location whose address is stored in the* `bx` register.

The first character of the string can be accessed as follows:

```
cmp  byte ptr [bx], 0  ; is this end of string?
```

This instruction compares the character (indicated by `byte ptr`) pointed to by `bx` with `0`. How do we store the address of the string in `bx` in the first place? The special operator `offset` allows us to specify the address of a memory variable. For example, the instruction:

```
mov  bx, offset message
```

will store the **address** of the variable `message` in `bx`. We can then use `bx` to access the variable `message`.

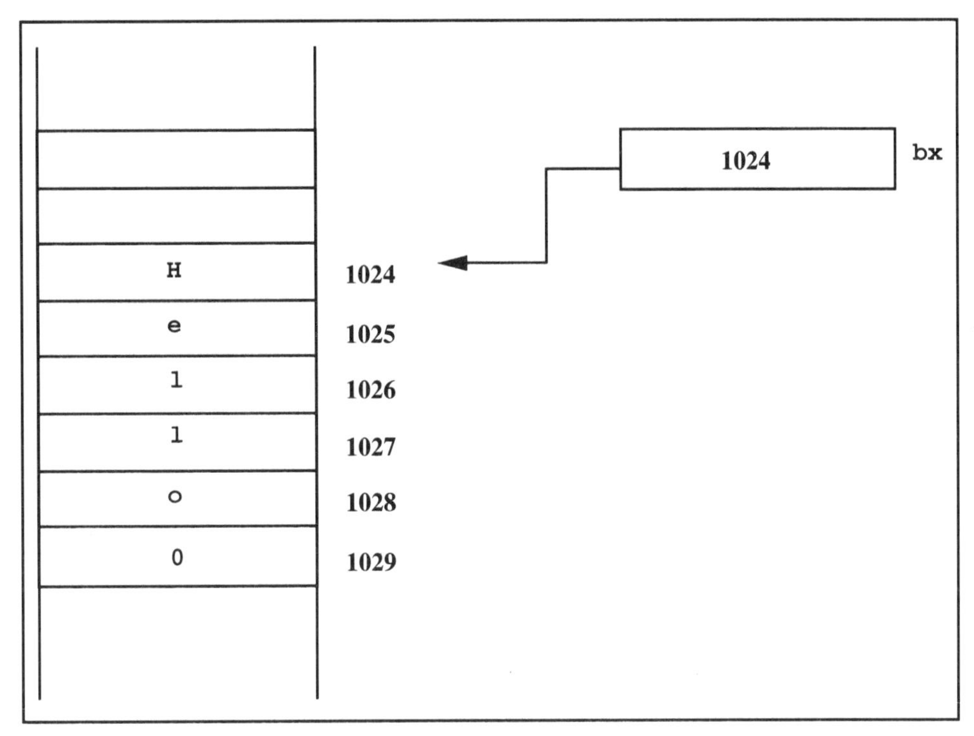

Figure 2.3 Using the bx register for indirect addressing.

Example 2.10

The following code fragment illustrates the use of indirect addressing. It is a loop to count the number of characters in a string terminated by the Null character (ASCII 0). It uses the cx register to store the number of characters in the string.

```
message     db      'Hello', 0
.......
........
        mov cx, 0               ; cx stores number of
                                ; characters
        mov bx, offset message  ; store address of
                                ; message in bx
start:
        cmp byte ptr [bx], 0    ; is this end of string?
        je  fin                 ; if yes goto Finished
            inc  cx             ; cx = cx + 1
            inc  bx             ; bx points to next
                                ; character
        jmp start
                                ; cx now contains the
                                ; number of
                                ; characters in message
fin:
```

The label `start` indicates the beginning of the loop to count the characters. After the `mov` instruction is executed, register `bx` contains the address of the first character in the string. We compare this value with `0` and if the value is not `0`, we count it by incrementing `cx`. We then increment `bx` so that it now points to the next character in the string. We repeat this process until we reach the `0` character that terminates the string.

When indirect addressing is used, the register containing the address may be treated as pointing at a single character (a byte) or as pointing at a word (two consecutive bytes). The use of `byte ptr` in the `cmp` instruction specifies that `cmp` is to compare with `0` the byte pointed to by `bx`.

Note: If you omit the 0 character when defining the string, the program will fail. Why? The reason is that the loop continues to execute until `bx` points to a memory location containing `0`. If `0` has been omitted from the definition of the message, then we do not know when, if ever, the loop will terminate. This is the same as an array subscript out of bounds error in a high-level language.

The form of indirect addressing described here is called **register indirect addressing** because a register is used to store the indirect address.

2.3.9 Indexed addressing

Another technique used to access the elements of a list is **indexing**. This is essentially the same as using subscripts with arrays in a high-level language. A register is used to hold the subscript value. Such a register is called an **index** register. Again the `bx` register may be used. The above example could be implemented using indexed addressing as shown in Example 2.11.

Example 2.11

Implementation of Example 2.10 using indexed addressing:

```
        message             db    'Hello', 0
 .......
 ........

        mov  cx, 0                ; cx = 0
        mov  bx, 0                ; bx = 0   ;index register
 start:
        cmp  message[bx], 0
        je   fin                  ; if message[bx] == 0 goto fin
             inc  bx              ; bx = bx + 1
             inc  cx              ; cx = cx + 1
        jmp  start                ; goto start
 fin:                             ; cx contains the count
```

The notation `message[bx]` is interpreted in the same way as an array subscript in a high-level language. We first access element `0`, then element `1` and so on. This is easier to read than indirect addressing as it closely mirrors the facility available in a high-level language. However, we have to know the name of the array in order to access elements of the array. If we wish to write a sub-program which is to process different arrays from call to call (such as get__str from Chapter 1), we cannot use this technique since it would mean that the array name would have to be specified in the sub-program and only that particular array could be accessed by the sub-program. In writing such sub-programs, we pass the address of the array as a parameter and use indirect addressing to access the array elements. This means that the same sub-program can access any number of different arrays since the sub-program is not concerned with the name of the array it is accessing. This will be made clearer by way of examples in the following chapters.

2.4 The stack

A **stack** is an *area of memory* which is used for storing data on a temporary basis. In a typical computer system the memory is logically partitioned into separate areas. Your program code is stored in one such area, your variables may be in another such area and another area is used for the stack. Figure 2.4 is a crude illustration of how memory might be allocated when a user program is running.

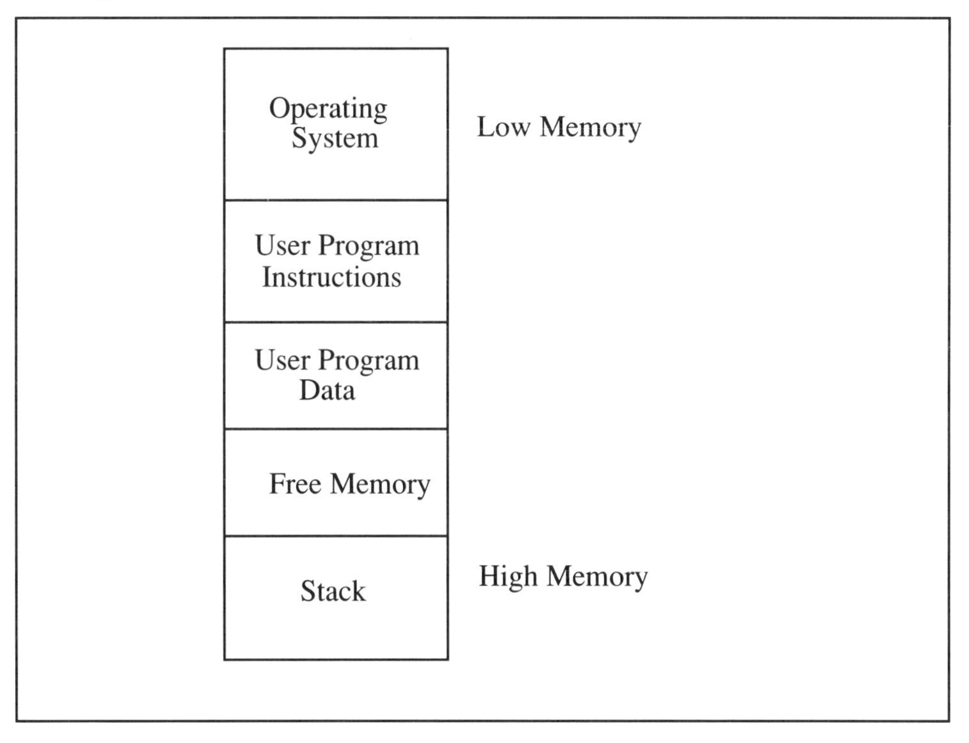

Figure 2.4 Memory allocation: user programs share memory with the operating system software.

The area of memory with addresses near 0 is called low memory, while high memory refers to the area of memory near the highest address. The area of memory used for your program code is fixed, so that, once the code is loaded into memory, it does not grow or shrink. The stack on the other hand may require varying amounts of memory. The amount actually required depends on how the program uses the stack. Thus the size of the stack varies during program execution. We can store information on the stack and retrieve it later.

One of the most common uses of the stack is in the implementation of the sub-program facility. This usage is transparent to the programmer; the programmer does not have to explicitly access the stack and the instructions to call a sub-program and to return from a sub-program automatically access the stack. They do this in order to return to the correct place in your program when the sub-program is finished. The point in your program where control returns after a sub-program finishes is called the **return address**. The return address of a sub-program is placed on the stack by the `call` instruction. When the sub-program finishes, the `ret` instruction retrieves the return address from the stack and transfers control to that location. The stack may also be used to pass information to sub-programs and to return information from sub-programs, i.e. as a mechanism for handling high-level language parameters.

Conceptually a stack, as its name implies, is a *stack of data elements*. The size of the elements depends on the processor and for example, may be 1 byte, 2 bytes or 4 bytes. We will ignore this for the moment. We can illustrate a stack as in Figure 2.5. To use the stack, the processor must keep track of where items are stored on it. It does this by using the **stack pointer** (`sp`) register. This is one of the special registers mentioned earlier and it points to the *top* of the stack, that is, its contains the address of the stack memory element containing the value last placed on the stack. When we place an element on the stack, the stack pointer contains the address of that element on the stack. If we place a number of elements on the stack, the stack pointer will always point to the last element we placed on the stack. When retrieving elements from the stack we retrieve them

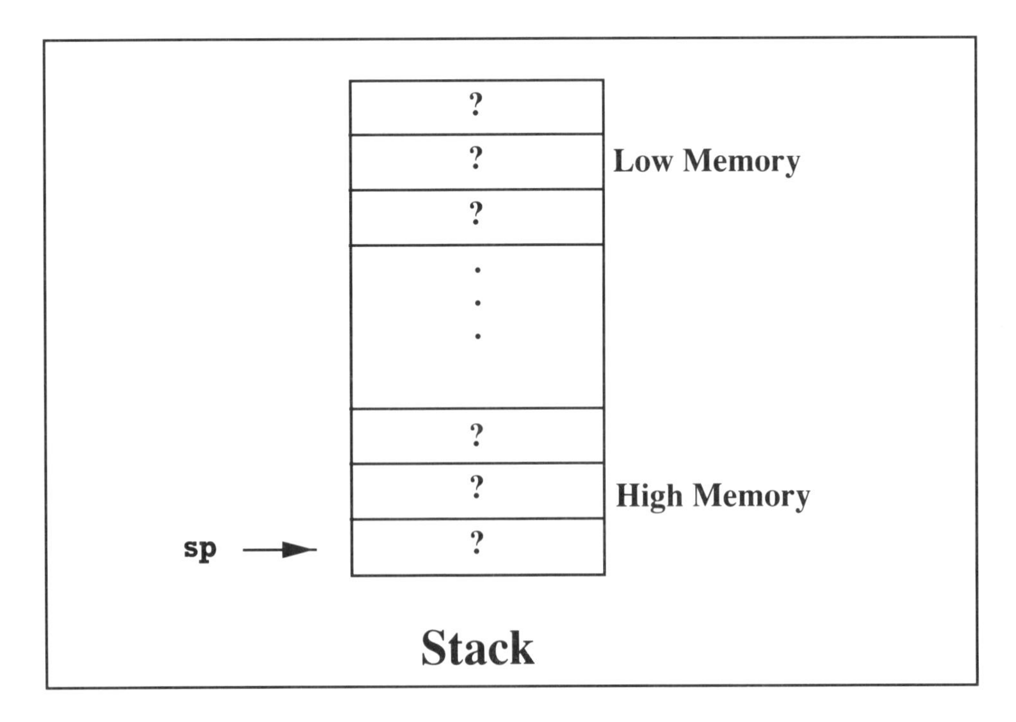

Figure 2.5 Simple model of the stack.

in reverse order. This will become clearer when we write some stack manipulation programs.

There are two basic stack operations that are used to manipulate the stack and these are usually called `push` and `pop`. The 8086 `push` instruction places (pushes) a value on the stack. The stack pointer is left pointing at the value pushed on the stack. For example, if `ax` contains the number `123`, then the instruction:

```
push  ax
```

will cause the value of `ax` to be stored on the stack. In this case the number `123` is stored on the stack and `sp` *points* to the location on the stack where `123` is stored. The 8086 `pop` instruction is used to retrieve a value previously placed on the stack. The stack pointer is left pointing at the next element on the stack. Thus `pop` conceptually removes the value from the stack. Having stored a value on the stack as above, we can retrieve it by:

```
pop  ax
```

which transfers the data from the top of the stack to `ax` (or any register); in this case the number `123` is transferred. Information is stored on the stack starting from high memory locations. As we place data on the stack, the stack pointer points to successively lower memory locations. We say that the stack grows downwards. If we assume that the top of the stack is location `1000` (`sp` contains `1000`) then the operation of `push ax` is as follows. First, `sp` is decremented by the size of the element (2 bytes for the 8086) to be pushed on the stack. Then the value of `ax` is copied to the location pointed to by `sp`, `998` in this case. If we then assign `bx` the value `212` and carry out a `push bx` operation, `sp` is again decremented by two, giving it the value `996`, and `212` is stored at this location on the stack. We now have two values on the stack.

As mentioned earlier, if we now retrieve these values, we encounter the fundamental feature of any stack mechanism. Values are retrieved in *reverse order*. This means that the last item placed on the stack is the first item to be retrieved. We call such a process a **Last-In-First-Out** or **LIFO** process. So, if we now carry out a `pop ax` operation, `ax` gets as its value `212`, the last value pushed on the stack. If we now carry out a `pop bx` operation, `bx` gets as its value `123`, the second last value pushed on the stack. Hence, the operation of `pop` is to copy a value from the top of the stack, as pointed to by `sp`, and to increment `sp` by 2 so that it now points to the previous value on the stack. We can push the value of any register or memory variable on the stack. We can retrieve a value from the stack and store it in any register or a memory variable. The above example is illustrated in Figure 2.6; steps (1) to (4) correspond to the states of the stack and stack pointer after each instruction.

The stack may be used in programs to store temporary variables, as is illustrated in Example 2.12.

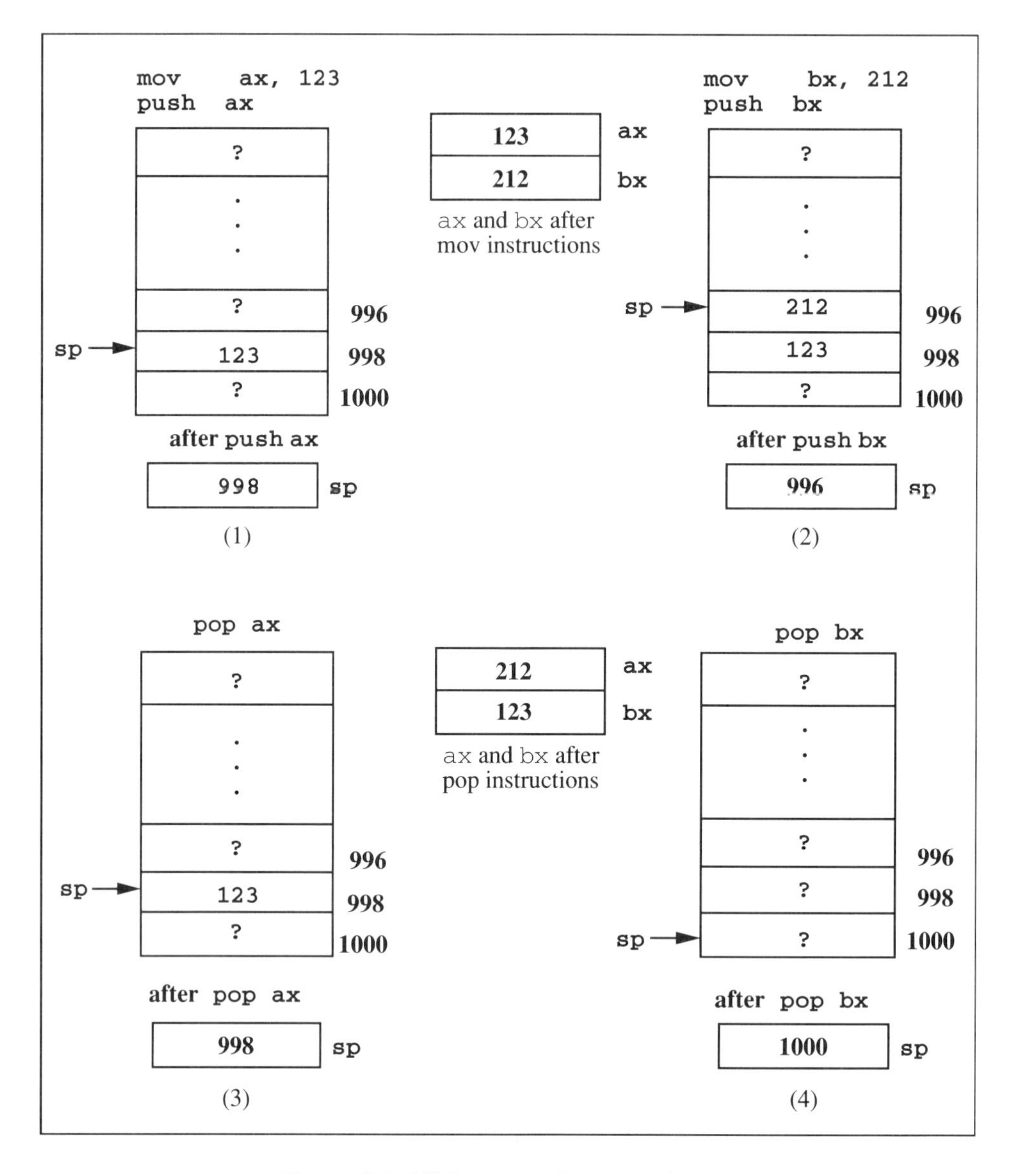

Figure 2.6 LIFO nature of push and pop.

Example 2.12

Using the stack, swap the values of the ax and bx registers, so that ax now contains what bx contained and bx contains what ax contained. (This is not the most efficient way to exchange the contents of two variables.) To carry out this operation, we need at least one temporary variable:

Version 1:

```
push    ax              ; Store ax on stack
push    bx              ; Store bx on stack
pop     ax              ; Copy last value on stack to ax
```

```
pop     bx                  ; Copy first value to bx
```

The above solution stores both ax and bx on the stack and utilizes the LIFO nature of the stack to retrieve the values in reverse order, thus swapping them in this example. We really only need to store one of the values on the stack, so the following is a more efficient solution.

Version 2:

```
push    ax                  ; Store ax on stack
mov     ax, bx              ; Copy bx to ax
pop     bx                  ; Copy old ax from stack
```

When using the stack, the number of items pushed on should equal the number of items popped off. This is vital if the stack is being used inside a sub-program. This is because, when a sub-program is called its return address is pushed on the stack. If, inside the sub-program, you push something on the stack and do not remove it, the return instruction will retrieve the item you left on the stack instead of the return address. This means that your sub-program cannot return to where it was called from and it will most likely crash (unless you were very clever about what you left on the stack!).

2.5 Format of assembly language instructions

The format of assembly language instructions is relatively standard. The **general format** of an instruction is (where square brackets [] indicate the **optional** fields) as follows:

```
[Label]   Operation   [Operands]   [; Comment]
```

The instruction may be treated as being composed of four **fields**. All four fields need *not* be present in every instruction, as we have seen from the examples already presented. Unless there is only a comment field, the **operation field** is *always* necessary. The label and the operand fields may or may not be required, depending on the operation field.

Example 2.13

Examples of instructions with varying numbers of fields.

```
                                        Notes
L1:  cmp bx, cx  ; Compare bx with cx   all fields present
     add ax, 25                         operation and two operands
     inc bx                             operation and one operand
     ret                                operation field only
; Comment only                          comment field only
```

When two operands are specified, they must be separated by a comma. Spaces around the comma are optional but enhance readability. The comment field is used to provide information to the programmer and those reading the program. A semicolon must precede a comment. The assembler ignores comments totally. They have no effect whatsoever on the machine code program generated by the assembler.

2.6 Assembling programs

The assembler translates a program to machine code, but this is not the whole story. The machine code program produced by the assembler (called the **object** program) is *not* ready for execution. In particular, the addresses generated by the assembler are **relocatable**. This means that they can be manipulated so that the program can be located anywhere in memory. The **linker/loader** program takes these relocatable addresses and translates them to **absolute** addresses which can be loaded directly into memory for execution. (This is the purpose of the MS-DOS **link** command.)

In addition, a given program may be composed of a number of sub-programs, which are stored in separate files. One file contains the main program, which is where execution begins. The other files store *external* sub-programs. All of these files must be assembled to produce object code and then the linker is used to combine them to produce a single executable program. A collection of sub-programs may also be organized to form a **library**. The linker also allows you to link the sub-programs in a library with a main program to form a single executable program. In fact, it can be arranged so that the linker automatically links specified library sub-programs with your main program. Figure 2.7 summarizes the assembly process.

The assembler can also produce a **listing file**, which lists the assembly language instructions and their machine code equivalents. This is a good way to become familiar with the details of assembly language program translation.

A compiler or assembler must scan through the complete source program to translate it to machine code. Such a scan is called a **pass**. The assembler checks the syntax, keeps track of symbols (variables and labels) and generates machine code. Some assemblers carry out all of this in a **single pass**, but most use **two passes**. The first pass keeps track of symbols and checks the syntax of each statement, reporting errors if there are any. The second pass generates the machine code, but only if there are no syntax errors.

2.7 Summary

This chapter has described the basic concepts required for writing and understanding assembly language programs. The implementation of programming concepts, such as variables and conditional statements was introduced. This involved describing assembly language directives and instructions. We also looked at the stack and examined its operation. We omitted a detailed discussion of I/O in this chapter and this is one of the major topics in Chapter 3.

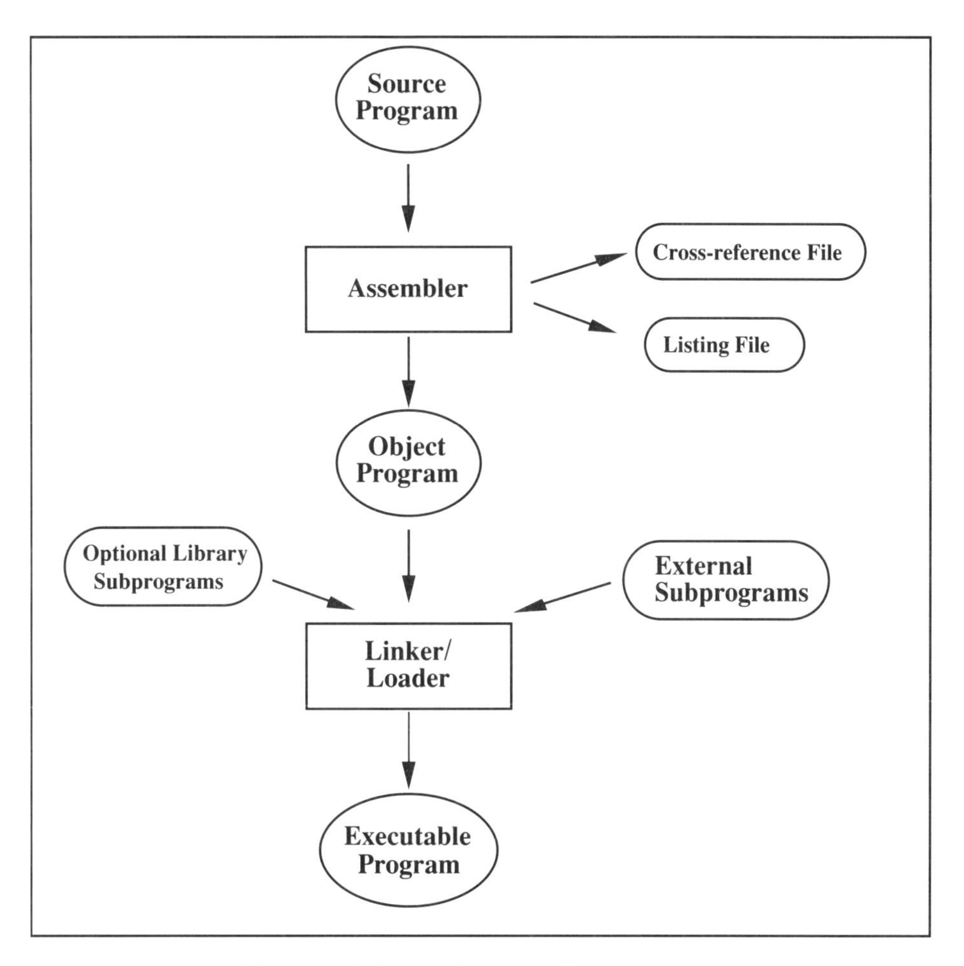

Figure 2.7 Assembling and linking a program.

Exercises

2.4 Explain the purpose of the stack pointer, status register and program counter.

2.5 How are instructions formatted?

2.6 Explain briefly the operation of the assembler.

2.7 Write a code fragment to count the number of occurrences of the letter 'e' in the string "Hello everyone" using (a) indirect addressing and (b) indexing to access the elements of the string. Show the definition of the string variable.

2.8 Explain the operation of the `push` and `pop` instructions and their effect on the stack pointer.

2.9 What is the difference between the following instructions?

```
cmp ax, bx
cmp ax, [bx]
```

2.8 Reading list

Brey, B.B. (1993) *8086/8088, 80286, 80386 and 80486 Assembly Language Programming*, Merrill (MacMillan), New York.

Hawkley, C. and Neil White, N. (1987) *Assembly Language Programming on the IBM PC*, Addison Wesley, Wokingham.

Liu, Yu-Cheng and Gibson, G.A. (1986) *Microcomputer Systems: The 8086/8088 Family*, Prentice Hall, Englewood Cliffs, NJ.

Microsoft Macro Assembler 5.1 Programmers Guide, (Manual available with MASM), 1987, Microsoft Corporation, Redmond, WA.

Morneau, P. (1992) *PC Assembly Language: An Introduction to Computer Systems*, West Publishing Co., St. Paul, MN.

Skinner, T. (1985) *An Introduction to Assembly Language Programming for the 8086 Family*, Wiley Press, New York.

Thorne, M. (1986) *Programming the 8086/8088*, Benjamin Cummings, Menlo Park, CA.

Uffenbeck, J. (1987) *The 8086/8088 Family: Design, Programming and Interfacing*, Prentice Hall, Englewood Cliffs, NJ.

3

8086 assembly language programming

In Chapter 2, assembly language programming concepts were introduced. To write assembly language programs you need to have a basic understanding of:

- the machine's register set: the registers available to the programmer;
- the machine's instruction set: the instructions for processing information and carrying out I/O;
- the assembler's directives: the directives to declare variables and perform other tasks. In addition, you need to know how to assemble, link and execute programs. In this chapter, we build upon the concepts developed in Chapter 2 to describe 8086 assembly language programming. First of all, we look at the 8086 register set. We mentioned some of the 8086 registers in Chapter 2, but now we take a more detailed look at the complete set of registers.

3.1 The 8086 register set

The 8086 microprocessor has a total of 14 registers that are accessible to the programmer, as illustrated in Figure 3.1. Each of the registers is *16 bits long*, so that each can contain a 16-bit number. Four of the registers are referred to as **data** registers and are the `ax`, `bx`, `cx` and `dx` registers. Another four are referred to as **index/pointer** registers and they are the `sp`, `bp`, `si` and `di` registers. These eight registers are collectively known as **general purpose** registers, that is, they can be used by the programmer for data manipulation. Four more registers are called **segment** registers and they are `cs`, `ds`, `es` and `ss`. The two remaining registers are the **instruction pointer** register **ip** and the **flags** register.

The general purpose registers are just that – they can be used by the programmer for whatever task is required. However, certain registers may have special importance. For example, as we mentioned in Chapter 2, the `bx` register may be used in indirect addressing. The `ax`, `cx` and `dx` registers may not be used for this purpose. While the four index registers can be used for arithmetic operations, their use is usually concerned with accessing data in memory. For example, the `sp` and `bp` registers are concerned with accessing the stack.

An important feature of the four data registers is that they can each be treated

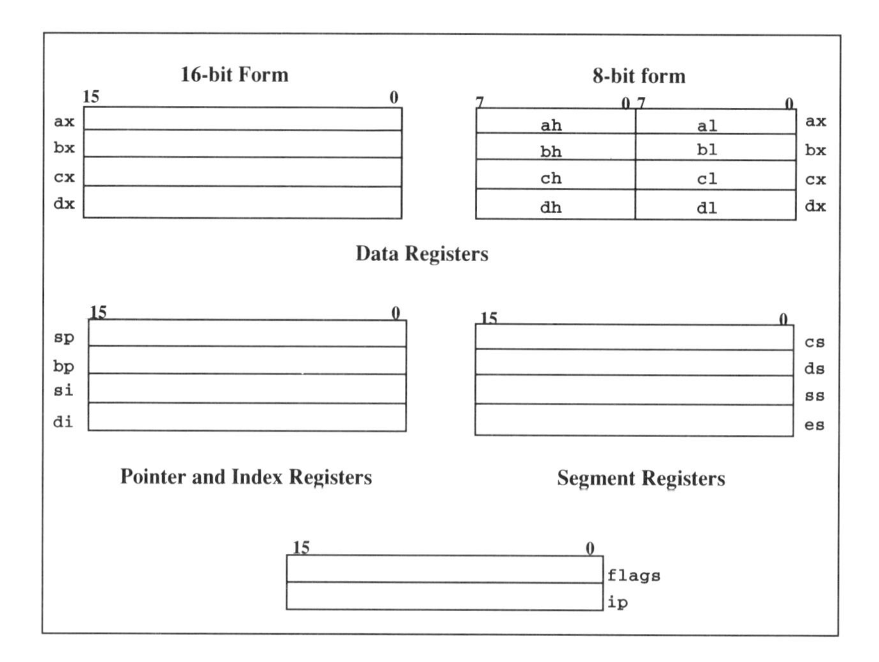

Figure 3.1 The Intel 8086 register set.

as either a 16-bit register or as *two 8-bit registers*. Each 8-bit register can be used independently. The ax register may be accessed as ah and al. The h stands for high-order byte (bits 8 to 15 of the 16-bit register) and the l stands for low-order byte (bits 0 to 7). Similarly, bx may be accessed as bh and bl, cx may be accessed as ch and cl and dx may be accessed as dh and dl. If you use a data register as an 8-bit register, you cannot use its 16-bit parent *in the same instruction*. So, an instruction such as mov ax, al is illegal.

The segment registers are concerned with accessing memory. The processor uses these registers to access instructions, data and the stack. The code segment register (cs) stores the starting address of the instructions making up a program. The data segment register (ds) stores the starting address of the variables used in the program, the extra segment register (es) has a similar function for additional variables. The stack segment register stores the starting address of the stack.

The ip register, or as it is more usually called, the **program counter**, is a 16-bit register used to contain the memory location of the next instruction to be executed. This register is updated automatically by the processor and the programmer cannot *directly* access it in a program. Instructions to transfer control, such as jmp, call, ret and the conditional jump instructions, modify the program counter, in order to transfer control to another point in a program.

The flags register (also called the **status** or **condition codes register**) is really a collection of bits called flags. Only nine bits of the status register are used. They are divided into two groups, one known as **control** flags (3 bits) and the other as **status** flags (6 bits). The remaining 7 bits are not used. A flag can only take on the values 0 and 1. We say a flag is *set* if it has the value 1. The status flags are used to record status information resulting from the execution of arithmetic and logical instructions. For example, the **zero flag (Z-flag** or **ZF)** is set to 1 if the result of an arithmetic operation is zero. An instruction such as `sub ax, ax` would result in the Z-flag being set to 1. The control flags are used to control certain processor modes, such as whether interrupts are allowed. The overflow flag is set when the result of an arithmetic operation is too large to fit in a register. The sign flag is set when a negative result is generated. The interrupt flag is used to control interrupts (to disable or enable them; see Chapter 6). Figure 3.2 illustrates some of the flags used in the status register.

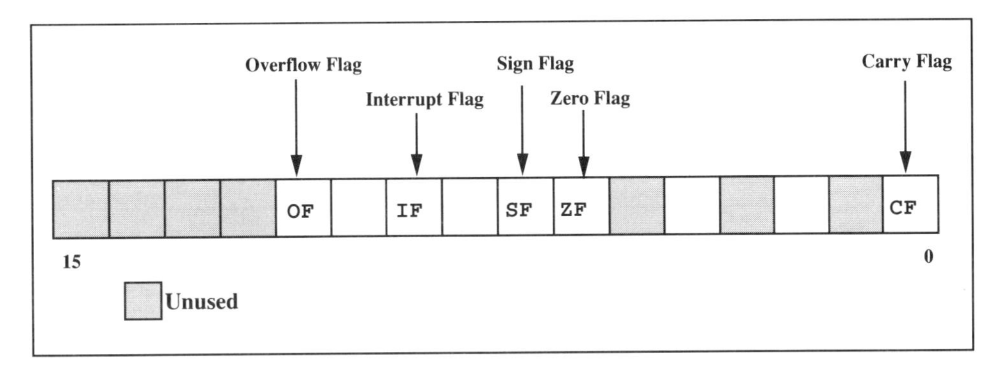

Figure 3.2 The `flags` register with the names of some of the flags.

3.2 The 8086 instruction set

There are over 120 instructions in the 8086 instruction set. Fortunately, we can write a large range of programs using a small sub-set of these 120 instructions. Instructions can be classified into four main groups: data-manipulation instructions, arithmetic/logical instructions, I/O instructions and transfer-of-control instructions. In this section, we look at some of the commonly used instructions in each class by giving examples of their usage. The equivalent C code is presented as comments where appropriate.

3.2.1 *Data-manipulation instructions:* `mov` *instruction*

These instructions are concerned with moving data inside the computer system. The `mov` instruction is one the most frequently used data manipulation instructions. The `mov` instruction allows us to transfer data between registers or between memory and registers. You may not transfer data from one memory variable to another in a single `mov` instruction. The general format of the `mov` instruction is:

```
mov    destination, source
```

This copies the data specified by the source operand to the destination operand, which must be either a register or a memory variable. Some examples of the use of the `mov` instruction are given below.

Example 3.1

The mov instruction is one of the most frequently used 8086 instructions:

```
mov  ax, 2        ; ax = 2
mov  cx, ax       ; cx = ax
mov  x, ax        ; x = ax     (x is a memory variable)
mov  dx, y        ; dx = y     (y is a memory variable)
mov  bx, 'a'      ; bx = 'a'
mov  dl, '?'      ; dl = '?'
mov  ah, 21h      ; ah = 0x21 (21h is 0x21 in C notation)
```

Figure 3.3 illustrates the effect of the second mov instruction in Example 3.1. This instruction loads into cx the value (2) stored in ax.

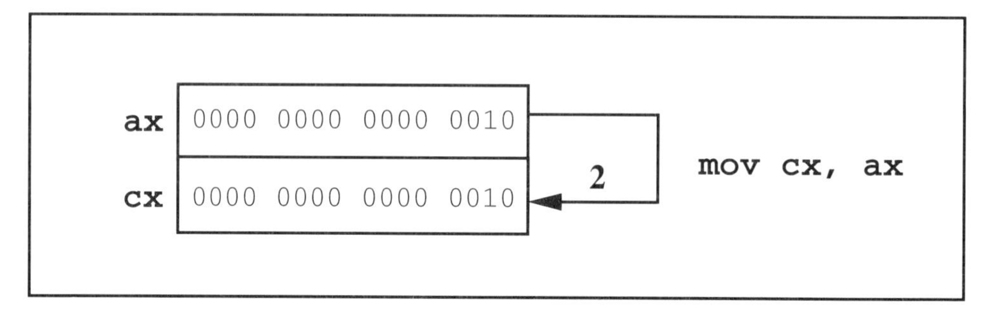

Figure 3.3 The effect of executing mov cx, ax.

Note, there is an important difference between the following two instructions:

```
mov  dl, 3        ; dl = 3
mov  dx, 3        ; dx = 3
```

In the first case, only the dl register gets changed, the dh register remaining unchanged by the mov instruction. In the second case, the entire register gets changed; dl will store 03h, but dh is overwritten by 00h. This is illustrated by Figure 3.4, where we assume we have used mov dx, ffffh to give dx an initial

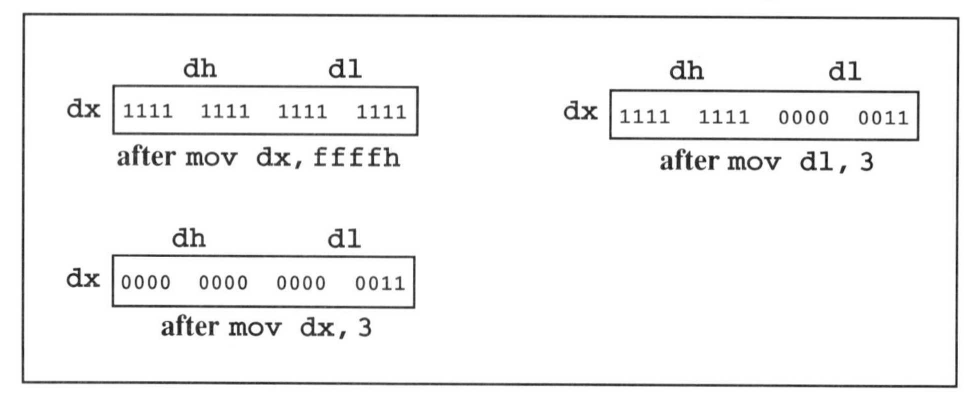

Figure 3.4 Comparing mov dl, 3 with mov dx, 3.

value of ffffh (1111 1111 1111 1111 in binary). In other words, when we store a value in a 16-bit register, all 16 bits of the register get changed, that is, the value is represented as a 16-bit number, padded with zeros on the left hand side if necessary.

Register names and hexadecimal numbers

There is an ambiguity problem if you wish to use the hexadecimal value A written as AH (or ah) since there is also a register called ah. In order to avoid ambiguity between register names and hexadecimal numbers that begin with a letter, we prefix the hexadecimal numbers with 0. Thus 0ah refers to a number and ah refers to a register. Thus, to assign the hexadecimal value ah to the bh register, we write:

```
mov    bh, 0ah
```

Hexadecimal numbers may be written using either upper-case or lower-case letters, so that 0ah is the same as 0AH.

The push and pop instructions (described in Chapter 2) which transfer information to and from the stack are also examples of data manipulation instructions.

3.2.2 *Arithmetic instructions*

These carry out the normal arithmetic operations. In this example we only consider a few of them: the add, inc, dec and sub instructions.

Example 3.2

```
mov  ax, 5     ; ax = 5
add  ax, 3     ; ax = ax + 3       (ax now contains 8)
inc  ax        ; ax = ax + 1       (ax now contains 9)
dec  ax        ; ax = ax - 1       (ax now contains 8)
sub  ax, 6     ; ax = ax - 6       (ax now contains 2)
mov  cx, 8     ; cx = 8
add  ax, cx    ; ax = ax + cx      (ax now contains 10)
sub  ax, cx    ; ax = ax - cx      (ax now contains 2)

mov  sum, 0    ; sum = 0           (sum is a memory variable)
add  sum, ax   ; sum = sum + ax    (sum now contains 2)
sub  cx, sum   ; cx = cx - sum     (cx now contains 6)
```

The add instruction adds the second operand to the first operand, leaving the result in the first operand. The inc instruction takes one operand and adds 1 to it. The dec instruction, like inc, takes one operand and subtracts 1 from it. The sub instruction subtracts the second operand from the first, leaving the result in the first operand. As we can see, operands may be constants, registers or (memory) variables. As for the mov instruction, you may not operate on two memory variables in a single 8086 instruction.

Note: The destination operand (first one) of all the instructions we have seen so far (mov, add, inc, dec, sub) *must* be a storage location, either a register or a memory location.

Some microprocessors do not provide instructions for multiplication or division (for example, the M6800 does not provide multiplication and division operations; it is not to be confused with the more powerful M68000 processor, which does provide such operations). With such microprocessors, multiplication and division have to be programmed using repeated addition, subtraction and shift operations (discussed later) which slows down computations involving multiplication and division. The 8086 provides the `mul` and `div` (and `imul` and `idiv`) instructions for multiplication and division.

The `mul` instruction is used to carry out multiplication and is used for unsigned numbers. It takes a single operand, either a register or a memory variable (a constant cannot be used). The other operand *must* be the `al` or `ax` register. The result, when two 8-bit numbers are multiplied, will be stored in the `ax` register. When 16-bit numbers are multiplied, the result will be in the pair of registers `dx:ax` (`ax` containing the low-order bits and `dx` containing the high-order bits). You can visualize this as if register `ax` was appended to the right-hand side of `dx`, as shown in Figure 3.5.

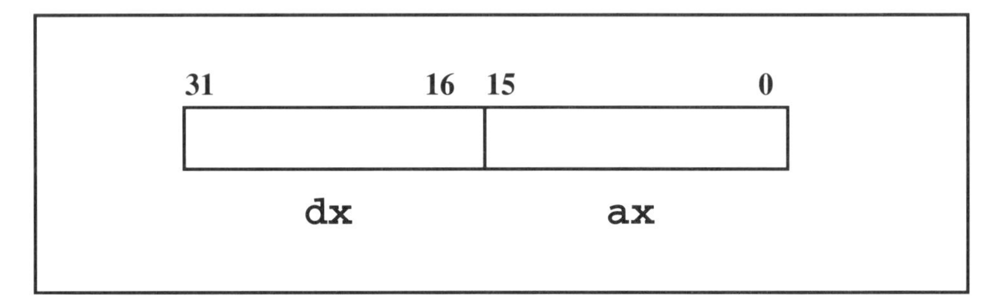

Figure 3.5 Representing a 32-bit number using the `dx:ax` registers.

Example 3.3

Multiply 7 by 9:

```
mov   al, 7
mov   bl, 9
mul   bl              ; ax = al * bl = 63
```

In this example, the `mul` instruction multiplies the contents of the `al` register by the contents of the `bl` register, storing the result in the `ax` register, overwriting the previous contents of the `ax` register. Note that the `mul` instruction takes a single operand and the `al` (`ax`) register is *implicitly* used for the second operand.

The `div` instruction carries out division and is used for dividing unsigned numbers. It allows you to divide an 8-bit number into a 16-bit number (byte division) or divide a 16-bit number into a 32-bit number (word division). In the case of byte division the number to be divided must be stored in the `ax` register and the divisor may be in another register or memory location (a constant cannot be used). In the case of word division, the 32-bit number must be stored in two registers since registers are limited to 16 bits. The `dx` and `ax` registers must be used. The high-order bits are stored in dx and the low-order bits are stored in ax, as in Figure 3.5.

The div instruction performs **integer division**, which means that the result will always be an integer. Dividing 7 by 4 using integer division gives the result 1 with remainder 3. Dividing 7 by 8 gives the result 0 and remainder 7. In the case of word division, the result is stored in ax and the remainder in dx. In the case of byte division the result is stored in al and the remainder in ah.

Example 3.4

Divide 1235 by 10:

```
mov   ax, 1235
mov   cl, 10
div   cl              ; divide ax by 10
                      ; al now contains 123 and ah
                      ; contains 5
```

The div instruction takes a single operand as does the mul instruction, with the second operand always being stored in the ax register (or the dx:ax registers).

The instructions imul and idiv are used for signed numbers, but otherwise they are identical to the div and mul instructions.

Exercises

3.1 Write instructions to:
load the character '?' into register bx;
load the space character into register cx;
load 26 (decimal) into register ax;
copy the contents of ax to bx and dx.

3.2 What errors are present in the following instructions?:

```
mov  ax    3d
mov  23,   ax
mov  cx, ch
move ax, 1h
add  2, cx
add  3, 6
inc  ax, 2
```

3.3 Write instructions to evaluate the arithmetic expression 5 + (6 – 2) leaving the result in ax using (a) one register, (b) two registers and (c) three registers.

3.3 Input and output (I/O) in 8086 assembly language

Each microprocessor provides instructions for I/O with the devices that are attached to it, for example the keyboard and screen. The 8086 provides the instructions in for input and out for output. These instructions are quite complicated to use, so we usually use the operating system to do I/O for us instead. The operating system in this case is most often MS-DOS and it provides a range of I/O sub-programs, in much the same way as there is an extensive library of sub-programs available to the C programmer. In C, to perform an I/O operation, we call a sub-program using its name to indicate its operations, for example `putchar()`, `printf()`, `getchar()`. In addition, we may pass a parameter to the sub-program; for example, the character to be displayed by `putchar()` is passed as a parameter to `putchar()`. In assembly language we must have a mechanism to call the operating system to carry out I/O and we must be able to tell the operating system what kind of I/O operation we wish to carry out, say, to read a character from the keyboard, to display a character or string on the screen or to do disk I/O. Finally, we must have a means of passing parameters to the operating sub-program.

In 8086 assembly language, we do not call operating system sub-programs by name, instead, we use a software interrupt mechanism (see Chapter 6 for a discussion of interrupts). An interrupt signals the processor to suspend its current activity (running your program) and to pass control to an interrupt service program, which is part of the operating system. A software interrupt is one generated by a program (as opposed to one generated by hardware). The 8086 `int` instruction generates a software interrupt. It uses a single operand, a number indicating which MS-DOS sub-program is to be invoked. For I/O and some other operations, the number used is `21h` (these numbers are usually written in hexadecimal in reference books and this text adopts the same practice). Thus, the instruction `int 21h` transfers control to the operating system, to a sub-program that handles I/O operations. This sub-program handles a variety of I/O operations by calling appropriate sub-programs. Therefore you must also specify which I/O operation (say read a character or display a character) you wish to carry out. This is done by placing a specific number in a register. The `ah` register is used to pass this information.

Initially, we will consider character I/O with the keyboard and screen. Each MS-DOS I/O operation is identified by a unique number. We need to pass this number as a parameter when using the `int` instruction. For example, the sub-program to display a character is sub-program number `2h`. This number must be stored in the `ah` register. We are now in a position to describe character I/O. When the I/O operation is finished, the interrupt service program terminates and our program will be resumed at the instruction following `int`. In this regard, the `int` instruction operates in a similar fashion to the `call` instruction. It transfers control to an operating system sub-program which carries out a particular task and returns control to the correct point in your program when the sub-program finishes.

3.3.1 Character output

The task here is to display a single character on the screen. There are three elements involved in carrying out this operation using the `int` instruction:

(1) We specify the character to be displayed. This is done by storing the character's ASCII code in a specific 8086

register. In this case we use the `dl` register, that is, we use `dl` to pass a parameter to the output sub-program.

(2) We specify which of MS-DOS's I/O sub-programs we wish to use. The sub-program to display a character is sub-program number `2h`. This number is stored in the `ah` register.

(3) Using the `int` instruction, we call MS-DOS to carry out the I/O operation. This means that we **interrupt** our program and transfer control to the MS-DOS sub-program that we have specified using the `ah` register.

As mentioned earlier, each MS-DOS sub-program may be identified by a number and in this text we will refer to an MS-DOS sub-program using this number, for example sub-program number `2h` displays a character.

Example 3.5

Write a code fragment to display the character `'a'` on the screen:

C version:

```
putchar( 'a' ) ;
```

8086 version:

```
mov  dl, 'a'   ; dl = 'a' which is to be displayed
mov  ah, 2h    ; character output sub-program is number 2
int  21h       ; call ms-dos to display character
               ;
```

As you can see, this simple task is quite complicated in assembly language. First, the MS-DOS I/O sub-program is invoked. It then uses the `ah` register value to determine which I/O operation is to be used. In this example, the number `2h` indicates that a character, stored in the `dl` register, is to be displayed.

3.3.2 Character input

The task here is to read a single character from the keyboard. There are also three elements involved in performing character input:

(1) As for character output, we specify which of MS-DOS's I/O sub-programs we wish to use, that is, the character input from the keyboard sub-program. This is MS-DOS sub-program number **1h**. This number must be stored in the `ah` register.

(2) We call MS-DOS to carry out the I/O operation using the `int` instruction as for character output.

(3) The MS-DOS sub-program uses the `al` register to store the character it reads from the keyboard.

Example 3.6

Write a code fragment to read a character from the keyboard:

C version:

```
c = getchar() ;
```

8086 version:

```
mov  ah, 1h   ; keyboard input sub-program
int  21h      ; call ms-dos to do character input operation
              ; character entered is stored in al
mov  c, al    ; copy character from al to variable c
```

Note: In the case of character input, the `ax` register is used for two purposes: first, it is used to indicate which MS-DOS sub-program is to be called (`ah` specifies the sub-program number). Second, it is used to store the character read from the keyboard (`al` stores this character).

The following example combines the two previous ones, by reading a character from the keyboard and displaying it.

Example 3.7

Reading and displaying a character:

C version:

```
c = getchar() ;
putchar( c ) ;
```

8086 version:

```
mov  ah, 1h   ; keyboard input sub-program
int  21h      ; call ms-dos to read character into al

mov  dl, al   ; copy character to dl

mov  ah, 2h   ; character output sub-program
int  21h      ; call ms-dos to display character in dl
```

A complete program

We are now in a position to write a complete 8086 program. You must use an **editor** to enter the program into a file. The process of using the editor (**editing**) is a basic form of word processing. This skill has no relevance to programming. In this text, we use Microsoft's `MASM` and `LINK` programs for assembling and linking 8086 assembly language programs. `MASM` program files should have names with the **extension** (three characters after the period) `asm`. We will call our first program `io1.asm` and it displays the letter `'a'` on the screen. (You may use any name you wish. It is a good idea to choose a meaningful file name.)

Having entered and saved the program specified in Example 3.6, using an editor, you must then use the MASM and LINK commands to translate it to machine code so that it may be executed as follows:

```
C> masm io1
```

If you have syntax errors, you will get error messages at this point. You then have to edit your program, correct them and repeat the above command, otherwise proceed to the link command, pressing Return in response to prompts for file names from masm or link.

```
C> link io1
```

To execute the program, simply enter the program name and press the Return key:

```
C> io1
a
C>
```

Example 3.8

A complete program to display the letter 'a' on the screen:

```
; io1.asm: displays the character 'a' on the screen
; Author:  Joe Carthy
; Date:    March 1994

         .model small
         .stack 100h

         .code
start:
         mov  dl, 'a'    ; store ascii code of 'a' in dl

         mov  ah, 2h     ; ms-dos character output
                         ; function
         int  21h        ; displays character in dl
                         ;

         mov  ax, 4c00h ; return to ms-dos
         int  21h
         end  start
```

The first three lines of the program are comments to give the name of the file containing the program, explain its purpose and give the name of the author and the date when the program was written. While such comments are optional, it is a good idea to begin all programs in this fashion. After the comments, the next three lines contain assembler directives. The first two directives, .model and .stack are concerned with how your program will be stored in memory and how large a stack it requires. The third directive, `.code`, indicates where the program instructions (the program code) begin. Later we will use a `.data` directive to indicate where memory variables are defined. For the moment, suffice it to say that you need to start all assembly language programs in a particular format (not necessarily that given above), in the same manner as C programs begin with a `main()` sub-program. Your program must also finish in a particular format; the `end` directive indicates where your program finishes. In the middle comes the code that you write yourself. Here, the code is that of the Example 3.5.

You must specify where your program starts, that is which is the first instruction to be executed. This is the purpose of the label, `start`. (Note that we could use any label, say `begin` in place of `start`.) This same label is also used by the `end` directive. When a program has finished, we return to MS-DOS. Like carrying out an I/O operation, this is also accomplished by using the `int` instruction. This time MS-DOS sub-program number `4c00h`, to terminate a program and return to MS-DOS, is used. This number is passed to the operating system using the `ax` register. Hence, the instructions:

```
mov  ax, 4c00h  ; Code for return to MS-DOS
int  21H        ; Terminates program returning to MS-DOS
```

terminate a program and return you to MS-DOS.

Time-saving tip: Since your programs will start and finish using the same format, you can save yourself time by not entering this code for each program. You create a template program called for example, `template.asm`, which contains the standard code to start and finish your assembly language programs. Then, when you wish to write a new program, you copy this template program to a new file, say for example, `io2.asm`, as follows (using the MS-DOS copy command):

```
C> copy template.asm io2.asm
```

You then edit `io2.asm` and enter your code in the appropriate place.

Example 3.9

The following template could be used for our first programs:

```
; <filename goes here>.asm:
; Author:
; Date:

            .model small
            .stack 100h

            .code
start:

;           < your code goes here >

            mov    ax, 4c00h ; return to ms-dos
```

```
            int     21h
            end     start
```

To write a new program, you enter your code in the appropriate place as indicated above.

More sample programs

Example 3.10

Write a program to read a character from the keyboard and display it on the screen (based on Example 3.7):

C version:

```
main()
{
  int c;

  c = getchar() ;        /* read character */
  putchar( c ) ;         /* display character entered */
}
```

8086 version:

```
; io2.asm: read a character and display it
; Author:  Joe Carthy
; Date:    March 1994

           .model small
           .stack 100h

           .code
start:

  mov  ah, 1h      ; keyboard input sub-program
  int  21h         ; call ms-dos to read character into al

  mov  dl, al      ; copy character to dl

  mov  ah, 2h      ; display sub-program
  int  21h         ; call ms-dos to display character in dl


  mov  ax, 4c00h   ; return to ms-dos
  int  21h
  end  start
```

Assuming you enter the letter B at the keyboard when you execute the program, the output will appear as follows:

```
C> io2
BB
```

The first **B** is the one entered and the second is the one output from the program. This program is not very user friendly in that it gives the user no prompt for input and the output appears beside the input. To improve the situation, we rewrite the program to display a ? as a prompt for input and separate the output from the input by a space character. Thus when we run the program we get the following effect:

```
C>io3
?B B
```

Example 3.11

C version:

```
main()
{
        int c;
        putchar( '?' );      /* display ? */
        c = getchar() ;      /* read character */

        putchar(' ');        /* display a space character */
        putchar( c ) ;       /* display character entered */
}
```

8086 version:

```
; io3.asm: prompt user with ? , read character and display a
;          space followed by the    character entered.
; Author:  Joe Carthy
; Date:    March 1994

           .model small
           .stack 100h
           .code
start:
; display ?
           mov  dl, '?'      ; copy ? to dl
           mov  ah, 2h       ; display sub-program
           int  21h          ; call ms-dos to display ?

; read character from keyboard
           mov  ah, 1h       ; keyboard input sub-program
           int  21h          ; call ms-dos to read character
                             ; into al

; we want to save character entered while we display a space
```

```
            mov  bl, al       ; copy character to bl

; display space character
            mov  dl, ' '      ; copy space to dl
            mov  ah, 2h       ; display sub-program
            int  21h          ; call ms-dos to display space

; display character read from keyboard
            mov  dl, bl       ; copy character entered to dl
            mov  ah, 2h       ; display sub-program
            int  21h          ; call ms-dos to display
                              ; character in dl

; terminate program and return to MS-DOS
            mov  ax, 4c00h    ; return to ms-dos
            int  21h
            end  start
```

Note: In this example we must save the character entered (we save it in `bl`) so that we can use `ax` for the display sub-program number.

Example 3.12

Modify the previous program so that the character entered is displayed on the following line giving the effect:

```
C> io4
? x
x
```

In this version, we need to output the Return and Linefeed characters, instead of the space character used in Example 3.11. Return (Carriage Return, ASCII 13D) is the control character to bring the cursor to the start of a line and Linefeed (ASCII 10D) is the control character that brings the cursor down to the next line on the screen. (We use the abbreviations CR and LF to refer to Return and Linefeed in comments.)

C version:

```
main()
{
        int c;
        putchar( '?' );     /* display ? */
        c = getchar() ;     /* read character */
        putchar('\n');      /* display a newline character */
        putchar( c ) ;      /* display character entered */
}
```

In a C program, while a single character (`'\n'`) is used to cause output to start on a new line, when the program is actually executed, the Return and Linefeed characters are actually output by the operating system. However, in assembly language programs under MS-DOS we must output the two control characters to start a new line.

8086 version:

```
; io4.asm: prompt user with ?, read character and display
;       the CR, LF characters    followed by the character
        entered.
; Author:   Joe Carthy
; Date:     March 1994


            .model small
            .stack 100h
            .code
start:
; display ?
            mov  dl, '?'      ; copy ? to dl
            ov   ah, 2h       ; display sub-program
            int  21h          ; call ms-dos to display ?

; read character from keyboard
            move ah, 1h       ; keyboard input sub-
                              program
            int  21h          ; call ms-dos to read
                              character

; save character while we display a Return and Line-feed
            mov  bl, al       ; copy character to bl

;display Return
            mov  dl, 13d      ; dl = CR
            mov  ah, 2h       ; display sub-program
            int  21h          ; call ms-dos to display CR

;display Line-feed
            mov  dl, 10d      ; dl = LF
            mov  ah, 2h       ; display sub-program
            int  21h          ; call ms-dos to display LF


; display character read from keyboard
            mov  dl, bl       ; copy character to dl
            mov  ah, 2h       ; display sub-program
            int  21h          ; call ms-dos

            mov  ax, 4c00h    ; return to ms-dos
            int  21h
            end  start
```

As you can see, assembly language programs tend to be long and complicated.

This is especially noticeable when you compare the C version of a program with the 8086 version. This is why there is an emphasis on using high-level language programs where possible.

Note: Indentation and documentation, as mentioned before, are the responsibility of the programmer. Program 3.13 below is a completely valid way of entering the program presented earlier in Example 3.12:

Example 3.13

Program 3.13 without indentation and comments.

```
.model small
.stack 100h
.code
start:
mov  dl,'?'
mov  ah,2h
int  21h
mov  ah,1h
int  21h
mov  bl,al
mov  dl,13d
mov  ah,2h
int  21h
mov  dl,10d
mov  ah,2h
int  21h
mov  dl,bl
mov  ah,2h
int  21h
mov  ax,4c00h
int  21h
end  start
```

The absence of indentation, blank lines and comments are of no consequence to the assembler, but make the program very difficult for a programmer to read and understand. It is a good idea to lay out and document your program as you enter it. This gives your code a more professional appearance and has the added advantage that, if you need to get someone to read your program (say, to help find a bug), it will be easier for them to understand your code.

3.3.3 String output

A string is a list of characters treated as a unit. In programming languages we denote a string constant by using quotation marks, for example `"Enter first number"`. In 8086 assembly language, single or double quotes may be used. The C language only allows double quotes to be used to define strings (Pascal uses single quotes). In Chapter 2, we saw that strings are defined using the `db` directive. The following 3 definitions are equivalent ways of defining a string `"abc"`:

```
version1  db  97, 98, 99       ; individual ASCII codes
version2  db  'a', 'b', 'c'    ; individual characters
version3  db  'abc'            ; string constant
```

The first version defines a string by specifying a list of the ASCII codes that make up the string. The second version is similar, except that character constants are used instead of the ASCII codes, which makes it easier to understand. The third version uses the method of high-level languages and simply encloses the string in quotes. We may also combine the above methods to define a string as in the following example:

```
message  db  'Hello world', 13, 10, '$'
```

The string `message` contains `'Hello world'` followed by Return (ASCII 13), Linefeed (ASCII 10) and the `'$'` character. This method is very useful if we wish to include control characters (such as Return) in a string. We terminate the string with the `'$'` character because there is an MS-DOS sub-program (number `9h`) for displaying strings that expects the string to be terminated by the `'$'` character.

String variables may be defined by using the `dup` operator with the `db` data definition directive, for example

```
buffer  db  100 dup (?)   ; buffer may contain up to 100
                          ; characters
colour  db  70 dup (?)    ; colour may contain up to 70
                          ; characters
```

The `dup` operator allows us to define arrays of bytes (use with `db`), words (use with `dw`) and long words (use with `dd`). It defines a block, of the specified size, of consecutive memory locations.

In order to display a string we must know where the string begins and ends. The beginning of a string is given by obtaining its address using the `offset` operator. The end of a string may be found by either knowing in advance the length of the string or by storing a special character at the end of the string to act as a sentinel. (The Null character (`'\0'`) serves this purpose in C strings.) We have already used MS-DOS sub-programs for character I/O (number `1h` to read a single character from the keyboard and number `2h` to display a character on the screen). MS-DOS provides sub-program number `9h` to display strings which are terminated by the `'$'` character. In order to use it we must:

(1) Ensure that the string is terminated with the `'$'` character.

(2) Specify the string to be displayed by storing its address in the `dx` register.

(3) Specify the string output sub-program by storing `9h` in `ah`.

(4) Use `int 21h` to call MS-DOS to execute sub-program `9h`.

The following code illustrates how the string `'Hello world'`, followed by the Return and Linefeed characters, can be displayed.

Example 3.14

Write a program to display the message `'Hello world'` followed by Return and Linefeed :

```
; io8.asm: Display the message 'Hello World', 13,10
; Author:  Joe Carthy
; Date:    March 1994

            .model small
            .stack 100h

         .data
message db      'Hello World', 13, 10, '$'
                                        ; note the terminating $
         .code
start:
         mov   ax, @data
         mov   ds, ax

         mov   dx, offset message ; copy address of
                                  ; message to dx
         mov   ah, 9h             ; sub-program for string
                                  ; output
         int   21h                ; call ms-dos to display
                                  ; string

mov      ax, 4c00h
         int   21h

end      start
```

In this example, we use the `.data` directive. This directive is required when memory variables are used in a program. In the examples to date, we have used registers to represent variables and this directive was, thus, not required. It is concerned with allocating memory space for variables. In addition, we have modified the starting code of the program. The instructions

```
mov  ax, @data
mov  ds, ax
```

are concerned with accessing memory variables. The `ds` (data segment) register is used by the 8086 processor when we access memory variables in a program. The `@data` operand in the first instruction is an assembler symbol, and is used to obtain the address of the data segment. The `ds` register must be assigned this value before variables can be accessed in a program. In addition, the `ds` register can only be given a value that is already stored in another register such as the `ax` register. Hence we need to use two mov instructions to assign the ds register the value of @data.

The offset operator was mentioned in Chapter 2. It allows us to access the address of a variable. In this case, we use it to access the address of message and we store this address in the dx register. Sub-program 9h can access the string message (or any string), using indirect addressing, once it has been passed the starting address of the string.

In practice, we use memory variables in programs, so a new template should be created, to replace that presented in Example 3.9, which contains the .data directive and the appropriate code to initialize the ds register.

Exercises

3.4 Modify the program in Example 3.11 to produce a program called io3B which will display a space after the ? prompt so that the following appears on the screen:

```
C> io3B
? B B
```

3.5 Write a program to display 'MS-DOS' (a) using character output and (b) using string output.

3.6 Write a program to display the letter 'A', followed by two blank lines followed by the letter 'B'.

3.7 Write a program called ex_37.asm to read two characters and display them on the following line, so that they appear as follows:

```
C> ex_37
ab
ab
```

3.8 Write a program to display the message 'Ding! Ding! Ding!' and output ASCII code 7 three times. (ASCII code 7 is the Bel character. It causes your machine to beep!)

3.9 Write a program to display the letter 'A' and to beep twice.

3.10 Write a program to beep, display '?' as a prompt, read a character and display it on a new line.

3.4 Control flow instructions: sub-programs

We introduced the concept of sub-programs in Chapter 1 and briefly discussed their use in assembly language in Chapter 2. As explained, a sub-program allows us to give a name to a group of instructions and to use that name when we wish to execute those instructions, instead of having to write the instructions again.

For example, the instructions to display a character could be given the name putc (or whatever you choose). Then to display a character you can use the name putc, which will cause the appropriate instructions to be executed. This is referred to as **calling** the sub-program. In 8086 assembly language, the instruction call is used to invoke a sub-program, so, for example, a putc sub-program would be called as follows:

```
call  putc      ; Display character in dl
```

The process of giving a group of instructions a name is referred to as **defining** a sub-program. This is only done once. The putc sub-program may be defined as follows:

Example 3.15

Definition of putc sub-program.

```
putc:
          mov  ah, 2h
          int  21h
          ret
```

The ret instruction terminates the sub-program and arranges for execution to resume at the instruction following the call instruction. We usually refer to that part of a program where execution begins as the **main program**. In practice, programs consist of a main program and a number of sub-programs. It is important to note that sub-programs make our programs easier to read, write and maintain even if we only use them once in a program.

Example 3.16

Using sub-programs, rewrite the program in Example 3.10 to read a character and display it. We define two sub-programs: putc to display a character stored in the dl register and getc to read a character into the al register.

```
; io6.asm: read and display character using sub-programs
; Author:  Joe Carthy
; Date:    March 1994

           .model small
           .stack 100h
           .code

;  main program
start:
        call getc        ; read character into al register

        mov  dl, al      ; copy character in al to dl

        call putc        ; display character in dl register
```

```
        mov  ax, 4c00h  ; return to ms-dos
        int  21h

; user defined sub-programs

putc:                   ; display character in dl
        mov  ah, 2h
        int  21h        ; call ms-dos to display character
        ret             ; return to caller

getc:                   ; read character into al
        mov  ah, 1h
        int  21h        ; call ms-dos to read character
        ret             ; return to caller


        end  start
```

This program is easier to read and understand than its equivalent presented in Example 3.10.

Note: Sub-programs are defined *after* the code to terminate the program, but *before* the end directive. If we placed the sub-programs earlier in the code, they would be executed without being called (execution would fall through into them). This should not be allowed to happen.

Example 3.17

Rewrite, using sub-programs, the program of Example 3.12, which reads a character and displays it on the following line.

```
; io7.asm: read a character and display it on the following
; line
; Author:  Joe Carthy
; Date:    March 1994

           .model small
           .stack 100h

CR      equu      13d
LF      equ       10d

        .code
start:
        call prompt     ; display ?<space>
        call getc       ; read character from keyboard

        mov  bl, al     ; copy character to bl

        call newline    ; output CR LF
```

```
        mov  dl, bl        ; copy input character to dl
        call putc          ; display character

        mov  ax, 4c00h     ; return to ms-dos
        int  21h

;  user defined sub-programs

putc:                      ; display character in dl
        mov  ah, 2h
        int  21h           ; call ms-dos to display character
        ret                ; return to caller

getc:                      ; read character into al
        mov  ah, 1h
        int  21h           ; call ms-dos to read character
        ret                ; return to caller

prompt:                    : display ? and space character
        mov  dl, '?'       ; dl = '?'
        call putc          ; display ?
        mov  dl, ' '       ; dl = ' '
        call putc          ; display space
        ret

newline:                   ; start a new line
        mov  dl, CR        ; dl = CR
        call putc          ; output CR character
        mov  dl, LF        ; dl = LF
        call putc          ; output LF character
        ret

        end  start
```

Note: A sub-program may call other sub-programs, as illustrated in this example. The main program firstly calls the `prompt` sub-program to display `'? '`. The `prompt` sub-program calls `putc` to display the relevant characters. The main program then calls `getc` to read a character into the `al` register. It saves this character in the `bl` register, because `al` will be used for other purposes. It then calls the `newline` sub-program to output Return and Linefeed. Finally, the main program displays the character initially read in, using `putc`.

The above example also uses the `equ` directive as described in Chapter 2, to define two constants `CR` and `LF`, to represent the ASCII codes of Return and Linefeed. These are used in the `newline` sub-program to make it easier to understand.

In Section 3.3.3 we used sub-program `9h` to display a string terminated by

'$'. We now define another useful sub-program, called puts, to display a string.

Example 3.18

The following program, which displays the message 'Hello World', defines and uses puts:

```
; io9.asm: Display the message 'Hello World' using puts
; Author:  Joe Carthy
; Date:    March 1994

         .model small
         .stack 100h
         .data

CR       equ   13d
LF       equ   10d

message  db          'Hello World', CR, LF, '$'

         .code
start:
         mov   ax, @data
         mov   ds, ax

         mov   dx, offset message
         call  puts                    ; display message

         mov   ax, 4c00h
         int   21h

; User defined sub-programs

puts:                   ; display a string terminated by $
                        ; dx contains address of string
         mov ah, 9h
         int 21h        ;call ms-dos to output string
         ret

         end    start
```

3.4.1 Character conversion: upper case to lower case

To convert an upper-case letter to lower case, we note that ASCII codes for the upper-case letters 'A' to 'Z' form a sequence from 65 to 90. The corresponding lower-case letters 'a' to 'z' have codes in sequence from 97 to 122. (We say that ASCII codes form a collating sequence and we use this fact to sort textual information into alphabetical order.) To convert from an upper-case character to its lower-case equivalent, we add 32 to the ASCII code of the upper-case letter to obtain the ASCII code of the lower-case equivalent. To convert from lower case to upper case, we subtract 32 from the ASCII code of the lower-case letter to obtain the ASCII code of the corresponding upper-case letter. The number 32 is obtained by subtracting the ASCII code for `'A'` from the ASCII code for `'a'` (`'A'` – `'a'` = 97 – 65 = 32).

Example 3.19

Write a program to prompt the user to enter an upper-case letter, read the letter entered and display the corresponding lower-case letter. The program should then convert the letter to its lower-case equivalent and display it, on a new line.

C version:

```
main()
{
  int c ;

  printf("Enter an upper-case letter: ");
  c = getchar() ;
  c = c + ( 'a' - 'A' ) ;      /* convert to lower case */
  printf("\nThe lower-case equivalent is: %c ", c);
}
```

8086 version:

```
; char.asm: character conversion: upper case to lower case

        .model small
        .stack 100h

CR      equ     13d
LF      equ     10d

     .data
msg1    db      'Enter an upper-case letter: $'
result  db      CR, LF, 'The lower-case equivalent is: $'

        .code
start:
        mov     ax, @data
        mov     ds, ax

        mov     dx, offset msg1
        call    puts            ; prompt for upper-case letter
        call    getc            ; read upper-case letter
```

```
        mov     bl, al                  ; save character in bl

        add     bl, 32d                 ; convert to lower case

        mov     dx, offset result
        call    puts                    ; display result
                                        ; message
        mov     dl, bl
        call    putc                    ; display lower-case
                                        ; letter

        mov ax, 4c00h
        int 21h                         ; return to ms-dos

; user defined sub-programs

puts:
        mov ah, 9h
        int 21h                   ; call ms-dos to output string
        ret

putc:                             ; display character in dl
        mov ah, 2h
        int 21h
        ret

getc:                             ; read character into al
        mov ah, 1h
        int 21h
        ret

        end start
```

Executing this program produces as output:

```
Enter an upper-case letter: G
The lower-case equivalent is: g
```

The string `result` is defined to begin with the Return and Linefeed characters so that it will be displayed on a new line. An alternative would have been to include the two characters at the end of the string `msg1`, before the `'$'` character:

```
msg1    db  'Enter an upper-case letter: ',CR, LF, '$'
```

After displaying msg1, as defined above, the next item to be displayed will appear on a new line.

Exercises

3.11 Modify the above program to convert a lower-case letter to its upper-case equivalent.

3.12 Write a program to convert a single digit number such as 5 to its character equivalent '5' and display the character.

3.4.2 I/O sub-program consistency

We have now written three I/O sub-programs: putc, getc and puts. One difficulty with these sub-programs is that they use different registers for parameters based on the requirements of the MS-DOS I/O sub-programs. This means that we have to be careful to remember which register (al, dl, dx) to use to pass parameters. A more consistent approach would be to use the same register for passing the parameters to all the I/O sub-programs, for example the ax register. Since we cannot change the way MS-DOS operates, we can do this by modifying our sub-programs. We will use al to contain the character to be displayed by putc and ax to contain the address of the string to be displayed by puts. The getc sub-program returns the character entered in al and so does not have to be changed.

Example 3.20

Revised versions of puts and putc:

```
puts:                   ; display a string terminated by $
                        ; ax contains address of string
        mov  dx, ax     ; copy address to dx for ms-dos
        mov  ah, 9h
        int  21h        ; call ms-dos to output string
        ret

putc:                   ; display character in al
        mov  dl, al     ; copy al to dl for ms-dos
        mov  ah, 2h
        int  21h
        ret
```

Example 3.21

To illustrate the use of the new definitions of putc and puts, we rewrite the program of Example 3.19, which converts an upper-case letter to its lower-case equivalent:

```
; char2.asm: convert upper case to lower case

        .model small
        .stack 100h

CR      equ   13d
        LF    equ              10d

        .data

sg1     db    'Enter an upper-case letter: $'
result  db    CR, LF, 'The lower-case equivalent is: $'

        .code
;                         main program
start:
        mov   ax, @data
        mov   ds, ax

        mov   ax, offset msg1
        call  puts
        call  getc              ; read upper-case letter
        mov   bl, al            ; save character in bl

        add   bl, 32d           ; convert to lower case

        mov   ax, offset result
        call  puts              ; display result message
        mov   al, bl
        call  putc         ; display lower-case letter

        mov ax, 4c00h
        int 21h                 ; return to ms-dos

; user defined sub-programs

puts:                ; display a string terminated by $
                     ; ax contains address of string
        mov   dx, ax
        mov   ah, 9h
        int   21h ; call ms-dos to output string
        ret

putc:                 ; display character in al
        mov   dl, al
        mov   ah, 2h
```

```
        int   21h
        ret

getc:                 ; read character into al
        mov ah, 1h
        int 21h
        ret

        end start
```

3.4.3 *Saving registers*

There is one disadvantage in using the above method of implementing putc and puts. We now use two registers where formerly we only used one to achieve the desired result. This reduces the number of registers available for storing other information. Another important point also arises. In the puts sub-program, for example, the dx register is modified. If we were using this register in a program before the call to puts, then the information stored in dx would be lost, unless we saved it before calling puts. This can cause subtle but serious errors in programs, which are difficult to detect. The following code fragment illustrates the problem:

```
mov   dx, 12             ; dx = 12
mov   ax, offset msg1    ; display message msg1
call  puts               ; dx gets modified
add   dx, 2              ; dx will NOT contain 14
```

In the above code fragment, after calling puts, the add instruction is carried out. The programmer might expect that dx should contain 14. This is not the case, however, because dx has been used in puts. It may be much later in the execution of the program before this error manifests itself. Beginners make this type of error quite frequently in assembly language programs. When a program behaves strangely, it is usually a good debugging technique to check for this type of situation, that is, check that sub-programs do not modify registers which you are using for other purposes.

This is a general problem with all sub-programs that change the values of registers. All of our sub-programs carrying out I/O change the value of the ah register. Thus, if we are using the ah register before calling a sub-program, we must save it before the sub-program is called. In addition, the MS-DOS sub-program invoked using the int instruction may also change a register's value. For example, sub-program number 2h (used by getc) does this. It modifies the al register to return the value entered at the keyboard. The MS-DOS sub-program may also change other register values and you must be careful to check for this when using such sub-programs.

There is, however, a straightforward solution to this problem. We can and should write our sub-programs so that before modifying any registers they first save the values of those registers. Then, before returning from a sub-program, we restore the registers to their original values. (In the case of getc, however, we would not save the value of the al register because we want getc to read a value into that register.) The stack, as introduced in Chapter 2, is typically used to save and restore the values of registers used in sub-programs.

Example 3.22

We now rewrite the `getc`, `putc` and `puts` sub-programs to save the values of registers and restore them appropriately. The following versions of `getc`, `putc` and `puts` are therefore safer in the sense that registers do not get changed without the programmer realizing it.

```
puts:                   ; display a string terminated by $
                        ; dx contains address of string
        push  ax        ; save ax
        push  bx        ; save bx
        push  cx        ; save cx
        push  dx        ; save dx

        mov   dx, ax
        mov   ah, 9h
        int   21h       ; call ms-dos to output string

        pop   dx        ; restore dx
        pop   cx        ; restore cx
        pop   bx        ; restore bx
        pop   ax        ; restore ax
        ret

putc:                   ; display character in al
        push  ax        ; save ax
        push  bx        ; save bx
        push  cx        ; save cx
        push  dx        ; save dx

        mov   dl, al
        mov   ah, 2h
        int   21h

        pop   dx        ; restore dx
        pop   cx        ; restore cx
        pop   bx        ; restore bx
        pop   ax        ; restore ax

        ret

getc:                   ; read character into al
        push  bx        ; save bx
        push  cx        ; save cx
        push  dx        ; save dx

        mov ah, 1h
```

```
int 21h

pop   dx      ; restore dx
pop   cx      ; restore cx
pop   bx      ; restore bx

ret
```

Note that we pop values from the stack in the reverse order to that in which we pushed them on, because of the last-in-first-out nature of stack operations. From now on, when we refer to `getc`, `putc` and `puts` in this and the following chapter, the definitions above are those intended.

Note: It is vital, when using the stack in sub-programs, to pop off all items pushed on the stack in the sub-program before returning from the sub-program. Failure to do so leaves an item on the stack which will be used by the `ret` instruction as the return address. This will cause your program to behave weirdly to say the least! If you are lucky, it will crash! Otherwise, it may continue to execute from any point in the program, producing baffling results. (I have burned my fingers on a number of occasions with such errors!) The point is worth repeating: when using the stack in a sub-program, be sure to remove all items pushed on, before returning from the sub-program.

3.5 Control flow: jump instructions

3.5.1 Unconditional jump instruction

The 8086 unconditional `jmp` instruction was described briefly in Chapter 2. This instruction takes a single operand, which specifies where control is to be transferred to. It may be to *any* instruction in your program.

Example 3.23

This example illustrates the use of the `jmp` instruction to implement an endless loop:

```
again:
            call getc; read a character into al
            call putc; display character
            jmp again; jump to again
```

This is an example of a backward jump as control is transferred to an earlier place in the program. The code fragment causes the instructions between the label `again` and the `jmp` instruction to be repeated endlessly. The program will execute forever unless you halt it with an interrupt, for example by pressing `ctrl/c` or by switching off the machine.

Example 3.24

The following code fragment illustrates a forward jump, as control is transferred to a later place in the program:

```
        call getc            ; read a character
        call putc            ; display the character
        jmp finish           ; jump to label finish

        <do other things>    ; Never gets done !!!

finish: mov  ax, 4c00h
        int  21h
```

In this case the code between `jmp` instruction and the label `finish` will not be executed because the `jmp` causes control to skip over it.

3.5.2 Conditional jump instructions

In Chapter 2 we also briefly described how conditional statements can be implemented in assembly language. You should recall that the status register records the result of arithmetic instructions. This result can be tested by any of a number of conditional jump instructions (for example `je`, `jne`, `ja`). The result is recorded by setting one or more flags such as the zero flag. If the Z-flag has value 1, it means that the result of the last instruction which affected the Z-flag was 0. If the Z-flag has value 0, it means that the result of the last instruction which affected the Z-flag was not 0. Instructions will also set or reset other flags in the status register such as the C-flag, S-flag, O-flag and so on, depending on the result of the instruction. By testing these flags, either individually or a combination of them, the conditional jump instructions can handle the various conditions (==, !=, <, >, <=, >=) that arise when comparing values. In addition, there are conditional jump instructions to test for conditions such as the occurrence of overflow or a change of sign.

The conditional jump instructions are sometimes called **jump-on-condition** instructions. They test the values of the flags in the status register (the value of the `cx` register is used by some of them). One conditional jump is the `jz` instruction which jumps to another location in a program just like the `jmp` instruction except that it only causes a jump if the Z-flag is set to 1, that is, if the result of the last instruction was 0. (The `jz` instruction may be understood as standing for 'jump on condition zero' or 'jump on zero'.)

Example 3.25

Using the `jz` instruction.

C version

```
ax = 2 ;
if ( (ax - bx) != 0) )
{
  ax = ax + 1 ;
```

```
}
bx = bx + 1;
```

8086 version:

```
        mov  ax, 2    ; ax = 2
        sub  ax, bx   ; ax = 2 - bx
        jz   nextl    ; jump if (ax-bx) == 0
        inc  ax       ; ax = ax + 1
nextl:
        inc  bx
```

In this example, the Z-flag will be set (to 1) only if `bx` contains 2. If it does, then the `jz` instruction will cause the jump to take place as the test of the Z-flag yields true. We are effectively comparing `ax` with `bx` and jumping if they are equal. The 8086 provides the `cmp` instruction for such comparisons. This works exactly like the `sub` instruction except that the operands are not affected, so that it subtracts the source operand from the destination but **discards** the result leaving the destination operand unchanged. However, it does modify the status register. All the flags that would be set or reset by `sub` are set or reset by `cmp`. So, if you wish to compare two values it makes more sense to use the `cmp` instruction.

Example 3.26

The above example could be rewritten using `cmp`:

```
        mov  ax, 2     ; ax becomes 2
        cmp  ax, bx    ; set flags according to (ax - bx)
        jz   equals    ; jump if (ax == bx)
        inc  ax        ; executed only if bx != ax
equals:
        inc  bx
```

Note: The `cmp` compares the **destination** operand with the **source** operand. The order is obviously important because, for example, an instruction such as `jng dest, source` will cause a branch only if `dest <= source` . (See Table 3.1 for the meaning of `jng`.)

Most jump-on-condition instructions have more than one name, for example the `jz` (jump on zero) instruction is also called `je` (jump on equal). Thus the above code could be written:

```
cmp  ax, bx
je   equals ; jump if ax == bx
```

This name for the instruction makes the code more readable in a situation where we are testing two values for equality. The jump-on-condition instructions may be used to jump forwards (as in the above example) or backwards and thus implement loops. There are 16 jump-on-condition instructions which test whether flags or combinations of flags are set or cleared. However, rather than concentrating on the flag settings, it is easier to understand them in terms of comparing numbers (signed and unsigned separately) as equal, not equal, less than, greater than, greater than or equal and less than or equal. Table 3.1 lists the jump-on-condition instructions. It also gives the alternative names for the instructions that have them.

Table 3.1 Conditional jump instructions.

Name(s)	Jump if	Flags tested
`je / jz`	equal/zero	`zf = 1`
`jne / jnz`	not equal/not zero	`zf = 0`
Operating with unsigned numbers		
`ja / jnbe`	above/not below or equal	`(cf or zf) = 0`
`jae / jnb`	above or equal/not below	`cf = 0`
`jb / jnae / jc`	below/not above or equal/carry	`cf = 1`
`ja / jnbe`	below or equal/not above	`(cf or zf) = 1`
Operating with Signed Numbers		
`jg / jnle`	greater/not less than nor equal	`zf=0` and `sf = of`
`jge / jnl`	greater or equal/not less	`sf = of`
`jl / jnge`	less /not greater nor equal	`sf <> of`
`jle / jng`	less or equal/not greater	`(zf = 1)` or `(sf != of)`
`jo`	overflow	`of = 1`
`jno`	not overflow	`of = 0`
`jp / jpe`	parity/parity even	`pf = 1`
`jnp / jpo`	no parity/odd parity	`pf = 0`
`js`	sign	`sf = 1`
`jns`	no sign	`sf = 0`

There are also four jump instructions involving the cx register: jcxz, loop, loope, loopne. For example, the jcxz instruction causes a jump if the content of the cx register is zero.

- cf, of, zf, pf and sf are the carry, overflow, zero, parity and sign flags of the flags register.
- (cf or zf) = **1** means that the jump is made if either cf or zf is set to **1**.
- The letter **a** can be taken to mean above and the letter **b** to mean below. Instructions using these letters (such as ja, jb etc.) operate on unsigned numbers. The letter **g** can be taken to mean greater than and the letter **l** to mean less than. Instructions using these letters (such as jg, jl etc.) operate on signed numbers. It is the programmer's responsibility to use the correct instruction depending on whether signed or unsigned numbers are being manipulated.

3.5.3 *Implementation of the* `if-then` *control structure*

The general form of the `if-then` control structure in C is:

```
if (condition )
{
  /* action statements */
}
<rest of program>
```

It consists of a condition to be evaluated and an action to be performed if the condition yields true.

Example 3.27

C version

```
if ( i == 10 )
{
  i = i + 5 ;
  j = j + 5 ;
}
/* Rest of program */
```

There are two ways of writing this in assembly language. One method tests if the condition `(i == 10)` is true. It branches to carry out the action if the condition is true. If the condition is false, there is a second unconditional branch to the next part of the program. This is written as follows:

8086 version 1:

```
         cmp  i, 10
         je   label1   ; if i == 10 goto label1
         jmp  rest     ; otherwise goto rest of program
label1:  add i, 5
         add j, 5
rest:                  ; rest of program
```

The second method tests if the condition `(i != 10)` is true, branching to the code to carry out the rest of the program if this is the case. If this is not the case, then the action instructions are executed.

8086 version 2:

```
         cmp  i, 10
         jne  rest      ; if i != 10 goto rest
           add i, 5     ; otherwise do action part
           add j, 5
rest:                   ; rest of program
```

The second method only requires a single branch instruction and is to be preferred. So, in general, to implement an `if-then` construct in assembly language, we test the inverse of the condition that would be used in the high-level language form of the construct, as in version 2 above.

3.5.4 *Implementation of the* `if-then-else` *control structure*

The general form of this control structure in C is:

```
if ( condition )
{
  /* action1 statements   */
}
else
{
  /* action2 statements    */
}
```

Example 3.28

Write a code fragment to read a character entered by the user and compare it to the character 'A'. Display an appropriate message if the user enters an 'A'. This code fragment is the basis of a guessing game program.

C version:

```
printf("Guessing game: Enter a letter (A to Z): ");
c = getchar() ;
if ( c == 'A' )
     printf("You guessed correctly !! ");
else
     printf("Sorry incorrect guess ") ;
8086 version:
```

```
        mov ax, offset prompt      ; prompt user for letter
        call puts
        call getc                  ; read character
        cmp al, 'A'                ; compare it to 'A'
        jne is_not_an_a            ; jump if not 'A'
        mov ax, offset yes_msg     ; if action
        call puts                  ; display correct guess
        jmp end_else               ; skip else action
 is_not_an_A:                      ; else action
        mov ax, offset no_msg
        call puts                  ; display wrong guess
                                   ; message

 end_else:
```

If the value read is the letter `'A'`, then the `jne` will not be executed, `yes_msg` will be displayed and control transferred to `end_else`. If the value entered is not an `'A'`, then the `jne` is executed and control is transferred to `is_not_an_A`.

Example 3.29

The complete program to play a guessing game based on the above code fragment is:

```
; guess.asm: Guessing game program. User is asked to guess
;             which letter the program 'knows'
; Author:    Joe Carthy
; Date:      March 1994

           .model small
           .stack 100h

CR         equ        13d
LF         equ        10d

           .data
prompt     db    "Guessing game: Enter a letter (A to Z): $"
yes_msg    db    CR, LF, "You guessed correctly !! $"
no_msg     db    CR, LF, "Sorry incorrect guess $"

           .code
start:
           mov  ax, @data
           mov  ds, ax
           mov  ax, offset prompt
           call puts                   ; prompt for input

           call getc                   ; read character
           cmp  al, 'A'
           jne  is_not_an_a            ; if (al != 'A') skip
                                       ; action
           mov  ax, offset yes_msg     ; if action
           call puts                   ; display correct
                                       ; guess message
           jmp  end_else1              ; skip else action
is_not_an_A:                           ; else action
           mov  ax, offset no_msg
           callputs                    ; display wrong guess
                                       ; message

end_else1:

finish:    mov  ax, 4c00h
           int  21h

; User defined sub-programs
;  <puts getc defined here>

           end  start
```

Note: In this program we use the label `end_else1` to indicate the end of the `if-then-else` construct. It is important, if you use this construct a number of times in a program, to use different labels each time the construct is used. So a label such as `end_else2` could be used for the second occurrence of the construct although it is preferable to use a more meaningful label such as `is_not_an_A`.

Example 3.30

Modify the program in Example 3.19, which converts an upper-case letter to lower case, to test that an upper-case letter was actually entered. To test if a letter is upper case, we need to test if its ASCII code is in the range 65 to 90 ('A' to 'Z'). In C such a test could be written as:

```
if ( c >= 'A' && c <= 'Z' )
  /* it is upper-case letter */
```

The opposite condition, to test if the letter is not upper case, may be written as:

```
if ( c < 'A' || c > 'Z' )
  /* it is not upper-case letter */
```

The variable `c` contains the ASCII code of the character entered. It is being compared with the ASCII codes of 'A' and 'Z'. The notation `&&`, used in the first condition, reads as AND, in other words if the value of `c` is greater than or equal to 'A' AND it is less than or equal to 'Z', then `c` contains an upper-case letter. The notation || used in the second condition reads as OR, in other words, if the value of `c` is less than 'A' OR if it is greater than 'Z', it cannot be an upper-case letter.

`&&` is an example of a logical operator. It allows us to combine two conditions, treating them as a single condition. The result of two conditions combined with AND is true only if both conditions yield true; otherwise the result is false. || is also a logical operator allowing two conditions to be combined. The result is true if either of the conditions evaluates to true. The result is false only if both conditions evaluate to false.

We use the first condition in the 8086 program below.

C version:

```
main()    /* char.c: convert letter to lower case */
{
  char c;
```

```
  printf("\nEnter an upper-case letter: ");
  c = getchar();
  if ( c >= 'A' && c <= 'Z' )
  {
    c = c + ( 'a' - 'A' ) ;      /* convert to lower case */
    printf("\nThe lower-case equivalent is: %c ", c);
  }
  else
    printf("\nNot an upper-case letter %c ", c );
}
```

8086 version:

```
; char3.asm: character conversion: upper case to lower
; case
; Author:   Joe Carthy
; Date:     March 1994

           .model small
           .stack 100h

CR         equ    13d
LF         equ    10d

           .data

msg1       db     CR, LF, 'Enter an upper-case letter: $'
result     db     CR, LF, 'The lower-case equivalent is: $'
bad_msg    db     CR, LF, 'Not an upper-case letter: $'

           .code                        ; main program
start:
           mov    ax, @data
           mov    ds, ax

           mov    ax, offset msg1

           call   puts
           call   getc          ; read upper-case letter
           mov    bl, al        ; save character in bl
           cmp    bl, 'A'
           jl     invalid       ; if bl < 'A' goto invalid
           cmp    bl, 'Z'       ; if bl > 'Z' goto invalid
           jg     invalid
                                ; otherwise its valid
```

```
          add   bl, 32d     ; convert to lower case

          mov   ax, offset result
          call  puts        ; display result message
          mov   al, bl
          call  putc        ; display lower-case letter
          jmp finish

invalid:  mov   ax, offset bad_msg     ; not upper-case
          call  puts        ; display bad_msg
          mov   al, bl
          call  putc        ; display character entered

finish:
          mov ax, 4c00h
          int 21h           ; return to ms-dos

; sub-programs getc, putc and puts should be defined here

          end start
```

This program produces as output, assuming the digit 8 is entered:

```
Enter an upper-case letter: 8
Not an upper-case letter: 8
```

It produces as output, assuming the letter Y is entered:

```
Enter an upper-case letter: Y
The lower-case equivalent is: y
```

Exercises

3.13 Write a program to read a digit and display an error message if a non-digit character is entered.

3.14 In the code fragments below, where will execution continue from when `<jump-on-condition>` is replaced by (a) `je lab1` ; (b) `jg lab1`; (c) `jle lab1`; (d) `jz lab1`?:

(a)
```
    mov ax, 10h
    cmp ax, 9h
    <jump-on-condition>
; rest of program
...........
```

```
 ...........
lab1:
(b) mov cx, 0h
    cmp cx, 0d
    <jump-on-condition>
    ; rest of program
    ...........
    ...........
lab1:
```

3.15 Write programs to read a character from the keyboard and transfer control to the label `ok_here` if the character is:

(a) a valid lower-case letter (`'a'` <= character <= `'z'`)

(b) either an upper-case or lower-case letter (`'A'` <= character <= `'Z'` OR `'a'` <= character <= `'z'`)

(c) is not a lower-case letter, (character < `'a'` OR character > `'z'`).

The programs should display appropriate messages to prompt for input and indicate whether the character satisfied the relevant test.

3.5.5 *Loops*

We have already seen how loops can be implemented using the `jmp` instruction to jump backwards in a program. However, we noted that, since `jmp` is an unconditional jump, it gives rise to infinite loops. The solution is to use jump-on-condition instructions. For example, a `while` loop to display the `'*'` character 60 times may be implemented as in Example 3.31.

Example 3.31

Display a line of 60 stars.

C version:

```
count = 1 ;
while ( count <= 60 )
{
    putchar('*') ;
    count = count + 1 ;
}
```

8086 version:

```
        mov  cx, 1d          ; cx = 1
        mov  al, '*'         ; al = '*'

disp_char:
        cmp  cx, 60d
        jnle end_disp        ; if cx > 60 goto end_disp
             call  putc      ; display '*'
```

```
                inc   cx          ; cx = cx + 1
          jmp   disp_char         ; repeat loop test

end_disp:
```

The instruction `jnle` (jump if not less than or equals) may also be written as `jg` (jump if greater than). We use a similar technique to that used in the implementation of an `if-then` construct in that we test the inverse of the condition used in the C code fragment `(count <= 60)`. This allows us to write clearer code in assembly language. The alternative is cumbersome, requiring an additional jump instruction, and should be avoided:

```
; POOR method of implementing above while loop
          mov   cx, 1d
          mov   al, '*'
disp_char:
          cmp   cx, 60d           ; while cx<= 60
          jle   loop_body         ; if cx <= 60 goto loop_body
          jmp   rest
loop_body:
                call  putc        ; display '*'
                inc   cx          ; cx = cx + 1
          jmp   disp_char         ; repeat loop test

rest::
```

Example 3.32

Write a code fragment to display the characters from `'a'` to `'z'` on the screen using the knowledge that the ASCII codes form a **collating sequence**. This means that the code for `'b'` is one greater than the code for `'a'` and the code for `'c'` is one greater than that for `'b'` and so on.

C version:

```
          c = 'a';                /* c = 97 (ASCII for 'a') */
          while ( c <= 'z' )
          {
                putchar( c );
                c = c + 1;        /* next character */
          }
```

8086 version:

```
          mov   al, 'a'
startloop:
          cmp   al, 'z'
          jnle  endloop           ; while al <= 'z'
                call  putc        ; display character
                inc   al          ; al = al + 1
          jmp   startloop         ; repeat test
endloop:
```

This program produces as output

```
abcdefghijklmnopqrstuvwxyz
```

In the last two examples, we specified how many times the loop action was to be carried out (such a loop is called a deterministic loop). We frequently encounter cases when we do not know how many times the loop will be executed. For example, at each iteration we may ask the user if the loop action is to be repeated and the loop continues to execute or is terminated on the basis of the user's response.

Example 3.33

The program in Example 3.19 reads an upper-case letter, converts it to lower case and displays the lower-case equivalent. We now modify it, so that the user may repeat this process as often as desired. The user is asked to enter `'y'` to carry out the operation, after each iteration.

C version:

```
main()
{
    char c, reply;

    reply = 'y';

    while ( reply == 'y' )
    {
        printf("\nEnter an upper-case letter: ");
        c = getchar();
        c = c + ( 'a' - 'A' ) ;      /* convert to lower case */
        printf("\nThe lower-case equivalent is: %c ", c);
        printf("\nEnter y to continue: ");
        reply = getchar();
    }

}
```

8086 version:

```
; char4.asm: character conversion: upper to lower case

        .model small
        .stack 100h

CR      equ     13d
LF      equ     10d
```

```
        .data
reply         db     'y'
msg0          db     CR, LF, 'Enter y to continue: $'
msg1          db     CR, LF, 'Enter an upper-case letter: $'
result        db     CR, LF, 'The lower-case equivalent is:
                     $'
        .code
;                              main program
start:
              mov    ax, @data
              mov    ds, ax
readloop:
              cmp    reply, 'y'           ; while (reply == 'y')
              jne    finish
                                          ; do loop body
              mov    ax, offset msg1
              call   puts                 ; prompt for letter
              call   getc                 ; read character
              mov    bl, al               ; save character in bl

              add    bl, 32d              ; convert to lower case

              mov    ax, offset
                     result
              call   puts                 ; display result
                                          ; message

              mov    al, bl
              call   putc                 ; display lower-case
                                          ; letter

              mov    ax, offset msg0
              call   puts                 ; prompt to continue

              call   getc                 ; read reply
              mov    reply, al            ; save character in
                                          ; reply
              jmp    readloop             ; repeat loop test


finish:
              mov ax, 4c00h
              int 21h                     ; return to ms-dos

; user defined sub-programs

; sub-programs getc, putc and puts should be defined here

              end start
```

Executing this program produces as output, assuming the user enters the characters `C`, `y`, `X` and `n`:

```
Enter an upper-case letter: C
The lower-case equivalent is: c
Enter y to continue: y
Enter an upper-case letter: X
The lower-case equivalent is: x
Enter y to continue: n
```

Exercises

3.16 Modify the program in Example 3.33 to test that the letter entered is a valid upper-case letter. If it is not, a suitable error message should be displayed and the program should continue executing for as long as the user wishes.

3.17 Modify the guessing game program (Example 3.29) to allow the user three guesses, terminating if any guess is correct.

3.18 Modify the guessing game program to allow users to guess as many or as few times as they wish, terminating if any guess is correct.

3.19 Modify the guessing game program to loop until a correct guess is made.

3.5.6 Counting loops

Counting loops, where we know in advance how many times to repeat the loop body, occur frequently in programming and as a result most high-level languages have a special construct called a **for-loop** to implement them. In Example 3.31, to display the `'*'` character 60 times, we counted upwards from 1 to 60, testing each time around the loop to see if we had reached 60. In assembly language programming, it is common to count downwards, say from 60 to 0. The loop could be implemented by the following code.

Example 3.34

Counting from 60 to 0.

```
              mov  al, '*'       ; al = '*'
              mov  cx, 60d       ; cx = 60
disp_char:
              cmp  cx, 0d
              je   end_disp      ; jump if cx == 0
                   call  putc    ; display '*'
                   dec   cx      ; cx = cx - 1
              jmp  disp_char
end_disp:
```

This code carries out exactly the same task as that of Example 3.31. It is no better or worse. However, there are 8086 jump-on-condition instructions that test the cx register. Recall the jcxz and loop instructions mentioned earlier. The jcxz instruction jumps if the value of the cx register is zero. We could rewrite the above code fragment using the jcxz instruction as follows.

Example 3.35

Rewriting Example 3.34 using the jcxz instruction:

```
                mov  al, '*'      ; al = '*'
                mov  cx, 60d      ; cx = 60

disp_char:
                jcxz end_disp     ; goto end_disp if cx == 0
                     call  putc   ; display '*'
                     dec   cx     ; cx = cx - 1
                jmp  disp_char
end_disp:
```

The code is shorter because jcxz essentially acts as a combination of the cmp and je instructions used in Example 3.34. Because this type of situation occurs frequently in programming, it can be implemented even more efficiently using the loop instruction. The loop instruction combines the test of cx with zero and the decrementing of cx in a single instruction, so that the loop instruction decrements cx by 1 and tests if cx equals 0. It causes a jump if cx does not equal 0. It can only be used in conjunction with the cx register (known as the count register) and the cx register is initialized with the number of times the loop is to be repeated. Example 3.35 can be rewritten to use the loop instruction as follows.

Example 3.36

Using the loop instruction:

```
                mov   al, '*'       ; al = '*'
                mov   cx, 60d       ; cx = 60   ; loop count

disp_char:
                call  putc          ; display '*'
                loop  disp_char     ; cx = cx - 1, if (cx != 0)
                                    ; goto disp_char
```

Here, cx is initialized to 60, the number of iterations required. The instruction loop disp_char first decrements cx and then tests if cx is not equal to 0, branching to disp_char only if cx does not equal 0.

General format for using the loop instruction:

The general format for using the loop instruction is:

```
                 mov   cx, count      ; count = no. of times to
                                      ; repeat loop
start__loop:                          ; use any label name

                  <loop body>         ; while cx > 0
                                      ; repeat loop body
                loop start__loop
```

To use the loop instruction, simply store the number of iterations required in the cx register and construct a loop body as outlined above. The last instruction of the loop body is the loop instruction.

Note 1: The loop body will always be executed at least once, since the loop instruction tests the value of cx after executing the loop body.

Note 2: What happens if cx is initialized to 0? The loop instruction decrements cx before testing the condition (cx != 0). Thus we continue around the loop, with cx becoming more negative. We will repeat the loop body 65,536 times. Why? The reason is because we keep subtracting 1 from cx until we reach 0. Eventually, by making cx more negative, the largest negative number that cx can contain is reached. Since cx is 16-bit register, we know from Appendix B, that this number is -32768d, which is the 16-bit number 1000 0000 0000 0000. Subtracting 1 from this yields the 16-bit number 0111 1111 1111 1111 or 32767d. We can subtract 1 from this number 32767 times before reaching 0, which terminates the loop instruction. Thus the total number of iterations is 32768 + 32767 + 1 which equals 65,535 + 1 (the extra 1 is because cx started at 0 and was decremented to -1 before the test).

3.6 More about I/O

3.6.1 Numbers

In Chapter 1, we presented two sub-programs getn() and putn() to read and display numbers. We also developed get__str() and put__str() to read and display strings. We are now in a position to implement these sub-programs in 8086 assembly language. The C code for the sub-programs is presented again for ease of reference. First, we rewrite the getn() sub-program, which reads a number from the keyboard and returns it. We maintain our convention of using the ax register to store the result of an I/O sub-program.

Example 3.37

Reading a Number: getn()

C version:

```
int getn()                       /* read a signed number and
                                 return it */
{
  int sign, digit, n;
```

```
    n = 0 ;
    sign = 1 ;                /* assume number is positive */

    c = getchar() ;           /* read first character */
    if ( c == '-' )           /* negative number ? */
    {
      sign = -1;              /* record its sign */
      c = getchar() ;         /* get next digit */
    }

    if ( c != '\n' )
    {
      digit = c - '0' ;       /* convert character to number
                              */
      n = digit ;             /* store number in n */
      c = getchar();          /* get next digit */
      while ( c != '\n' )     /* finished ? */
      {
        digit = c - '0' ;     /* convert c to number */
        n = (n * 10) + digit ; /* compute new value for n */
        c = getchar();        /* get next digit */
      }
    }

    return ( n * sign ) ;     /* return -n if sign == -1
                                 otherwise return +n */
  }
```

8086 version:

```
getn:  ; read a number from the keyboard
       ; return value in ax register
       ;                                    C variables
       ; dx records sign of number          sign variable
       ; bl stores each digit               digit variable
       ; cx stores the number read in so far n variable
       ; al stores each character read in.  c variable
       ; ax is also used in the mul instruction


            push bx           ; save registers on stack
            push cx
            push dx

            mov dx, 1         ; record sign, 1 for
                              ; positive
            mov bx, 0         ; initialise digit to 0
            mov cx, 0         ; initialise number to 0
```

```
                call getc          ; read first character
                cmp al, '-'        ; is it negative
                jne newline        ; if not goto newline
                mov dx, -1         ; else record sign

                call getc          ; get next digit
newline:
                push dx            ; save sign on stack
                cmp al, 13         ; (al == CR) ?
                je fin_read        ; if yes, goto fin_read
                                   ; otherwise
                sub al, '0'        ; convert to digit
                mov cl, al         ; cl = first digit
                call getc          ; get next character

read_loop:
                cmp al, 13         ; if (al == CR)
                je fin_read        ; then goto fin_read

                sub al, '0'        ; otherwise, convert to
                                   ; digit
                mov bl, al         ; bl = digit
                mov ax, 10         ; ax = 10
                mul cx             ; ax = cx * 10
                mov cx, ax         ; cx = ax n = n * 10
                add cx, bx         ; cx = cx + digit n = n +
                                   ; digit
                call getc          ; read next digit
                jmp read_loop

fin_read:
                mov ax, cx         ; number returned in ax
                pop dx             ; retrieve sign from stack
                cmp dx, 1          ; 1 for positive, -1 for
                                   ; negative
                je fin_getn
                neg ax             ; ax = -ax
fin_getn:
                pop dx
                pop cx
                pop bx
                ret
```

The 8086 version is written to mirror the C version as closely as possible. The various registers may have been used by the programmer before calling `getn`, so it is essential to save them on the stack at the beginning of `getn` and restore them to their original values at the end of the sub-program. The stack is also used to save the sign of the number, because the `dx` register, which we are using to record the sign, is modified by the `mul` instruction. Therefore, the sign recorded in dx at the start of getn will be overwritten by the mul instruction later on, so dx is saved on the stack. It is restored at the end of the sub-program to allow us to compute the sign of the value to be returned.

Note: We use an instruction in the above example that we have not mentioned before, the neg instruction. It negates its operand and in the above code is used if the number entered was preceded by '-' indicating it was negative. We read the number as a positive number and at the end of the sub-program, we convert it to its negative form using the neg instruction. We could also have used the method used in the C version, to multiply the number by –1 if it is negative, but the neg instruction is a simpler solution in assembly language. It is also more efficient than the mul instruction.

Before illustrating the use of getn we describe the implementation of putn to display a number on the screen. Again, the 8086 version is based on the C version.

Example 3.38

Displaying a number: putn()

C version:

```
putn( number )                    /* displays a signed number
                                  */
{
  int i, div, rem, numstr[13] ;

  if ( number < 0 )               /* number is negative */
  {
    putchar('-') ;                /* display sign */
    number = -number ;
  }

  i = 0 ;                         /* store characters from
                                  numstr[0 ] */

  div = number / 10;              /* div is result of division
                                  */
  rem = number % 10;              /* rem is remainder */

  while ( div != 0 )
  {
    numstr[i] = rem + '0';        /*convert to ASCII, store
                                  in numstr[i] */
    i = i + 1 ;                   /* i is index of next free
                                  element */
    number = div;                 /* new number is old one / 10
                                  */

    div = number / 10;
    rem = number % 10;
  }
```

```
    numstr[i] = rem + '0' ;           /* last digit */

    while ( i >= 0 )                  /* display characters
                                      numstr[i] to numstr[0] */
    {
      putchar( numstr[i] );
      i = i - 1;
    }
}
```

In the C version, to display the digits in reverse order (see discussion of `getn()` in Chapter 2), we store them in a string and display the string from the last element to the first. In assembly language there is a simpler alternative. Given that items are retrieved from the stack in reverse order, we can push the digits onto the stack as they are generated. We then display the numbers from the stack. Given the LIFO nature of the stack we will display the digits in the appropriate order, that is, most significant digit first. We have to know how many digits are pushed onto the stack. To solve this problem we push a non-digit value onto the stack at the start of the sub-program. We use the value 0, since the digits pushed on the stack have values 48 to 57 (corresponding to the ASCII codes of the digits 0 to 9). When we are retrieving the digit values from the stack, we stop when we retrieve the value 0.

8086 version:

```
putn:                       ; display number in ax
                            ; ax contains number (and also div
                            ; C in above)
                            ; dx contains remainder (rem in C
                            ; above)
                            ; cx contains 10 for division
    push  bx
    push  cx
    push  dx

    mov   dx, 0             ; dx = 0
    push  dx                ; push 0 on stack to act as
                            ; sentinel
    mov   cx, 10            ; cx = 10

    cmp   ax, 0
    jge   calc_digits       ; number is negative
    neg   ax                ; ax = -ax; ax is now positive
    push  ax                ; save ax
    mov   al, '-'           ; display - sign
    call  putc
    pop   ax                ; restore ax
```

```
calc_digits:
  div   cx              ; dx:ax = ax / cx
                        ; ax = result, dx = remainder
  add   dx, '0'         ; convert dx to digit
  push  dx              ; save digit on stack
  mov   dx, 0           ; dx = 0
  cmp   ax, 0           ; finished ?
  jne   calc_digits     ; no, repeat process

;
                        ; all digits are now on the stack
                        ; we display them in reverse
disp_loop:
  pop   ax              ; get last digit from stack
  cmp   ax, 0           ; is it sentinel
  je    end_disp_loop   ; if yes, we are finished
  call  putc            ; otherwise display digit in al
  jmp   disp_loop

end_disp_loop:
  pop dx                ; restore registers
  pop cx
  pop bx
  ret
```

We are now in a position to write a complete program to illustrate the use of getn and putn.

Example 3.39

Write a program to read two numbers, add them and display the result. The C version is presented in Example 1.5 in Chapter 1.

```
; calc.asm: Read and sum two numbers. Display result.
; Author:   Joe Carthy
; Date:     March 1994

            .model small

            .stack 256

CR          equ   13d
LF          equ   10d

            .data

prompt1     db    'Enter first number: $'
prompt2     db    CR, LF, 'Enter second number: $'
result      db    CR, LF 'The sum is $'

num1        dw    ?
```

```
num2        dw      ?       ; we use these variables for
                            ; illustrative purposes
                            ; but we could use registers in this
                            ; simple example
            .code
start:
            mov     ax, @data
            mov     ds, ax

            mov     ax, offset prompt1
            call    puts                    ; display prompt1
            call    getn                    ; read first number
            mov     num1, ax

            mov     ax, offset prompt2
            call    puts                    ; display prompt2
            call    getn                    ; read second number
            mov     num2, ax

            mov     ax, offset result
            call    puts                    ; display result

            mov     ax, num1                ; ax = num1
            add     ax, num2                ; ax = ax + num2
            call    putn                    ; display sum

            mov     ax, 4c00h
            int     21h                     ; finished, back to dos


    <definitions of getn, putn, puts, getc, putc go here>
            end start
```

Exercises

3.20 Write a program that reads characters from the keyboard and counts the number of characters entered. The program stops reading characters when the `'$'` character is entered. It should display the number of characters entered.

3.21 Write a program to sum the integers 1 to 99 and display the result using `putn`.

3.22 Write a program to read numbers and sum them. It should continue reading until `0` is entered. It should then display on a new line the sum of all numbers entered. The C version was presented in Chapter 1, Example 1.11.

3.23 Write a program to read in a list of numbers terminated by 0, as in Exercise 3.32, and display the largest number in the list.

3.6.2 String I/O

In Chapter 1 we developed C sub-programs get__str() and put__str() to read and display strings. A string in C or assembly language is represented by an array of characters. In C, strings are terminated by the '\0' character. We adopt the same convention here. This method of terminating a string has an advantage over that used for the puts sub-program defined earlier, where the '$' character is used to terminate a string. The use of the value 0 to terminate a string means that a string may contain the '$' character which can then be displayed, since '$' cannot be displayed by puts. In Chapter 2, Section 2.3.9 we described indirect addressing, a method of accessing the characters in an array. The idea is that we store the address of the array (which also corresponds to the address of the first element of the array) in a register, typically the bx register. We then use that register to access the elements of the array. We use this technique in the implementation of get__str() and put__str(). For ease of reference, we repeat the C versions of get__str() and put__str() here followed respectively by their assembly language implementations.

Example 3.40

Reading a string: get__str()

C version:

```
get__str( str )             /* Read a string terminated by \n
                            and store it in the array str,
                            terminated by \0 */
char str[];                 /* String parameter: length is not
                            specified*/
{
  int i;                    /* to index elements of string */

  i = 0;                    /* arrays always start at 0 */
  str[i] = getchar() ;      /* read first character */
  while ( str[i] != '\n' ) /* finished ? */
  {
    i = i + 1;              /* i indexes next free element */
    str[i] = getchar();
  }
  str[i] = '\0';            /* terminate with \0, overwriting
                            \n */
}
```

8086 version:

```
get__str:                   ; read string terminated by CR into
```

```
            push  ax                    ; save registers
            push  bx
            push  cx
            push  dx

            mov   bx, ax

            call  getc                  ; read first character
            mov   byte ptr [bx], al     ; In C: str[i] = al

get_loop:   cmp   al, 13                ; al == CR ?
            je    get_fin               ;while al != CR

            inc   bx                    ; bx = bx + 1
            call  getc                  ; read next character
            mov   byte ptr [bx], al     ; In C: str[i] = al
            jmp get_loop                ; repeat loop test

get_fin:    mov   byte ptr [bx], 0      ; terminate string
                                        ; with 0

            pop   dx                    ; restore registers
            pop   cx
            pop   bx
            pop   ax
            ret
```

The `get_str` sub-program reads characters one at a time until the user enters Return. Assume the user enters the characters `'abc'` followed by Return. Initially, `bx` points to the first element in the array and we copy the first character entered (`'a'`) into this element. We test if Return was entered and, if not, we increment `bx`. Then the next character (`'b'`) is read and stored as the second element of the array. The same happens with the character `'c'` and `bx` is incremented to point to the fourth element of the array. The user now enters the Return character which is stored in the fourth element of the array and the loop terminates. Finally, the Null character (ASCII 0) is stored in the fourth element of the array, overwriting the Return character.

The `put_str` sub-program is implemented in a similar manner to `get_str`.

Example 3.41

Displaying a string: put_str()

C version:

```
put_str(str)                    /* display string parameter */
char str[]
{
  int i;
  i = 0;
  while ( str[i] != '\0' )      /* finished ? */
  {
    putchar( str[i] ) ;             /* display element i */
    i = i + 1;
  }
}
```

8086 version:

```
put_str:                     ; display string terminated by 0
                             ; whose address is in ax

            push  ax                     ; save registers
            push  bx
            push  cx
            push  dx

            mov   bx, ax                 ; store address in bx
            mov   al, byte ptr [bx]      ; In C: al = str[0]

put_loop:   cmp   al, 0                  ; al == 0 ?
            je    put_fin                ; while al != 0
            call  putc                   ; display character
            inc   bx                     ; bx = bx + 1
            mov   al, byte ptr [bx]      ; In C: al = str[i]
            jmp   put_loop               ; repeat loop test
put_fin:
            pop   dx                     ; restore registers
            pop   cx
            pop   bx
            pop   ax
            ret
```

We can now write programs which read and display strings using our own I/O sub-programs. As an example, we implement the program to prompt a user to enter a colour and display a message followed by the colour, as presented in Chapter 1, Example 1.2.

Example 3.42

Read colour entered by the user and display a suitable message, using `get_str` and `put_str`.

```
; colour.asm: Prompt user to enter a colour and display a
; message
; Author:    Joe Carthy
; Date:      March 1994

           .model small

           .stack 256

CR         equ     13d
LF         equ     10d

; string definitions: note 0 terminator
           .data
msg1       db    'Enter your favourite colour: ', 0
msg2       db    CR, LF, 'Yuk ! I hate ', 0
colour     db    80 dup (0)

           .code
start:
           mov   ax, @data
           mov   ds, ax

           mov   ax, offset msg1
           call  put_str            ; display prompt

           mov   ax, offset colour
           call  get_str            ; read colour

           mov   ax, offset msg2
           call  put_str            ; display msg2

           mov   ax, offset colour
           call  put_str            ; display colour

           mov   ax, 4c00h
           int       21h            ; finished, back to dos

;  < get_str put_str getc and putc sub-programs defined
here >

           end start
```

This program produces as output:

```
Enter your favourite colour: yellow
Yuk ! I hate yellow
```

Exercises

3.24 Modify the guessing game program (Example 3.29) to use the `put_str` sub-program. Remember to modify the string definitions to terminate with `0`.

3.25 Write a program, using `get_str`, to read a string and count the number of characters in the string. The program should display the number of characters entered using `putn`.

3.26 Write a program to read a string and display a message indicating whether or not the string is a palindrome.

3.7 Summary

In this chapter we have presented the basic features of 8086 assembly language programming. We described how character I/O can be carried out using MS-DOS sub-programs and looked at the various conditional jump instructions used in control structures such as loops. Finally, we developed sub-programs for string and numeric I/O based on those presented in Chapter 1. You should now be in a position to write a host of useful 8086 assembly language programs. You should also have grasped the primitive nature of assembly language programming as compared to that of a high-level language such as C.

In the next chapter we take a look at some other aspects of 8086 programming such as bit manipulation operations, the different ways to access variables stored in memory and using the stack to pass parameters to a sub-program.

3.8 Reading list

Brey, B.B. (1993) *8086/8088, 80286, 80386 and 80486 Assembly Language Programming*, Merrill (MacMillan), New York.

Hawkley, C. and Neil White, N. (1987) *Assembly Language Programming on the IBM PC*, Addison Wesley, Wokingham.

Liu, Yu-Cheng and Gibson, G.A. (1986) *Microcomputer Systems: The 8086/8088 Family*, Prentice Hall, Englewood Cliffs, NJ.

Microsoft Macro Assembler 5.1 Programmers Guide, (Manual available with MASM), 1987, Microsoft Corporation, Redmond, WA.

Morneau, P. (1992) *PC Assembly Language: An Introduction to Computer Systems*, West Publishing Co., St. Paul, MN.

Skinner, T. (1985) *An Introduction to Assembly Language Programming for the 8086 Family*, Wiley Press, New York.

Thorne, M. (1986) *Programming the 8086/8088*, Benjamin Cummings, Menlo Park, CA.

Uffenbeck, J. (1987) *The 8086/8088 Family: Design, Programming and Interfacing*, Prentice Hall, Englewood Cliffs, NJ.

4
8086 programming continued

In this chapter we continue our discussion of 8086 programming. We introduce the **logical** instructions that are used for bit manipulation purposes and give some practical examples of using these instructions. We also look at the use of shift and rotate instructions for manipulating bits. The use of **macros** is described. We explain the different **addressing modes** that are used in 8086 programming. Finally, we discuss methods for passing parameters to sub-programs, paying particular attention to the use of the stack for passing parameters.

4.1 Bit manipulation

One of the features of assembly language programming is that you can access the individual bits of a byte (word or long word). You can **set** bits (give them a value of `1`), **clear** them (give them a value of `0`), **complement** them (change `0` to `1` or `1` to `0`), and **test** if they have a particular value. These operations are essential when writing sub-programs to control devices such as printers, plotters and disk drives. Sub-programs that control devices are often called **device drivers**. In such sub-programs, it is often necessary to set particular bits in a register associated with the device, in order to operate the device. The instructions to operate on bits are called **logical** instructions.

Under normal circumstances programmers rarely need concern themselves with bit operations. In fact most high-level languages do not provide bit manipulation operations (the C language is a notable exception). Another reason for manipulating bits is to make programs more efficient. By this we usually mean one of two things:

- the program is smaller in size and so requires less RAM, or
- the program runs faster.

Both of these can be important considerations in some situations. For example, in the case of a computer games machine, to keep the cost as low as possible, the machine may not have much memory or a powerful processor. The games software will need to be programmed as efficiently as possible if the machine is to perform at an acceptable level.

We can reduce the storage requirements for data by using individual bits to store information, instead of using bytes and words. For example, if we are storing information about people, we store such things as *name*, *address*, *salary*, *sex* and *marital status*. Items such as *sex* and *marital status* are **binary** in nature and we could use individual bits to represent them, say `1` for male, `0` for female; `1` for married, `0` for single. Thus we could store up to eight items of information about a person in a single byte, provided each item was of a binary nature. If we are storing information about large numbers of people, then the storage saving could be quite large. (The C language deals elegantly with such a situation by providing **bit fields** which can be used in a similar manner to the ordinary fields in a record.)

It should be noted that the issue of efficiency is secondary to that of **correctness**. A fast, small program that sometimes does not work is useless and possibly even dangerous (for example in aircraft control). Thus, a clear and elegant solution is usually preferred to an intricate, small and efficient solution. Obviously, programs can be written which are both correct and efficient and a balance should be struck.

4.1.1 *The logical instructions:* `and`, `or`, `xor`, `not`

As stated above, the logical instructions allow us operate on the bits of an operand. The operand may be a byte (8 bits), a word (16 bits) or a long word (32 bits). We will concentrate on byte-sized operands, but the instructions operate on word operands in exactly the same fashion.

4.1.2 *Clearing bits:* `and` *instruction*

A bit `and` operation compares two bits and sets the result to `0` if either of the bits is `0`, so that

```
1 and 0 returns 0
0 and 1 returns 0
0 and 0 returns 0
1 and 1 returns 1
```

The `and` instruction carries out the `and` operation on all of the bits of the source operand with all of the bits of the destination operand, storing the result in the destination operand (like the arithmetic instructions such as `add` and `sub`). The operation `0 and x` always results in `0` regardless of the value of `x` (`1` or `0`). This means that we can use the `and` instruction to clear a specified bit or collection of bits in an operand. If we wish to clear, say bit 5, of an 8-bit operand, we `and` the operand with the value `1101 1111`, that is, a value with bit 5 set to `0` and all other values set to `1`. This results in bit 5 of the 8-bit operand being cleared, with the other bits remaining unchanged, since `1 and x` always yields `x`. (Remember, when referring to a bit number, we count from bit 0 upwards, that is, from the right.)

Example 4.1

To clear bit `5` of a byte we `and` the byte with `1101 1111`

```
mov     al, 62h          ; al =          0110 0010
```

```
and     al, 0dfh            ; and it with       1101 1111
                            ; al is 42h         0100 0010
```

Note: You can use binary numbers directly in 8086 assembly language, for example

```
mov  al, 01100010b
and  al, 11011111b
```

but it is easier to write them using their hexadecimal equivalents.

The value in the source operand, 0dfh in this example, is called a **bit mask**. It specifies the bits in the destination operand that are to be changed. Using the and instruction, any bit in the bit mask with value 0 will cause the corresponding bit in the destination operand to be cleared.

In the ASCII codes of the lower-case letters, bit 5 is always 1. The corresponding ASCII codes of the upper-case letters are identical except that bit 5 is always 0. Thus to convert a lower-case letter to upper case we simply need to clear bit 5 (set bit 5 to 0). This can be done using the and instruction and an appropriate bit mask, such as 0dfh, as shown in the above example. The letter 'b' has ASCII code 62h. We could rewrite Example 4.1 above as:

Example 4.2

Converting a lower-case letter to its upper-case equivalent:

```
mov  al, 'b'        ; al = 'b' (= 98d or 62h)     0110 0010
and  al, 0dfh       ; mask =                      1101 1111
                    ; al now = 'B' (= 42h)        0100 0010
```

The bit mask 1101 1111 when used with and will always set bit 5 to 0 leaving the remaining bits unchanged as illustrated below:

```
      xxxx xxxx   ; destination bits
and   1101 1111   ; and with mask bits
      xx0x xxxx   ; result is that bit 5 is cleared
```

If the destination operand contains a lower-case letter, the result will be the corresponding upper-case equivalent. In effect, we have subtracted 32 from the ASCII code of the lower-case letter which was the method we used in Chapter 3 for converting lower-case letters to their upper-case equivalents.

In general, to clear a bit or group of bits, you define a mask consisting of 0s for the bits to be cleared and 1s everywhere else. Hence the mask to clear bit 5 has a 0 in bit position 5 and 1s everywhere else. The bits cleared in this fashion are said to be **masked out.**

Example 4.3

Consider the problem of converting the ASCII code of a digit to its numeric equivalent. If we look at the ASCII codes of the digits in binary (Table 4.1) we see that the four low-order bits actually give the magnitude of the digit while the four high-order bits are always the same (0011).

Table 4.1 The ASCII codes of the digits in binary

Digit	ASCII Code
0	0011 0000
1	0011 0001
2	0011 0010
3	0011 0011
4	0011 0100
5	0011 0101
6	0011 0110
7	0011 0111
8	0011 1000
9	0011 1001

Thus, to convert the ASCII code of a digit to its numeric equivalent, we mask out bits 4 and 5. The required mask is 1100 1111 (0cfh) which clears bits 4 and 5, leaving the remaining bits unchanged. If al contains '2', we can convert it to the number 2 as follows:

```
mov  al, '2'        ; al = '2' =      0011 0010
and  al, 0cfh       ; 0cfh =          1100 1111
                    ; now al = 2 =    0000 0010
```

4.1.3 Setting bits: or instruction

A bit or operation compares two bits and sets the result to 1 if either bit is set to 1, so that

```
1 or 0 returns 1
0 or 1 returns 1
1 or 1 returns 1
0 or 0 returns 0
```

The or instruction carries out an or operation with all of the bits of the source and destination operands and stores the result in the destination operand. The or instruction can be used to set bits to 1 regardless of their current setting since x or 1 returns 1 regardless of the value of x (0 or 1). The bits set using the or instruction are said to be **masked in**.

Example 4.4

To convert a digit to its equivalent character, we need to set bits 4 and 5. This can be accomplished using an or instruction and the bit mask 0011 0000. In this example we convert the number 7 to the ASCII code for 7, that is '7':

```
mov    al, 7               ; 7 is          0000 0111
or     al, 0011 0000b      ; or with       0011 0000
                           ; '7' is        0011 0111
```

In general, to set a bit or group of bits to 1s, you define a bit mask with 1s in the positions to be set and 0s everywhere else. Thus, the bit mask 1000 1001 when used with the or instruction will set bits 0, 3 and 7 of the destination operand.

As a second example, take the conversion of an upper-case letter to lower case, the opposite of Example 4.2 discussed above. Here, we need to **set** bit 5 of the upper-case letter's ASCII code to 1 so that it becomes lower case and leave all other bits unchanged. The required mask is 0010 0000 (20h).

Example 4.5

Convert an upper-case letter, stored in al to its lower-case equivalent. If we store 'A' in al then it can be converted to 'a' as follows:

```
mov    al, 'A'          ; al = 'A' =       0100 0001
or     al, 20h          ; or with          0010 0000
                        ; gives al = 'a'   0110 0001
```

In effect, we have added 32 to the upper-case ASCII code thus obtaining the lower-case ASCII code. Before changing the case of a letter, it is important to verify that you have a letter in the variable you are working with. We now define two sub-programs tolower and toupper which convert a character in al to lower case and to upper case respectively. These sub-programs first check the character, leaving it unchanged if it not an upper-case or lower-case letter.

Example 4.6

Sub-programs toupper and tolower for case conversion:

```
toupper:                        ; convert character in
                                ; al to lower case
          cmp    al, 'A'        ; testing first that it is
                                ; upper case
          jb     notupper       ; if al < 'A' then don't
                                ; convert
          cmp    al, 'z'
          ja     notupper       ; if al > 'Z' then don't
                                ; convert
                                ; otherwise it must be
                                ; between A and Z
                                ; convert to lower case
          or     al, 20h        ; or al with 00100000,
                                ; setting bit 5
notupper:
          ret

tolower:                        ; convert character in
                                ; al to upper case
          cmp    al, 'a'        ; testing first that it is
                                ; lower case
```

```
            jb      notlower     ; if al < 'a' then don't
                                 ; convert
            cmp     al, 'z'
            ja      notlower     ; if al > 'z' then don't
                                 ; convert
                                 ; otherwise it must be
                                 ; between a and z
                                 ; convert to upper case
            and     al, 0dfh     ; and al with 11011111,
                                 ; clearing bit 5
notlower:
            ret
```

It is always a good idea to verify the information being manipulated, where possible, as exemplified by the above sub-programs. The C programming language library provides a range of sub-programs such as `tolower` and `toupper` for dealing with characters.

Exercises

4.1 Specify the instructions and masks you would use to
(a) set bits 2, 3 and 4 of the `ax` register
(b) clear bits 4 and 7 of the `bx` register

4.2 How would `al` be affected by the following instructions?:

```
(a) and al, 00fh
(b) and al, 0f0h
(c) or  al, 00fh
(d) or  al, 0f0h
```

4.3 Write sub-programs `todigit` and `tocharacter`, which convert a digit to its equivalent ASCII character code and vice versa. They should test the operand being converted, in the same way as `toupper` and `tolower`.

4.1.4 The `xor` *instruction*

The `xor` operation compares two bits and sets the result to `1` if the bits are different, so that

`1 xor 0` returns `1`
`0 xor 1` returns `1`
`1 xor 1` returns `0`

`0 xor 0` returns `0`

The `xor` instruction carries out the `xor` operation with its operands, storing the result in the destination operand.

The `xor` instruction can be used to **toggle** the value of specific bits (reverse them from their current settings). The bit mask to toggle particular bits should have 1's for any bit position you wish to toggle and 0's for bits which are to remain unchanged.

Example 4.7

Toggle bits 0, 1 and 6 of the value in al (here 67h):

```
mov     al, 67h        ; al =             0011 0111
xor     al, 08h        ; xor it with      0100 0011
                       ; al is 34h        0111 0100
```

A common use of xor is to clear a register (set all bits to 0); for example, we can clear register cx as follows:

```
xor  cx, cx
```

This is because when the identical operands are xored, each bit cancels itself, producing 0:

0 xor 0 produces 0
1 xor 1 produces 0

Thus abcdefgh xor abcdefgh produces 00000000 where abcdefgh represents some bit pattern. The more obvious way of clearing a register is to use a mov instruction as in:

```
mov  cx, 0
```

but this is slower to execute and occupies more memory than the xor instruction. This is because bit manipulation instructions, such as xor, can be implemented very efficiently in hardware. The sub instruction may also be used to clear a register:

```
sub  cx, cx
```

It is also smaller and faster than the mov version, but not as fast as the xor version. My own preference is to use the clearer version, the mov instruction. However, in practice, assembly language programs are used where efficiency is important and so clearing a register with xor is often used.

4.1.5 The not instruction

The not operation complements or inverts a bit, so that

not 1 returns 0
not 0 returns 1

The not instruction inverts **all** of the bits of its operand.

Example 4.8

Complementing the `al` register:

```
mov     al, 33h          ; al =      00110011
not     al               ; al =      11001100
```

Table 4.2 summarizes the results of the logical operations. Such a table is called a **truth table.**

Table 4.2 Truth table for logical operators.

		not	A and	A or	A xor
A	B	A	B	B	B
0	0	1	0	0	0
0	1	1	0	1	1
1	0	0	0	1	1
1	1	0	1	1	0

Efficiency

As noted earlier, because of its efficiency, the `xor` instruction is often used to clear an operand. For similar reasons of efficiency, the `or/and` instructions may be used to compare an operand to `0`.

Example 4.9

Comparing an operand to `0` using logical instructions:

```
or      cx, cx          ; compares cx with 0
je      label
and     ax, ax          ; compares ax with 0
jg      label2
```

Doing `or/and` operations on identical operands does not change the destination operand (`x or x` returns `x`; `x and x` returns `x`), but they do set flags in the status register. The `or/and` instructions above have the same effect as the `cmp` instructions used in Example 4.10, but they are faster and smaller instructions (each occupies two bytes) than the `cmp` instruction (which occupies three bytes).

Example 4.10

Comparing an operand to `0` using the `cmp` instruction:

```
cmp  cx, 0
je   label
cmp  ax, 0
jg   label2
```

4.1.6 Testing bits: the `test` instruction

All of the logical instructions (`and`, `or`, `xor`, `not`) affect the flags in the status register. This means that you can use the conditional jump instructions after executing one of these instructions, as in the example of using `or` to test if a register equals `0`. To determine if a particular bit is set to a `1` or `0`, we can use the `and` instruction and a mask which clears the remaining bits (a mask with the bit to be tested set to `1`). For example, if we wish to test if bit 1 of `al` is `1` or `0`, we use a mask with bit 1 set, the mask: `00000010`.

Example 4.11

Test if bit 1 of `al` is clear (`0`).

```
and    al, 00000010b       ; mask has bit 1 set
jz     bit1_clear          ; goto to bit1_clear if bit 1 == 0
............               ; if its 1 we end up here
```

The `and` instruction will clear all bits in `al` except bit 1. The value of bit 1 remains unchanged by the `and` instruction. If it is `1`, then it remains `1`, with the `and` instruction returning a non-zero result, so the Z-flag will not be set. If bit 1 in `al` is `0`, then the `and` instruction returns a zero result and the Z-flag will be set. A conditional jump instruction can then be used to test whether the bit was set or clear. The disadvantage of testing a bit in this fashion is that the contents of `al` are destroyed (akin to the use of `sub ax, ax` to compare `ax` with `0`). The `test` instruction operates exactly like the `and` instruction, except that the contents of the destination register are not modified (akin to using `cmp ax, 0`).

Example 4.12

Test if bit 1 of `al` is clear using the `test` instruction:

```
test   al, 00000010b       ; mask has bit 1 set
jz     bit1_clear          ; goto to bit1_clear if bit 1 = 0
............               ; if its 1 we end up here
```

Here `al` remains unchanged after the `test` instruction. You can test more than one bit at a time using either the `and` or the `test` instruction. The mask contains a `1` in each bit position you wish to test. If *any* of the corresponding bits in the destination is set, the result will be non-zero.

Example 4.13

Test if any of bits `0`, `1`, `6` or `7` are set:

```
test   al, 11000011b       ; if any of the bits 0,1,6 and 7
                           ; are set
jnz    bit_set             ; goto bit_set
```

We use the `jnz` instruction to test if the bits are set, since if any of the bits are set, then the result of the test instruction will be non-zero.

Exercises

4.4 Write a code fragment to transfer control to label `L`, using a conditional jump instruction combined with the `test` instruction:

(a) if bit 15 of ax is set
(b) if bit 7 of al is clear
(c) if bits 2 and 4 of cx are clear
(d) if any of bits 1, 2 and 3 of bx are set
(e) if bit 5 of al is set
(f) if bit 5 of bl is clear.

4.1.7 *Shifting and rotating bits*

We sometimes wish to change the positions of all the bits in a byte, word or long word. The 8086 provides a complete set of instructions for shifting and rotating bits. Bits can be moved right (towards the 0 bit) or left towards the most significant bit. Values shifted off the end of an operand are lost (one may go into the **carry flag**). **Shift** instructions move bits a specified number of places to the right or left. The last bit in the direction of the shift goes into the carry flag. When we **shift left** a 0 is always shifted into the lower-order bit position (bit 0). When we **shift right**, two results are possible. There is an arithmetic shift right instruction (sar) which causes the sign bit to be shifted into itself. The sign bit, as described in Appendix B, is the most significant bit (bit 7 in a byte or bit 15 in a word or bit 31 in a long word) of an operand. There is also a logical shift right instruction (shr) which causes a 0 to be shifted into the high-order position.

Rotate instructions move bits a specified number of places to the right or left. For each bit rotated, the last bit in the direction of the rotate is moved into the first bit position at the other end of the operand.

With all the shift and rotate instructions, the destination operand contains the value to be manipulated and the source operand specifies the number of bits to shift or rotate. The source operand may be the immediate value 1 or the value contained in the cl register. No other value or register may be used with the 8086 microprocessor. The shift instructions are frequently used to carry out multiplication and division. As an example consider multiplying a number by 10 in decimal. You simply shift the number left one digit and add a 0 on the right hand side. Division by 10 shifts the decimal point in the opposite direction. The shift instructions are used when multiplying or dividing by 2 as opposed to 10. The number 0000 0100 (4), when shifted left one bit, gives 0000 1000 (8). Thus, shifting left one bit is equivalent to multiplying by 2. Shifting left by two bits effectively multiplies by 4 (2^2). Shifting left n bits multiplies by $\mathbf{2}^n$. The shl (shift left) instruction is used to shift bits to the left. There is also a sal (shift arithmetic left) instruction but it is the same as the shl instruction .

Example 4.14

Given that al contains 0000 0100, it can be multiplied by 2 as follows:

```
mov   al, 04h      ; al =                 0000 0100
shl   al, 1        ; shift left 1 bit
                   ; al now contains      0000 1000
```

al could be multiplied by 16 by shifting it left four bits:

```
mov   al, 05h      ; al =                 0000 0101
```

```
mov    cl, 4
shl    al, cl        ; shift left 4 bits
                     ; al now contains 80d     0101 0000
```

The second example is illustrated in Figure 4.1, where we note that four 0's are shifted into the rightmost bit positions and four 0's are lost on the left hand side, the last one moving into the carry flag.

Note: We can only perform unsigned multiplication with shl (sal), since the sign bit gets overwritten in the shift process.

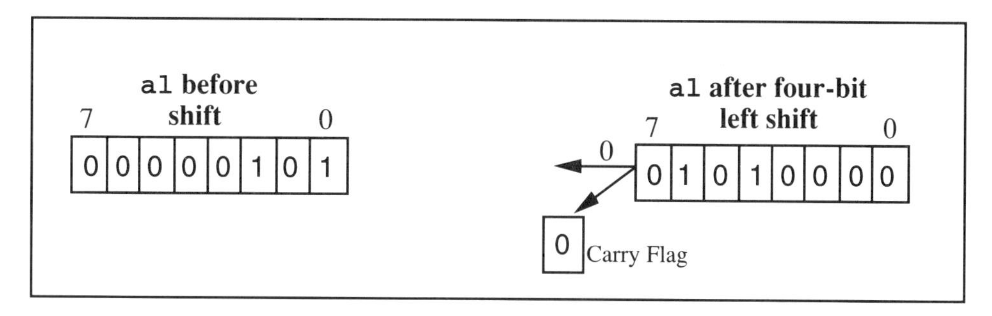

Figure 4.1 Multiplying al by 16 using the shl instruction.

In the case of **division**, a right shift of n bits divides a number by 2^n. We use the sar (shift arithmetic right) instruction if we wish to preserve the sign bit; otherwise we use the logical shift right instruction shr. It is obviously important to use the shift arithmetic right instruction when dealing with signed numbers.

Example 4.15

Dividing al (which contains 12) by 2 using the sar instruction:

```
mov    al, 12        ; al =                    0000 1100
sar    al, 1         ; divide by 2
                     ; al now contains 6       0000 0110
```

Example 4.16

Here we see the difference between the sar and shr instructions:

```
mov    al, 0afh      ; al = -96d = 10100000 in 2's complement
mov    cl, 3         ; divide by 8
sar    al, cl        ; al = -12d = 11110100 in 2's complement

mov    al, 0afh      ; al = 160d = 1010000 as unsigned number
mov    cl, 3         ; divide by 8
shr    al, cl        ; al = 20d = 00010100 in 2's complement
```

In this example, we are using two's complement numbers as described in Appendix B. The number 0afh represents -96d as a two's complement number, while as an unsigned number it represents 160d. By using the sar instruction for the negative number, we get the correct result, `-12d`, whereas for the unsigned number we need to use the `shr` instruction to get the correct result, `20d`. Figure 4.2 illustrates the difference between the `sar` and `shr` instructions, based on Example 4.16.

In the case of the `sar` instruction the sign bit is preserved. Thus `1` bits are shifted in by the `sar` instruction for a negative number such as -96 as in the example. If the number is positive, the sign bit will be `0` and so `0` bits will be shifted and the operation will be the same as for the `shr` instruction. The `shr` instruction always shifts `0` bits in from the right regardless of sign, that is, it treats its operand as an unsigned number.

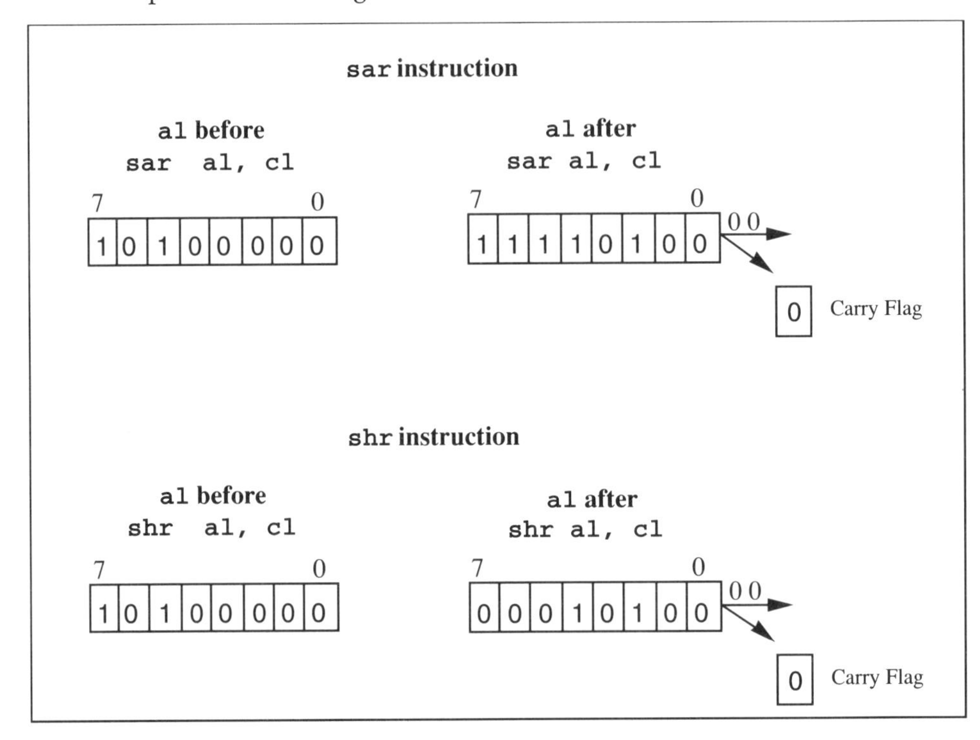

Figure 4.2 Division by 2 using the `sar` and `shr` instructions.

The reason for using shift instructions for multiplication and division is that they are faster than the `mul` and `div` instructions. In the case of the 8086 processor, multiplication or division by `2` using shift instructions can be faster by a factor of ten or more than multiplication or division using the equivalent `mul` or `div` instructions.

Exercises

4.5 Write the shift instructions to multiply `ax` by `8` and `bx` by `32`.

4.6 Write the shift instructions to divide `ax` by `4` and `dx` by `16`.

Displaying the registers

It can be useful when using bit manipulation instructions to display the value of a register in binary and hexadecimal. We now develop two sub-programs, put_bin and put_hex, which display the contents of ax in binary and hexadecimal form. Such sub-programs can be very useful for debugging purposes, because we can use them, for example, to examine the effects of the bit manipulation instructions on operands.

Example 4.17

Write a sub-program to display the contents of the ax register as a binary number. The sub-program is called put_bin:

```
put_bin:                            ; Display ax as binary
                                    ; number
             push  ax               ; save registers
             push  bx
             push  cx
             push  dx

             mov   dx, ax           ; al will be used to
                                    ; display bits
             mov   cx, 16           ; loop counter - 16
                                    ; iterations
             mov   bx, 8000h        ; bl = 1000 0000 0000
check:
             test  dx, bx           ; test if bit set in bx
                                    ; is also set in dx
             jnz   display_1        ; if it's not set,
                                    ; display a 1
             mov   al, '0'          ; otherwise display a
                                    0
             jmp   display_bit
display_1:
             mov   al, '1'
display_bit: call  putc             ; display bit value
             shr   bx, 1            ; adjust mask 1 bit to
                                    ; the right
             loop  check            ; repeat for all 16
                                    ; bits

             pop   dx               ; restore registers
             pop   cx
             pop   bx
             pop   ax

             ret
```

In this example, we use the test instruction to test each bit of the dx register. The bx register contains the mask for testing. The sub-program loops so that the bx register is shifted right one bit each time around the loop, effectively dividing bx by 2. This shifts the 1 bit in bx to the next bit position to be tested.

The put_hex sub-program which displays the contents of ax as a four-digit hexadecimal number operates in the same way as the putn sub-program, which displays a decimal number. It repeatedly divides the contents of ax by 16, storing the remainder on the stack each time. After four digits have been generated (a 16-bit number is represented by four hexadecimal digits) it pops the digits from the stack and displays them.

Example 4.18

Sub-program put_hex to display ax in hexadecimal form:

```
put_hex:                            ; display ax in hexadecimal
            push ax
            push bx
            push cx
            push dx

            mov bx, 16
            mov cx, 4               ; there are 4 hex digits
gethx:                              ; repeatedly divide ax by 16
            mov dx, 0
            div bx                  ; ax/bx: rem in dx, result in
                                    ; ax
            push dx                 ; store digits on stack
            loop gethx
                                    ; now pop digits from stack
                                    ; and display them
            mov cx, 4               ; there are 4 hex digits to be
                                    ; displayed
disphx:
            pop ax                  ; get digit from stack
            cmp ax, 10              ; if ax > 10, then letter a-f
                                    ; must be displayed
            jge displetter
            add ax, '0'             ; otherwise convert to ASCII
                                    ; and display digit
            call putc
            jmp next                ; process next digit
displetter:                         ; digit values 10-15 map onto
                                    ; a-f
                                    ; (digit value + 'a'-10)
                                    ; gives correct ASCII code
            add ax, 'a' - 10
            call putc               ; display the letter

next:       loop disphx
            mov al, 'h'             ; display h for hex at end
            call putc

            pop dx                  ; restore registers
```

```
        pop cx
        pop bx
        pop ax
        ret
```

Values in the range 10 to 15 must be displayed as hexadecimal digits a to f. This is carried out by adding the constant 'a' - 10 (87) to the digit value. For example, value 11 + 'a' - 10 gives 98, which is the ASCII code for the letter 'b', the hexadecimal digit corresponding to decimal number 11.

Example 4.19

This example illustrates the use of put_bin and put_hex and shows the operation of the and instruction being used to clear the eight low-order bits of ax.

```
; clear.asm: Set all bit in ax and display ax.
; Clear 8 low-order bits and display ax.

    .model small
    .stack 100h

    .data
s1 db    'ax before and operation: ', 0
s2 db    13, 10, 'ax after and operation: ', 0

    .code

start:
    mov  ax, @data
    mov  ds, ax

    mov  ax, offset s1 ; display before message
    call put_str

    mov  ax, 0ffffh    ; set all bits in ax
    call put_bin       ; display ax in binary
    call put_tab       ; display a tab
    call put_hex       ; display ax in hex:     ffffh

    mov  ax, offset s1 ; display after message
    call put_str
    mov  ax, 0ffffh    ; set bits in ax again
    and  ax, 0ff00h    ; clear 8 low-order bits
    call put_bin       ; display ax in binary
```

```
    call put_tab        ; display a tab
    call put_hex        ; display ax in hex:    ff00h

    mov  ax, 4c00h      ; terminate program
    int  21h

;   Insert code for put_bin, put_hex, put_str, putc

put_tab:                ; display a tab
    push ax
    mov  al, 9          ; ASCII code for tab is 9
    call putc
    pop ax
    ret

    end start
```

Executing this program produces as output:

```
ax before and operation: 1111111111111111  ffffh
ax after and operation: 1111111100000000  ff00h
```

4.1.8 *Rotate instructions*

Rotate instructions, as the name suggests, allow you to rotate the bits in an operand – rotating left means that the leftmost bits are moved to the right-hand side. For example, if we rotate the `al` register by two bits then bit 7 rotates to position 1 and bit 6 to position 0. Bits 0 and 1 move two positions to the left, as do bits 2, 3, 4 and 5. Similarly for a right rotation of two bits, bit 0 is moved to position 6, bit 1 to position 7 and bits 3, 4, 5, 6 and 7 all move two positions to the right.

The `rol` (rotate left) instruction rotates bits so that the leftmost bit is initially moved into bit zero. The `ror` (rotate right) instruction rotates bits so that bit 0 is initially moved into the leftmost position.

Example 4.20

If `al` contains `0110 0011`, then after rotating by one bit to the right `al` will contain `1011 0001`. If we then rotate `al` two bits to the left `al` will contain `1100 0110`:

```
mov  al, 47h        ; al =                0110 0011
ror  al, 1          ; al now contains     1011 0001
mov  cl, 2          ; cl = 2
rol  al, cl         ; al now contains     1100 0110
```

Example 4.21

Use the ror instruction to swap the high-order bits with the low-order bits of bl:

```
mov  bl, 0110 0111b  ; bl =                 0110 0111
mov  cl, 4
ror  bl, cl          ; bl now contains      0111 0110
```

4.2 Macros

We have already used the equ directive to define constants in our programs, for example

```
CR   equ   13
```

The assembler replaces all occurrences of CR with the number 13 before the program is translated to machine code. Essentially, the equ directive provides a text substitution facility. One piece of text (CR) is replaced by another piece of text (13) in your program. Such a facility is often call a **macro** facility. Most assemblers provide more powerful macro facilities in addition to the equ directive. They allow you to assign a name to a group of instructions, and anywhere we use the name, it is replaced by the group of instructions. The process of assigning a name to a group of instructions (or indeed any text) is referred to as **defining a macro**. A macro called sample may be defined as follows:

```
sample  macro  [parameter-list]

        ; text (body) of macro may be one or many lines

        endm
```

The keyword macro indicates the start of the macro and the keyword endm indicates the end of the macro. It is a good idea to use meaningful names for macros, just as for variables and sub-programs. Parameters may also be used with macros, as we shall see later.

Example 4.22

Define macros to swap the contents of ax with bx and to add the registers ax, bx, cx and dx, leaving the sum in ax:

```
swap        macro
              mov cx, bx
              mov bx, ax
              mov ax, cx
            endm

add_regs    macro
```

```
    add ax, bx
    add ax, cx
    add ax, dx
endm
```

A macro may be used by writing its name in the program where you want the task defined by the macro to be carried out. When we use a macro we say that the macro name is **expanded** into the full text of the macro. Macros may be defined anywhere in your program, but they must be defined before they are first called. The above macros may be used as in the following example:

Example 4.23

Using the swap and add_regs macros:

```
mov     ax, 10
mov     bx, 20
swap                    ; the swap macro is expanded here
mov     cx, 4
mov     dx, 6
add_regs                ; the add_regs macro is expanded here
```

It is very important to realize that the assembler simply replaces the macro name with the code making up the macro body, everywhere the macro name occurs. Thus the above example would be converted by the assembler into the following form, before the code is translated to machine code (we use indentation to highlight the macro expansion):

```
mov     ax, 10
mov     bx, 20
  mov   cx, bx          ; code of swap is expanded
  mov   bx, ax
  mov   ax, cx
mov     cx, 4
mov     dx, 6
  add   ax, bx          ; code of add_regs is expanded
  add   ax, cx
  add   ax, dx
```

Note: The 8086 provides the xchg instruction to swap the contents of two registers or a register with a memory variable, for example

```
xchg    ax, bx          ; swap ax with bx
xchg    dx, y           ; swap dx and memory variable y
```

This is the most efficient way to swap values on the 8086.

Example 4.24

As another example, we define a macro save__regs to save the registers on the stack and the macro restore__regs to restore the registers:

```
save__regs      macro
                        push ax
                        push bx
                        push cx
                        push dx
                      endm

restore__regs   macro
                        pop dx
                        pop cx
                        pop bx
                        pop ax
                      endm
```

To save the registers in the `putc` sub-program and to restore them afterwards, we could use the macros defined above, as in the next example.

Example 4.25

Using save__regs and restore__regs:

```
putc:
save__regs
mov  dl, al
mov  ah, 2h
int  21h
restore__regs
ret
```

The above sub-program would be converted by the assembler to:

```
  push ax
  push bx
  push cx
  push dx
mov  dl, al
mov  ah, 2h
int  21h
  pop dx
  pop cx
  pop bx
  pop ax
ret
```

Note: Macros should be clearly distinguished from sub-programs. A sub-program exists in one place only. The call instruction **transfers control** to the sub-program and the ret instruction transfers control from the sub-program at run-time. A macro results in the assembler expanding the name of the macro into the defined set of instructions and inserting them at that point in the program, just as if you entered them there. There is no transfer of control involved in the use of macros. They provide a text substitution facility. In fact, this is one reason why macros may sometimes be preferred to sub-programs. When we use sub-programs, the return address has to be pushed on the stack by the call instruction and retrieved from there by the ret instruction. This represents an overhead in the time taken to carry out these operations. If time is critical in an application, this overhead can be reduced by not using sub-programs, but by repeating the sub-program code everywhere it is required. By defining this code in the form of a macro, we can make programs easier to read (one of the goals of using sub-programs) without sacrificing speed of execution.

However, there is a price, since the code is to be repeated everywhere it is needed, the program will be larger, occupying more memory space. This is a fundamental trade off in computing. To make programs faster, they usually need to use more memory space. A balanced approach is required in programming. The macro facility is very useful and well worth exploring if you have to write assembly language programs.

4.2.1 *Macros with parameters*

Macros can be passed parameters, which greatly increases their usefulness. We could write a macro add_regs which sums any three registers that are passed as parameters. The result is stored in the first parameter.

Example 4.26

Using macros with parameters:

```
add_regs    macro r1, r2, r3          ; r1, r2, r3 are the
                                      ; parameters
                add  r1, r2
                add  r1, r3
            endm
```

We can use add_regs to sum any three registers, for example

```
add_regs    ax, bx, cx      ; ax = ax + bx + cx
add_regs    cx, dx, si      ; cx = cx + dx + si
```

The assembler will replace r1, r2 and r3, which are called **dummy parameters**, by the values specified in the macro call, which are referred to as **actual parameters**.

Thus in add_regs ax, bx, cx the dummy parameter r1 is replaced by ax, r2 by bx and r3 by cx. In add_regs cx, dx, si, the parameter r1 is replaced by cx, r2 by dx and r3 by si.

This greatly increases the power and usefulness of macros. In this example, we are not confined to passing registers as parameters; we can also pass memory variables as long as we are careful not have a memory variable as both the source and destination operand when the macro is expanded.

Exercises

4.7 What is the difference between dummy and actual parameters?

4.8 What is a macro? How are macros defined and called?

4.9 What is the difference between a macro and a sub-program? What are their relative advantages?

4.10 Write macros to implement the `put__str` and `get__str` sub-programs developed in Chapter 3.

4.3 Addressing modes

Assembly language instructions access operands stored in memory or registers. The way an instruction accesses its operands is called its **addressing mode**. In our programs, we have accessed operands in a number of ways, using registers, memory variables and constants. Consider the instructions in the following example.

Example 4.27

Some addressing modes we have already used:

```
mov ax, 10        ; register and constant
add i, 25         ; memory variable and constant
cmp ax, i         ; register and memory variable
mul bx            ; registers (ax, dx and bx)
loop label1       ; memory label and cx register
```

Each of the above instructions accesses operands stored either in memory, registers or in a combination of registers and memory. It is important to realize that *all* operands used by an instruction must be located either in memory or in a register. Even constants such as `25` and `10`, as used in the above example, are stored in memory. In this case, the constants are stored with the code of the instructions in memory. The location of an operand value is called the **effective address** (**EA**) of the operand. We can classify the different addressing modes (ways an instruction accesses its operands) into two groups: register addressing and memory addressing. Memory addressing may be further classified as one of the following: immediate, direct, register indirect, based, indexed, based indexed and relative addressing. It should be noted that not all microprocessors provide the same set of addressing modes. We now describe the commonly used addressing modes used in 8086 programming.

4.3.1 Register addressing

If a register is designated as the source or destination of an instruction, the operand value is stored in the register itself. This is called register addressing. The effective address of the operand is the register. There may be restrictions as to what registers an instruction may access. For example, the segment registers may only be accessed by the `mov` instruction. The shift and rotate instructions are such that the `cl` register must be used to hold the number of bits to be manipulated (if greater than one). Some instructions use registers *implicitly*. The `loop` instruction, for example, decrements the `cx` register, the `mul` and `div` instructions modify the `ax` register (and possibly the `dx` register). This is sometimes called **implied** addressing.

4.3.2 Memory addressing

When memory addressing is used for an operand, the effective address will be a location in memory. We consider the following memory addressing modes: immediate, direct, register indirect, based, indexed addressing and relative addressing.

Immediate addressing

When a constant is used as an operand, we refer to the type of addressing as immediate addressing because the operand is immediately available with the instruction itself, for example

```
mov ax, 30
```

The source operand `30` is stored with the instruction in memory. The effective address of the operand is the location in memory of the one or more bytes that specify the constant value. Expressions such as `30 * 15` may be used as immediate operands provided they can be evaluated to a constant value by the assembler.

Direct addressing

This is one of the commonest addressing modes. A direct memory address is specified by using a variable or label as in the following instructions:

```
mov ax, value
jmp endloop
```

where `value` is a variable whose effective address is located in the data segment of memory and `endloop` is a **label** specifying an address in the code segment of memory. We should note here that not all labels are treated as memory addresses. In particular, labels used with the conditional jump instructions are treated in a completely different fashion, as is described later in the section on relative addressing.

Register indirect addressing

With **indirect addressing** the address of the operand is held in another memory location or a register, and the instruction identifies this intermediate address. In the 8086 we have **register indirect addressing**, with which we place the address of the variable we wish to access in an appropriate register. The bx, bp, si or di registers may be used for this type of addressing. Thus the effective address is found indirectly by accessing a register and using its contents to compute the address, for example

```
mov  bx, offset string

cmp  byte ptr [bx], 0     ; register indirect addressing
```

The address of string is stored in bx and the elements of string may be accessed indirectly using the bx register. Accessing the elements of an array is one of the common uses of register indirect addressing. We used this addressing mode in our string I/O sub-programs get_str and put_str.

Based addressing

Based addressing is similar to indirect addressing, except that we use a displacement with the indirect address. Thus to access the second and third elements of a list pointed to by bx we can write:

```
mov  bx, offset string      ; first element is at [bx]
mov  al, byte ptr [bx + 1]  ; accessing second element
mov  bl, byte ptr [bx + 2]  ; accessing third element
```

The displacement must be a constant. We use this form of addressing to access parameters passed to sub-programs on the stack (see Section 4.4).

Indexed addressing

Indexed addressing is also used to implement arrays in assembly language. The effective address is calculated by adding the value contained in an index register (called a displacement) to a base address, for example the address of the array being manipulated. In the 8086, only the bx, si, di and bp registers may be used as index registers.

Example 4.28

Given an array of characters called str, the following loop initializes the first 10 individual characters to blank:

```
          mov cx, 10
          mov si, 0
init:     mov str[ si ] , ' ' ; store blank in each element
          inc si
          loop init
```

The notation str[si] means access the effective address computed by adding the value of si to the base address str. In simple terms this means access element si of the array str. This allows us to access an individual element of the array str. By incrementing the si register, we can access the successive elements of the array str. It should be noted that when we increment the index by one we access the next byte of the array. This is fine if we are dealing with an array of characters, as in the case of str above, because each element is one byte in size. If, however, we have an array of words (two-byte elements), we must increment the index in steps of two. For example, take an array of seven 16-bit elements called day__totals, which is defined as follows:

```
day__totals     dw    7 dup(0)
```

Assuming that the array has been assigned actual values elsewhere, it could be summed using indexed addressing as shown in the next example.

Example 4.29

Accessing an array of word-sized elements using indexed addressing:

```
            mov   cx, 7
            mov   si, 0
calc__sum:  add   sum, day__totals[ si ]
            add   si, 2
            loop  calc__sum
```

In the case of an array of double words (four-byte elements), the index must be incremented in steps of four. The same rules apply when using register indirect addressing. The above example could be implemented using indirect addressing as follows.

Example 4.30

Accessing an array of word-sized elements using indirect addressing:

```
            mov   cx, 7
            mov   bx, offset day__totals
calc__sum:  add   sum, word ptr [bx] ; word ptr specifies
                                     ; that bx points
            add   bx, 2              ; to a word and not a
                                     ; byte
            loop  calc__sum
```

Relative addressing

This is different to the addressing modes above. Here the address used in the instruction is relative to some base address, such as the address of the instruction itself or more accurately the value of the program counter (which stores the address of the next instruction in the program). The conditional jump instructions use this type of addressing. This is because many transfers of control are local in the sense that the jump is made forwards or backwards over a few instructions. So, instead of specifying the actual address of where to transfer control, it takes less space to store a short relative address in the operand field of the instruction. For example an 8-bit operand field will allow a relative addressing range of +127 to -128 bytes from the program counter address. The 8086 uses this type of relative addressing when you use a conditional jump such as

```
je some_label
```

The assembler works out the number of bytes from the program counter to the label some_label and stores this relative address in the machine code version of the program. If the label occurs before the instruction, then the number will be negative, so it will be subtracted from the program counter to give the program counter its new value. If the label occurs after the instruction, the number will be positive, so it will be added to the program counter to give the program counter its new value.

The location specified by the label some_label must be *within range of* +127 to -128 bytes of the address in the program counter. There is *no such restriction* with the unconditional jmp instruction since it uses the address of the label in memory, that is, it uses direct memory addressing. What happens if you wish to have a conditional jump instruction to jump over a longer distance? One approach to the problem is to use a combination of conditional and unconditional jumps. For example, assume you wish to transfer control, using a conditional jump instruction, to a label called distant, which is more than 128 bytes from the current instruction. You can achieve this as follows, assuming that the label distant is out of range for relative addressing:

```
            <test some condition>
            je near_label      ; if true goto near_label
                               ; and from there goto
                               ; distant
            jmp rest           ; if false goto rest

near_label: jmp distant        ; goto distant

rest:
```

In practice, the majority of conditional jump instructions involve short jumps and relative addressing takes advantage of this to make programs smaller because the label can be implemented using one byte. A label (or memory variable address) will be implemented using at least two bytes with direct addressing.

4.4 The stack and sub-program parameter passing

We frequently need to pass information both to and from sub-programs. For example, the getc sub-program we have being using reads a character from the keyboard and passes it back in the al register. Similarly, we pass information to putc via the al register and putc displays the character stored in al on the screen. We use the ax register with the getn, putn, get_str and put_str sub-programs. Sub-programs may access all the registers and memory variables defined in the main program. In high-level language terms we would say that these variables are **global**. High-level languages such as Pascal and C allow you to write sub-programs and pass information into them in a more convenient fashion using parameters, for example

```
putn( x ) ;                /* display the number stored in x */
get_str( colour );         /* read characters into string */
```

In assembly language programming, we lack the expressive power of high-level languages to pass parameters to sub-programs. Three common methods are used to pass parameters in assembly language. The first method is one we have used frequently and is to place the parameters in registers. Our I/O sub-programs have used the ax register to act as a parameter. This method is fine as long as we have enough spare registers to use, but in practice we will only have two or three registers available for parameter passing purposes.

Another method of passing parameters is to pass the address of a list of parameters to the sub-program. The parameter list may be of arbitrary length, so long as the list is stored contiguously in memory. We used this method of parameter passing with the put_str and get_str sub-programs. Here the list was a list of characters. We can consider each character in the list as a separate parameter (although conceptually it is easier to think of it as a string). We used the ax register to store the address of the list to be passed to put_str. We used bx in put_str to access the elements of the list. As an another example of this method we write a sub-program called sum which takes the address of a list of four numbers, passed as a parameter in the bx register, and returns the sum of the numbers in the ax register.

Example 4.31

Defining and using the sum sub-program, which accesses a list of four parameters passed via the bx register.

```
; sum.asm: sums 4 numbers

        .model small
        .stack 100h

        .data
arg1    dw    3             ; these 4 variables form a list
arg2    dw    7             ; since they are defined together
arg3    dw    4
arg4    dw    11

        .code
start:
        mov   ax, @data
        mov   ds, ax
```

```
        mov   bx, offset arg1    ; bx = address of list
        call  sum                ; compute sum and store it
                                 ; in ax
        call  putn               ; display result

        mov   ax, 4c00h
        int   21h

sum:                             ; returns sum of 4 element
                                 ; list in ax
        mov   ax, [bx]           ; ax = arg1
        add   bx, 2              ; bx points to arg2
        add   ax, [bx]           ; ax = ax + arg2
        add   bx, 2              ; bx points to arg3
        add   ax, [bx]           ; ax = ax + arg3
        add   bx, 2              ; bx points to arg4
        add   ax, [bx]           ; ax = ax + arg4
        ret

;       Insert code for putn etc
              end start
```

The bx register is increased by 2 to point to successive elements in the list, because the elements are word sized (16 bits). Executing this program produces, as output, the number 25.

The above code could be made more efficient by eliminating the need for the add instructions to increase bx to point to the next parameter. We can write [bx+2], [bx+4], and [bx+6] to specify the addresses of the parameters, that is, we can use based addressing to access the parameters. Thus we could rewrite sum as follows:

```
sum:                             ; returns sum of 4 element
                                 ; list in ax
        mov   ax, [bx]           ; ax = arg1
        add   ax, [bx+2]         ; ax = ax + arg2
        add   ax, [bx+4]         ; ax = ax + arg3
        add   ax, [bx+6]         ; ax = ax + arg4
        ret
```

A third method of passing parameters to a sub-program is to use the stack. In fact, when a high-level language sub-program is translated to machine code, this is a common technique that is used for passing parameters to the sub-program. As many parameters as desired may be pushed on the stack before the sub-program is called. The sub-program can then access them on the stack. However, there is a potential problem because the call instruction pushes the return address on the stack. If the sub-program were to simply pop the stack to obtain a parameter, it would first pop off the return address. This would have to be saved and pushed back on the stack in order for the ret instruction to work. This is messy and a much better solution is possible. We can use the bp register to indirectly access items on the stack in the same manner as using the bx register to indirectly access memory.

As an example, we will rewrite the last sub-program, which sums four numbers, to use the stack for accessing its parameters. In order to use the new version we must first push the parameters on to the stack:

```
push  arg4
push  arg3
push  arg2
push  arg1
call  sum
```

The above would give rise to a stack of the form illustrated in Figure 4.3 where **parameter1, parameter2, parameter3** and **parameter4** refer to the parameters that the sub-program is to use. Here they represent the values of arg1, arg2, arg3 and arg4.

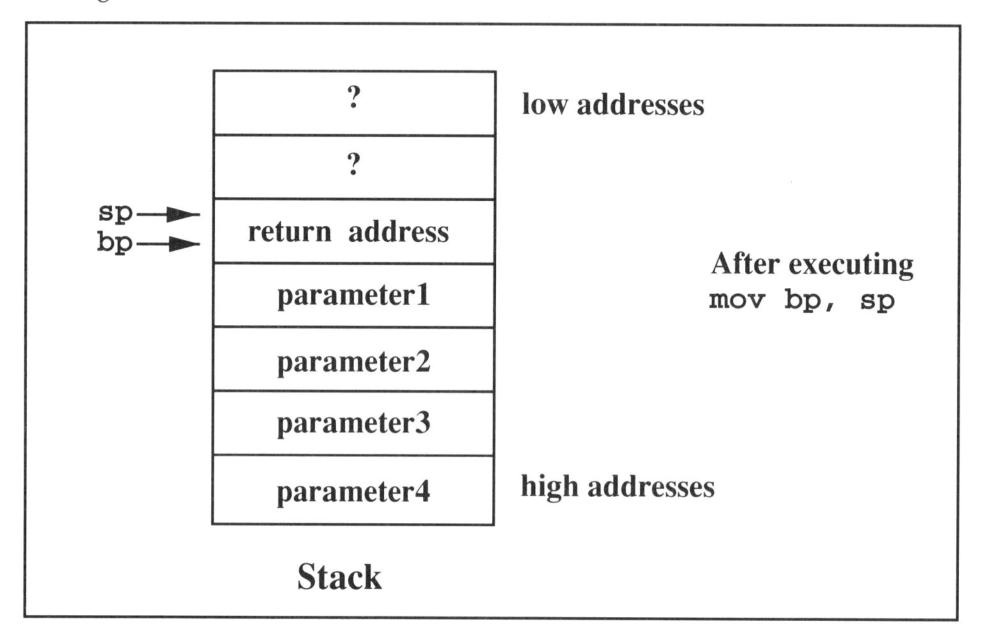

Figure 4.3 State of stack after mov bp, sp instruction has been executed.

We need to access the stack without changing sp. The bp register is used for this purpose. The bp register, like the sp register, always references the stack segment. Thus, by copying the value of sp into bp we can access the stack without modifying sp. We can use bp to indirectly access the parameters on the stack. The notation [bp] refers to the value on the stack pointed to by bp and we can used based addressing to access the parameters. In the above example, we know that the first parameter is 2 bytes above the value in sp, because the stack grows downwards from high memory. Thus, we can access each element on the stack, as in the following implementation of sum:

```
sum:                        ; sum 4 elements from stack and
                            ; return result in ax
        mov  bp, sp         ; bp = sp
        mov  ax, [bp+2]     ; ax = parameter1 i.e. arg1
        add  ax, [bp+4]     ; ax = ax + parameter2 i.e. arg2
        add  ax, [bp+6]     ; ax = ax + parameter3 i.e. arg3
        add  ax, [bp+8]     ; ax = ax + parameter4 i.e. arg4
        ret
```

In the above code fragment, we set bp equal to sp and then, by using based addressing with a displacement of 2 ([bp+2]), we access the first parameter. We store this parameter value in ax and then we then use [bp+4] to access the second parameter. We add this to the first parameter value, which is in ax. We access the two remaining parameters in the same fashion. We are finally left with the sum in ax. Because we have not modified sp, the ret instruction causes our program to return appropriately. However, there is still one important issue to be taken care of. When using the stack, we should always clear items from the stack when we have finished using them. In this example, we pushed four numbers onto the stack before calling sum and these should be cleared from the stack when sum finishes. There are three solutions to this problem:

- The caller uses a pop for each value pushed on, for example

```
call  sum
pop   dx        ; any register or memory variable may be
                ; used
pop   dx
pop   dx
pop   dx
```

- The caller could modify sp directly, by adding 2 for each push instruction, after calling the sub-program. We pushed four items on the stack for the sum sub-program, so we need to add 8 to the sp register to clear the stack:

```
call  sum
add  sp, 8
```

- The 8086 provides for an operand to be included with the ret instruction. If this operand is present, the ret instruction will automatically add this value to sp *after* the return address has been obtained. The sub-program sum could have been terminated with:

```
ret  8
```

This ret instruction will add 8 to sp after obtaining the return address. This is probably the most elegant solution, as it removes responsibility from the sub-program user to clear the stack. The sub-program may be part of a library used by different programmers, who need not concern themselves with details of its implementation. Thus we could rewrite sum as follows:

```
sum:                          ; sum 4 elements from stack and
                              ; return result in ax
        mov    bp, sp         ; bp = sp
        mov    ax, [bp+2]     ; ax = arg1
        add    ax, [bp+4]     ; ax = ax + arg2
        add    ax, [bp+6]     ; ax = ax + arg3
        add    ax, [bp+8]     ; ax = ax + arg4
        ret 8
```

Exercises

4.11 Rewrite `putc` to take its parameter from the stack and show how it would be called.

4.12 Write a sub-program called `max` to compute the largest of three numbers passed as parameters on the stack. It should return the largest value in the `ax` register.

4.5 Summary

In this chapter, we have described the instructions provided for bit manipulation by the 8086 microprocessor and have given some examples of their usage. The `and` instruction is typically used to clear bits, the `or` instruction is typically used to set bits and the `xor` instruction is used to toggle bits. In addition, for efficiency purposes the `and/or` instructions may be used to compare an operand with `0`, while the `xor` instruction may be used to clear an operand to `0`. These instructions occupy less storage when translated to machine code and execute more quickly than the `cmp` and `mov` instructions that we typically use for comparisons and assigning operand values.

We described the use of macros, which constitute a powerful text replacement facility and may be used as an alternative to sub-programs when speed of execution is paramount. However, they cause programs to be larger. We then described the commonly used addressing modes of the 8086 microprocessor. The addressing mode of an instruction refers to the way the instruction accesses its operands. Finally, we described the use of the stack as a mechanism for passing parameters to sub-programs.

This concludes our introduction to 8086 assembly language programming. We have described the commonly used instructions and programming techniques used for the 8086. It should be noted that there are a number of features that we have not discussed and these include the string-handling instructions and the instructions for handling binary coded decimal numbers. These and other features of 8086 assembly language programming are described in the texts on the reading list.

4.6 Reading list

Brey, B.B. (1993) *8086/8088, 80286, 80386 and 80486 Assembly Language Programming*, Merrill (MacMillan), New York.

Hawkley, C. and Neil White, N. (1987) *Assembly Language Programming on the IBM PC*, Addison Wesley, Wokingham.

Liu, Yu-Cheng and Gibson, G.A. (1986) *Microcomputer Systems: The 8086/8088 Family*, Prentice Hall, Englewood Cliffs, NJ.
Microsoft Macro Assembler 5.1 Programmers Guide, (Manual available with MASM), 1987, Microsoft Corporation, Redmond, WA.
Morneau, P. (1992) *PC Assembly Language: An Introduction to Computer Systems*, West Publishing Co., St. Paul, MN.
Skinner, T. (1985) *An Introduction to Assembly Language Programming for the 8086 Family*, Wiley Press, New York.
Thorne, M. (1986) *Programming the 8086/8088*, Benjamin Cummings, Menlo Park, CA.
Uffenbeck, J. (1987) *The 8086/8088 Family: Design, Programming and Interfacing*, Prentice Hall, Englewood Cliffs, NJ.

Part II
Introduction to Computer Architecture

- Chapter 5

  Introduction to computer systems

- Chapter 6

  Computer architecture

- Chapter 7

  Enhancing the basic architecture

- Chapter 8

  Case studies

5

Introduction to computer systems

This chapter provides a general introduction to computer systems. A computer system is made up of both **hardware** and **software**. Software is another term for computer programs. Software controls the computer and makes it do useful work. Without software a computer is useless, akin to a car without someone to drive it. Hardware refers to the physical components that make up a computer system. These include the computer's processor, memory, monitor, keyboard, mouse, disk drive, printer and so on. In this chapter we take a brief look at the functions of the different hardware components. In addition we describe some of the essential software required for the operation of a computer system.

5.1 Hardware

It is crucial to understand that all information is represented inside a computer system in **binary** form, that is, using the binary numbers 1 and 0. The hardware of a computer system has no other way of representing information. Thus when you press a key on a computer's keyboard, a binary number (code) which represents that key is transmitted to the computer and not the symbol, for example, A, displayed on the key. Similarly, when a computer transmits a character to be displayed on the monitor, it is the binary code representing that character that is sent to the monitor. The monitor hardware takes this binary code and displays the corresponding symbol on the screen. To reiterate, all information is transmitted and manipulated inside a computer system in the form of binary numbers. Appendix B describes the representation of information in a computer system in more detail.

A binary digit (1 or 0) is called a **bit** and a group of eight bits is called a **byte**. The fundamental unit of storage is the byte (also called character). Since this is a small amount of information, we group bytes into larger units so that we can easily refer to thousands, millions or billions of them. When counting bytes we deal in powers of 2 such as 2^{10} which is called a kilobyte (**kb**), 2^{20} called a megabyte (**Mb**), 2^{30} called a gigabyte (**Gb**) and 2^{40} called terabyte (**Tb**). When describing transmission speeds, the number of bits per second (bps) is the unit used. The units of measurement used in computer systems are outlined in Appendix A.

The hardware of a computer system is made up of a number of electronic devices connected together. Figure 5.1 is a block diagram of a typical computer system. We make a distinction between a computer and a computer **system**. In this chapter, the term computer refers to that part of the computer system which runs computer programs. A computer system includes the other necessary equipment and software that allow us to use the computer.

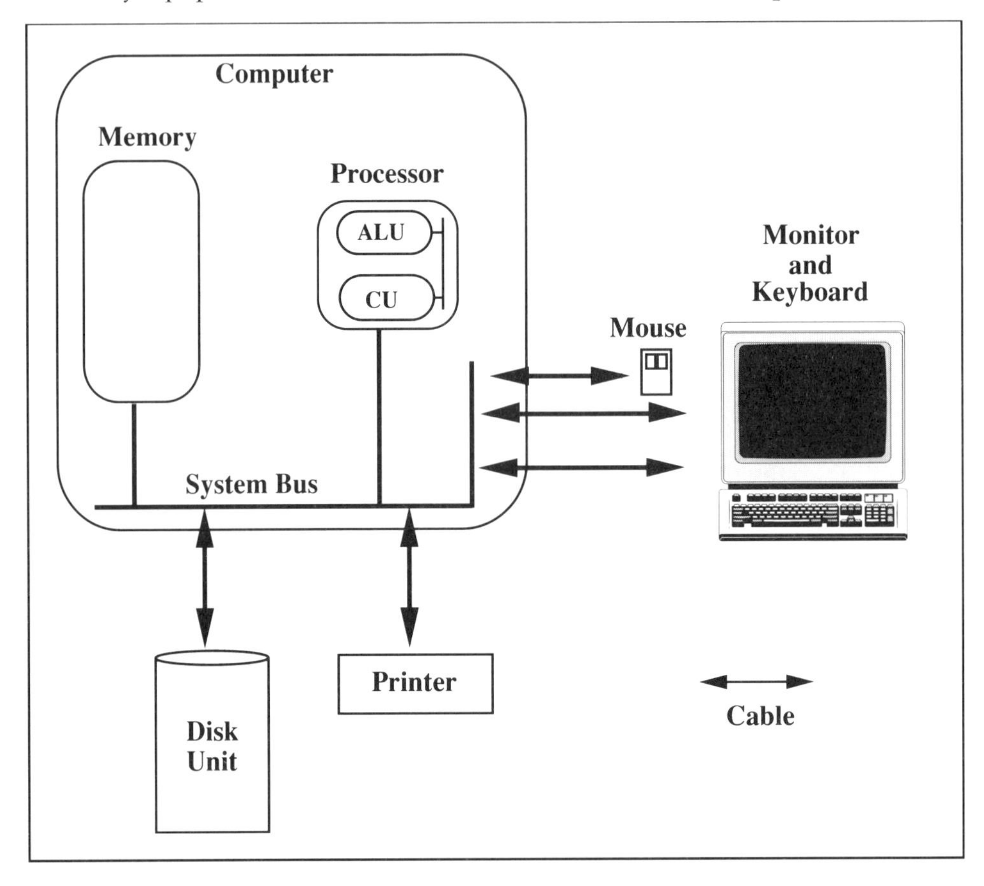

Figure 5.1 A typical computer system.

A computer has two major internal components that are of particular interest to us, namely its **processor** and its **memory**. There is also a power supply unit (not shown in Figure 5.1) to handle electrical power for the system. The term **device** is used to describe any piece of hardware that we connect to a computer, such as a keyboard, monitor, disk drive, printer and so on. Such devices are also described as **peripheral devices** or simply **peripherals**. They may be classified as **input/output** (I/O) devices and **storage** devices. As the name suggests, I/O devices are responsible for communicating with the computer, providing input for the computer to process and arranging to display output for computer users. The keyboard and mouse are commonly used input devices. The monitor is the commonest output device, followed by the printer for **hard copy** (permanent) output. Storage devices are used to store information in a computer system. The memory is used to store information inside the computer while the computer is switched on. Disk storage is the commonest form of external storage, followed by the tape storage. External storage devices can store information indefinitely or, more realistically, for some number of years. A very important component of a computer system is the **system bus**, which is used to transfer information between all system components.

5.1.1 The processor

The processor as its name suggests is the unit that does most of the work of the computer system, that is, it executes computer programs. Software, as we have seen in earlier chapters, is composed of instructions which are executed (obeyed) by the processor. These instructions tell the processor when and what to read from a keyboard, what to display on a screen, what to store and retrieve from a disk drive and so on. A computer program is a set of such instructions that carries out a meaningful task. It is worth remembering at this stage that the processor can only perform a limited range of operations. It can do arithmetic, compare numbers and perform input/output (read information and display or store it). It has no magical powers. It is instructive to bear in mind that *all* computer programs are constructed from sequences of instructions based on such primitive operations.

The processor itself is made up of a number of components such as the **arithmetic logic unit** (**ALU**) and the **control unit** (**CU**). The ALU carries out arithmetic operations (for example, addition and subtraction) and logical operations (for example, `and`, `or`, `xor` operations), while the CU controls the execution of instructions. Traditionally, the processor is referred to as the **central processing unit** or **CPU**. With the advent of microprocessors, the term **MPU** or **microprocessor unit** is also used. A **microprocessor** is simply a processor contained on a *single* silicon chip.

In addition to the ALU and CU, the processor has a small number (usually less than 100) of storage locations to store information that is currently being processed. These locations are called **registers** and, depending on the processor, a register may typically store 8, 16, 32 or 64 bits. The register size of a particular processor allows us to classify the processor. Processors with a register size of n-bits are called **n-bit** processors, so that processors with 8-bit registers are called **8-bit processors**, while there are also **16-bit**, **32-bit** and **64-bit** processors. An n-bit processor is said to have an n-bit word size, so a 32-bit processor has a 32-bit word size. The greater the number of bits, the more powerful the processor, since it will be able to process a larger amount of information in a single operation. For example, a 32-bit processor will be able to add two 32-bit numbers in a single operation, whereas an 8-bit processor will only be able to add two 8-bit numbers in a single operation. An n-bit processor will *usually* be capable of transferring n bits to or from memory in a single operation. This number of bits is also referred to as the memory **word** size. So, while a byte refers to an 8-bit quantity, a word can mean 8, 16, 32, 64 or some other number of bits. On some machines (such as the 8086 and M68000 families) a word is taken to mean a 16-bit quantity and the term **long word** is used to refer to a 32-bit quantity.

An alternative method of classifying a processor is to use the width of the data bus (described later), in which case an n-bit processor describes one operating with a data bus of n bits. This means that the CPU can transfer n bits to another device in a single operation. Using this classification, the Intel 8088 microprocessor is an 8-bit processor since it uses an 8-bit data bus, although its CPU registers are in fact 16-bit registers. Similarly the Motorola 68000 is classified as a 16-bit processor, even though its CPU registers are 32-bit registers. Sometimes a combination of the two classifications is used, so that the 8088 might be described as 8/16-bit processor and the Motorola 68000 as a 16/32-bit processor. In this text, we use the register size as the method for classifying the processor.

The data bus width is very important in a computer system, since it determines the amount of information that can be transferred to or from the CPU in a single operation. This means, for example, that the Motorola 68000 would have to transfer two 16-bit items to the CPU to fill a 32-bit register, since the data-bus width is 16 bits. As we shall see later, I/O devices and memory operate at very slow speeds compared to the speed of the CPU. As a result, the CPU is frequently delayed by these slower devices, waiting for information to be transferred along the data bus. So, the more information we can transfer between an I/O device and the CPU in a single operation, the less time the CPU will spend waiting for information to process. This in turn means that we should strive to have the data bus as wide as possible.

An important component not shown in Figure 5.1 is the CPU **clock**. The clock controls the rate at which activities are carried out by the CPU. It generates a stream of **cycles** or **ticks** and an action can only be carried out on the occurrence of a clock tick. Obviously, the more cycles per second, the more actions that the CPU can carry out. The speed of the clock is measured in millions of cycles per second. One cycle per second is one hertz (Hz), a kilohertz (kHz) is 1000 Hz and a megahertz (MHz) is 1000 kHz. Currently, low-cost PCs are being marketed with clock rates range from 25 to 66 MHz. More powerful machines operate at clock rates in the range from 100 to 200 MHz and the rate continues to increase.

5.1.2 Bus system

The processor must be able to communicate with all devices. They are connected together by a communications channel called a **bus**. A bus is composed of a set of communication lines. A simple bus configuration is shown Figure 5.2. We refer to this bus as the **system bus** as it connects the various components in a computer system. Internally, the CPU has a **CPU bus** for transferring information between its components (the control unit, the ALU and the registers).

In order to attach any device to a computer, it must be connected to the computer's bus system. This means that we need a unit that connects the device to the bus. The terms device **controller** and device **interface** are used to refer to such a unit. So, for example, a disk controller would be used to connect a disk drive to the system bus and the term I/O controller refers to the controller for any I/O device to be connected to the bus system. A computer system will have some standard interfaces, such as a **serial interface** (see Section 5.1.5) which can be used with a number of different I/O devices. The serial interface, for example, can be used to attach a printer, a mouse or a modem (a device allowing a computer to handle communications over a telephone line) to the computer. So, if you wish to construct a new type of I/O device, you could use the

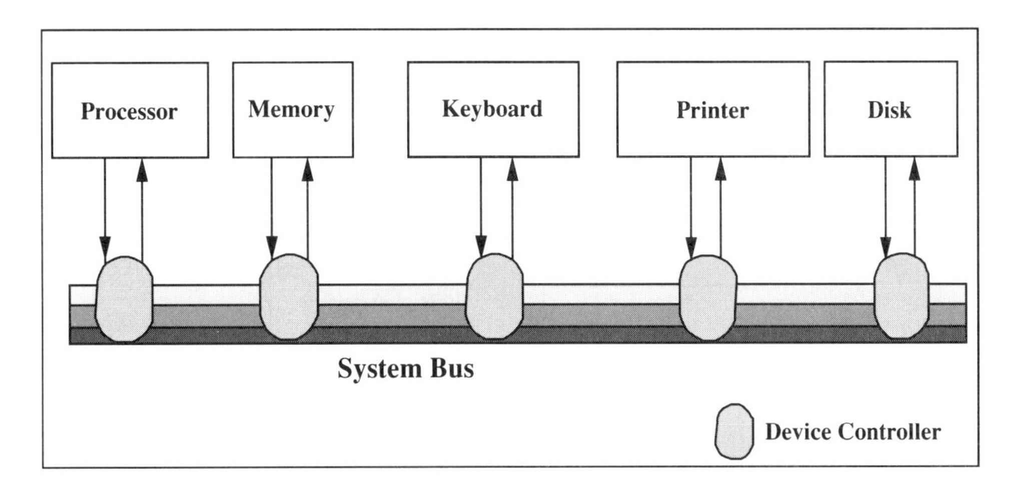

Figure 5.2 The system bus, via which the processor communicates with all devices.

standard laid down for the serial interface (the RS-232 standard) and you could then attach your device to the computer, using the serial interface.

Information is transferred from one device to another on the bus. For example, information keyed in at the keyboard is passed along the bus to the processor. The processor executes programs made up of instructions, which are stored in the computer's memory. These instructions are transferred to the processor using the bus. As indicated in Figure 5.2, the lines of the bus may be classified into three groups. One group of lines, the **data** lines, is used to carry the actual data along the bus from one device to another. A second group of lines, the **address** lines, allows the CPU to specify where the data is going to or coming from, that is, which memory location is to be accessed or which I/O device is to be used. The third group of lines, the **control** lines, carries control signals which, among other things, allow the CPU to control the transfer of information along the bus. For example, the CPU must be able to indicate whether information is to be transferred from memory or to memory; it must be able to signal when to start the transfer and so on. We will refer to these groups of lines as separate buses in this text, so we refer to the **data bus**, **address bus** and **control bus** as separate entities. It is important to realize that a computer system may have a number of separate bus systems so that information can be transferred between more than one pair of components at the same time. For example, it is common to have one bus for communicating between memory and the CPU at high speeds. This bus is called a CPU-memory bus. In addition, this bus would be connected to a second I/O bus via a bus adapter, as illustrated in Figure 5.3. This second bus would be used for the slower I/O devices.

This allows the processor more efficient access to memory, as the CPU-memory bus can operate at very high speeds. These high speeds are only possible if the physical bus length is quite short. Thus, by providing a second I/O bus to accommodate the various I/O devices that may be connected to the computer, the length of the CPU-memory bus can be kept shorter than it would be if the I/O devices were to be directly attached to a single system bus. On the

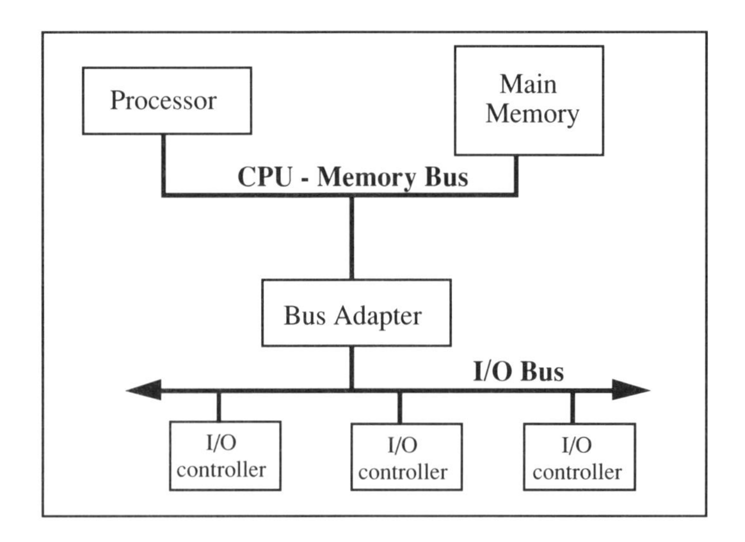

Figure 5.3 The CPU-memory bus and the I/O bus.

other hand, to keep the cost of a computer system low, a single bus running at a slower speed may be used to connect all devices to the CPU.

5.1.3 Memory

Memory is used to store the information (programs and data) that the computer is currently using. It is sometimes called **main** or **primary** memory. One form of memory is called **RAM**, which stands for random access memory. This means that any location in memory may be accessed in the same amount of time as any other location. Memory access means one of two things, either the CPU is reading from a memory location or the CPU is writing to a memory location. When the CPU reads from a memory location, the contents of the memory location are *copied* to a CPU register. When the CPU writes to a memory location, the CPU copies the contents of a CPU register to the memory location, overwriting the previous contents of the location.

RAM is a form of short-term or **volatile** memory. Information stored in short-term storage is *lost* when the computer is switched off (or when power fails, say, if you pull out the power lead!). There is therefore a requirement for permanent or long-term storage which is also referred to as **secondary storage.** This role is fulfilled by disk and tape storage. RAM consists of a large number of cells, each one capable of storing a small amount of information, typically a single byte. These cells are numbered or **addressed** starting at zero, up to some maximum number determined by the amount of RAM present, as illustrated in Figure 5.4. At the time of writing this book, PCs typically have 4 to 8 Mb of RAM installed, but the figure is constantly being revised upwards.

The address of a memory cell is used when we wish to access that particular memory location. This means that we must know the address of a cell in memory before we can access its contents. A byte is a small unit of storage, capable of storing unsigned numbers in the range 0 to 255. In order to allow you to store larger quantities in memory, the hardware allows you to treat a number of consecutive cells as a unit. For example, by using two consecutive cells, 16

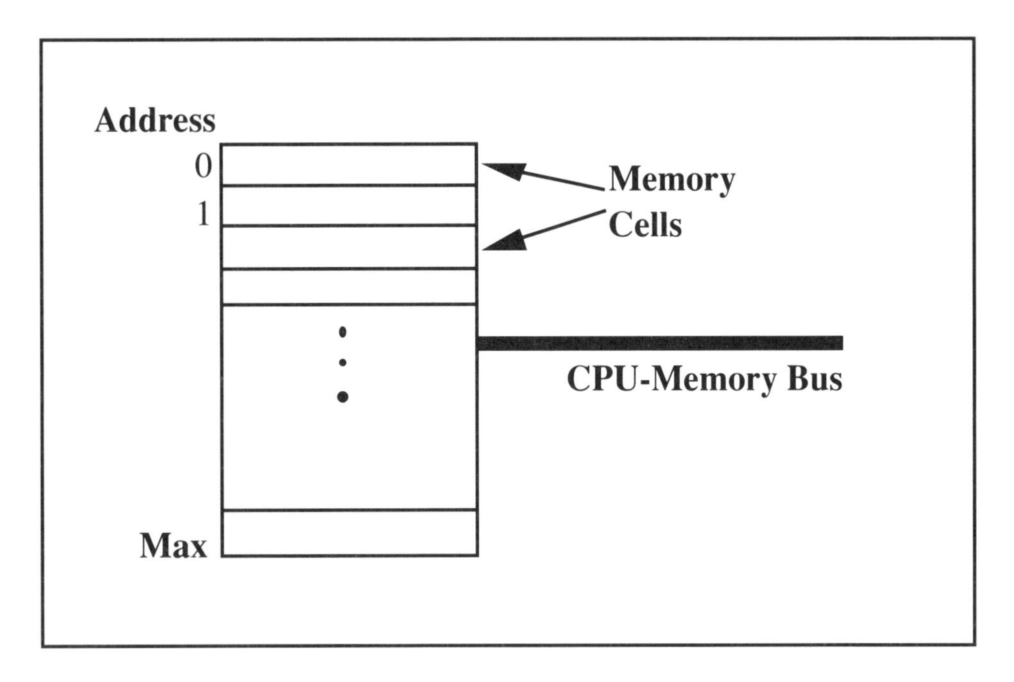

Figure 5.4 Memory organization.

bits are available for storing information, giving an unsigned number range from 0 to $2^{16} - 1$ (65 535). By using four consecutive cells, 32 bits are available, allowing numbers in excess of one billion to be manipulated. What about text, such as that on this page? In the case of text, each character is stored separately in a single byte. So, if there are 2 000 characters on a page, then 2 000 consecutive bytes could be used to store the text.

An important issue arises as to how to interpret the contents of memory. For example, if we are told that a 16-bit number N is stored in memory locations 4 and 5, two possibilities arise. The low-order byte of N may be stored in location 4 (little end) and the high-order byte of N stored in location 5. This is called **little endian** byte order and is used by the Intel 8086 family and the Digital VAX family. The other possibility is that the low-order byte is stored in location 5 (big end) and the high-order byte is stored in location 4. This is called **big endian** byte order and is used by the Motorola 68000 family of microprocessors.

There are two major forms of RAM called **static RAM** (**SRAM**) and **dynamic RAM** (**DRAM**). SRAM is the more expensive of the two as it is more complex to manufacture, but it is considerably faster to access than DRAM. DRAM has an access time in the range of 60–100 ns (nanoseconds) upwards, while SRAM access times range from 4 or 5 to 20 ns upwards. It is not uncommon for a computer system to have a small amount of SRAM and a larger volume of DRAM making up its total RAM capacity. The SRAM is used to construct a **cache** memory, which stores frequently accessed information and so speed up memory access for the system. Cache memory is described in more detail in Chapter 7.

There are other forms of primary memory such as **ROM, PROM, EPROM**

EEPROM and **flash memory**. ROM (**Read Only Memory**) is the same as RAM in so far as any location can be **read** at random, but it cannot be written to. ROM is pre-programmed by the manufacturer and its contents cannot be changed, hence its name 'read only'. This means that ROM is a form of permanent storage. However, since the user cannot store information in ROM, its usefulness is restricted. ROM is typically used to store programs and data that are required to start up a computer system. When a computer is powered on, its RAM will contain no useful information, but the processor is designed to run programs that it finds in memory. One major use of ROM is to store the initial program used by the processor when the machine is started. This use is described in the section on booting up a computer in the second half of this chapter. Another use of ROM in personal computers is to store operating systems sub-programs for carrying out I/O and other activities. The term **firmware** is used for the combination of ROM and the software stored in it.

PROM stands for **programmable** ROM, which means that the memory chip manufacturer provides a form of ROM that can be programmed via the use of a special hardware device. This allows computer system designers to place their own programs on the PROM chip. If their programs do not operate correctly, the designer can program another PROM chip, as opposed to getting the memory manufacturer to do it, as is the case when a designer uses ROM. **EPROM** is a form of ROM that is **erasable**, which means that the contents of the EPROM chip can be erased in their entirety and the chip can be reprogrammed (a limited number of times). As in the case of PROM, EPROM can only be programmed and erased (via exposure to ultraviolet light) by a special hardware device, outside the computer system.

EEPROM is **electrically erasable** PROM. EEPROM can be erased inside a computer system using an electrical current. Its major advantage is that it does not have to be removed from the computer system. In recent years, work has advanced on such **non-volatile** RAM (**NVRAM**) devices. **Flash memory** is one such device. This memory can be accessed (read and written) like RAM, but is non-volatile and so it is a form of permanent storage. At the time of writing, flash memory is available in the 1 to 16 Mb range. One disadvantage of current NVRAMs is that they cannot be written to as quickly as ordinary RAM. However, they are much faster to access than disk storage systems and they consume less power, so that in small portable computer systems they offer an alternative low-powered option to disk storage. However, NVRAMs are more expensive than disk storage devices.

NVRAM should not be confused with a device called a **RAM card** which is made up of normal RAM with a battery power supply. A RAM card can be removed from a computer and is about half the size of a floppy disk. At the moment RAM cards are available in the kilobyte to low-megabyte storage range. Because of the battery power supply, RAM cards retain their contents when removed from a computer.

5.1.4 Permanent storage devices

Long-term storage is also described using the terms secondary, auxiliary, mass, and external. The two commonest forms of secondary storage are disk and tape storage.

Disk storage

Disk storage is the most popular form of secondary storage. It is more versatile than tape storage and it is faster to access than tape, as information on any part of the disk can be accessed independently of its position (**direct access**) on the disk. Its disadvantage is that it is more expensive than tape storage.

The surface of a disk is divided into **tracks** and each track is divided into **sectors** (**blocks**). There may be from 40 to hundreds of tracks on a disk surface. Each sector of a track will typically have a capacity from 32 to 1024 bytes (1024 bytes = 1 kb). Information is stored on or read from a disk magnetically, using a read/write head. To access information on a disk, the head must be moved to the correct track (the time taken to do this is called the **seek time**); the correct **sector** must **rotate** around to the head (the time taken to do this is called the **rotational delay** or **latency**) and finally the information may be transferred (transfer time). On a typical hard disk, the average seek time is around 20 ms (milliseconds). Based on a disk rotation speed of 3 600 rotations per minute, the average rotational delay is the time for half of one rotation, about 8 ms. The transfer time is so small, compared to the seek time and latency, that it can be ignored.

Note: It is approximately 100 000 times slower to access information on disk than to access information in RAM. This is because of the electromechanical nature of the disk drive, involving disk rotation and read/write head movement. While the speeds used in disk drives are quite fast in human terms, in CPU terms they are extremely slow. For example, the CPU can access information stored in RAM in of the order of 20 to 100 ns. The CPU can access information in its registers in a few nanoseconds. So from the CPU's perspective, if information has to be fetched from disk and this takes of the order of 28 ms, then a long wait ensues. As a result of the mismatch in speed between the CPU and disks, much work is concerned with making disk I/O as efficient as possible. For example, you can arrange to do disk I/O so that when you read something from disk, you read a big chunk (at least one sector). Then when you need another piece of information, it may have been read into memory already, as part of the large chunk. You can also arrange information on disk so that it is stored on the same track or neighbouring tracks, which means that the seek time can be significantly reduced.

The physical size of disk drives has decreased dramatically over the years. Only a few years ago, a disk drive of 100 Mb capacity would have been larger than a domestic washing machine. Nowadays such a disk drive fits easily inside a notebook computer. The cost of disk storage has fallen in a similar manner. The shrinking size and low cost of disk drives has led to the use of systems with several disk drives or arrays of disk drives. In addition, to increase availability of data, **redundant arrays of independent disks** (**RAID**) systems have been developed.

In a RAID system, information is distributed over a number of disk drives in such a fashion that if one of the disk drives is removed from the system (due to failure), the information can still be accessed. A simple version of a RAID system is called mirroring, whereby two disks, whose contents are mirror images of each other, are maintained. Whenever information is stored (updated) on one disk, it is automatically stored (updated) on the mirror disk. In the event of one of the disks failing, the second disk can be used to access the information. In this case we have 100% redundancy, with a complete copy of all information on one disk stored on a second disk. This increases the availability of data in the system at the expense of a second disk. Using clever software, however, similar availability can be achieved in a system without the overhead of 100% redundancy. For example, a RAID system might be composed of nine disks where eight of the disks are used to store information and one is used to store redundant information. This redundant information can be used to *reconstruct* data from any of the disks in the event of a disk failing. In this case, we have only a little more than 11% redundancy, but the system can operate successfully (albeit more slowly) without information loss, if a disk drive becomes faulty.

In brief, the decreasing cost and size of disk drives is leading to computer systems having very large storage capacities with very high data availability.

Tape storage

Tape storage is *cheap* with a *large capacity*, for example 50 Mb upwards for a typical tape. Exabyte tapes, which are also used in video camcorders, can store 2 Gb (billion bytes). The disadvantage of tape as a storage medium is that tape is a **sequential storage medium**. This means that to access the *n*th item of information, you have to skip over the first $n - 1$ items, in the same fashion as fast forwarding to play music from the middle of an audio tape cassette. This makes tape very slow to access in comparison with disks. Typically, tape storage is used to keep a **backup** of the information stored on a disk. Thus, in the event of a loss of information from disk, you can retrieve it from your tape backup. Tape is also used to transfer information (data and software) between computers. Tape is especially popular in large computer installations where large amounts of data have to be kept for years. On personal computers it is more common to use disks as a form of backup storage and as a means of transferring information between computers.

Aside: An important principle: always have a backup. A backup is a second copy of information stored on disk or tape. This crucial principle is a matter of common sense. Much time is spent entering data and programs (days, weeks, even years). However, it must be remembered that computer storage media can easily be damaged, lost or even stolen. In addition, users may inadvertently delete information. All computer users lose information at some stage. The seriousness of this is greatly reduced, or even eliminated, if regular backups are taken. In the event of information loss, you simply use the backup copy. If the information is particularly valuable (in terms of time spent to enter it or in financial terms) then it may be a wise precaution to have several backups. Backup copies should be stored separately from the main copy to avoid a disaster destroying all copies at the same time.

There are a number of different types of tape available: reel tapes, cartridge tapes, digital audio tapes and optical tapes. The capacity ranges from tens of megabytes upwards for reel tapes, from hundreds of megabytes for cartridge tapes, from one or two gigabytes for video tapes and from a terabyte for optical tapes. The huge capacity of optical tapes is useful for organizations, such as weather forecasting services, storing enormous amounts of data.

CD-ROM

CD-ROM (Compact Disk Read Only Memory) is another form of secondary storage that is increasing in popularity. It is a low-cost storage medium with a very large capacity. Unlike disk storage, CD-ROM is a WORM (Write Once Read Many times) device, a **read only** storage device. This means that, like ROM, the disk comes with information already stored on it. Thus one of the main uses of CD-ROM is to disseminate information such as library catalogues, reports, manuals, journals, directories and software. It has also become a very popular medium for computer games. Many software vendors and computer manufacturers such as Sun and Apple distribute their software and manuals on CD-ROM. Many publishers now use CD-ROM especially for educational material and it is possible to buy encyclopaedias and various texts in CD-ROM form. The CD-ROM has sufficient capacity not only to store the written text, but also video and audio material which require large amounts of storage; for example, a digital version of a small photograph may require up to a megabyte of storage.

CD-ROM uses the same technology as the compact audio disk or CD and such disks can also be used in a CD-ROM drive. Optical scanning techniques, using lasers, are employed with CD-ROMs, which allow massive amounts of data to be stored in a compact area. A CD-ROM drive is about the same size as a floppy disk drive. CD-ROM is currently more reliable and durable than magnetic media (disks and tapes). In terms of capacity, a single CD-ROM may store up to 600 Mb. In terms of text this is equivalent to about 200 books of 1 000 pages each.

A disadvantage of CD-ROM is that it takes longer to access information, compared to a hard disk. However, clever software tailored for particular applications often means that this is not a serious problem. **Video disks** are similar to CD-ROM (but have a larger capacity) and are used for similar applications.

Rewritable CD storage (CD-R) is now becoming more widely used. This storage combines the reliability and storage capacity of CD-ROM with the flexibility of magnetic disks in that users can store their own information on them. They are still slower to access than conventional hard disks. Magneto-optical (MO) disks combine the use of magnetic and optical principles to store information. MO disks have a smaller capacity than CD-ROMs (for example, a 3.5 inch MO disk stores 128 Mb) and are quite expensive in comparison to conventional hard disks.

Taking short-term and long-term storage together, we can represent the relative capacity and access times in the form of a storage hierarchy as illustrated in Figure 5.5. At the top of the hierarchy we have storage on the CPU chip (in registers). This is the fastest form of storage in terms of CPU access time, but it also has the smallest capacity. Register capacity ranges from a few tens to a few hundreds of bytes. We then have **cache** memory with a capacity of typically less than 1 Mb. Nowadays we also have CPU cache memory, that is, cache memory on the CPU chip itself. This is in the low-kilobyte range, 8 to 64 kb at the moment. Cache memory has an access time of typically less than 20 ns. The next level is that of main memory with a capacity in the megabyte range and access times of less than 100 ns. Disk storage is in the high megabyte to gigabyte capacity range with typical access times of microseconds. Tape storage provides from high megabyte to terabyte storage capacity with access times as slow as seconds for reel tapes. It should be noted that the access time for the newer optical tapes is much better than that of reel tapes.

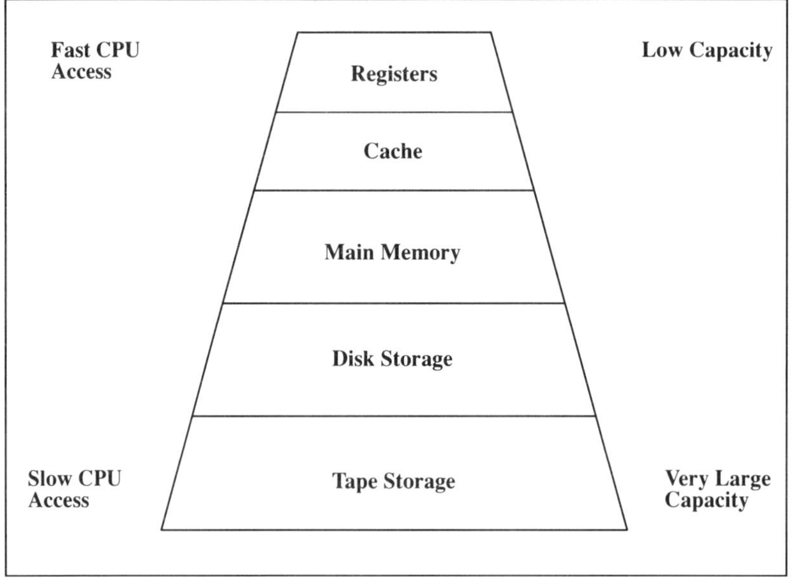

Figure 5.5 The storage hierarchy of a computer system.

5.1.5 I/O devices

In this section we survey some of the commonly used I/O devices encountered in computer systems.

Input devices

The **keyboard** and **mouse** are the most widely used input devices at the moment. The QWERTY keyboard, so called because the keys q, w, e, r, t and y are adjacent, is the commonest form of keyboard. But other types of keyboard are available, some being specially designed for people with special needs. It should be noted that the layout of keys on the QWERTY keyboard owes its origins to typewriter designers, who were actually trying to slow down the speed at which a typist could type. The reason being that the original lever-based typewriters were liable to levers getting interlocked if two keys were pressed in rapid succession. Typewriter designers laid out the keys in a fashion that made it difficult to type quickly, the QWERTY layout being the product of this design. Because so many people trained on such keyboards, the layout still remains with us today, many years after the engineering problem, which it was designed to alleviate, disappeared. It is worth noting that in some non-English speaking countries the layout is slightly different, giving rise to QWERTZ and AZERTY keyboard layouts.

The **mouse** is used as a pointing device and to select options from menus. A **tracker ball** is used for the same purposes as a mouse and is popular on laptop computers. Another input device is called a **light pen** which can be used to point at a monitor, serving a similar function to a mouse. A **touch-sensitive screen** is a method of input based on touching a specially designed screen in particular places. It is typically used in applications such as a tourist information system, where information can be obtained by touching menu options displayed on the screen.

A very common requirement for business is the processing of payments. Take an insurance company, for example, where very many customers return payment for their insurance with some form of printed statement from the company. In order to automate processing such payments, a form of input called **optical character recognition** (**OCR**) was developed. An OCR device can scan a document and recognize characters. Originally, text had to be printed in a special OCR font for OCR to operate but nowadays OCR can handle almost any font. The advantage of OCR for companies is that when statements are returned with payments, they can be scanned in and the customer accounts automatically credited. A less sophisticated but similar device is an **optical mark reader**, which can scan a specially designed form and recognize the presence of marks in particular positions. One use for such a device is in lottery games machines, where a user marks numbers on a pre-printed form, which is then read by an OCR reader connected to a lottery computer.

Magnetic ink character recognition (MICR) is similar to OCR but this time the characters are not scanned optically. Instead they are scanned magnetically as they have been printed with magnetized ink, each character having a very distinct shape. This is used on cheques by banks, to encode bank account numbers.

Bar-code scanners are very popular input devices in supermarkets and stores. These devices scan bar-codes which identify products. This is a form of OCR. The bar-code is translated to a number that can be used by the computer to identify the product and look up its price in a database. In addition the software can keep track of stock levels by recording the number of sales of each item.

Image scanners are devices which scan an image (document, photograph) and produce a digital version of the image, that is, the image is stored as a sequence of binary numbers. Special software can then display the digital version of the image on a monitor. They effectively 'photocopy' the image into the computer. This type of technology is very useful for storing legal documents, application forms and anywhere there is a requirement to access the contents of an original document very quickly. The term **document image processing** (**DIP**) is used to describe the application of this technique and it is becoming an important application in insurance and banking organizations. OCR may also be used in conjunction with DIP in document management software packages.

Aside: It should be noted that digital images require large amounts of storage. To alleviate this problem, various **data compression** techniques may be used. Data compression software can reduce storage requirements dramatically, with savings ranging from 10 to 90% depending of the type of data being compressed. Some PCs use this type of software to effectively double their hard-disk storage capacity – all data stored on the hard disk is compressed, so that an 80 Mb disk appears as if it has 160 Mb capacity. Data compression is also used by software vendors who typically compress their software when distributing it on floppy disks, since it reduces the number of floppy disks required. Data compression is also very important in data communications, since if data is compressed, it can be transmitted in less time. This is important because users are charged either for transmission time or for the amount of data transmitted, or both. Compression techniques reduce both costs. Fax machines have hardware to compress the images being transmitted and because of the nature of most faxes (lots of blank lines or white space) reductions of up to 90% can be achieved, so that an image requiring 1 Mb can be compressed to 100 kb for transmission. The receiving fax machine automatically decompresses the image as it receives it.

There is available a whole range of cards, such as ATM (Automatic Teller Machine) and credit cards, which encode information magnetically. These cards can be read by card readers and allow you to carry out various transactions, such as paying for goods or obtaining cash.

Voice input is perhaps the most exciting form of computer input. While some devices and applications are available, a good deal of work remains to be done before we will easily be able to use computer software without the need for a keyboard and mouse.

Output devices

Monitors are the commonest output device for a computer system. They range from the lowly dumb terminal screen to the high-quality bit-mapped colour screen of workstations. A basic monitor displays up to 24 lines of 80 columns of standard characters. Advanced monitors range from monochrome to full colour and are bit-mapped which means that each point on the screen (called a **pixel** which stands for picture element) corresponds to at least one bit in memory. By modifying the bits in memory, the image on the screen is modified. A colour screen may have in memory up to 24-bits corresponding to each pixel, since the colour of the pixel must be recorded. Such monitors vary in size and in the number of colours they support.

Printers are the commonest **hard-copy** output device. They range from cheap low-quality dot-matrix to high-speed, high-quality laser printers with a variety of intermediate-quality devices available.

Aside: A word of caution is appropriate regarding the management and use of printers. Paper inevitably jams in printers at some stage, no matter whether it's an expensive laser printer or a cheap dot-matrix one. There are very few more irate users than those who have spent a few hours preparing documents only to find that they cannot get them printed! So, if you have anything to do with managing or installing a computer system, be warned, make sure your users know the basics of clearing paper jams or face the consequences!

Connecting a printer to a computer

Computers are connected to printers with cables using plugs and sockets as illustrated in Figure 5.6. The sockets are usually called **interfaces** or **ports**. Since we use these ports to send information into or out of a computer, they are also called **input/output ports** or **I/O ports**. The cable used to connect the printer to the computer is often called a **line**. There are two types of cable which may be used. One is called a **serial** cable and the other a **parallel** cable. The parallel cable is made up of many lines running in parallel, hence its name. A different interface (socket) is required for each. You use a **serial interface** for a serial line and a **parallel interface** for a parallel line. Most computers and printers have both types of interface, allowing you to use whichever one you please. The serial line and interface is made up according to an international standard referred to as the RS-232 standard. Hence a serial line and the interface for a serial line (a serial interface) are often referred to as an **RS-232 line** and an **RS-232 interface.**

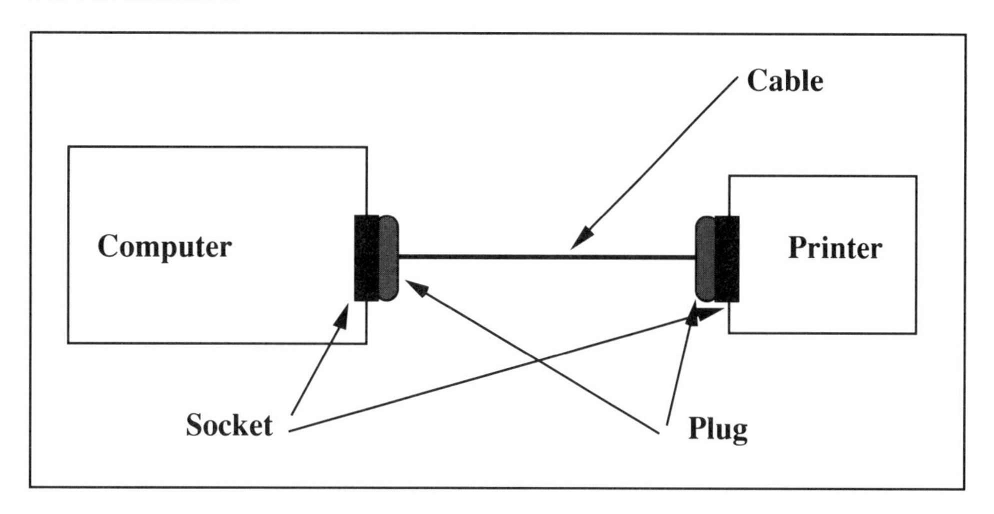

Figure 5.6 Connecting a computer to a printer.

You may also use a serial or parallel interface if you wish to communicate with other computers over a telephone line. A device called a **modem** (modulator/demodulator) is used for such communication. It connects your computer to a telephone line via the serial or parallel port. In fact, a whole variety of I/O devices may be connected to a computer using either the serial or parallel interfaces. For example, on multi-user computers which use computer terminals, each terminal (keyboard and screen) may be connected to the computer via a serial line connected to a serial port on the computer. Such a computer will have a serial port for each terminal. (Alternatively terminals may be connected to a mainframe using some form of **network** link; see Section 5.1.8.)

Plotters are output devices used for graphical output, such as architectural and engineering drawings produced by CAD (Computer Aided Design) packages. They can handle a range of paper sizes and operate at various speeds.

5.1.6 Embedded computer systems

So far we have been describing a conventional computer system, as might be used in an office or at home. However, strange as it may seem at first, the vast majority of computer processors are not used in such computer systems. One of the world's largest customers for processors is General Motors, the US automobile manufacturer, where they are used in automobiles, for example in the braking system or to monitor fuel and oil consumption. In the home, appliances such as microwave ovens, washing machines, sound systems, alarms and so on are usually controlled by microprocessors. The computer system used in such applications is called an **embedded computer system**, as it is a component of another system.

Embedded processors are much the same (and sometimes are the same) as those used in a conventional computer system. For example, Patriot missiles are guided by a Digital VAX processor (a pretty suicidal task for a processor!). For many embedded systems, only very simple microprocessors are required and in many cases primitive 4-bit processors are adequate, while 8-bit microprocessors are still very commonly used.

An obvious difference between an embedded computer system and a conventional one is in the type of I/O device used. Embedded systems take their input from a range of devices such as **switches** and **sensors** including temperature, pressure, light, humidity, sound, vibration sensors. The output of such systems typically goes to switches to activate lights and other devices.

These I/O devices are usually electrical devices and use analogue electrical signals. A computer, on the other hand, uses digital (binary) signals. The conventional I/O devices described earlier all use digital signals and so they can be directly connected to an appropriate device controller. Sensors and switches must be connected to an analogue-to-digital (A/D) converter for input to the computer system and to a digital-to-analogue (D/A) converter for output from a computer system.

5.1.7 *Classifying computers*

A few years ago, a computer was easily classified as being one of **mainframe**, **minicomputer** or **microcomputer**. Mainframe computers were physically large and powerful systems capable of supporting hundreds of users. They had relatively large amount of RAM (1 to 2 Mb) and disk storage (100 to 400 Mb). Minicomputers were smaller, less powerful machines than mainframes, but were still multi-user machines. Microcomputers were small humble machines with 8-bit or 16-bit processors, 16 to 256 kb of RAM and 5 to 10 Mb of disk storage, used mainly for games and basic word processing.

Developments in microprocessor technology, however, mean that today's desktop microcomputer will easily have more RAM and disk storage than the above mentioned mainframe, as well as having a more powerful CPU. Minicomputers today are really no more than very powerful microcomputers. The differences between such a machine and a desktop model may more likely be in the software that is being used as opposed to the hardware. For example, a multi-user operating system, such as UNIX, would typically be used, as opposed to the MS-DOS or Windows systems of PCs. Mainframe computers are still powerful machines (physically much smaller than their ancestors) with tens of megabytes of RAM and gigabytes of disk storage. They have very powerful CPUs that allow them cope with large numbers of users.

Supercomputer is the term used for the most powerful computer available at any time. These are typically tailored for very fast processing of what are known as **number crunching** applications. Such applications require a tremendous number of arithmetic calculations to be carried out. Weather forecasting is the classic example of such an application where complex equations taking account of huge numbers of observations have to be solved. Other applications are to be found in astro-physics and some branches of chemical analysis and modelling.

Supercomputers at the moment can carry out billions of operations per second! The Cray is perhaps the most well known supercomputer and is named after its designer Seymour Cray.

5.1.8 Computer networks

The trend, at the time of writing this text, is for organizations to install **distributed** computer systems in a move away from large mainframe systems. In a distributed system, computers are connected together to form networks. Networks often provide **services** (for example, electronic mail, printing, database access) on one machine for all users of the network. The machine providing the service is called a **server**. The machines (users) using the service are called **clients**. A typical organization might provide each user with their own desktop machine, connected on a network to a central **file server** machine. The file server is simply a microcomputer with high-capacity disk drives, dedicated to the task of storing user files and applications software. A user can load software from the file server and run it on their own machine. In addition, they can have shared access to data stored on the file server. Because the machines are networked, it is easy to provide electronic mail (**e-mail**) applications to allow users to communicate with each other.

One of the problems with a distributed system is that of management. With a centralized mainframe-based system, it is easier for the system manager to keep track of software and data, as well as users! With a distributed system, users may store software and data on their local hard disks (even if they are advised not to do so!). This can cause problems in keeping data consistent (everybody should have access to the **same** data) and problems due to different versions of a software package being used.

A computer network that is local to a building or campus is called a **local area network** or **LAN**. The advantages of such a system include decreased cost (it is cheaper to install a network of PCs than a powerful mainframe) and increased availability since users are not dependent on a single mainframe computer. LANs are to be found in offices, schools, colleges, hospitals and most large organizations. They do not provide for new applications that could not be carried out on a single mainframe with terminals, but they have significant cost and availability advantages. While mainframe computers are capable of running the same applications as those used on PCs, it is frequently the case that user friendly software for many common applications, such as for word processing, is not readily available on mainframe computers and this has been an important advantage in the promotion of PCs.

Wide area computer networks (**WANs**) are interconnected computer systems where the distance between the machines making up the network is anything from a few kilometres to the other side of the globe. Many WANs are based on phone lines for their connections. WANs are widely used in banking and the airline industry. The financial markets are also heavily dependent on WANs. They provide for **remote database access** (accessing a database in a computer system that may be hundreds or thousands of miles away), which is the basis for airline reservations and home banking applications. They also provide global e-mail for users.

The connection of two networks is called **internetworking**. The term internetwork or **internet** is used to describe the composite network. This may involve the connection of: a LAN to a WAN; or a LAN to another LAN; or a WAN to another WAN. The term **Internet** is now often employed to refer to a specific global network of computers that is widely used by people all over the world to communicate with each other. The Internet has millions of computers connected to it and an estimated 25 million users. The number of users connected to the Internet is still growing at a phenomenal rate. Organizations are connecting their LANs or WANs to the Internet and individual users can also access the Internet from home, using a modem. The term **information superhighway** is being applied to this network and its planned high-capacity successor. The information superhighway will allow users to employ the network for all of their communication requirements, including e-mail, voice mail, fax, tele-conferencing and television and radio programs. It will be based on optical fibre links, capable of transferring vast amounts of information very quickly.

5.2 Software

Software, as we mentioned earlier, is another term for computer programs. In this text we have described how to write software using assembly language for the 8086 microprocessor family. Some important software that usually comes with your computer is called **systems** software or the **operating system** and in this section we discuss some of the important components of operating systems. There is a whole field of computer science concerned with the study of operating systems because of its fundamental importance in the use of computers. We can only take a cursory look at the nature of operating systems in this text and the reader can explore the field further by consulting some of the reference text books listed at the end of the chapter.

5.2.1 *Operating systems*

The operating system is the software that enables you to use a computer. Without an operating system, a computer would be useless. It is the software that allows you to give the computer commands, such as to start a word processor or to list the files you have stored on the computer's disk. For programming purposes the importance of the operating system becomes apparent when we wish to perform input and output (I/O). The operating system controls the computer's I/O operations, allowing us to deal with keyboards and screens without getting bogged down in the details of their hardware interfaces. It is worth noting, at this point, that the operating system is software just like the software presented in Part I of this text. The programmers who write operating system software use the same techniques as other programmers and they cannot walk on water! They do, however, have to concern themselves with details of hardware and operating system software, which most programmers do not have to worry about.

An operating system **manages** both the computer's hardware and software for you. It allows you to use the computer by providing a user interface which enables you to give the computer commands. **Graphical user interfaces (GUIs)** are becoming very popular nowadays. A GUI allows you to use a mouse to select commands from menus, which are usually displayed in windows on the screen. Microsoft Windows and the Apple Macintosh operating system interface are widely used GUIs. The Apple Macintosh GUI can take a lot of the credit for bringing the advantages of a GUI to a wide audience. A **command interpreter** is a user interface program that displays a prompt on the screen and the user enters a command using the keyboard. MS-DOS and UNIX provide such command interpreters. Note that many systems now provide both GUIs and keyboard-oriented command interpreters. So, on a UNIX system, you may use the UNIX command interpreter or a windows-based GUI (usually X-Windows). On an IBM-compatible PC you may choose to use MS-Windows or MS-DOS. We describe command interpreters in more detail in Section 5.2.6.

One way to look at an operating system is to view it as being composed of two major sub-systems: a **file handling** sub-system and a **program execution** sub-system. The file handling sub-system is responsible for the **management of files.** A file may be defined as a named computerized container for information. The program execution sub-system is responsible for allowing you to **run** or **execute** programs. A running program is called a **process** in operating systems terminology, so this sub-system is also called the **process sub-system.**

You must not confuse the term process with the term program. A program is a set of instructions and as such is a static entity, that is, it does not change (unless of course you modify it). A process on the other hand is defined as a program in execution. This means that a process includes not only the instructions making up the program but also the values of the CPU registers and memory variables that are associated with a running program. Thus a process changes after each instruction executes, causing some change in a register or memory variable. A process is therefore a dynamic entity. It may pass through different states, such as executing, waiting for I/O to complete or waiting for the CPU to be allocated to it.

5.2.2 *Computers and operating systems*

There are numerous different types of computers, ranging from microcomputers to supercomputers being manufactured by many computer companies. Each manufacturer's hardware is typically different from that of their competitors. For this reason, traditionally, each computer type had its own operating system developed for it. This was because the operating system was totally dependent on the hardware of the computer it was to manage. The operating system could only be used on the particular machine it was designed for. This meant that if you bought a different type of computer, you had to learn how to use a new operating system. While this may have suited manufacturers, who did not want you to buy a competitor's machine, it certainly did not suit users. For example, Digital developed the **VMS** operating system for their VAX range of computers and IBM developed the **OS/360**, **MVS**, **VM** and other operating systems for their mainframe series of computers. The VAX series is a very popular range of computers from micro to mainframe power. The VMS operating system was designed to run on only the VAX computer series.

In the 1970s a new operating system called **UNIX** was developed at Bell

Labs. UNIX was designed to be **portable**. This meant that it could be moved from one type of computer to another different type of computer using **different** hardware, without too much difficulty. UNIX has to be *tailored* for each machine, but it is designed to make this tailoring relatively straightforward. By the late 1980s, UNIX had been implemented on every common make of computer, from the Digital VAX to IBM mainframes, from the humble microcomputer to powerful supercomputers. It is the only operating system that has been implemented on such a diverse range of hardware platforms. As a result, it is now one of the most commonly used operating systems in the world, becoming a *de facto* standard in operating systems.

In the microcomputer world, the **MS-DOS** operating system is very widely used on IBM microcomputers (**PC**s) and their **clones**. When IBM introduced their PC to the market, many of their competitors in effect copied the machine producing IBM **compatibles** or clones. The competitors then acquired the same operating system for the clones, from a company called Microsoft who had developed the operating system for IBM! The IBM PC operating system was called **PC-DOS** while that of its clones was called MS-DOS. For practical purposes they are almost identical. MS-DOS is the most widely used operating system, since there are in excess of 200 million PCs in use around the world and this number is increasing at a rate of between 20 and 30 millions a year. The Apple Macintosh is another widely used microcomputer and is noted for its user friendly operating system.

It should be noted that a microcomputer operating system is usually much less sophisticated than an operating system for more powerful computers. A microcomputer typically only has to deal with a single user at any point in time, that is, it is a **single-user** system. Operating systems like UNIX and VMS may have to cope with hundreds of users simultaneously, that is, they are **multi-user** systems. This means that the operating system has to deal with the programs of a number of users at the same time. Even a single-user system may have to do this if it provides multi-tasking. A multi-tasking system is one whereby a number of programs can be executed at the same time. Multi-user systems have to be multi-tasking and this makes them harder to design and implement than single-user systems, which are usually single tasking.

A major design problem in a multi-user system is due to **concurrent access**, users accessing the machine at the same time. The problem is one of preventing them (their programs) from interfering with each other. For example, we must ensure that two or more users do not use the printer at the same time, otherwise their printouts would become mixed up. Text from different users would appear on the same page and the printouts would be useless! Thus, one important theme in a multi-user operating system design is that of *sharing resources*. Since a number of users are accessing the computer system concurrently, the operating system must arrange to share (allocate) the resources of the computer system among the users. Hence an operating system is sometimes called a **resource manager**. The computer system resources which must be shared are the CPU, memory, disk storage, printers, terminals and so on. Sharing the CPU is called **scheduling** and the part of the operating system that carries out this function is called the **scheduler**. Sharing memory is called **memory management** and the **memory manager** is the operating system component that carries out this function. Scheduling and memory management are fundamental functions of the process sub-system.

5.2.3 Scheduling

It is crucial to understand that in a single processor (**uni-processor**) computer system, *only one program can execute at any point in time*. Yet on a multi-user system *all* users have the *impression* that their program is the one currently executing. This is an illusion which is achieved by the speed of the processor. The processor can execute millions of instructions per second. So the operating system scheduler allocates the CPU to each user's program for a short period of time called a **quantum**, usually a fraction of a second, for example 100 ms. The CPU then executes that program until its time fraction expires. The scheduler then switches the CPU to another program for a fraction of a second and so on. When the scheduler returns to executing the first program, it resumes the program at the point it stopped executing. Because of the speed of the CPU a program will normally have resumed execution before a user realizes that it had not being executing for a while.

The scheduler is a small, but important, program whose basic function is to decide which program to run next and to start that program executing. There are numerous **scheduling policies** used to decide which process gets the CPU next. One such policy is called the **round robin** policy, where everyone gets an equal amount of CPU time in sequence so that no process gets a second CPU quantum until every process has received a first CPU quantum. Another scheduling policy is a **priority** scheduling policy, where user processes are assigned higher or lower priorities. The scheduler gives high-priority processes preference over low-priority processes, executing the process with the highest priority.

While priority scheduling seems very unfair, it works quite well in practice because of one important feature of program execution, which is that most programs carry out I/O. This is important because of the mismatch in speed between the CPU and the I/O devices of a computer system. As mentioned earlier, it is 100 000 times slower to access information on disk than to access information stored in RAM. Keyboard input compares to CPU speed the same way as snail speed compares to jet-aircraft speed! Thus, while the CPU is waiting for an I/O operation to complete for one program, it can be switched by the scheduler to another program. As a result, a high-priority process that carries out I/O will not unduly hog the CPU from other programs. It has been observed that process execution involves periods of CPU execution and periods of I/O wait (waiting for an I/O operation to complete). Processes alternate between these two states. Programs may be classified as **I/O bound** if they exhibit many short CPU bursts (typical file processing program) intermingled with I/O waits. They are **CPU bound** if they exhibit a few very long CPU bursts. A high-priority CPU-bound process will indeed hog the CPU and the response time for other users will suffer as a consequence.

5.2.4 Memory management

The operating system memory manager must arrange for programs to share memory. For example, a multi-user system, running four user programs, might have its memory shared as illustrated in Figure 5.7. Note that the operating system itself is a program and so it must also be stored in memory and, indeed, it occupies a significant portion of memory. It also occupies a significant amount of disk storage space. It is important to be aware of the fact that the operating system, in managing the computer's resources, uses a significant amount of those resources itself in terms of CPU time, memory and disk storage space.

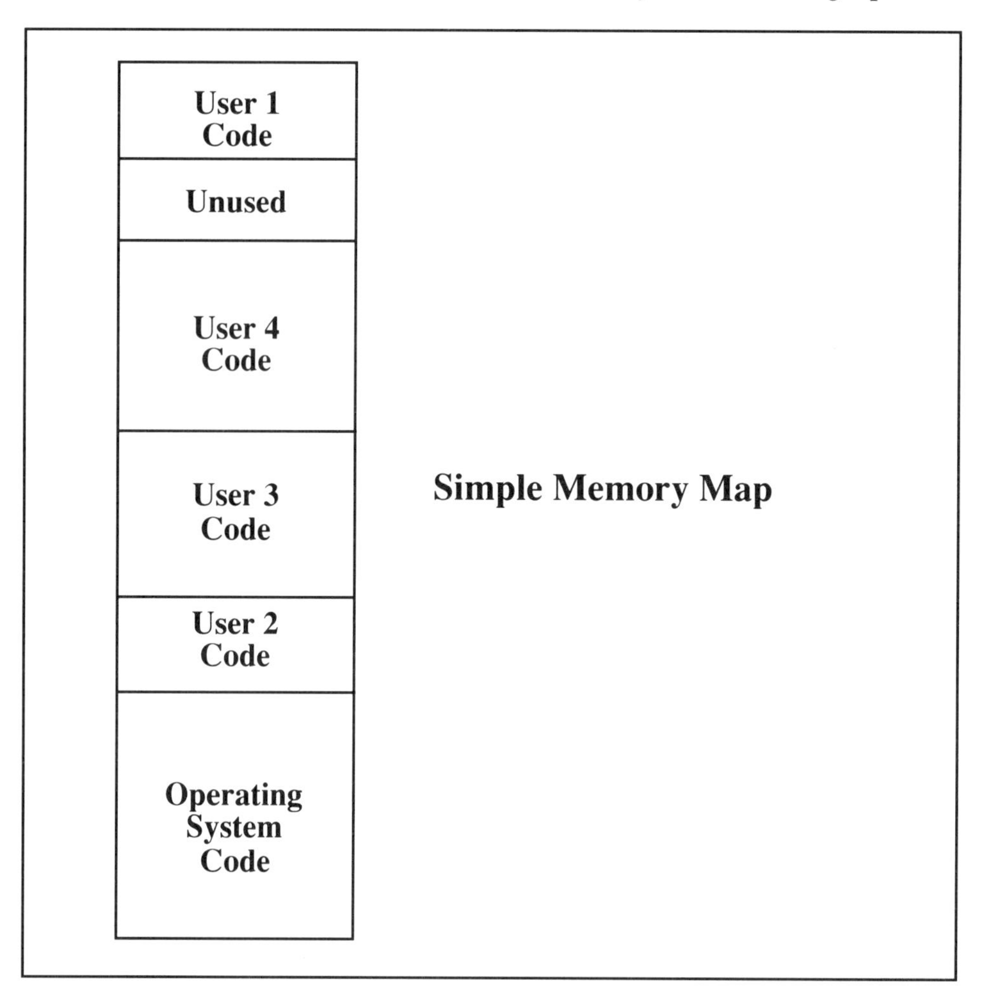

Figure 5.7 Sharing memory.

A fundamental problem for computing systems is the lack of sufficient RAM capacity to store very large programs or to store a large number of programs, in their entirety. As RAM capacity increases (doubles every 1.5 years approximately), so too does program size, including the size of the operating system. The basic solution to this problem is to use disk storage to store portions of programs not currently required by the processor and to swap information between disk and RAM as it is required by the processor. The disadvantage of this solution is that it slows down program execution, given the time it takes to access disk storage.

One strategy, called **swapping**, swaps **entire programs** between disk storage and RAM. When a program has been swapped into RAM it can execute for a while until the scheduler decides to execute another program; then the current program is swapped out to disk and the next program is swapped into RAM. This allows you to execute many more programs than you have RAM capacity to cater for.

However, swapping does *not* allow you to write programs larger than the available RAM. One solution to this problem, to allow you to write programs larger than the available RAM size, involves the use of **overlays**, an old technique dating from the early days of computing, but widely used in the PC world today. The idea is simple, instead of writing one large monolithic program, you write a number of smaller programs, each of which can fit into RAM. You write the programs in such a way that the first program carries out part of the task and before it terminates it loads in or **overlays** itself with a second program. This program carries out a further part of the task and overlays itself with a third program and so on.

As an example of the use of overlays, consider a menu driven program with three options (A, B and C). It could be constructed using four separate programs so that each option is carried out by a separate program:

```
program1:    (Main Program)
             display menu
             read user option
             overlay with program for user option
                  (i.e. one of program2, program3 or
                  program4)

program2:    carry out task for option A
             verlay with program1 (main program)

program3:    carry out task for option B
             overlay with program1 (main program)

program4:    carry out task for option C
             overlay with program1 (main program)
```

The user executes the main program and chooses an option from the menu. The main program responds by overlaying itself with the appropriate program to carry out the user's option. When this program has finished, it overlays itself with the main program. This allows the user to choose another option and the procedure is repeated. Overlays can be used on single-user, single-tasking machines and are frequently used in PC software applications where insufficient RAM is available to hold very large application programs.

Virtual memory

The use of a **virtual memory** system also solves the problem of insufficient RAM storage. A virtual memory system employs disk storage to provide the illusion that a machine has a very large RAM which is called its virtual memory. In this manner, a machine that has only a few megabytes of actual RAM can operate as if it had many megabytes of RAM. The trick is to store much of the information on disk and copy it into RAM as it is required. The operating system and memory management hardware keep track of what is stored in RAM and what is stored on disk, transferring information from disk as it is required. Information is usually transferred in units called **pages**, the technique being referred to as **paging**. There is also another technique called **segmentation**, which is not as widely used.

Virtual memory may be visualized as a large linear address space, much larger than the actual physical address space, as illustrated in Figure 5.8. A mapping function is required to map addresses between the two address spaces. Programs use **virtual addresses**, for example, given a machine with 4 Mb of RAM and a 16 Mb virtual address space, a program will use addresses (for data and instructions) in the range from 0 to 16 million. It is one of the functions of the memory management unit (**mmu**, a hardware device) to perform the mapping between the virtual address used in the program and the actual physical address in RAM.

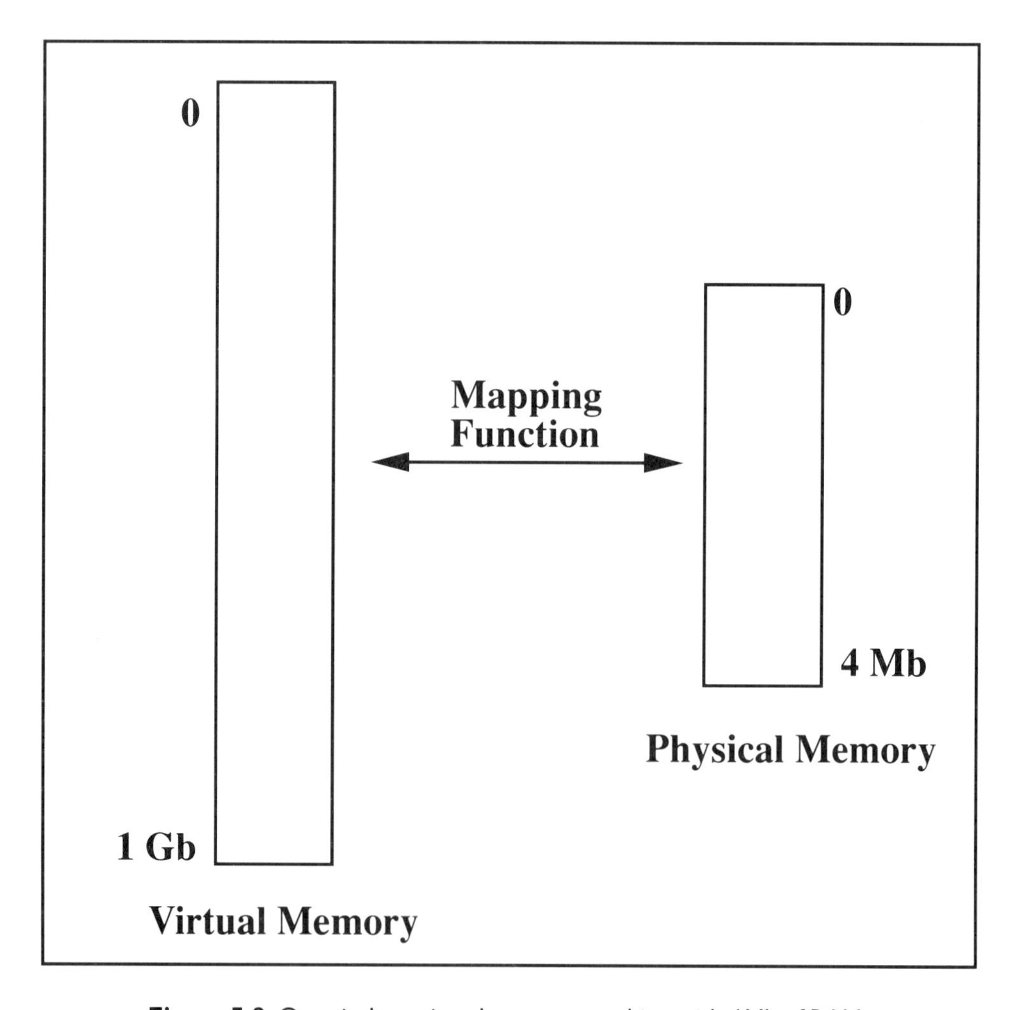

Figure 5.8 One gigabyte virtual memory machine with 4 Mb of RAM.

Virtual memory, as mentioned above, is typically composed of units called **pages**, ranging in size from 512 bytes to 4 kb. Physical memory is treated as if it were made up of **page frames** of the same size as pages. A **page table** is used to indicate which page frame contains which virtual memory page. The page table has a reference bit to indicate if the page is already in the page frame. A **page fault** occurs if we attempt to access a virtual memory address that is not currently in physical memory. This causes an **interrupt** (see Section 6.9.2 in Chapter 6) which results in the transfer of the required page from disk to memory. A problem arises if all the page frames in memory are full, that is, where do we store the incoming page? The solution is to replace a page in one of our page frames with the incoming page. The previous page will be copied to disk if it has been changed since it was last loaded from disk.

How do we choose which page to replace? There are a number of **page replacement** algorithms that may be used. The optimal algorithm would be to replace the page that will not be needed for the longest period of time. However, we have no way of knowing this in advance, so we cannot implement this method. We could replace a page at random, although performance is greatly improved if we do not choose a heavily used page. This is because such a page would be required very soon and would have to be transferred back into RAM and another page replaced. Other algorithms that may be used include Least Recently Used (LRU), Not Recently Used (NRU) and First In First Out (FIFO). The reader will find details of these algorithms in the operating system texts listed at the end of this chapter.

Working-set model

Most programs exhibit a phenomenon known as **locality of reference**. This means that most programs access a small number of their pages during any phase of their activity. For example, for many applications up to 90% of CPU time is frequently spent executing 10% of the program code. Another way of looking at this is to observe that most programs spend long periods of time executing loops. During the execution of a particular loop, only those instructions composing the loop and the variables accessed in the loop are required. This phenomenon also forms the basis in computer architecture for using cache memory to improve performance. Cache memory is described in Chapter 7, Section 7.4.2. The set of pages in current use is called the **working set.** If the entire working set is in memory, there will be few page faults. If the working set is not in memory, then there will be many page faults and performance degrades significantly as more time is spent servicing page faults than executing the program instructions. This phenomenon is called **thrashing.**

Virtual memory systems often use a mechanism known as **demand paging.** They only load pages into RAM as they are required (demanded). An alternative approach is to pre-load the working set of a program into memory (called **prepaging**), before beginning to execute the program, if you know in advance what the working set is. Virtual memory systems may also use swapping. For example, in an interactive situation, a user editing a file may go for a coffee break and the program remains inactive until the return of the user. The system can detect this and swap the program pages out of memory until the program is reactivated by the user.

5.2.5 *File sub-system*

The file sub-system provides facilities for managing files such as:

- space allocation for files;
- security of files;
- creation and modification of files;
- organizing files (directory management);
- backup utilities for file system.

An important function of the filing sub-system is **space management**. It must keep track of both the allocated space used by files (so that the contents of files can be accessed) and the free space available for use. Space is usually allocated in **blocks** of 512 or 1024 bytes. A file containing a single character will still use up an entire block of storage. While this may appear wasteful, it makes space management much simpler. When a file is deleted, the filing sub-system reclaims the space used by that file, so that it can be reused.

A multi-user operating system allows users to share disk storage. This is an additional function of the filing system of a multi-user system. Usually the filing system arranges to **partition** the disk so that each user has an area of disk for their sole use. This area is called a **directory** (**folder**). A user's directory contains the user's files and perhaps other directories. The operating system itself will also have its own directory where its programs are stored. The filing system allows each user to access only their own files or files which they have been given permission to access. In other words, the filing sub-system also maintains information about the access rights users have to files. This provides a level of security for users of a multi-user system. The area of file protection and operating system security is very important and more details can be obtained from the references at the end of the chapter.

5.2.6 *Command interpreter*

The command interpreter, as mentioned earlier, is a program that allows you to execute commands (run programs) on a computer. This means that it is an important component of an operating system. Every command you give is associated with running a program. When you start up (boot up) a microcomputer or log onto a multi-user computer, the command interpreter is usually started automatically for you, so that you can immediately execute commands. A GUI allows you to give commands by selecting options from a menu with a pointing device such as a mouse. A command interpreter carries out commands, usually loading programs from disk to do so. A small number of commands are **built in** to the command interpreter program and do not have to be loaded from disk. For example, in MS-DOS, commands such as **diskcopy** and **format** are the names of programs which reside on disk (**external** commands). When a user issues one of these commands, the command interpreter loads the appropriate program from disk and executes it. The command **dir** on the other hand is a built-in command and does not have to be loaded from disk. Each command interpreter will have some built-in commands and will load programs from disk to carry out other commands.

Most operating systems provide the facility of allowing you to create a file of commands which will be executed automatically, by the command interpreter, each time you log on to (boot up) your machine. This file is called a **login command file** or **startup file**. For example, if you wished to use a word processor every time you start your machine, you could put the command to start the word processor program in your startup file. Then, when you start your machine, the command interpreter will run your word processor program automatically. Each operating system uses a special name for the startup file. In MS-DOS this file is called **autoexec.bat**; in UNIX it is called either **.login** or **.profile** and in VMS it is called **login.com.**

The operation of a text based command interpreter program is quite simple and can be shown in pseudo-code as follows:

```
while (not finished)
{
        Prompt user
        Read command
        Execute command or display error message
        if the command is invalid
}
```

The prompt tells you that the command interpreter is waiting for your command. Various systems use different prompts:

```
MS-DOS      C>      (or A> or B>)
UNIX        %       (or $)
VMS         $
```

It is usually possible for you to change the prompt to whatever text you wish. The MS-DOS command interpreter is stored in a file called **command.com.** When MS-DOS is booted, it loads and executes this program. UNIX provides a choice of three or more command interpreters, called shells in UNIX terminology.

Command names

One problem with having different operating systems available is that they use different names for commands which carry out the same task. This can be a cause of confusion and frustration for users. As an example, Table 5.1 shows the names used for some file handling commands for the MS-DOS, VMS and UNIX operating systems. (Note that VMS commands may be abbreviated, so that `ty` may be used for `type` and `dir` for `directory`.) While the MS-DOS and VMS commands are similar, the UNIX commands are quite different. There is some evidence to show that new computer users can learn the commands for any operating system in about the same amount of time. UNIX advocates cite this when confronted with the charge that UNIX command names are unfriendly! It is the author's opinion that much of the debate about so-called friendly command names is spurious and that users are very influenced by the command names of the first computer system they encounter and are familiar with. If subsequent computer systems have similar command names to those of the first one used, then these may be regarded by users as being 'friendly', while if the command names differ greatly from those a user is familiar with, they may be regarded as 'unfriendly'. A user with a good grasp of the underlying functionality of commands should have little difficulty coming to grips with a new set of command names. An operating system should be evaluated on issues such as its reliability, efficiency and security as opposed to the names chosen for commands.

Table 5.1 Names of file-handling commands in different operating systems.

MS-DOS	VMS	UNIX
`type`	`type`	`cat`
`copy`	`copy`	`cp`
`del`	`delete`	`rm`
`dir`	`directory`	`ls`
`print`	`print`	`lpr`
`cd`	`set default`	`cd`

5.2.7 *Operating systems: programming perspective*

So far we have described the operating system from a user perspective. Programmers and, in particular, systems programmers need to interact with the operating system from their programs, that is, they need to create files and directories, execute and terminate programs, read and write various I/O devices. The operating system provides a comprehensive set of sub-programs to enable programmers to carry out these functions. Such sub-programs are called **system calls** and they provide an interface between a program and the operating system. In other words, if you require the operating system to perform a function on your behalf, you invoke the appropriate system call for that function. In a program, a system call looks like a normal sub-program call. However, there is a major difference. When a system call is invoked, control is transferred to the operating system and the user program is no longer running. The operating system carries out a task on behalf of the user program. The switch from the running program to the operating system is called a **context switch**. When the system call is finished, control is returned to the user program, again via a context switch.

Frequently, programmers do not realize how much work is carried out, by way of system calls, when a program is executed. The most frequent tasks carried out via system calls are I/O operations. All I/O operations take place via system calls. This means that programmers do not have to know any details about the devices they are using. They allow the system calls to look after the details. In addition, the operating system can carry out the I/O in an optimal fashion for a group of users. For example, take the case of disk I/O, if each user was allowed carry out their own disk I/O operations, the read/write head would be carrying out many seek operations. Because the operating system is responsible for I/O, it can take the disk I/O operations for a group of users and organize them so that when it seeks to a particular track, it carries out all operations for that track, and so on. The idea is similar to a postman delivering letters on a street. The postman sorts the letters, so that he can deliver them, in order, as he goes down the street, thus saving time and energy. Another important reason for the operating system to control I/O is to prevent users accessing data belonging to other users. The operating system can check a user's I/O request to ensure that the user has permission to carry out that operation.

When a programmer uses a high-level language I/O sub-program such as C's `printf` or Pascal's `writeln` to carry out I/O operations, it is important to realize that these sub-programs invoke system calls to carry out the actual I/O operation. In Part I of this text we used MS-DOS system calls to carry out I/O operations. These system calls were invoked using an interrupt mechanism. In a high-level language, we may use I/O sub-programs provided with the language (which in turn use system calls) to carry out I/O operations or we may be able to invoke system calls directly to carry out I/O and other operations.

An operating system must be capable of allowing users to handle a variety of I/O devices, such as terminals, disk drives, tape drives, plotters and printers. Each device has its own characteristic and unique features. This means, for example, that the sub-program to write to a terminal screen is different from the sub-program required to write to a printer. Every device requires its own sub-programs to allow the operating system to use the device. The collection of sub-programs used for a specific device is called its **device driver**. Every device driver contains sub-programs to allow you to **read** from, **write** to and **control** that particular device. All I/O is carried out via device drivers. The I/O system calls will invoke the appropriate device driver sub-program to carry out an I/O operation on any particular device.

System calls may be regarded as sub-programs providing low-level access to the operating system. In order to write **systems software** a programmer must know how to use the system calls provided by the operating system. Such software includes programs such as compilers, interpreters, assemblers, linkers, command interpreters and operating system commands for file handling (copy, delete, display, print, edit) and process handling. Such programs constitute the systems software that accompanies an operating system. Programs similar to those mentioned above, which invoke system calls directly, would be regarded [by the author] as **systems programs** and programmers whose work is concerned with the development of such programs are called systems programmers.

In addition to system calls, it is also common to find libraries of useful sub-programs such as an I/O library with an operating system, or provided with a programming language. The I/O library will contain a collection of I/O sub-programs to carry out frequently used operations. For example, C programmers can use library functions such as `gets`, `printf`, `scanf` and so on. These functions make the programmer's life much easier; they carry out I/O operations by using system calls but hide the low-level details of using system calls from the programmer.

5.2.8 Operating system structure

Figure 5.9 illustrates the overall structure of a hypothetical, but UNIX-like, operating system. It should be noted that it is very difficult to present an accurate view of an operating system in the form of a diagram.

The **kernel** is the most machine-dependent part of the operating system. It is the interface between the operating system and the raw hardware of the computer system. Operating-system programmers access the hardware via

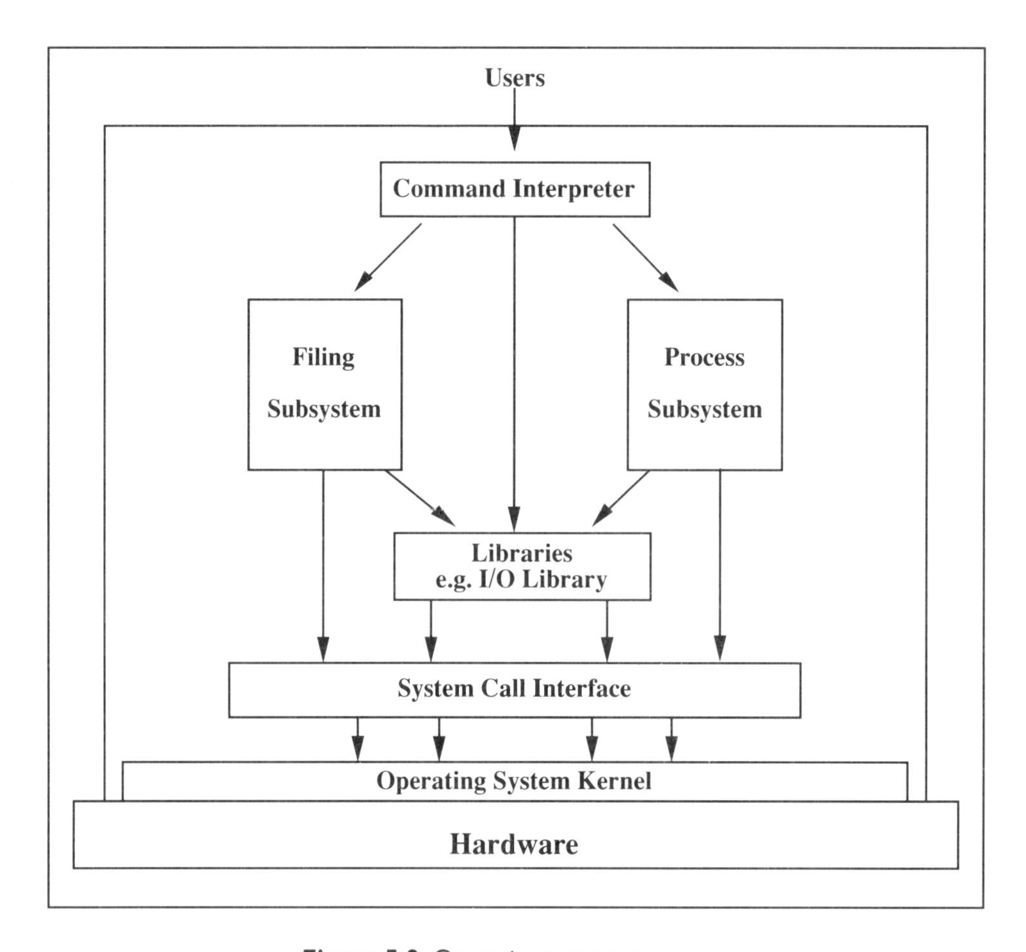

Figure 5.9 Operating system structure.

sub-programs that make up the kernel. If this is the only way that programmers access the hardware, then to make the operating system work on a new machine, most of the work involves rewriting the kernel. If the kernel is well designed and kept quite small, then rewriting it for a new machine is not a major task.

5.2.9 *Booting up a computer*

The question arises as to how the operating system gets started? Remember, this is the software that allows you use the computer. In order for any program to execute, it must be in the computer's memory. But the RAM of a computer loses its contents when the computer is switched off. How then is the operating system loaded into RAM and executed when a computer is switched on? The answer lies in using **ROM**, because, as mentioned in Section 5.1.3, ROM retains its contents permanently. The operating system itself is not stored in ROM. There is normally only a small amount of ROM available and it would not be large enough to hold an operating system. Also, since its contents cannot be modified, it would not be possible to correct any of the errors that unfortunately arise in complex programs like operating systems. Thus, it would not be a good idea to store the operating system in ROM even if it was possible.

Instead, what happens is that a small program is stored in ROM which is used to get the operating system loaded from disk and executed. The ROM program loads a part of the operating system, called the **bootstrap program**, from a fixed location on disk (called the **boot block**) into RAM and switches control to this program. This bootstrap program in turn loads the rest of the operating system from disk into RAM and switches control to it. This process is called **bootstrapping** (**booting**) after the notion of pulling yourself up by your boot laces! One advantage of this technique is that it means that the same computer can use a different operating system by placing in the boot block an appropriate bootstrap program for the operating system you wish to boot up.

In summary, when you switch on (boot up) a computer, a program in ROM is executed, which loads in a second program from disk and starts it. This bootstrap program in turn loads the operating system program from disk and starts it. The operating system then starts the command interpreter to allow you to give the computer commands. Each operating system has its own command interpreter, which will be executed on booting. IBM PCs and their compatibles are unusual in that the ROM does not only contain a bootstrap program as described above, but it also contains code for device drivers for the screen, keyboard and disk and so on. This code is referred to as the ROM **BIOS** (Basic Input Output System). In other operating systems this code would usually reside on disk with the rest of the operating system code. In addition, the ROM contains self-test code to ensure that the hardware is functioning properly when the machine is switched on. This code is called **power-on self test** (**POST**) code .

5.3 Programming support

In order to write programs, language translators such as compilers, interpreters and assemblers are required. These translators have to have knowledge of the operating system in order to produce machine code programs that can be executed by the operating system. In addition, programs called linkers and loaders are used to allow external sub-programs, such as library functions and system calls, to be invoked from a program. Linkers and loaders arrange for the external sub-programs to be integrated with a program and look after the loading of the program into a suitable area of memory. Such software may come with an operating system or be purchased separately. In either case, it is essential to have such software if users intend to write computer programs.

5.4 Real-time operating systems

Embedded computer systems, such as those used in an alarm system or a washing machine, are controlled by relatively small programs as compared to the operating system of a conventional computer system. The control programs for such systems will typically be stored in ROM. More elaborate embedded computer systems, such as those used for aircraft flight control, require a type of operating system that is referred to as a **real-time** operating system. A conventional operating system such as UNIX or VMS is in control of the environment in which it works. Users and devices are dealt with as and when the operating system is ready to deal with them. Real-time operating systems, on the other hand, are controlled by their environments. To monitor or control *external* events with its own timing characteristics, the operating system must respond according to the dictates of the I/O devices and delays in response are usually unacceptable. Applications for real-time systems vary from uses in air traffic control and laboratory experiments, to car braking systems, alarm systems and environmental control.

Many real-time applications are in life-critical areas such as patient monitoring, nuclear systems and aircraft flight control, where failure could result in loss of life or major destruction. In many such situations the computer is a **dedicated system** – all or most of its time is devoted to a single job. The crucial point about a real-time system is that it *must* produce an appropriate response to certain events and conditions *within a specified time* and failure to respond can lead to serious if not catastrophic consequences. Imagine the consequences of a life-support system not responding for five minutes instead of an expected 5 ms! In a conventional operating system, a poor response time leads to user frustration, whereas in a real-time system, such a poor response can literally lead to a loss of life.

The software for real-time systems is usually contained in ROM and many small real-time systems have no distinct operating system at all, but consist of a special purpose program to carry out a single task. However, most complex real-time applications require similar facilities for memory management and device handling. While it may be more efficient to produce a special purpose system for each application, it is often more effective to use an existing operating system if its overhead can be tolerated. A number of limited operating systems known as **real-time executives** have been designed to meet the general needs of real-time systems. These include RSX-11 from Digital and VRTX and RTE-1 from Hewlett-Packard.

5.5 Summary

In this chapter we have presented a broad overview of the software and hardware that make up a computing system. Important hardware components such as the CPU, memory, bus system, various I/O and storage devices were briefly described. Operating system software and its components were also described and the concept of virtual memory was explained. In the next chapter we will look at the processor in more detail and examine how program instructions are actually executed.

Exercises

5.1 How is computer storage capacity measured?

5.2 What peripheral devices would you expect to find in a typical computing system?

5.3 What components make up the CPU and how does the CPU communicate with other devices?

5.4 Explain the functions of the different buses used in a computer system. Why is it useful to have a separate I/O bus?

5.5 Explain the difference between primary and secondary memory. Compare the access times and storage capacities of the different types of storage device.

5.6 Why is the difference in access time between RAM and disk storage so important?

5.7 What is ROM and why is it used? Explain the difference between PROM and EEPROM.

5.8 Compare the use of disk and tape as secondary storage media. What are the major uses of CD-ROM?

5.9 List five different input devices and explain where each one might be used.

5.10 Explain how computers may be classified.

5.11 What is the difference between a LAN and a WAN?

5.12 Why is operating system software so important? Name three operating systems, giving the name of a computer system on which each might be found.

5.13 Explain how overlays can alleviate the problem of insufficient RAM in a computer system.

5.14 Explain why virtual memory is so important and how it operates.

5.15 How does a program communicate with the operating system and why is it necessary for programs to communicate with the operating system?

5.16 Explain how a typical computer system is booted up.

5.6 Reading List

Anderson, J.A. (1994) *Foundations of Computer Technology*, Chapman & Hall, London.

Baron, R.J. and Higbie, L.(1992) *Computer Architecture*, Addison Wesley, Reading, MA.

Deitel, H.M. (1990) *Introduction to Operating Systems*, Addison Wesley, Reading, MA.

Harvey, D.A. (1992) Downsizing Media: 3.5-inch MO Drives Arrive, *Byte*, May 1992, **17**(5), 240–50.

Hennessy, J.L. and Patterson, D.A. (1990) *Computer Architecture A Quantitative Approach,* Morgan Kaufmann, San Mateo, CA.

Silberschatz, A., Peterson, J.L. and Galvin P. (1991) *Operating System Concepts*, Addison Wesley, Reading, MA.

Rafiquzzaman, M. and Chandra R. (1988) *Modern Computer Architecture*, West Publishing Co., St Paul, MN.

Stern, N. and Stern, R.A.(1993) *Computing in the Information Age*, John Wiley, New York.

Tannenbaum, A.S. (1992) *Modern Operating Systems*, Prentice Hall, Englewood Cliffs, NJ.

6
Computer architecture

Computer architecture involves the design of computers. In this text we concentrate almost exclusively on the design of the processor. Processor design involves the design of the instruction set and the organisation of the processor. Instruction set architecture (ISA) describes the processor in terms of what the assembly language programmer sees, the instructions and registers. Organization is concerned with the internal design of the processor, the design of the bus system and its interfaces, the design of memory and so on. Two machines may have the same ISA, but different organizations. The organization is implemented in hardware and in turn, two machines with the same organization may have different hardware implementations, for example, a faster form of silicon technology may be used in the fabrication of the processor. So, computer architecture involves the instruction set architecture, the organization and the hardware implementation of the organization. In this text, we introduce the basic concepts of the instruction set architecture and organization, but we will not concern ourselves with details of the hardware implementation.

6.1 Introduction

The first point that must be made about computer architecture is that there is no standard computer architecture, in the same way as there is no such thing as a standard house architecture or standard motor car design. Just as different car manufacturers produce different types of car, different computer manufacturers produce a variety of computers. However, just as all cars have some basic features in common, so too do computers. In this chapter, we take a high-level look at the components of computer architecture that are common to all computers, noting that any particular computer will differ in various details from the general model presented. This chapter approaches computer architecture from the standpoint of how instructions are executed by the processor. This can be described at a number of levels, from the very general to details of the electrical signals used by the computer's hardware. In this text we do not concern ourselves with electrical or electronic details, but concentrate, at a higher level, on the process of instruction execution and the functionality of the components, such as the control unit and ALU, that are involved in the execution of instructions. It is worth emphasizing that the general principles, described here, apply to most uni-processor computer systems, but some simplifications have been made to make the material easier to understand.

In the first part of this text we have been concerned with computer programming and, in particular, with assembly language programming. We have described some of the internal components of a computer: the CPU and its registers, the memory and the buses linking the components together. As we have seen earlier, computer programs are translated to machine code for execution by the CPU. We will address later the question of translating an instruction to machine code. Once a program has been loaded into the computer's memory (carried out by the operating system on our behalf), the program may then be executed. This means that the CPU obeys the instructions making up the program and carries them out one at a time.

It is worth noting, at this point, the *primitive* nature of the CPU. The CPU does not *understand* programs, rather it *obeys* individual instructions. The fact that a group of such instructions makes up a meaningful program (or not!) is something that only the programmer is aware of. In the same way, a motor car does not *know* what route the car is travelling on, that is the driver's responsibility. However, when a computer program does not perform correctly, the computer is often blamed for the error, rather than the programmer. Imagine a driver blaming his car because he took a wrong turn on the road! Unfortunately, people learning to use computers are frequently told that the computer *understands* their commands and *knows* what to do; for example, it knows how to save files or how to print them. While this anthropomorphism makes it easy to explain certain concepts to beginners, it also allows incompetent programmers and users to blame a dumb machine for their mistakes. Having noted the disadvantage of this style of explanation, we will continue to use it in this text!

6.2 Instruction set

One of the crucial features of any processor is its **instruction set**, the set of machine code instructions that the processor can carry out. Each processor has its own unique instruction set specifically designed to make best use of the capabilities of that processor. The actual number of instructions provided ranges from a few dozen for a simple 8-bit microprocessor to several hundred for a 32-bit VAX processor. However, it should be pointed out that a large instruction set does not necessarily imply a more powerful processor and, as discussed in the next chapter, many modern processor designs are so-called RISC (Reduced Instruction Set Computer) designs, which use relatively small instruction sets, in contrast to so called CISC (Complex Instruction Set Computer) designs, such as the VAX and machines based on the Intel 8086 and Motorola 68000 microprocessor families. A brief discussion of RISC and CISC machines is presented in the next chapter.

6.2.1 Classification of instructions

The actual instructions provided by any processor can be broadly classified into the following groups:

- **Data movement** instructions: These allow the processor to move data between registers and between memory and registers (for example 8086 `mov`, `push`, `pop` instructions). A `move` instruction and its variants are among the most frequently used instructions in an instruction set.
- **Transfer-of-control** instructions: These are concerned with branching for loops and conditional control structures as well as for handling subprograms (for example 8086 `je`, `jg`, `jmp`, `call` and `ret` instructions). These are also commonly used instructions.
- **Arithmetic/logical** instructions: These carry out the usual arithmetic and logical operations (for example 8086 `cmp`, `add`, `sub`, `inc`, `and`, `or` and `xor` instructions). Surprisingly, these are not frequently used instructions and, when they are used, it is often in conjunction with a conditional jump instruction rather than for general arithmetic purposes. Note that we have included the `cmp` instruction with the arithmetic/logical instructions because it actually behaves like a `sub` instruction, except it does not modify its destination register.
- **Input/output** instructions: These are used for carrying out I/O (for example 8086 `in` and `out` instructions) but a very common form of I/O called **memory mapped I/O** uses `move` instructions for I/O.
- **Miscellaneous** instructions (for example 8086 `int`, `sti`, `cti`, `hlt` and `nop`) for handling interrupts and such activities. The `hlt` instruction halts the processor and the `nop` instruction does nothing at all! [Most processors provide a non-operation (`nop`) instruction. Its execution takes one clock cycle, the purpose of which is simply to use time. It is used (frequently in a loop) to delay some time while the processor waits for an event, such as an I/O device to respond to an I/O request, to happen.] These instructions are again not that frequently used relative to data movement and transfer-of-control instructions. The `int` instruction could also be classified as a transfer of control instruction and interrupts are described in more detail below.This is not the only way to classify instructions. For example, the arithmetic/logical instructions mentioned above may be classified as **operate** instructions. Operate instructions also include instructions that move data between registers and manipulate stacks. **Memory-access** instructions refer to those that transfer data between registers and memory.

6.2.2 *Format of assembly language instructions*

The format of assembly language instructions used by different processors is usually very similar, taking the form:

```
[label:]  operation [operand...] [; comment ]
```

where the square brackets `[]` indicate an optional field and the ellipsis (`...`) indicates one or more operands.

An instruction may be treated as being composed of *four fields* some of which may be omitted. Unless a comment field appears on its own, the **operation** field is *always* necessary. The label and the operand fields may or may not be required depending on the operation field. There are rules specifying how the names of variables, labels and subprograms should be composed, depending on the assembler and processor being used. For the 8086 masm assembler, names must always begin with a letter and only the first 31 characters are significant. Spaces or tabs may be used as separators between the fields making up an instruction or between the operands making up the operand field. We also use **delimiters** such as commas to separate operands; these are compulsory with the `masm` assembler.

Example 6.1

The following 8086 instructions are the typical instruction formats that are used in an assembly language program:

```
lab1:   cmp bx, cx   ; compare bx with cx
        add ax, 25
        inc bx
        ret
```

The label field

If the label field is present, it contains a label name. The label may represent the address of an instruction in memory, as in the above example, or it may be used to represent the name of a variable or constant as in the following:

```
val    db     100          ; variable definition
max    equ    1000         ; constant definition
```

The operation field

The operation field contains either a (**machine code**) instruction or an **assembler directive** (**pseudo-op**). It is important to understand the difference between directives and instructions. Each machine code instruction has a special symbol or **mnemonic** associated with it (such as `mov`, `add` and so on). If the operation field contains a machine instruction, the assembler will generate machine code, corresponding to the instruction, to be placed in memory. This machine code will be executed by the processor. Assembler directives (such as `equ`, `db`, `dw` and `.stack`) have different names to instructions, which allows the assembler to differentiate between the two. Directives are used for such tasks as defining variables and constants and providing information about stack size and where a program starts. They are commands to the assembler program and are not translated to machine code instructions.

The comment field

This field is used to provide information to the programmer and those reading the program. A semicolon or some such character (say *) must precede a comment. Comments are an important part of the documentation of any program, but are particularly important for assembly language programs, which are usually difficult to understand. The assembler *ignores comments completely* and they are not stored in the machine code program output by the assembler.

The operand field

Many instructions and directives require one or more operands, which are provided by the operand field. An operand may be a **constant**, **variable** or **special symbol** (for example `@data`). When two operands are specified, they must be separated by a comma for the masm assembler. Processors vary as to how many operands may be specified in an instruction. Traditionally, machines were classified as **one-address**, **two-address** or **three-address** machines, according to whether only one operand was allowed, two operands were allowed or three operands were allowed. Example 6.2 illustrates what the instructions for such machines look like.

Example 6.2

One-address code (for example Motorola 6800)

```
ldaa  #$2          ; load accumulator A with 2h
adda  #$4          ; add 4H to accumulator A
```

Two-address code (for example Intel 8086)

```
add  ax, y          ; ax = ax + contents of memory variable y
```

Three-address code (Digital VAX)

```
addl3  i, j, k          ; i = j + k
```

It should be noted that the Intel 8086 is not a two-address machine as it also allows single-address instructions. Similarly, the VAX is not a three-address machine as it allows all three instruction formats to be used. A one-address machine uses an implied operand, usually called an **accumulator**, as its destination operand. The Motorola 6800 provides two such accumulators (A and B) and has separate instructions for manipulating them (for example, the instructions `ldaa` and `ldab` load accumulator A and B respectively). The 8086 programming examples from Part I of this text illustrate typical two-address instructions. Three-address instructions, such as those used in VAX assembly language, allow us carry out more work in a single instruction and, as such, are easier to use from a programming perspective.

Given that a machine such as the VAX can have instructions with one, two or three operands, it is obvious that an instruction with three memory variables as operands will be longer (occupy more storage locations) than say an instruction with only one operand. This is because a memory variable may have a 32-bit address. So the above VAX `addl3` instruction could require 12 bytes of storage for the variable addresses alone (and this is not the longest VAX instruction). The same situation arises with 8086 instructions, which range from 1 byte to a maximum of 6 bytes in length. Such instructions are called **variable-length** instructions and are commonly used on CISC machines. The advantage of using such instructions is that each instruction can use exactly the amount of space it requires, so that variable length instructions reduce the amount of memory space required for a program. This was very important when memory was a very expensive commodity, right up until the 1980s. On the other hand, it is possible to have **fixed-length** instructions, where, as the name suggests, each instruction has the same length. Fixed-length instructions are commonly used with RISC processors such as the PowerPC and Alpha processors. Since each instruction occupies the same amount of space, every instruction must be long enough to specify a memory operand, even if the instruction does not use one. Hence, memory space is wasted by this form of instruction. The advantage of fixed-length instructions, it is argued, is that they make the job of fetching and decoding instructions easier and more efficient, which means that they can be executed in less time than the corresponding variable length instructions.

Thus the comparison between fixed- and variable-length instructions comes down to the classic computing trade-off of memory usage versus execution time. In general, computer programs that execute very quickly tend to use larger amounts of storage, while programs which carry out the same tasks, but do not use so much storage, tend to take longer to execute. It is therefore suggested that variable-length instructions, while using less storage, take longer to execute than fixed-length instructions, which use more storage. It should be noted, however, that there is *not* universal agreement that CISC instructions actually do take longer to execute than RISC instructions.

6.3 SAM architecture and assembly language

As we have said, the CPU executes the instructions that it finds in the computer's memory. In order to execute an instruction, the CPU must first fetch (transfer) the instruction from memory into one of its registers. This is a non-trivial task requiring several steps. The CPU then decodes the instruction, that is, it decides which instruction has been fetched and arranges for this instruction to be executed. The CPU then repeats this procedure: it fetches an instruction, decodes it and executes it. This process is repeated continuously and is known as the **fetch-execute** cycle. This cycle continues until the CPU is halted (via a halt instruction, say the 8086 `hlt` instruction, or the machine is switched off).

Instead of looking at the details of a particular microprocessor's architecture at this point, we will use a simple, but hypothetical, microprocessor to explain the basic concepts of computer architecture, underlying the execution of programs. We call the machine SAM (Simple Architecture Machine). Figure 6.1 illustrates the major components of SAM. It is a 16-bit microprocessor with four general purpose registers `r0` to `r3`, a program counter register `PC`, a stack pointer register `SP` and status register `SR`. The status register is made up of similar flags to the 8086 flags register, a zero flag, an overflow flag, a carry flag and so on. Bit 0 of the `SR` register corresponds to the zero flag, which will be set to `1` when an instruction generates a zero result.

SAM is programmed using an assembly language called **SAL** (Simple Assembly Language). SAM instructions have been chosen to resemble the 8086 instructions used in Part I of this text. A notable difference between SAM and 8086 instructions is that there are only two SAM instructions which access memory. These are the `load` and `store` instructions which load a value from memory into a register and store the value of a register in memory. All other instructions operate on SAM registers. This type of architecture is called a **load/store architecture** and is typically used with RISC machines. A typical SAL instruction takes the form:

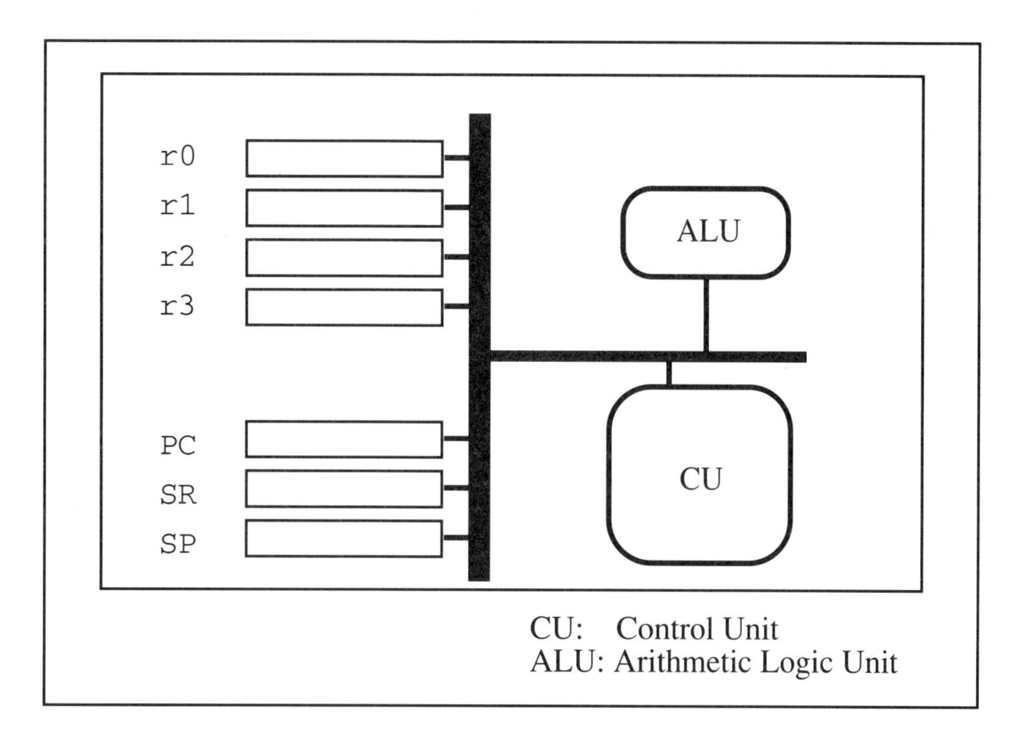

Figure 6.1 SAM architecture: programming model.

```
[label:]  operation  destination, source  [; comment]
```

and, as such, resembles the 8086 instructions presented earlier. Example 6.3 illustrates how a C assignment statement might be implemented in SAL, assuming that we use memory variables for the corresponding C variables.

Example 6.3

SAL code to carry out a C assignment statement:

C Code

```
i = j + k - 1;
```

SAL code

```
load   r1, j       ; r1 = j
load   r2, k       ; r2 = k
add    r1, r2      ; r1 = r1 + r2
load   r3, 1       ; r3 = 1
sub    r1, r3      ; r = r1 - r3
store  i, r1       ; i = r1
```

The first `load` instruction loads its source operand `j` (a memory variable) from memory into register `r1`. The `add` instructions adds its operands, which must be in registers, storing the result in the destination register, `r1` in this case. Finally the `store` instruction transfers its source operand `r1` to memory variable `i`. Other SAL instructions include the `move` and `cmp` instructions, as well as the transfer-of-control instructions. The transfer-of-control instructions use the same mnemonics as the corresponding 8086 instructions and are carried out in the same fashion as the 8086 instructions. Example 6.4 illustrates how a loop to sum the integers 1 to 10 might be written in SAL.

Example 6.4

SAL code to sum the integers 1 to 10 and store the result in a memory variable called `sum`:

```
          move   r0, 0        ; r0 = 0 running total
          move   r1, 1        ; r1 = 1 loop count
begin:    cmp    r1, 11       ; if (r1 == 11)
          je     endloop      ;   goto endloop
          add    r0, r1       ; r0 = r0 + r1
          add    r1, 1        ; r1 = r1 + 1
          jmp    begin        ; goto begin
endloop:  store  sum, r0      ; sum = r0
```

In this example, register `r1` contains the loop count and the loop terminates when it reaches `11`. On each pass through the loop, the loop count in `r1` is added to `r0`, which contains the running total. The `cmp` instruction tests if `r1` equals `11`, setting the zero flag if this is the case. The `je` instruction transfers control to `endloop` only when the zero flag is set.

Now that we have specified the programming model for SAM, we can look at a more detailed architectural model to explain how information is transferred between the processor and memory.

6.4 Accessing memory

In order to execute programs, a microprocessor fetches instructions from memory and executes them, fetching data from memory if it is required. Figure 6.2 illustrates the SAM architecture in more detail so that we can gain an understanding of how information is transferred between the processor and memory.

In Figure 6.2 we introduce two registers that we have not mentioned before, namely the **memory address register** `MAR` and the **memory data register** `MDR`. There are a number of such CPU registers that do not appear in the programming model of a CPU. We shall refer to these registers as **hidden** CPU registers to distinguish them from the programming model registers `r0` to `r4`, `PC`, `SR` and `SP` registers. The `MAR` and `MDR` registers are used to communicate with memory (and other devices attached to the system bus). In addition, Figure 6.2 shows the buses that allow the devices making up a SAM computer system to communicate with each other.

The `MAR` register is used to store the address of the location in memory that is to be accessed for reading or writing. When we retrieve information from memory, we refer to the process as **reading** from memory. When we store an item in memory, we refer to the process as **writing** to memory. In either case,

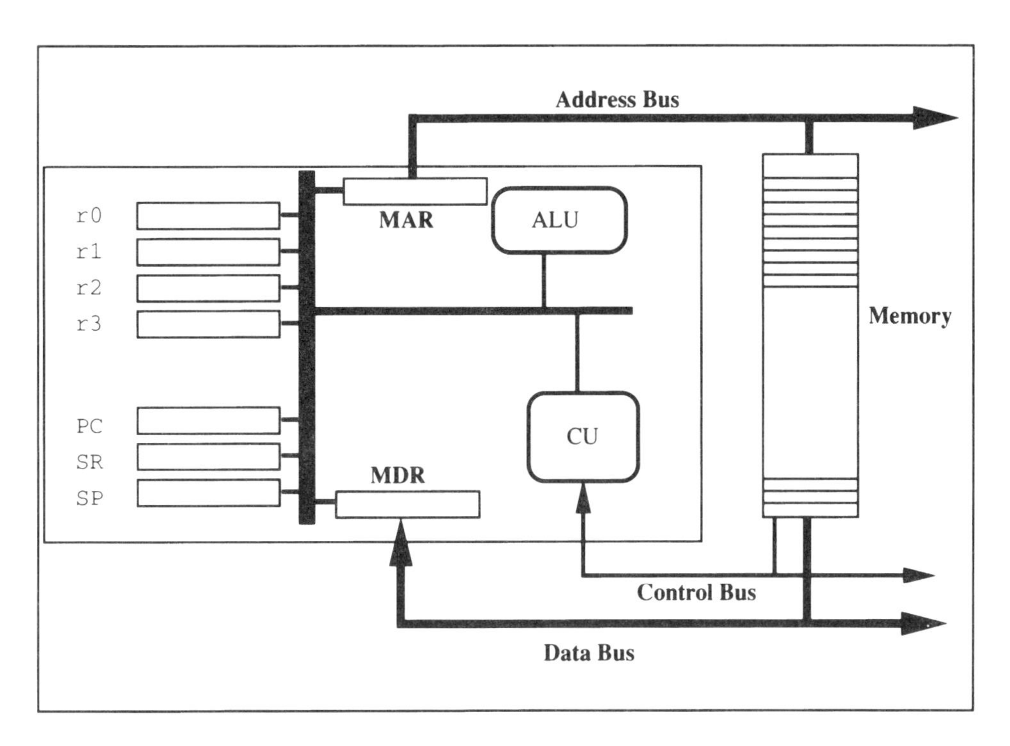

Figure 6.2 SAM architecture: accessing memory.

before we can access memory, we must specify the location we wish to access, the address of the location in memory. This address must be stored in the MAR register. The MAR register is connected to memory via the **address bus**, whose function is to transfer the address in the MAR register to memory. In this way the memory unit is informed as to which location is to be accessed. The address bus is a uni-directional bus, so information can only travel along it in a single direction, from the CPU to memory and other devices. The MAR register is a 16-bit register like all the other SAM registers. This means that the maximum address it can contain is $2^{16} - 1$ (65 535) bytes, that is, it can address up to 64kb of memory.

The MDR register is used either to store information that is to be written to memory or to store information that has been read from memory. The MDR register is connected to memory via the **data bus**, whose function is to transfer information to or from memory and other devices. The data bus is a bi-directional bus, so information can travel along it both to and from the CPU.

The control bus plays a crucial role in I/O. It carries control signals specifying what operation is to be carried out and signals to synchronize the transfer of information. For example, one line of the control bus is the **read/write** (**R/W**) line, which is used to specify whether a read or write operation is to be carried out. Another line is the **valid memory address** (**VMA**) line, which indicates that the address bus now carries a valid memory address. This tells the memory unit when to look at the address bus to find the address of the location to be accessed. A third line is the **memory operation complete** (**MOC**) line which signals that the read/write operation has now completed. We should note at this point, that the other devices attached to the computer, such as I/O and storage devices, usually communicate with the CPU in a similar fashion to that described for communicating with memory (see Section 6.9). We are now in a position to describe the steps involved in reading from and writing to memory.

6.4.1 *Reading from memory*

The following steps are carried out by the SAM microprocessor to read an item from memory. The item may be an instruction or a data operand.

(1) The address of the item in memory is stored in the `MAR` register.

(2) This address is transferred to the address bus.

(3) The VMA line and R/W line of the control bus are used to indicate to memory that there is a valid address on the address bus and that a **read** operation is to be carried out.

(4) Memory responds by placing the contents of the desired address on the data bus.

(5) Memory enables the MOC line to indicate that the memory operation is complete, that is, the data bus contains the required data.

(6) The information on the data bus is transferred to the `MDR` register.

(7) The information is transferred from the `MDR` register to the specified CPU register.

6.4.2 *Writing to memory*

This procedure is similar to that for reading from memory:

(1) The address of the item in memory is stored in the `MAR` register.

(2) This address is transferred to the address bus.

(3) The item to be written to memory is transferred to the `MDR` register.

(4) This information is transferred to the data bus.

(5) The VMA line and R/W line of the control bus are used to indicate to memory that there is a valid address on the address bus and that a **write** operation is to be carried out.

(6) Memory responds by placing the contents of the data bus in the desired memory location.

(7) Memory uses the MOC line to indicate that the memory operation is complete, that is, the data has been written to memory.

We can see from the above descriptions (which have been simplified!) that accessing memory or any device is quite complicated from an implementation viewpoint. So, when an instruction such as

```
load r1, i
```

to load a register with the contents of a memory variable is to be executed, a lot of work has to be carried out. First, the instruction, including the address of the variable `i`, must be fetched from RAM, then the value of `i` must be fetched from RAM and finally the transfer of the value of `i` to register `r1` is carried out. It is important to realize that every operation concerning memory involves either reading or writing memory. Memory is a *passive* device. It can only store information. No processing can be carried out on information in memory. The information, stored in memory, must be transferred to a CPU register for processing and the result written back to memory. So, for example, when an instruction such as the 8086 `inc` instruction is carried out to increment a memory variable (as in `inc memvar`), its execution involves *both* a memory read operation and a memory write operation. Firstly, the value of `memvar` must be transferred to the CPU, where it can be incremented by the ALU. This transfer is carried out via a memory read operation. Then, once this value has been incremented by the ALU, the new value of `memvar` must be written out to `memvar`'s address in memory, via a memory write operation. Fortunately, even the assembly language programmer is spared from this level of implementation detail.

6.5 Encoding instructions in machine code

Instructions are represented in **machine code** as binary numbers in the same way as all other information is represented in a computer system. We noted earlier that assembly language instructions for most processors are broadly similar and have the form:

```
[label] operation [operand ..] [;comment]
```

It is important to realize that this similarity ends at the assembly syntax level and the way instructions are encoded in machine code (the actual binary codes used) differs significantly from processor to processor. Appendix D provides a brief introduction to 8086 instruction encoding, while in this section we look at how SAM instructions are encoded. The general form of a machine code instruction is illustrated in Figure 6.3 with the bits making up the instruction being grouped into **opcode** and **operand** fields.

The opcode field contains a binary code that specifies the operation to be carried out (say an addition or a transfer of control). Each operation has its own unique opcode. The operand field specifies the operand or operands on which the operation is to be carried out. For the SAM microprocessor, each instruction is made up of an **8-bit opcode** field followed by either an **8-bit** or **24-bit operand field**. The 24-bit operand field is made up of the 8-bit operand field followed by a 16-bit operand field. The 8-bit operand field is referred to as the **B-field** and the 16-bit operand field is called the **W-field** (B for byte and W

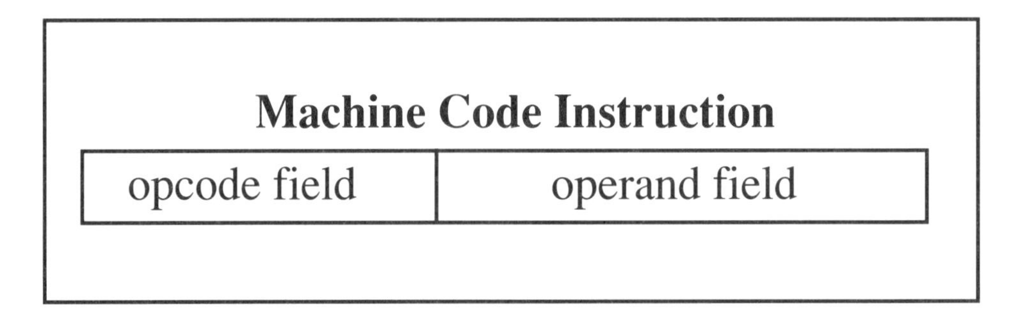

Figure 6.3 Machine code instruction format.

for word). Thus SAM instructions are encoded using either 16 bits or 32 bits, as illustrated in Figure 6.4.

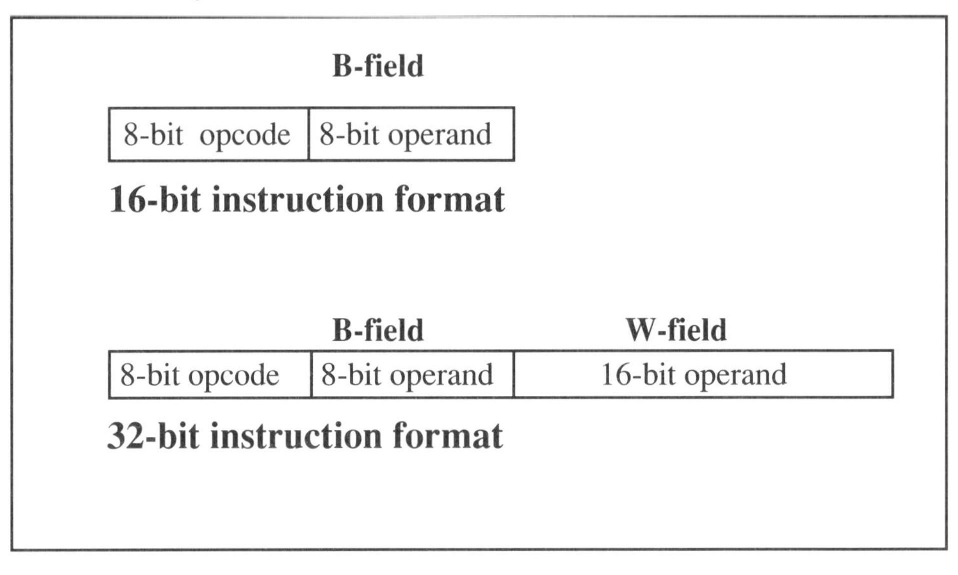

Figure 6.4 SAM instruction encoding.

The 8-bit opcode field allows us to represent up to 256 distinct instructions. We only need a fraction of that number of instructions, but we choose to use an 8-bit field for the sake of simplicity. The B-field is used to indicate which registers (if any) are being used by an instruction. It also specifies the addressing mode of the instruction, indicating, for example, if an operand is a memory variable, label or an immediate value. When an operand is stored in memory, the address of the operand (memory addressing for variables) or the actual value (immediate addressing for constants) is stored in the W-field, giving a 24-bit operand size. Since the B-field specifies the addressing mode of the instruction, we can have many more instructions than the 8-bit opcode field allows. While the following are two forms of the `add` instruction, the machine code used is different for each of them:

```
add  r1, r2
add  r0, 4
```

The first instruction operates on operands stored in registers, while the second operates on an immediate operand stored as part of the instruction itself. Obviously, at the machine level, there are important differences in the way two instructions are implemented. In fact, Motorola 68000 assemblers allow programmers to use different assembly language instructions to express the difference between instructions that take an immediate operand from those that do not. The letter `'i'` at the end of an M68000 instruction indicates the use of immediate addressing; for example, `addi #10, d0` adds the number `10` to `d0` whereas `add d1, d0` is the instruction to add the register `d1` to `d0`. The point is that separate machine code instructions are used for the different addressing modes that arise in instructions. One way of implementing this is to use a distinct opcode for each type of addressing mode, giving rise to the use of a large number of opcodes. Another approach, which is adopted with SAM instructions, is to use one opcode for each instruction and to use one or more bits in the operand field to specify the addressing mode. In either case, when an instruction is decoded, the control unit knows exactly what steps have to be carried out to implement the instruction, by examining either the opcode on its own or the opcode in combination with addressing mode information in the B-field.

It should be noted that, when the number of instructions in an instruction set is being cited, this number sometimes represents the total number of instructions obtained by counting each instruction with its different addressing modes as separate instructions. This means, for example, that if there are ten addressing modes that can be used with an `add` instruction, the instruction set would be treated as if it had ten `add` instructions. Such a method for counting instructions gives the impression of very large instruction sets. An alternative method of describing an instruction set is to say that there are x instructions with y addressing modes.

It should be emphasized that the instruction encoding for SAM is designed for illustration purposes. The aim is to keep it as simple as possible, while remaining basically similar to the encoding of instructions on real processors. The reader is encouraged to look at ways the instructions could be more efficiently encoded.

Table 6.1 lists the opcodes of the commonly used SAM instructions in binary and hexadecimal.

Table 6.1 SAM opcodes.

Instruction	Binary Code	Hex Code
move	0000 0001	01
load	0000 0010	02
store	0000 0011	03
add	0000 1000	08
sub	0000 1001	09
cmp	0000 1111	0F
jmp	0001 1111	1F
je	0010 1111	2F

The operand field of an instruction must be able to specify the registers, memory addresses or constants that the instruction is to operate on. (The term **literal** is also used for constant, particularly in assembly language. It is used because constants are stored as immediate values with the instruction, that is, they are literally part of the instruction.) SAM instructions have at most two operands. If there are two operands, then one is always a register. If a memory address is specified (say in the case of a memory variable or label) then the instruction is encoded using 32 bits with the memory address stored in the W-field. The B-field stores the addressing mode as well as specifying the register or registers to be used by an instruction. Since SAM has four general purpose registers we can represent them using 2-bit codes as follows:

00 for r0
01 for r1
10 for r2
11 for r3

Thus, four bits of the B-field are required to represent the two registers that may be used in an instruction. Bit numbers 0 and 1, of the B-field, represent the source register and bit numbers 2 and 3 represent the destination register. The four high-order bits of the B-field are used to specify the addressing mode. In the case of register addressing where both operands are registers, these bits are all set to 0. Where one of the operands is a memory address or immediate value, bit number 7 is a 1 and the address of the variable is stored in the W-field of the instruction. The machine code form of a number of SAM instructions, in binary and hexadecimal, is presented in Example 6.5.

Example 6.5

SAM instructions and their machine code equivalents. In the following instructions, val refers to a memory variable stored at location FFF3H in memory, Loop and Label are labels for the instructions stored at locations 3000H and 301CH in memory. The instruction and its binary encoding are given on the left and the hex encoding is given on the right, below the comment.

The load instruction:

```
        load          r1,     val                    ; r1 = val
0000  0010    1000  01 00 1111 1111 1111 0011   0284 FFF3H
                            (address of val)
```

is encoded using 32 bits. The opcode for load is 0000 0010 (02H), the destination register r1 is encoded as 01, while the source register is encoded as 00, but is not used because the load instruction looks for its source operand in memory, hence bit 7 of the B-field is set to 1, indicating a memory operand. Finally, the address of the memory variable val (FFF3H) is stored in the W-field.

The add instruction, encoded using 16-bits:

```
        add           r1, r2                         ; r1 = r1 + r2
0000  1000    0000  01 10                            0806H
```

The opcode for add is 0000 1000, the destination and source registers r1 and r2 are encoded as 01 and 10 respectively, while the four high-order bits of the B-field are clear since no memory addressing is required.

The add instruction using immediate addressing:

```
        add          r2,          7                   ; r2 = r2 + 7
0000    1000    1000 10 00 0000 0000 0000 00111 0888 0007H
                          (immediate value 7)
```

The immediate addressing is indicated by setting bit 7 of the B-field to 1. The destination register r2 is encoded as 10, and the source register is not used. The immediate value to be added, 7 in this case, is stored in the W-field.

The store instruction

```
        store        val, r2                          ; val = r2
0000    0011    1000 00 10 1111 1111 1111 0011   0382 FFF3H
                          (address of val)
```

The opcode for store is 0000 0011, the source register r2 is encoded as 10, while the destination register is not used in this instruction. Bit 7 of the B-field is set to 1, indicating memory addressing with the memory variable address stored in the W-field.

The cmp instruction:

```
        cmp          r0, r1
0000    1111    0000 00 01                        0F01H
```

The opcode for the cmp instruction is 0000 1111 and the source and destination registers are encoded as 0001, representing source register r0 and destination register r1.

The jmp instruction:

```
        jmp          Loop                             ; goto Loop
0001    1111    1000 0000 0011 0000 0000 0000    1F80 3000H
                          (label address)
```

The opcode for jmp is 0001 1111. The source and destination registers are not used, while bit 7 of the B-field is set to 1, indicating that the operand (Loop) is a memory address, which is stored in the W-field. In this case, the label Loop corresponds to address 3000H of the program.

The je instruction:

```
        je           Label
0010    1111    0000 1000                         2F08H
```

The opcode for je is 0010 1111 and the source and destination registers are not used by je. The seven low-order bits of the B-field are used to store what is called a **byte offset**. Conditional jump instructions use **relative addressing**. This means that instead of storing the address of the label, as in the jmp instruction above, the number of bytes (the byte offset) between the program counter and that indicated by the label, is stored in the B-field. In implementing the conditional jump instruction, this value is added to the address in the program counter, to effect the branch to the label. A negative value is used for a backwards jump. In this example, the instruction indicated by `Label` is eight bytes forward from the current value of the program counter, so the seven low-order bits of the B-field represent the value `8`. As explained below, this allows us to encode such instructions in an efficient fashion.

The `move` instruction:

```
        move           r0,  6                          ; r0 = 6
0000    0001    1000   00 00 0000 0000 0000 0110      0180 0006H
                             (immediate value 6)
```

The opcode for `move` is `0000 0001`. The destination register `r0` is encoded by `00`, while the source register is not used in this instruction. This `move` instruction illustrates the use of immediate addressing as for the second `add` instruction above. The immediate value, `6`, in this case, is stored in the W-field.

Notes

- Instructions, such as `load` and `store` and instructions with immediate operands, where only one register is being used, encode the register not being used as `00`, but any value could be used, since these bits will be ignored when the instruction is executed.
- Relative addressing is frequently used with conditional jump instructions because the majority of such jumps tend to be only a few bytes backwards or forwards from the conditional jump instruction. By encoding this number of bytes, for example, in a 7-bit field, we can jump `64` bytes backwards or `63` bytes forwards from the current value in the program counter, since we can represent numbers in the range `-64` to `+63` in a 7-bit two's complement number. A conditional jump instruction, using relative addressing, occupies less memory space than if we encode the label address using memory addressing. An additional benefit, because the instruction is encoded in fewer bytes, is that it can be fetched more quickly from memory. But what happens if you wish to jump more than `64` bytes in either direction? In this case we use bit 7 of the B-field to indicate that this has arisen and we store the byte offset in the W-field, in the same fashion as an immediate operand is stored. So a `je` instruction that wishes to jump, say, `127` (`FFH`) bytes forwards would be encoded as:

  ```
          je                      lab
  0010    1111    1000    0000    0000 0000 1111 1111    2FC0 00FFH
                                  (byte offset = 127)
  ```

  In other words the assembler, when translating a conditional jump instruction to machine code, must first calculate the number of bytes to be jumped, before encoding the instruction in one of the two appropriate forms. The 8086 encodes the byte offset of relative addresses using eight bits allowing branches in the range from `-128` to `127` bytes from the program counter to be implemented.

- Immediate addressing is indicated by setting bit 7 of the B-field to `1`. Immediate addressing is not allowed with our versions of the `load` and store instructions or the transfer of control instructions. This means that, without confusion, we can use bit 7 to indicate a memory variable or label as an operand with these instructions. We use the full 16 bits of the W-field to encode the immediate value for the sake of simplicity. In practice, immediate values are usually quite small and may be stored in eight bits. If optimizing memory usage was an important consideration, then we could allow either 8- or 16-bit immediate values to be used, depending on the size of the value.

6.6 Executing instructions: the fetch-execute cycle

We have described how information can be read from or written to memory and how instructions can be encoded in machine code. We are now in a position to describe, in more detail, how instructions are executed. Let us assume that a particular program has been loaded into memory and is currently being executed. Program execution has reached a certain point and the next six instructions of the program are listed in Example 6.6. To illustrate how the fetch-execute cycle operates, we will trace the execution of these instructions. We assume that these instructions are stored in memory beginning at location 3000H. The instructions and their machine code equivalents (in hexadecimal) are listed below. We use hexadecimal instead of binary as it is easier to work with, but you must remember that it is the binary form of the instructions that is actually stored in memory.

Example 6.6

The following is a SAL program fragment and its machine code version. It also shows the addresses of where the instructions are stored in memory. The label Loop corresponds to address 3000H. The memory variable x is stored at location 0100H in memory, which contains the value 6. The label Next is 16 (10H) bytes forward from the je instruction.

	SAL code	SAM code	Memory address Hex	Decimal
	move r0, 6	0180H	3000H	4096
		0006H	3002H	4098
Loop:	load r1, x	0284H	3004H	4100
		0100H	3006H	4102
	cmp r0, r1	0F01H	3008H	4104
	je Next	2F10H	300AH	4106
	.....		300CH	4108
	.....			
Next:	add r0, r2	0802H	301CH	4124
	jmp Loop	1F80H	301EH	4126
		3004H	3020H	4128

This code fragment assigns register r0 the value 6, assigns register r1 the value of x (also 6) and compares the values of registers r0 and r1. If the registers are equal, which they are in this case, control transfers to the instruction stored at Next (memory location 301CH, in this example),which is the instruction to add r2 to r0. We omit the instructions between the je instruction and the label Next, for the sake of simplicity, but assume for this example that they occupy 16 (10H) bytes of storage. Finally, the jmp instruction transfers control back to the load instruction, labelled by Loop.

The fetch-execute cycle operates by first fetching an instruction. The program counter register PC always contains the address of the next instruction to be executed. For the code fragment under consideration, the move instruction is stored at location 3000H in memory. Thus, the program counter contains this value at the point where we begin tracing execution of the program. In order to fetch this instruction, a memory read operation must be carried out. This means that the value 3000H is transferred from the PC register to the memory address register MAR and the read operation is performed, as described earlier, to fetch the instruction in location 3000H. Having fetched an instruction, the control unit updates the program counter to point to the next instruction to be fetched. The control unit increments the program counter by the size of the current instruction, in this case the PC register is incremented by 4, giving it the value 3004H. When the memory read operation is complete, the MDR register contains the instruction fetched from memory and this is transferred to the instruction register IR. The instruction register is another of the CPU's hidden registers which we have not encountered to date. It is logically part of the control unit and its function is to store an instruction so that it can be decoded for execution.

Figure 6.5 illustrates the state of the SAM registers *after* the move instruction has been fetched. Only the relevant portions of memory are shown. We assume that the general purpose registers have the value 0 except for r2 which has the value 1. The SP register is shown to have ? as its value to indicate that, in this example, we are not interested in its contents. The status register SR has value 0, indicating that the flags are all set to 0. Figure 6.5 also indicates how the SAM instructions are stored in memory, showing the SAL code equivalents for clarity.

As can be seen from Figure 6.5, the instruction encoded as 0180H (move r0, 6) has been fetched and transferred to the instruction register IR. Figure 6.5 also illustrates the **decoder**, which is the part of the control unit responsible for decoding the instruction stored in the instruction register. On decoding the move instruction 0180H, it is recognized that an immediate operand must be fetched from the next memory address, 3002H. It should be understood that while we said earlier that we fetched the move instruction, in fact we only fetched half of the instruction, the opcode and the B-field. This particular instruction is a 32-bit instruction and we have still to fetch the rest of the instruction's operand field. Thus, another memory read operation is initiated. This time, the control unit updates the value contained in the MAR register, by transferring it to the ALU, where it is incremented to 3002H. This is the address of the 16-bit immediate operand which is to be fetched from memory. This address is transferred back to the MAR register and a memory read initiated. On completion of this read operation, the MDR register contains the value 6. The execution of the move instruction may now be completed. In this case, it

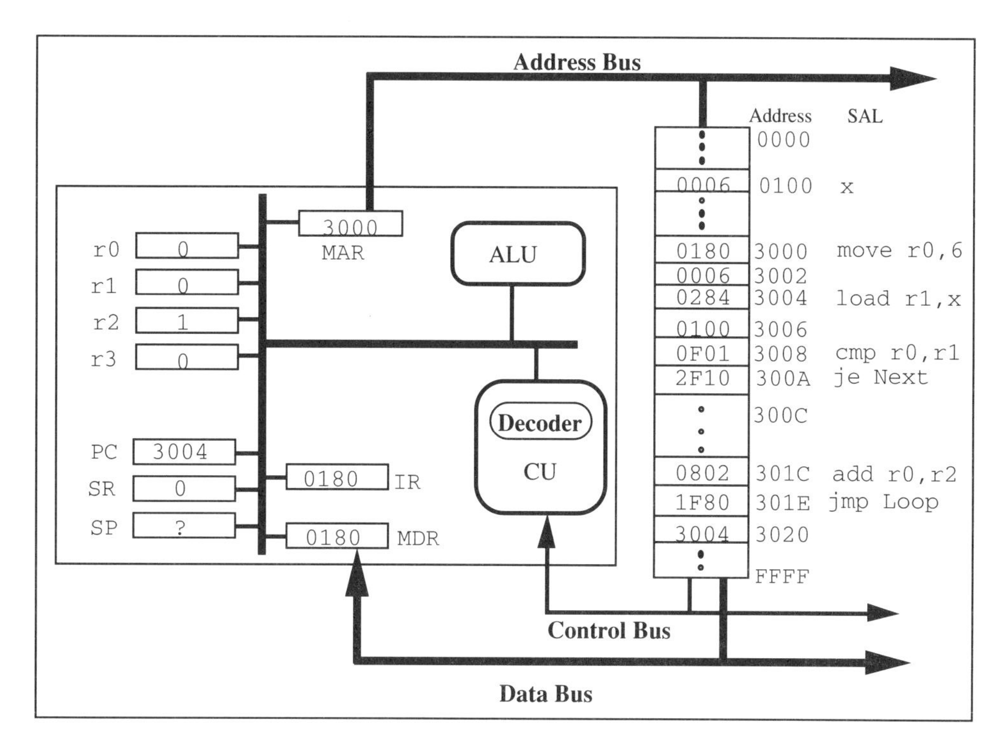

Figure 6.5 SAM register state having fetched the instruction at address 3000H.

involves the control unit transferring the contents of the `MDR` register to the `r0` register, using the internal CPU bus. On completion, the control unit repeats the fetch-execute cycle for the next instruction. You should note the number of steps involved in fetching and executing a relatively simple instruction.

Instruction `0284H` (`load r1, x`) is now fetched from memory and stored in the instruction register. The program counter is incremented to `3008H`, since this is also a 32-bit instruction. On decoding the instruction, it is recognized that another fetch is required to retrieve the W-field of the instruction, the address of the variable `x`. Thus, a second read operation is carried out, as for the `move` instruction above, to fetch the *address* of `x` (`0100H`) to the `MDR` register. The `load` instruction can now be executed. In this case, a third read operation is required to fetch the *value* of `x` (the contents of location `0100H`) before the instruction can be completed. This entails transferring the address of `x` (`0100H`) from the `MDR` register to the `MAR` register and initiating the third read operation to fetch the contents of location `0100H`. On completion of this read operation, the `MDR` register contains the value of `x`, which is `6`. Now we can complete execution of the load instruction by transferring the contents of the `MDR` register to register `r1`.

The execution of `load r1, x`, as described above, illustrates that instructions, which in assembly language look very similar, can have very different execution times. For example, the previous `move` instruction only required two memory read operations and the `cmp` instruction (explained below), as we shall see only requires a single memory read operation. This is important because the CPU can execute instructions much more quickly that it can fetch them from memory. Thus the CPU is idle while waiting for information to come from memory. This means that an instruction that requires three memory read operations will be much slower to execute than one which only requires a single memory read operation.

Having completed execution of the `load` instruction, we now fetch the next instruction from address `3008H` which has been transferred to the `MAR` register. The state of the system at this point is illustrated in Figure 6.6. The *previous* contents of the `IR` and `MDR` registers are shown and we also see the updated values of `r0` and `r1`.

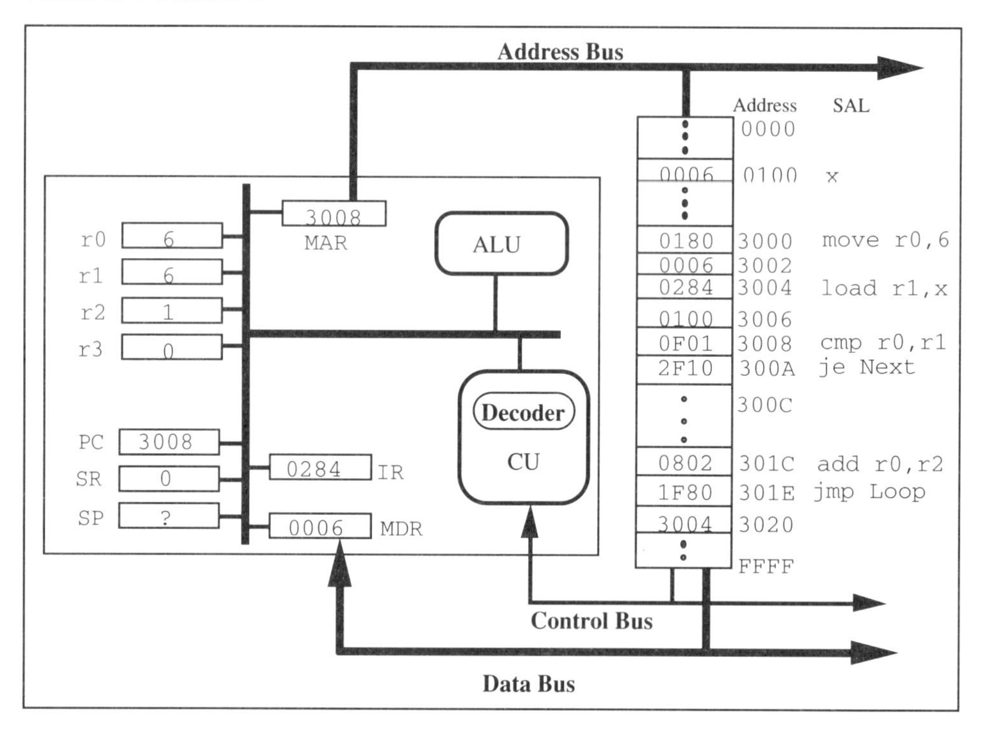

Figure 6.6 State of system after executing `load r1, x`.

The `cmp` instruction (`0F01H`) is now fetched and the program counter incremented to `300AH`. This means that the `MDR` register now contains `0F01H` and this value is transferred to the instruction register. The instruction is now decoded for execution. A `cmp` instruction is executed by subtracting the destination operand from the source operand (as for a `sub` instruction) and the status register flags are set appropriately. The result of the subtraction is not retained. This subtraction is carried out by the ALU. So, to execute the `cmp` instruction, the contents of the registers `r0` and `r1` are transferred to the ALU, which subtracts `r1` from `r0`. The ALU then sets the flags in the status register `SR` to appropriate values. In this case, since the registers `r0` and `r1` contain the same value, the zero flag (bit 0 of `SR`) will be set. The state of the system at this stage is shown in Figure 6.7.

The next instruction (`je Next`) is now fetched in the usual manner and transferred to the instruction register, which as a result contains the value `2F10H`. As usual, the program counter is incremented and now contains

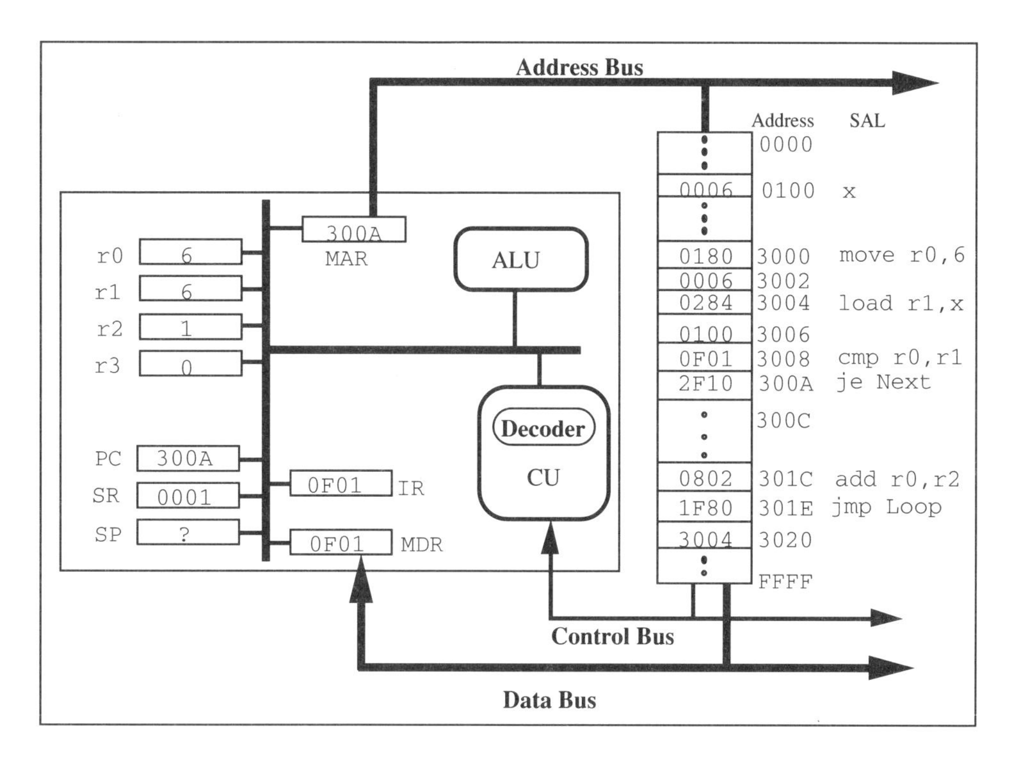

Figure 6.7 State of system after executing `cmp r0, r1`. Note that the SR register has the value 0001H indicating that the zero flag has been set to 1.

300CH. To execute this instruction, the flag settings in the status register are examined and, in particular, the zero flag is checked. If the zero flag is not set, the instruction simply completes and the next instruction is fetched. If the zero flag is set, as is the case in this example, then the program counter is updated. The conditional jump instructions, as explained earlier, use relative addressing. The B-field of these instructions contains a 7-bit two's complement number, which is added to the program counter. In this case the number 10H (16) will be added to the program counter, which contains the value 300CH, thus giving a new value for the program counter of 301CH. This addition is carried out by the ALU, which in this case stores the result in the program counter. This effectively transfers control to the instruction in location 301CH, that is, it branches to the `add r0, r2` instruction pointed at by `Next`.

The `add` instruction (0802H) is now fetched and decoded in the usual manner, with the PC being updated to 301EH. The contents of r0 (0006H) and r2 (0001H) are transferred to the ALU, where they are summed. The result (7) is then transferred to r0 and, since the result of the `add` instruction was not zero, the zero flag of SR will be cleared. The next instruction (`jmp Loop`) is now fetched.

In the case of the unconditional `jmp` instruction, the address to which control is to be transferred is stored in the W-field. Once the first part of the `jmp` instruction (1F80H) has been fetched and decoded, this address is then fetched from memory. The `jmp` instruction is executed by transferring this address to the program counter to bring about the transfer of control, that is, the program counter is overwritten with the value `3004H` in this case. This means that the next instruction to be fetched will be from address `3004H`, the location pointed at by the label `Loop`.

This completes our trace of the execution of the six instructions in our program fragment. The reader might like to continue the trace for another pass through the loop as an exercise.

One crucial element in the fetch-execute cycle is that the program counter is always updated to point to the next instruction. This is carried out by the ALU. In the case of the SAM microprocessor, it simply means adding either `2` or `4` to the program counter value, depending on the size of the instruction that has been fetched. For example, a `load` instruction is encoded in four bytes (two bytes specify the opcode and destination register and two bytes specify the address of the variable to be loaded), whereas an `add` instruction with two register operands is encoded in two bytes. When it decodes an instruction, the control unit must determine how many bytes the instruction occupies, so that the program counter can be updated by the appropriate amount. In general, instructions may be encoded using from one byte to many bytes depending on the machine. The 8086, for example, encodes instructions using from one to a maximum of six bytes. Many RISC machines encode all instructions using the same number of bytes, for example four bytes. In addition, high-performance processors may have an additional special purpose ALU (an **adder**) as part of the control unit. This adder updates the program counter directly so that it can be updated in parallel with the execution of other arithmetic instructions such as an `add` or `sub` instruction, which use the ALU.

6.7 Executing instructions: the control unit

So far in our discussion, we have looked at the steps involved in the fetch-execute cycle. In this section we look at the role of the control unit in the execution of instructions. The control unit is responsible for the execution of instructions. This means that it controls the fetch-execute cycle. When an instruction is decoded by the control unit, then a set of steps must be initiated to execute the instruction. There are two ways of implementing a control unit to enable it to carry out these steps. One is to **hardwire** the control unit so that each instruction is executed in hardware. This lends itself to very high execution speeds. The earliest computers used this approach and nowadays RISC machines also tend to use it. The other approach to implementing a control unit is to use a technique known as **micro-programming**.

Micro-programming was developed by Maurice Wilkes at Cambridge University. It has been employed in most computers built during the 1970s and 1980s and continues to be used in CISC machines. In simple terms, a micro-programmed control unit behaves likes a processor inside the CPU. The instruction, fetched by the CPU, is implemented by the control unit executing a **micro-program** which carries out the steps required by the instruction. These steps are called **micro-instructions**. These micro-instructions are stored in memory called **control memory**, usually in ROM. The control unit has a micro-program program counter which, like the `PC` of the CPU, keeps track of the next micro-instruction to be executed. There are micro-programs to control all activities of the CPU, so that each instruction in the instruction set has a corresponding micro-program. There is also a micro-program to implement the fetch operation.

In a micro-programmed processor, program execution proceeds via the fetch-execute cycle as described earlier. The point is that the fetch operation is under the control of a fetch micro-program. When an instruction (say, `add`) has been fetched, it is executed by executing its corresponding micro-program (an `add` micro-program). Having executed the `add` micro-program, the fetch micro-program is executed again to repeat the cycle. The micro-instructions themselves are actually made up of **micro-orders**, which are in turn executed by the hardware of the computer.

Let us look at an instruction to add the contents of `r2` to `r0` leaving the result in `r0`:

```
add r0, r2
```

As stated earlier, the ALU is responsible for carrying out arithmetic operations. To execute this `add` instruction, a set of steps such as the following are carried out (whether the control unit is hardwired or micro-programmed).

(1) The contents of one of the registers (say `r2`) is transferred to an ALU register. This involves:
- signalling `r2` to write its contents to the CPU bus;
- signalling the ALU to read the contents of the CPU bus into one of its registers.

(2) The contents of the other register (`r0`) is transferred to the ALU in a similar fashion, by:
- signalling `r0` to write its contents to the CPU bus;
- signalling the ALU to read the contents of the CPU bus into another of its registers.

(3) The ALU is signalled to carry out an add operation.

(4) The ALU transfers the result from its internal result register to the destination register. This involves:
- signalling the ALU register to write its result register contents to the CPU bus;
- signalling `r0` to copy the value from the CPU bus.

The sub-steps making up the micro-instructions (1), (2) and (4) may be considered to correspond to micro-orders. Similar sequences of steps must be carried out to execute any instruction. It must be emphasized that such steps have to be carried out regardless of how the control unit is implemented. A hard-wired control unit carries out the same steps as would a micro-programmed control unit. A block diagram of a micro-programmed control unit is illustrated in Figure 6.8.

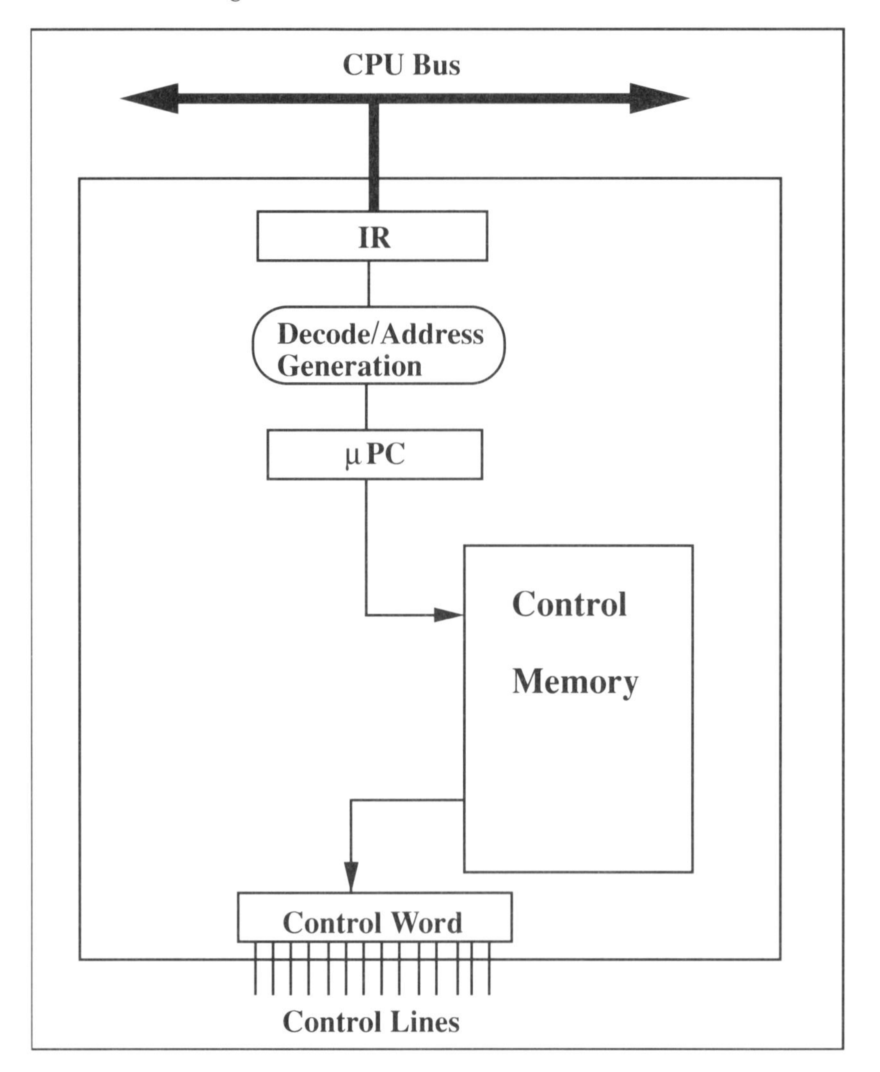

Figure 6.8 Micro-programmed control unit.

The instruction register `IR` contains the instruction to be executed. This instruction must be decoded and the address of the first micro-instruction of the corresponding micro-program must be generated. The micro-program counter `μPC` is initialized with this address and the first micro-instruction is fetched from the control store that contains all the micro-programs for the control unit. Each micro-instruction specifies a set of control signals that are responsible for executing that particular micro-instruction. These control signals are loaded into the **control word**, which is connected to all CPU components via control lines. These lines allow, for example, a micro-instruction to specify that a register write its contents to the CPU bus. In this case the control word would have set to `1` the particular bit that specifies which register is to write to the CPU bus. Each register is identified by a particular bit (or group of bits) in the control word. A separate bit is used to specify that a register load a value from the CPU bus or write its contents to the CPU bus.

In order to execute a micro-instruction, the control unit must be able to send signals to many components, including all of the registers (the general purpose registers, the ALU registers, MAR, MDR, IR, PC, SP, status register and so on), the ALU (specifying the operation to be carried out, for example add, sub, shifts, rotates, and, or and xor), RAM (specifying a read or write operation) and to the various I/O devices attached to the system. The set of signals that will be sent to implement a micro-instruction are stored in the control word. If the control word uses one bit for each signal to each component, then it is going to be very wide, that is, have a large number of bits. Taking the signals for the registers and instructions alone, for even a modest machine, might require a control word containing in excess of 100 bits. When such a control word is used the term **horizontal micro-programming** is used because of the width of the control word.

Another approach is possible. Since for any micro-instruction only one register will be specified, instead of having a bit for every possible register, why not use a field to encode the register possibilities. Thus a 5-bit field would allow you to specify any one of 32 possible registers. Similarly an 8-bit opcode field would allow you to specify any of up to 256 possible instructions. With this approach the width of the control word can be greatly reduced and the technique is known as **vertical micro-programming**. The disadvantage of this technique, however, is that the control word must be decoded in order to interpret what signals are to be sent to the various components. This means some extra hardware, in the form of decoders, is required.

Once the first micro-instruction has been executed, the address of the next micro-instruction must be generated. This may be done, as for the processor program counter, by incrementing the μPC by the appropriate amount. Alternatively, each micro-instruction may contain the address of the next micro-instruction to be executed. Once the last micro-instruction in a micro-program for a particular instruction has been executed, the μPC is loaded with the address of the fetch micro-program so that the fetch-execute cycle may continue.

The advantage of a micro-programmed control unit is that it is easier to design and modify than a hard-wired control unit. The instruction set can be completely changed without changing the hardware; all that is required is that the micro-programs in the control memory be changed. Similarly, it is easy for a designer to add a few new instructions to the instruction set of a micro-programmed machine. All that is required is that micro-programs for the new instructions be written and stored in the control memory. This may be done to make some applications run faster, by creating instructions specifically for a particular application. CISC machines typically use micro-programmed control units.

6.8 Executing instructions: the ALU

The other major unit involved in the execution of many instructions is the ALU. The ALU is the functional unit concerned with carrying out arithmetic and bit manipulation operations. The term **integer unit** is used for an ALU that deals with integer arithmetic, while **floating-point unit** or **FPU** denotes an ALU that handles real (floating-point) numbers. A **floating-point co-processor** (**accelerator**) is a processor that is dedicated to carrying out floating-point operations. Such co-processors are often available as options for a computer system, so that a user with applications software requiring extensive floating-point support may have such an option installed. When a co-processor is installed, the CPU allows the co-processor to handle the floating-point operations, while it may proceed to carry out other work in parallel, thus greatly speeding up the operation of the system. While an FPU is typically provided on a separate chip from the CPU, modern microprocessors, such as the Pentium, PowerPC and SuperSparc, have an FPU on the microprocessor chip. This means that information can be transferred between the FPU and CPU registers much more quickly than if a co-processor on a separate chip is used.

It should be noted that the arithmetic capabilities of the ALU may be quite limited. Some 8-bit processors only provide facilities for the addition and subtraction of 8-bit numbers. On such machines, operations such as multiplication and division (or 16-bit addition and subtraction) have to be implemented by the programmer in software. Even on quite powerful processors, multi-word arithmetic (such as adding two 32-bit numbers on a 16-bit processor) may have to be carried out in such a fashion. It is also possible for multiplication and division to be carried out in micro-code as opposed to being hard-wired into the ALU. The advantage of hardwired operations is that they can be carried out quickly, but they are more expensive to implement. The advantage of a software implementation is that they are cheaper, in that they do not require special hardware support, but they have the penalty of being slower.

As with other computing components there are many ways of designing an ALU. A very simplified ALU design is illustrated in Figure 6.9. An ALU has a number of internal registers, of which we only show three, `input1`, `input2` and `result`. A programmer has no direct access to any of these registers. The two input registers are used to store operands to be manipulated by the ALU and the result register, as the name suggests, stores the result of the ALU operation.

The ALU, like all CPU components, is attached to the CPU bus. Information to be manipulated by the ALU is transferred to the ALU via the CPU bus and results are returned likewise. In addition, the ALU must be signalled as to what operation is to be carried out. The ALU design, outlined here, indicates that carrying out an `add` operation, for example, requires that the two operands that are to be summed should be transferred to the ALU input registers `input1` and `input2`. The ALU then receives a signal indicating that an `add` operation is to be performed. It sums the operands in the input registers and stores the result in the output register `result`. The contents of this register are then transferred to the destination operand. One important additional operation also occurs. Status information concerning the result of the operation (for example, did overflow

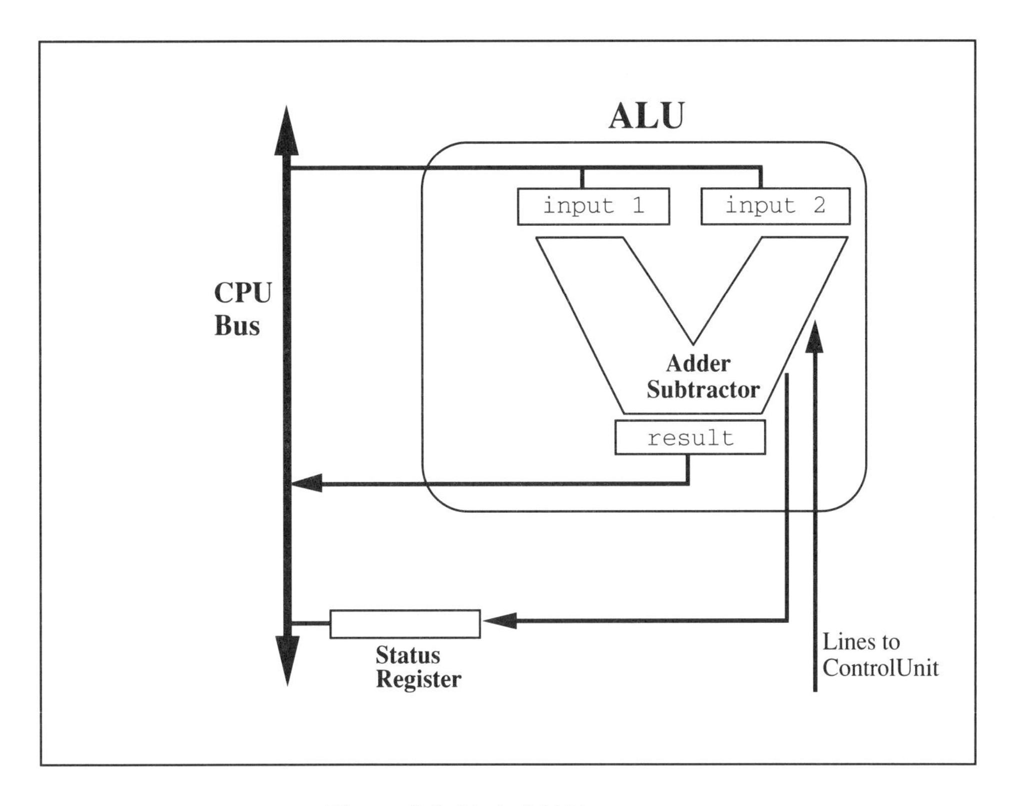

Figure 6.9 Typical ALU structure.

occur? was the result equal to zero or was it negative?) is transferred to the status register, where it is recorded in one or more of the flags. These flags can be tested by a conditional jump instruction in order to implement the various control structures required in programming, such as loops.

There are many possible variations on this design. For example, one of the general purpose registers may be designated as an input or output register, which reduces the number of internal ALU registers required. An ALU is often represented in diagrams in the form illustrated in Figure 6.10.

6.9 Executing instructions: I/O and storage devices

One of the fundamental classes of instruction executed by the CPU is that concerned with carrying out I/O. A computer system must have I/O devices that allow it to communicate with its environment. In addition to I/O devices, a computer system usually provides long-term storage devices in the form of disk and tape drives, but from the CPU's perspective, these may also be treated as I/O devices. We are familiar with I/O devices such as keyboards, monitors, printers and mice. However, many computers are embedded inside other equipment, such as televisions, radios, telephones, washing machines and cars. In fact, there are many more processors used in these applications than are used in conventional computer systems. Such processors are often referred to as

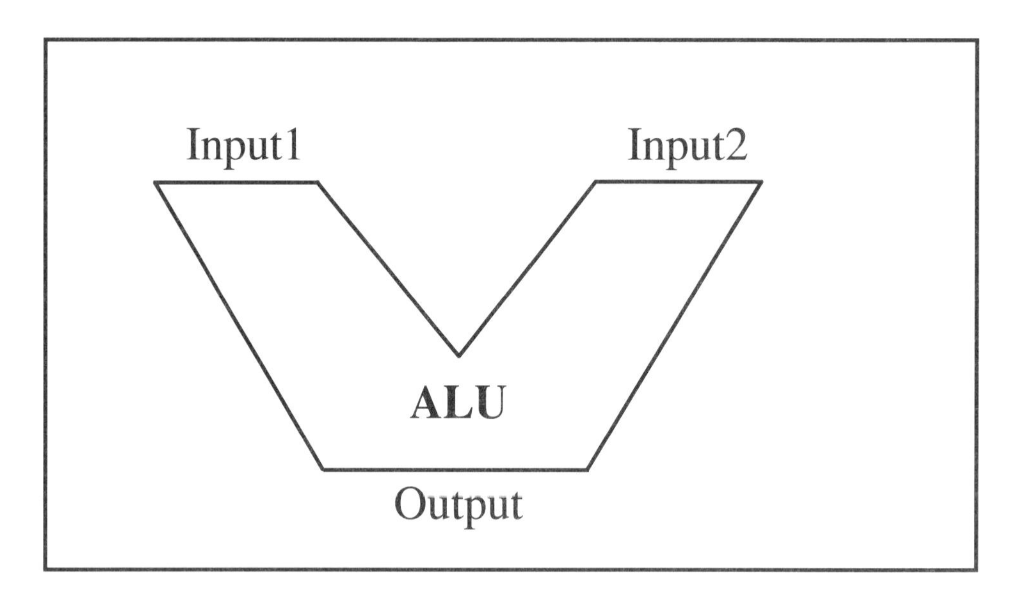

Figure 6.10 ALU schematic form.

micro-controllers and they interact with their environment via switches, lights, sensors, analogue/digital converters and so on.

Every device is connected to the system buses via an **interface** or **controller**. The device controller converts signals from the device to a form compatible with the system buses and vice versa. A single controller may actually control a number of identical devices, so that a disk controller, for example, may act as interface for a number of disk drives. Figure 6.11 illustrates a typical computer system showing the CPU, memory and three I/O device controllers. The device controllers are in turn connected to their respective devices by appropriate cables (not shown in Figure 6.11).

6.9.1 Memory-mapped I/O

One common form of I/O is called **memory-mapped I/O**. Here, the CPU communicates with the device *exactly* as if it was communicating with memory. It reads from and writes to the device in exactly the same fashion as it accesses memory. This means that the same instructions that are used to access memory (such as `load` and `store`) may also be used to carry out I/O. This has the advantage that no special instructions are required for I/O. In contrast to this, it is possible to have dedicated I/O buses, in which case special I/O instructions are required to perform I/O.

Consider a microcomputer monitor. The monitor **interface** (video card) is connected to the three buses (**address**, **data** and **control**). It uses specific memory addresses, so that when the CPU writes to these addresses (using some form of `move` or `store` instruction) the information is transferred to the monitor and is displayed appropriately. Each I/O controller will have its own set of memory addresses associated with it. Thus, in order to perform I/O, the programmer must know in advance what these addresses are. This means that certain addresses in the address space are not used by the computer's RAM but

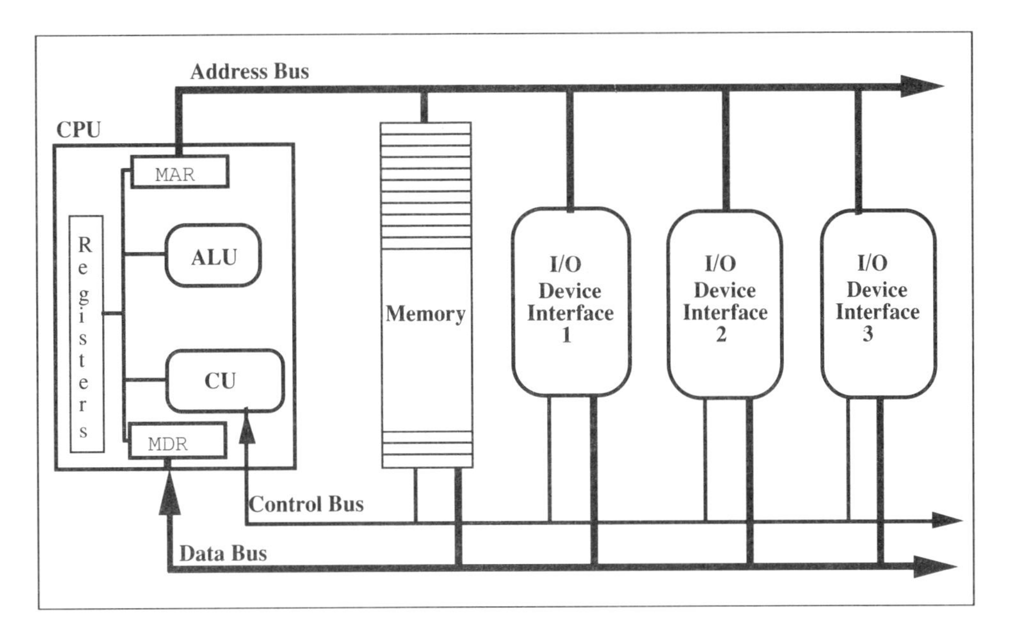

Figure 6.11 CPU, memory, buses and I/O device controllers.

are reserved for I/O purposes. So an 8086 microprocessor with the capability of addressing 1 Mb of RAM cannot actually use that amount of real RAM memory. Specific parts of the address space are allocated for the various devices that can be interfaced to an 8086.

The CPU can initiate I/O with a device by placing the device address on the address bus and activating control lines (read or write) on the control bus. Each device effectively listens to the address bus and becomes active when its address appears on the bus. Typically each controller will use a number of memory addresses, for example, one address will be used to specify a **device data register** and another to specify a **device status register**, both of which are part of the I/O device's hardware. The status register will contain information such as whether the device is ready, busy or has completed an I/O operation. The data register will contain the data to be read from the device or the data to be written to the device. Because devices are so slow when compared with CPU speeds, the CPU may have to wait for the device to become ready. For example, a printer prints characters at a vastly slower rate than the CPU can deliver them. Thus the CPU must wait until the printer has printed one batch of characters before sending the next batch. The CPU can check if the device is busy by testing the status register. One technique that can be used to allow the CPU to wait for a busy device is called **busy waiting**. The CPU repeatedly tests the status register until the device is not busy, in which case it can proceed with the I/O operation. The following C code fragment illustrates the process:

```
while (status == BUSY)
{
      status = test (status_register) ;
}
```

When I/O is controlled in this fashion it is called **program-controlled I/O**. However, busy waiting is a technique that is only suitable in certain restricted situations. The reason is that while the CPU is busy waiting, no other work can be carried out and so CPU time is wasted. In addition, if the I/O device fails, the CPU may be left in an infinite loop as the device status never changes! In multi-tasking computer systems, CPU time is shared between programs. If one program does not have useful work for the CPU, then another program is allowed to run. So, rather than be busy waiting for I/O operations to complete, the CPU can be allocated to another program. But how do we handle busy devices? Another type of I/O is possible called **interrupt-driven I/O**.

6.9.2 *Interrupt-driven I/O*

An interrupt is a signal to the CPU that some event has occurred and that a specific action must be taken to cope with that event. The term **interrupt** is well chosen as it mirrors human activity quite well. Imagine that you are reading a book (as an analogy to the CPU executing a program) when the telephone rings and interrupts you. You stop reading the book, answer the phone and carry on a conversation (equivalent to the CPU executing a different program) for a while. Then when the phone call is over, you resume reading the book from where you left off. In a computer system, a very similar process happens on the occurrence of an interrupt.

An interrupt is a signal to the processor to stop executing the current program and transfer control to another program. This second program is called an **interrupt service routine** or **interrupt handler** and has been written to cope with the event that has occurred. On completion of this routine, program control will be returned to the interrupted program, allowing it to continue as if nothing had happened. In order for this to happen, that is, to resume the program where it stopped executing, the **state** of the program at the time of the interrupt must be **saved**. This means that the CPU must take a copy of all information that is required to restart the program at the same place. This information is called the **volatile environment** of a program. In order to restart a program you need to have the correct values of the program counter, stack pointer and status registers. In addition, you need a copy of all registers used by the program. This information can be stored in the computer's memory, typically on the stack. When the interrupt has completed, this information must be restored to these registers.

Interrupt-driven I/O allows the CPU to initiate an I/O operation, say send some information to the printer, and then continue with another activity. When the printer has processed the information, it can then interrupt the CPU, signalling that it is ready for more output. The CPU can respond to the interrupt by resuming the printing program to send more information to the printer, after which the CPU can resume another program. It is important to remember that it is the high speed of the CPU that makes this possible. A typical CPU can execute several million instructions per second. In a few milliseconds the CPU can send the printer enough information to keep it busy for several seconds. Thus the CPU can process millions of instructions for other programs, while the printer is printing, in parallel. We say a little more about interrupts at the end of this section.

6.9.3 *Direct memory access (DMA) I/O*

This type of I/O is used for transferring large quantities or **blocks** of data (for example 512 bytes, 1024 bytes) between the CPU and a device. It is typically used for fast devices such as disks. These devices are block-structured devices, by which we mean that they store information in blocks. Thus, a typical disk drive will transfer an entire block of data to the CPU as opposed to transferring a single byte of data. Such devices use a DMA controller to interface to the CPU buses. The CPU initiates an I/O operation by informing the DMA controller of the number of bytes and the address of the data to be transferred. The DMA controller then takes over and carries out the transfer between the device and memory. This means that the DMA controller is in control of the data bus for the duration of the transfer. The CPU is no longer involved and it is left free to do other processing that does not require use of the data bus. When the DMA controller has completed the transfer, it can let the CPU know, by using an interrupt. This means that the CPU can continue processing in parallel with the DMA transfer, which increases the amount of processing that can be carried out.

6.9.4 *I/O processors*

In large computer systems, special I/O processors may be present which look after I/O operations, freeing the CPU for other activities. These processors are sometimes called I/O channels or peripheral processors. The CPU communicates with the I/O processor, instructing it as to which I/O operation to carry out. The I/O processor then looks after the I/O operation, allowing the CPU to continue processing in parallel. An I/O processor might be an actual computer system, for example, Digital's Dec-20 computer system used a PDP-11 as a **front-end machine** to handle I/O processing and such machines are sometimes called **front-end processors (FEPs)**.

Note: An important point to remember about I/O operations and even memory access operations is that the CPU can process information much more quickly than it can obtain it from memory or I/O devices. Accessing a disk for example is of the order of 100 000 times slower than accessing RAM which in turn, is around five to 20 times slower than accessing a CPU register. Thus, even accessing memory causes a bottleneck, because, given the speed of the CPU, it is frequently waiting for information to be transferred to or from memory. This is known as the **von Neumann bottleneck**. Various techniques have been developed to alleviate this problem and these include **caching** and **pipelining**, which are described in Chapter 7.

6.9.5 *More about interrupts*

There are two types of interrupt that arise, one is called a **hardware (external) interrupt** and the other is called a **software (internal) interrupt**. A software interrupt is initiated by an interrupt instruction such as the 8086 `int` instruction. The interrupt instruction passes information that allows the CPU to determine which interrupt handler program to invoke for the interrupt. When the interrupt handler has finished executing, the original program is resumed at the next instruction after the interrupt instruction. This mechanism is used in 8086 assembly language programming to access operating system services to carry out I/O and other tasks.

A hardware interrupt is generated by a peripheral device, such as a keyboard, mouse, printer or disk drive, seeking the attention of the processor. A virtual-memory page fault is another example of a hardware interrupt. A hardware interrupt occurs as a result of device interfaces manipulating **control** signals on the bus. This means that an executing program can potentially be interrupted at any time; as a result, we say that interrupts are **asynchronous** events. When the CPU is interrupted, it finishes executing the current instruction and transfers control to a program sometimes called the **first level interrupt handler** (**FLIH**). The FLIH saves the volatile environment of the program and transfers control to an interrupt handler program This means that the FLIH has the task of identifying the device that generated the interrupt and transferring control to a particular interrupt handler program that has been written to deal with that particular device. In other words, there is an interrupt handling program for each device attached to the system. When a particular device, such as a printer, generates an interrupt, the CPU must transfer control to the interrupt handler for the printer. The function of the FLIH is to identify the source of the interrupt and transfer control to the interrupt handler appropriate to that device.

This gives rise to the question as to how the FLIH identifies the interrupting device. There are two popular techniques for identifying an interrupting device. One method is called **polling**. In this case the FLIH checks the status register of each device in turn, until it locates the device whose status register indicates that it has generated an interrupt. The FLIH can then invoke the appropriate interrupt handler for that device. The sequence in which the FLIH checks the device status registers determines their importance; thus it will check important devices before less important ones. Importance is usually related to the speed of the device. A slow device, such as a terminal or printer, will not have to be serviced as quickly as a faster device, such as a disk drive. The disadvantage of this technique is that it is a relatively slow method of identifying the interrupting device.

The second method for identifying an interrupting device uses **vectored** interrupts. In this case, each device has a unique identification code. When a devices generates an interrupt by sending a signal on the interrupt control line to the CPU, it also places its identification code (a number) on the data bus. The CPU can now immediately identify the device by reading the identification code from the data bus. This code, may in fact, be the starting address of the interrupt handler for that device, so by loading this address into the program counter, control can very quickly be transferred to the appropriate interrupt handler.

An important question in the handling of interrupts is what happens if two devices generate interrupts at the same time? In this situation the system usually uses some form of **priority** scheme. This means that some devices are regarded as more important than others, that is, they require service from the CPU more quickly than others. Such devices are given a higher priority than less important devices. With the polling approach, priority is automatically associated with the order in which devices are polled. The first device polled will have a higher priority than the second and so on. Thus, if two devices generate an interrupt simultaneously, the first one to be polled will be serviced first. One approach with vectored interrupts is that interrupt requests are passed through a special unit which associates priorities (fixed in advance by the computer designer) with each device. This unit then passes on the code of the highest-priority device to the CPU.

Another issue is that of a second interrupt occurring while a first interrupt is being processed. Again this can be solved using priority levels. When an interrupt of a high-level priority is being serviced it cannot be interrupted by a lower-priority interrupt. When a low-priority interrupt is being serviced, then it can be interrupted (in the same manner as any other program) by a device with a higher priority level.

Finally, there are times when the CPU may not wish to be interrupted, because it is executing a program fragment that is of critical importance. For example, the operating system may be about to update an internal data structure and it is important that only the updated value be made available to other programs. If the CPU were switched to another program before finishing the update, then serious problems could arise because other programs might access out of date information. The section of the program that was carrying out this action is called a **critical section**. To prevent the CPU from being interrupted while it is in a critical section, there are instructions to *disable* and *enable* interrupts. For example on a multi-user machine used by travel agents to book seats on flights, if one travel agent is booking a seat, then no-one else should be able to access that seat until the travel agent is finished booking it. This can be accomplished in the program by **disabling interrupts** before the part of the program that carries out the booking task. This means that the program cannot be stopped until interrupts are **enabled** again. Thus, the program can complete the seat booking operation, without interference. Enabling interrupts means that the program may be interrupted. So, when the required task has been completed, interrupts are enabled. In the case of the travel-agent program, this means that another person may run a program that accesses the seats on the flight. This technique is used by the operating system to carry out critical tasks. We can represent this idea in pseudo-code:

```
program code
disable interrupts

        Code for task to        ; Called Critical Section
        be completed

enable interrupts
more program code
```

It should be pointed out that controlling access to shared data, as in the travel-agent example, is a major area in operating systems and database management systems and there are high-level techniques for carrying out these tasks. In operating systems a technique using **semaphores** is popular, whilst in database systems there are various **locking** techniques that are used.

6.10 Other CPU components

In this section we look at other important CPU components that have been mentioned in this chapter: registers, decoders and the CPU bus.

6.10.1 Registers

Registers are storage areas inside the CPU. We have used very simple diagrams for registers in our figures. Figure 6.12(a) illustrates the simple picture of a register we have being using, while Figure 6.12 (b) is a more detailed illustration of the design of an 8-bit register.

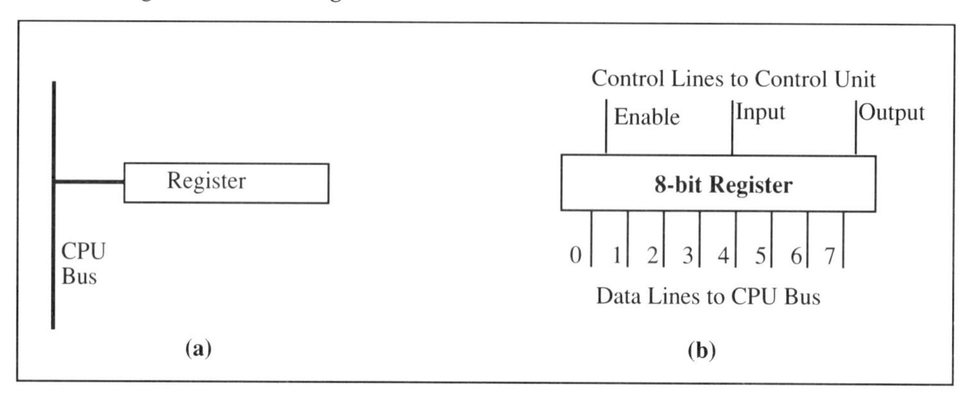

Figure 6.12 Typical register.

As shown in Figure 6.12(b), there must be a line connecting each bit of a register to the CPU bus. (This also applies to memory locations, so that a 32-bit memory word must have 32 lines connecting it to the data bus.) In addition, Figure 6.12(b) shows three control lines that govern the activity of the register. The **enable** control line activates the register so that it may read data from the bus or write data to the bus. The **input** control line causes the register to read data from the bus while the **output** control line causes the register to write its data to the bus. Figure 6.12(b) is still a simplified illustration of the register. For example, it does not show a clock signal, which is also required for the correct operation of registers. The register will only transfer data when it has been enabled by the enable control line. In a micro-programmed processor, micro-instructions are used to activate the control lines so as to operate the register.

6.10.2 Decoders

A decoder is a device that decodes its input to generate a single corresponding output. For example, a three-input decoder can be regarded as taking a 3-bit input and mapping it on to one of eight output signals, as illustrated in Figure 6.13. In this case we see that, given an input of 110 (6), output line 6 (highlighted) will be activated. An n-input decoder will activate one of 2^n output lines. The opcode of an instruction may be decoded in this fashion, thus an eight-input decoder could be used to decode the SAM opcodes described earlier. In addition, the register fields of the B-field could be decoded using two-input decoders. A decoder is also used by the memory hardware to decode the memory address received on the address bus, so as to activate the memory location indicated by the address. For example, a memory system with a 16-bit address scheme would require a 16-bit decoder to decode addresses.

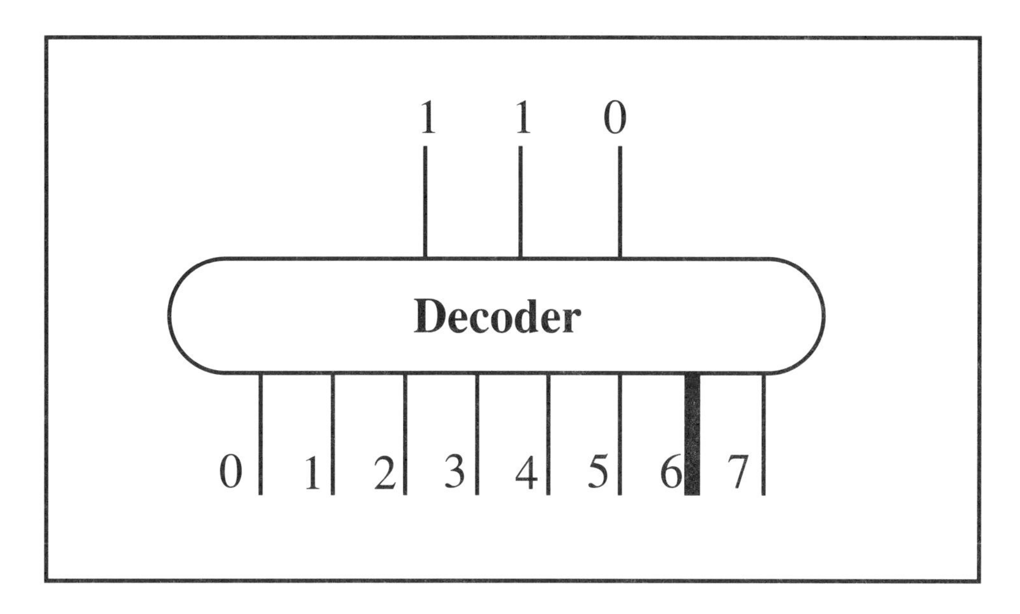

Figure 6.13 Three-input decoder.

6.10.3 CPU bus

In this chapter we have described the CPU as having a single internal bus for transferring information to the various CPU components such as the registers and ALU. The CPU bus must have the same number of lines as the word size of the processor, so that a 32-bit processor will have 32 lines making up the CPU bus. In addition, we have referred to control lines from the control unit to the registers and the ALU. While this provides a simple conceptual view of how the CPU operates, it is not uncommon for a real CPU to have a number of internal buses to carry data between registers and the functional units. The major advantage of having more than one CPU bus is that information can be transferred between a number of locations at the same time. For example, a result may be transferred from the ALU to a register on one bus, at the same time as an instruction is being transferred from the memory data register to the control unit on another bus.

In the next chapter we will see that many CPUs use storage areas known as **cache memories** (or simply **caches**) to access information more quickly. One design employs separate caches for storing instructions and data. Thus, while an instruction is being fetched from the instruction cache, at the same time an operand may be fetched from the data cache, providing of course that there are two separate buses to transfer the information. In the same way as the internal CPU bus system is important, so too is the system bus linking the CPU to the other devices in a computer system. The system bus can become a bottleneck, degrading the performance of the system. The use of additional buses allows the

CPU to transfer information in parallel to a number of devices and so increases the performance of the system.

6.11 Summary

This chapter has been about instructions: what type of instructions make up the instruction set of a processor and how these instructions are executed. The architecture of a hypothetical machine, SAM, was used to clarify some of the concepts involved without getting lost in the details of a real processor. The fetch-execute cycle is the central activity of the CPU. As described, it involves fetching instructions and data from memory (a complex task in itself), decoding the instructions and executing them. The control unit is responsible for the execution of instructions, with the ALU carrying out any required arithmetic or logical operations. The control unit may be hardwired (as with many RISC machines) or it may be micro-programmed (as with many CISC machines). I/O is a fundamental operation in a computer system and different forms of I/O are available such as memory mapped I/O, DMA I/O and interrupt driven I/O.

The next chapter describes mechanisms for improving the performance of the CPU, so that it can execute programs more quickly.

Exercises

6.1 Take any assembly language program you have written or one of the examples in the first part of this text and classify the instructions used, as described in Section 6.2.1.

6.2 Take as large an assembly language program as you can and count the frequency of occurrence of each instruction class (**static instruction count**). Which are the most frequently used instructions?

6.3 Repeat Exercise 6.2, but try to count how many times each class of instruction would actually be executed. In other words, count the number of times instructions are executed in loops (**dynamic instruction count**). Which are the most frequently used instructions?

6.4 Write a SAL code fragment to compute which of the registers `r0` and `r1` has the larger value and store this value in a variable called `max`.

6.5 Trace the execution of the SAL code fragment from Exercise 6.4 in the fashion described in Section 6.6. You may assume that `max` is stored at memory location `0210H`.

6.6 Suggest ways that the encoding of SAM instructions could be made more efficient from a memory usage point of view. (Hint: You may use a one-byte encoding scheme for some instructions.)

6.7 What effect would insisting that all instructions occupy 32 bits have on the efficiency of encoding SAL instructions?

6.8 Redesign the SAM instruction set for a 32-bit processor with 16 registers `r0` to `r15` and with 24-bit memory addressing, specifying how the instructions are encoded.

6.9 What is meant by relative addressing and why is it used?

6.10 Explain how assembly language labels are implemented in machine code.

6.11 Why is micro-programming used in processor design?

6.12 How does memory-mapped I/O operate?

6.13 Explain the importance of interrupts and how they are handled by the CPU.

6.12 Reading list

Baron, R.J. and Higbie, L. (1992) *Computer Architecture*, Addison Wesley, Reading, MA.
Date, C.J. (1983) *Introduction to Database Systems*, Vol. II, Addison Wesley, Reading, MA.
Hennessy, J.L. and Patterson, D.A. (1990) *Computer Architecture A Quantitative Approach*, Morgan Kaufmann, San Mateo, CA.
Feldman, J.M. and Retter C.T. (1994) *Computer Architecture, a Designer's Text Based on a Generic RISC*, McGraw-Hill, New York.
Rafiquzzaman, M. and Chandra R. (1988) *Modern Computer Architecture*, West Publishing Co., St Paul, MN.

7

Enhancing the basic architecture

In Chapter 6 the basic features of a computer's architecture were presented. In this chapter we look at ways of improving the performance of a computer from an architectural perspective. Improving performance, as understood in this chapter, means making programs run faster. This is achieved by looking at ways for executing instructions more quickly. Each instruction takes a certain amount of time to execute, that is, a certain number of clock cycles are required to execute an instruction. The average number of **clock cycles per instruction (CPI)** can be calculated for a program, by dividing the number of clock cycles used by the number of instructions executed. To improve performance, we wish to decrease the CPI or, put another way, we wish to increase the number of instructions executed per clock cycle. For example, we shall describe a system called **pipelining** that greatly speeds up the fetch-execute cycle and in theory allows an instruction to be completed every clock cycle. Another technique (**superscalar** architecture) is to use more than one ALU, so that two instructions can be executed in parallel, which, in theory, can result in executing two instructions per clock cycle. In order to support pipelining and multiple ALUs, instructions and data must be accessible without long delays. Cache memory is a memory system designed to increase the speed at which the processor accesses information.

This chapter also describes the design of RISC machines and compares them to that of CISC machines. This is followed by a brief discussion of computer performance. Finally, a short description of semiconductor technology concludes the chapter.

7.1 The fetch-execute cycle and pipelining

The fetch-execute cycle was described in Chapter 6. Since this cycle represents the fundamental process in the operation of the CPU, attention has been focused on ways of making it more efficient. One possibility is to improve the speed at which instructions and data may be retrieved from memory, since the CPU can process information at a faster rate than it can retrieve it from memory. The use of a cache memory system, which is discussed later, can improve matters in this respect. Another way of improving the efficiency of the fetch-execute cycle is to use a system known as **pipelining**. The basic idea here is to break the fetch-execute cycle into a number of separate stages, so that when one stage is being carried out for a particular instruction, the CPU can carry out another stage for a second instruction, and so on. This idea originates from the assembly line concept used in manufacturing industry.

Consider a simplified car manufacturer's assembly line, as shown in Figure 7.1. The production of a car involves a number of stages, three of which are illustrated. The advantage of the assembly line system is that while one car is going through a particular stage (say stage 6), another car can be going through a different stage (stage 5 or stage 8). In fact, we can have a car in each stage of production *at the same time*. So, for example, if a car goes through ten stages before being completed, then we can have up to ten cars being operated on at the same time on the assembly line. If, for the sake of simplicity, we assume that each stage takes one hour to complete, then it will take ten hours to complete the first car since it will be processed for one hour at every stage on the assembly line. However, when the first car has moved to the second stage of the assembly line, we can start work on a second car at the first stage of the assembly line. When the first car moves on to the third stage, the second car can move on to the second stage and a third car can be started on the first stage of the assembly line. This process continues, so that when the first car reaches the tenth and final stage, there are nine other cars in the first nine stages of production. This means that when the first car is finished after ten hours, then another car will be completed every hour thereafter.

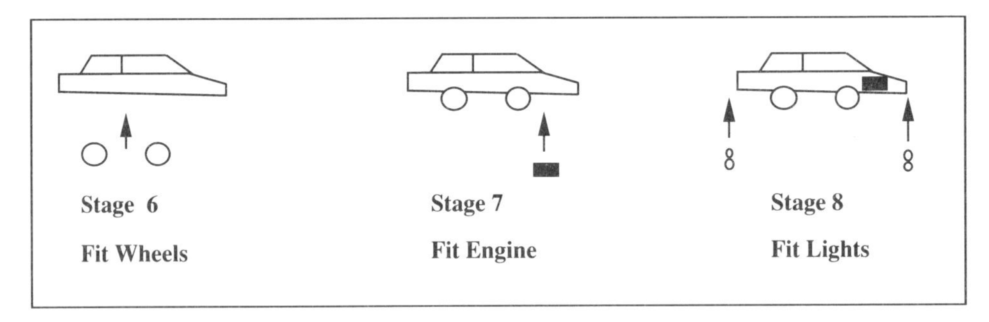

Figure 7.1 Assembly line production.

The great advantage of assembly line production is the increase in **throughput** that is achieved. After the first car is completed we continue production with a throughput of one car per hour. If we did not use an assembly line and worked on one car at a time, each car would take ten hours to produce and the throughput would be one car per ten hours. For example, the time taken to complete 20 cars on the assembly line is 29 hours, while without using the assembly line, the time taken would be 200 hours. It should be noted that each car still requires ten hours of processing on the assembly line, that is, it still takes ten hours of work to produce a car. The point is that, because we are doing the work in stages, we can work on ten cars at the same time, in parallel. The time taken for all stages of the assembly line to become active is called the **flow-through time**, the time for the first car to reach the last stage. Once all the assembly line stages are busy, we achieve maximum throughput.

We have simplified the analysis of the assembly line and, in particular, the assumption that all stages take the same amount of time is not likely to be true.

The stage that takes the longest time to complete creates a bottleneck in an assembly line. For example, if we assume that stage 5 in our car assembly line takes three hours then the throughput decreases to one car per three hours. This is because stage 6 must wait for three hours before it can begin and this delay is passed on to the remaining stages, slowing the time to complete each car to three hours. We can express this by saying the **clock period** of the assembly line (time between completed cars) is three hours. The clock period, denoted by T_p, of an assembly line is given by the formula:

$$T_p = max(t_1, t_2, t_3, ..., t_n)$$

where t_i is the time taken for the ith stage and there are n stages in the assembly line. This means that the clock period is determined by the time taken by the stage that requires the most processing time. In a non-assembly line system, the total time T taken to complete a car is the sum of the time for the individual stages:

$$T = t_1 + t_2 + t_3 + ... + t_n$$

In our example, if all stages take one hour to complete, then $T = 10$ hours and it takes ten hours to complete every car. If stage 5 takes three hours and the other stages take one hour to complete then T rises to 12 hours and it will take 12 hours to complete every car.

We can define the throughput of an assembly line to be $1/T_p$. Using this definition, the throughput for our assembly line where all stages take 1 hour is 1/1, 1 car/hour. If we assume stage 5 takes three hours to complete, the throughput falls to 1/3 or 0.333 cars/hour. For non-assembly line production the respective throughputs are 1/10 or 0.1 cars/hour and 1/12 or 0.083 cars/hour.

Pipelining

Assembly line production is an efficient production system, as is evidenced by its widespread use in industry. The same principle as that of the assembly line can be applied to the fetch-execute cycle of a processor where we refer to it as **pipelining**. In Chapter 6, we described the fetch-execute cycle as consisting of three stages, which are repeated continuously:

(1) Fetch an instruction

(2) Decode the instruction

(3) Execute the instruction

Assuming each stage takes one clock cycle, then in a non-pipelined system, we use three cycles for the first instruction, followed by three cycles for the second instruction and so on, as illustrated in Table 7.1.

Table 7.1 Fetch-execute cycle.

	Cycle 1	Cycle 2	Cycle 3	Cycle 4	Cycle 5	Cycle 6
Instruction 1	Fetch	Decode	Execute			
Instruction 2				Fetch	Decode	Execute

The throughput for such a system would be one instruction per three cycles. If we adopt the assembly line principle, then we can improve the throughput dramatically. Table 7.2 illustrates the fetch-execute cycle employing pipelining.

Table 7.2 Fetch-execute cycle with pipelining.

	Cycle 1	Cycle 2	Cycle 3	Cycle 4	Cycle 5	Cycle 6
Instruction 1	Fetch	Decode	Execute			
Instruction 2		Fetch	Decode	Execute		
Instruction 3			Fetch	Decode	Execute	
Instruction 4				Fetch	Decode	Execute

Using pipelining, we overlap the processing of instructions, so that while the first instruction is in the decode stage, the second instruction is being fetched. While the first instruction is in the execute stage, the second instruction is in the decode stage and the third instruction is being fetched. After three cycles the first instruction is completed and thereafter an instruction is completed on every cycle as opposed to a throughput of three cycles per instruction in a non-pipelined system. Again, as in the assembly line example, each instruction still takes the same number of cycles to complete; the gain comes from the fact that the CPU can operate in parallel on instructions in the different stages. The clock period and throughput of a pipeline are as defined for the assembly line above:

Clock period $T_p = \max(t_1, t_2, t_3, ..., t_n)$ (for an n stage pipeline)

Throughput $= 1/T_p$

The above description is quite simplified, ignoring the fact, for example, that all stages may not be completed in a single cycle. It also omits stages that arise in practice such as an **operand fetch** stage, which is required to fetch an operand from memory, or a **write back** stage to store the result of an ALU operation in a register or in memory. In practice, pipelined systems range from having three to ten stages; for example, Intel's Pentium microprocessor uses a five-stage pipeline for integer instructions.

There are difficulties in pipelining which would not arise on a factory assembly line, due to the nature of computer programs. Consider the following three instructions in a pipeline:

```
        jg       label
        move     y, 0
        move     x, 3
            ......
            ......
label:
```

When the `jg` instruction is being executed, the following two instructions will be in earlier stages, one being fetched and the other being decoded. However, if the `jg` instruction evaluates the condition to be true, it means that the two `move` instructions will not be executed and new instructions have to be loaded, starting at the instruction indicated by `label`. This means that we have to **flush** the pipeline and reload it with new instructions. The time taken to reload the pipeline is called the **branch penalty** and may take several clock cycles. Branch instructions occur very frequently in programs and so it is important to process them as efficiently as possible.

A technique known as **branch prediction** can be used to alleviate the problem of conditional branch instructions, whereby the system 'guesses' the outcome of a conditional branch evaluation before the instruction is evaluated and loads the pipeline appropriately. Depending on how successfully the guess is made, the need for flushing the pipeline can be reduced. When the branch has been evaluated, the processor can take appropriate action if a wrong guess was made. In the event of an incorrect guess, the pipeline will have to be flushed and new instructions loaded. Branch prediction is used on a number of microprocessors, such as the Pentium and PowerPC. Successful guesses, ranging from 80 to 85% of the time, are cited for the Pentium microprocessor. Another technique is to use **delayed branching**. In this case, the instruction following the conditional jump instruction is always executed. For example, if the conditional jump instruction is implementing a loop by jumping backwards, it may be possible to place one of the loop body instructions after the conditional jump instruction. If a useful instruction cannot be placed here, then a `nop` instruction can be used.

So far we have dealt with pipelining in the control unit and such a pipeline is called an **instruction unit** pipeline. Pipelining can also be used in the ALU, where the pipeline is referred to as an **arithmetic unit** pipeline. This speeds up the rate at which arithmetic operations can be carried out. The Pentium, PowerPC and other microprocessors use pipelined FPUs to greatly increase the execution speed of floating-point operations.

7.2 Increasing execution speed: more hardware

Consider the following two instructions:

```
add   i, 10
add   x, y
```

In a simple processor these instructions would be executed in sequence by transferring the operands to the ALU and carrying out the addition operations. One way of speeding things up is to have two ALUs, so that the instructions can be carried out at the same time, the two ALUs carrying out the instructions in parallel. This idea is now widely employed by the current generation of microprocessors, such as the Pentium, PowerPC and Alpha. The term **superscalar** is used to describe an architecture with two or more functional units, which can carry out two or more instructions in the same clock cycle. These may include integer units (IUs), floating-point units (FPUs) and branch processing units (BPUs, devoted to handling branch instructions). The **micro-architecture** of a hypothetical superscalar processor is illustrated in

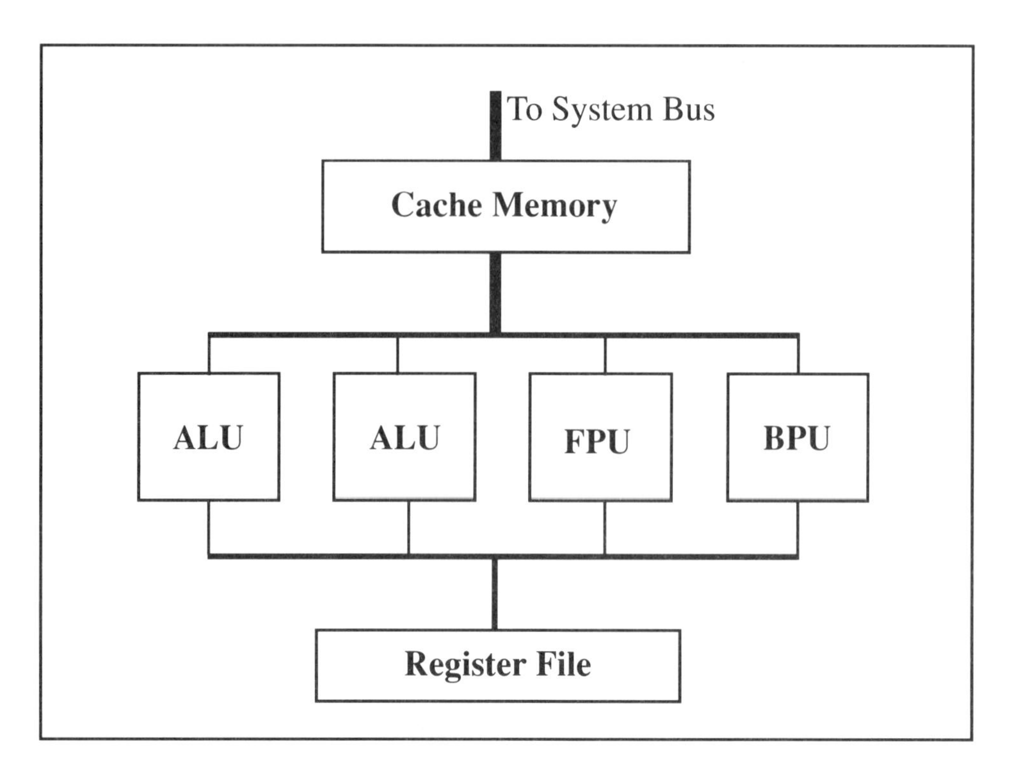

Figure 7.2 Micro-architecture of a superscalar processor.

Figure 7.2. The term micro-architecture is used to refer to the internal architecture of a processor.

The processor shown in Figure 7.2 has four execution units and could execute four instructions concurrently, in theory. The register file is the collective name given to the CPU's registers. A processor with an on-chip FPU would have a separate set of floating-point registers (**FPR**s) in addition to the usual general purpose registers (**GPR**s). The cache memory is used to speed up the processor's access to instructions and data (see Section 7.4.2). The extra functional units allow the CPU carry out more operations per clock cycle. Table 7.3 illustrates the fetch-execute cycle for a superscalar architecture, with **two** functional units operating in parallel.

Table 7.3 Superscalar architecture fetch-execute cycle.

	Cycle 1	Cycle 2	Cycle 3	Cycle 4	Cycle 5	Cycle 6
Instruction 1	Fetch	Decode	Execute			
Instruction 2	Fetch	Decode	Execute			
Instruction 3		Fetch	Decode	Execute		
Instruction 4		Fetch	Decode	Execute		
Instruction 5			Fetch	Decode	Execute	
Instruction 6			Fetch	Decode	Execute	
Instruction 7				Fetch	Decode	Execute
Instruction 8				Fetch	Decode	Execute

As can be seen from Table 7.3, two instructions are in each stage of the pipeline at the same time, doubling the throughput of the pipeline, *in theory*. If we consider cycle 3 we can see that the processor is handling six stages of six instructions at the same time. In practice, this can give rise to a number of problems, since there are situations that arise which mean that instructions cannot be executed in parallel. One problem that arises is that of **inter-instruction dependencies**. Consider the following three instructions:

```
sub  r1, x
add  r1, 2
sub  r0, r3
```

The first two instructions (`add` and `sub`) cannot be carried out in parallel as they both modify the same operand, `r1`, giving rise to a **data dependency**. A data dependency arises between two instructions if the destination operand of one instruction is accessed by the other instruction. In this particular example, a solution called **instruction reordering** (**scheduling**) is possible because by reordering the instructions in the sequence:

```
sub  r1, x
sub  r0, r3
add  r1, 2
```

the two `sub` instructions can now be executed in parallel, since their operands do not conflict with each other. This is a software solution and can be implemented by a compiler, when translating a program to machine code. The compiler software must be aware of the processor's superscalar architecture for this solution to be implemented. This is why **processor-aware compilers** and **native compilers** are very important, if programs are to take advantage of the advanced features of a processor. A **processor-aware** compiler is capable of producing efficient code for more than one processor, such as an Intel 80486 and a Pentium. A **native** compiler is designed to generate efficient code for a specific processor. So, although a compiler that only generates code for an Intel 80386 can also be used on a PC with Intel's Pentium processor, the code produced will not perform nearly as well as code produced by a native Pentium compiler.

There are various rules used by each microprocessor that determine which instructions can be issued in parallel and to which units they may be issued. For example, it may be possible to execute integer and floating-point instructions in parallel on one machine, while on another it may only be possible to issue two integer instructions in parallel. There may be rules such as preventing a jump instruction from being issued in parallel with another instruction. So, while in (simplified) theory a superscalar architecture doubles the throughput of a pipeline, in practice this is not achieved, although a significant improvement is produced. Processors may also provide special logic that facilitates the parallel execution of instructions. As an example, the Pentium provides such logic for handling updates to the flags register because many instructions modify the flags register. This logic operates so that, even if two instructions that update the flags register execute in parallel, they have the same effect on the register as if they were executed sequentially.

The number of functional units for a superscalar architecture typically varies from three to five, while the number of instructions that a machine may issue in a cycle typically varies from one to three. An important implication of the superscalar fetch-execute pipeline, as illustrated in Table 7.3, is that since two instructions are fetched at the same time, the CPU bus must be wide enough to transfer the two instructions to the control unit. It is important to point out that pipelining and superscalar designs require rapid access to data and instructions if they are to be successful in improving performance. The provision of on-chip cache memory, as described later, facilitates such rapid access.

Another very important technique for increasing a computer's performance is the use of more than one processor in a computer system, as for example, in a **multiprocessor** or **parallel** computer. Such machines may have from two to many thousands of interconnected processors. Each processor may have its own private memory or they may share a common memory. One of the difficulties with such machines is the development of software to take advantage of their parallel nature. It is important to note that such machines will only yield significant performance gains if the problems they are being used to handle can be expressed in a parallel form. The manipulation of matrices is one such problem. For example, given two 10 000 element matrices, which have to be summed to produce a third matrix, and a parallel machine with 10 000 processors, one processor can be dedicated to the addition of each pair of elements. Thus, in crude terms, the computation can be carried out in the time taken for the addition of one pair of elements, since the 10 000 processors can carry out the operation in parallel. The same operation on a conventional processor would require the time taken for all 10 000 additions. The performance gain is striking, but it must be stressed that this example is precisely suited to a parallel machine. A major design issue in the construction of parallel computers is how the processors communicate with each other and with memory. Various solutions, such as **crossbar** connections and **hypercube** connections, are possible. The area of parallel computing is a major field of computer science and the interested reader may consult some texts referenced at the end of the chapter for further information.

7.3 Increasing execution speed: faster clock

The clock speed of a computer determines the rate at which the CPU operates. It is measured in megahertz (MHz) or millions of cycles per second. Early microcomputers had a clock in the low MHz range, for example 1 to 4 MHz. With advancing chip technology, higher and higher clock speeds have been obtained. Standard personal computers currently run at typical speeds in the 25 to 66 MHz range, while the more powerful ones run at speeds up to 200 MHz. At the time of writing versions of Digital's Alpha run at 200 MHz, Intel's Pentium runs at speeds from 66 to 120 MHz and the IBM/Motorola PowerPC at 80 MHz. Manufacturers release different versions of a microprocessor which operate at different clock rates, with other features such as cache capacity also varying. The higher-performance versions are sold at higher prices.

To gain some insight into clock speed, consider a 100 MHz clock rate. At 100 MHz, each clock cycle takes one hundredth of a millionth of a second, which is 0.01 ms or 10 ns. Light travels at about one foot per nanosecond, so one clock cycle of a 100 MHz clock takes the same amount of time as the time light takes to travel ten feet! As mentioned above, Digital's Alpha microprocessor uses a 200 MHz clock and it is anticipated that clock speeds will continue to increase in the coming years. It should be noted that increasing the clock speed does not guarantee significant performance gains. This is because the speed of the processor is effectively determined by the rate at which it can fetch instructions and data from memory. Thus if the processor spends 90% of its time waiting on memory, the performance gained by doubling the processor speed (without improving the memory access time) is only 5%. For example, assume a task takes 100 units of time, and 90 units are spent waiting on memory access, with 10 units spent on CPU processing. By doubling the CPU speed, CPU processing time is reduced to 5 units and so the overall time is reduced to 95 time units, a 5% improvement. It is obviously important then to reduce the time the CPU has to wait for memory accesses. The processor will also usually have to wait for I/O operations to complete and, indeed, it is usually the case that I/O speeds determine the speed of program execution. Recall that it is of the order of 100 000 times slower to retrieve data from disk than it is to retrieve it from memory. This means that for programs that carry out I/O, the processor is idle most of the time, waiting for the I/O operations to complete. This, in turn, means that using a more powerful processor to execute such programs results in very little gain in overall execution speed.

7.4 Improving memory access time

In Chapter 6, we mentioned the von Neumann bottleneck, which is caused by the mismatch in speed between the CPU and memory. The CPU can process data at a low-nanosecond rate while RAM can only deliver it at a high-nanosecond rate. For example, if RAM delivers data to the CPU at a rate of 100 ns per data item (10 million items per second!) and the CPU can consume data at say 5 ns per item, then the CPU will still spend 95% of its time waiting on memory. Designers have come up with a number of mechanisms for improving memory access time (the time taken to complete one memory access). One such mechanism involves the use of **parallel memory architectures**, which allow a number of items to be accessed in memory at the same time. Another more important mechanism involves the use of a **cache memory system**.

7.4.1 *Parallel memory architectures*

Parallel memories fall into two classes: **banked memory** and **interleaved memory**. In a banked memory system, memory is divided into a number of independent segments called banks. Each memory bank will have its own address and data registers as well as independent buses, so that while one memory bank is being accessed for one data item, the other memory bank may be simultaneously accessed for another data item. Figure 7.3 illustrates the situation for a system employing two memory banks.

The system illustrated in Figure 7.3 allows the processor to access simultaneously information stored in the two banks, provided one of the items referenced is located in bank 0 and the other item is in bank 1. However, if the CPU needs to access two items located in the same bank, it must do so sequentially.

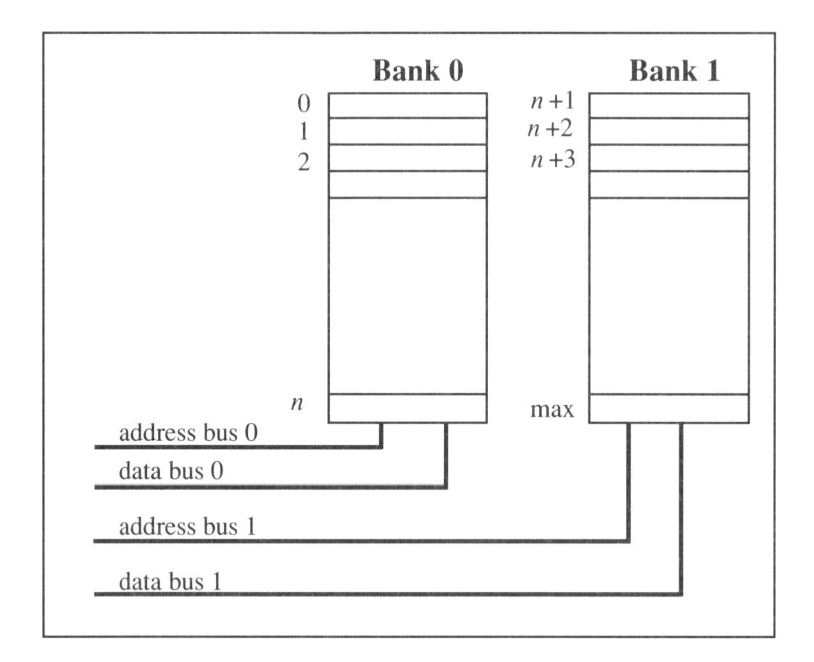

Figure 7.3 Banked memory.

Unfortunately, owing to the nature of computer programs, this occurs quite often, since instructions tend to be stored and accessed sequentially in memory. (In fact, cache memory works very well precisely because of this.)

Interleaved memory attempts to alleviate this problem. It has a similar structure to banked memory, but memory addresses alternate between the memory banks. Figure 7.4 illustrates the configuration for an interleaved memory system consisting of three memory banks. As with banked memory, the processor can have three memory accesses in operation, in parallel. Because the memory addresses are interleaved, it is more likely that the processor will be

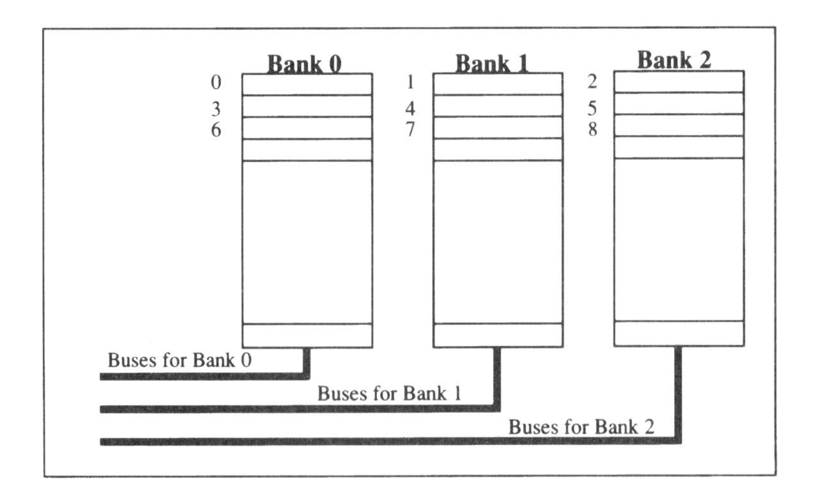

Figure 7.4 Interleaved memory.

able to take advantage of this parallelism. So, for example, if access is required to locations 4 and 5, they can be accessed in parallel, since they are in different memory banks.

Banked and interleaved memory architectures are one approach to improving memory access times. Another very important mechanism for improving memory access time is the use of cache memory, which can be employed with a normal memory architecture or in conjunction with banked or interleaved memory architectures.

7.4.2 *Cache memory*

The processor operates at its maximum speed if the data to be processed is in its registers. Unfortunately, register storage capacity is very limited and so memory is used to store programs and data. One, very effective, way of overcoming the slow access time of main memory is to design a faster intermediate memory system that lies between the CPU and main memory. Such memory is called **cache** memory (or simply cache) and it may be visualized as in Figure 7.5.

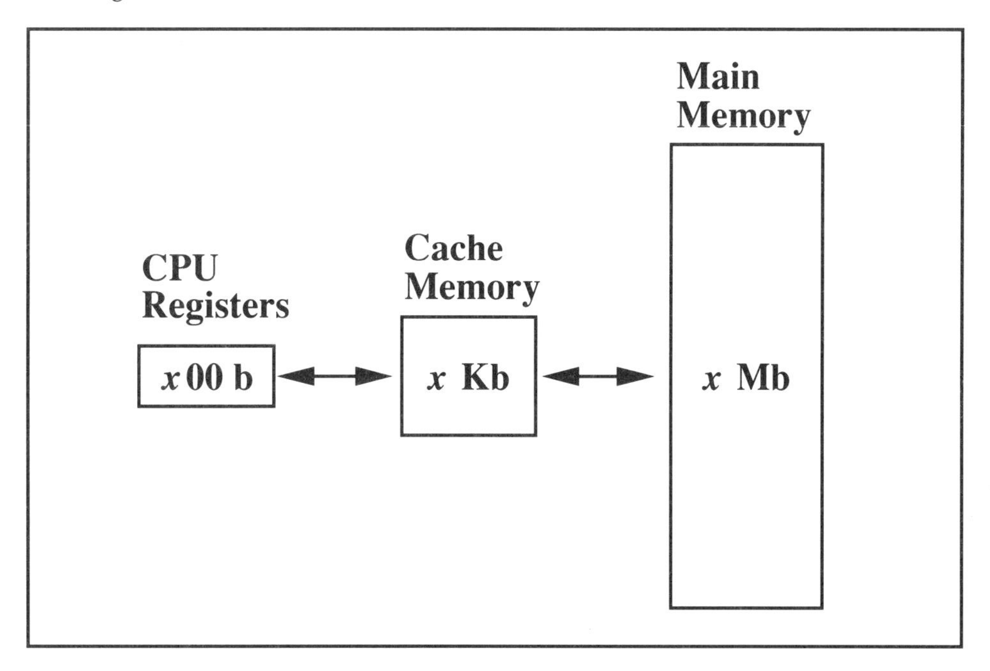

Figure 7.5 Cache memory: early systems had small cache memory systems measured in kilobytes, compared to today's megabyte cache memory systems.

Cache memory is high-speed memory (usually static RAM – SRAM), which can be accessed much more quickly than normal memory (usually dynamic RAM – DRAM). It has a smaller capacity than main memory and it holds recently accessed data from main memory. The cache memory system is usually not visible to the programmer (although some RISC machines may allow programmers to access cache memory). The reason why cache memory works so well in improving performance is due to what is known as the **principle of**

locality of reference. This roughly means that, having accessed a particular location in memory, it is highly likely that you will subsequently access neighbouring memory locations. This is because:

- programs tend to execute instructions sequentially and instructions are stored in neighbouring memory locations;
- programs often have loops, whereby a group of neighbouring instructions are repeatedly executed;
- arrays of data elements get accessed sequentially.

As a result, when an instruction or data element is fetched from memory, if you also fetch its neighbouring instructions or data elements and store them in cache memory, then it is very likely that the next item to be fetched will be in cache memory and can be obtained very quickly, relative to accessing it in main memory.

Cache memory operates so that when the CPU initiates a memory access (for data or an instruction), the cache memory is first checked to see if the information is already there. (Cache memory is designed so that it can be checked very quickly to ascertain if an item is stored in it.) If it is there (called a **cache hit**), it can be transferred to the CPU very quickly. If the information is not in cache memory (a **cache miss**), then a normal memory access occurs, but the information is passed to both the CPU and the cache memory. In addition, while the CPU is using the information, the cache memory system fetches nearby information from memory, independently of the CPU, so that if neighbouring information is required (a likely event), then it will already be in cache memory and can be accessed very quickly. If enough cache memory is available, the instructions making up a loop in a program could be stored in cache. This would mean that the loop could be executed an arbitrary number of times without causing any memory fetches for instructions, after the instructions have been initially fetched. This can yield great improvements in program execution speeds.

In this way a cache hit rate of 90% and greater is possible, that is, 90% or more of information requested by the CPU is found in cache memory, without the CPU having to access main memory. The speed of a memory system using cache memory is the weighted average of the cache speed and the main memory speed. For example, assume a 100 ns delay for main memory and 20 ns delay for cache memory with a 90% hit rate. Then the apparent speed of memory access is

$$(0.9 * 20) + (0.1 * 100) = 28 \text{ ns}$$

This is a significant improvement in memory access performance, since the access time is now on average 28 ns as opposed to 100 ns if cache memory is not used.

Cache memory is now also included on the CPU chip (**on-chip cache**) of many microprocessors such as Intel's 40486 and Pentium microprocessors, Digital's Alpha microprocessor and the IBM/Apple PowerPC microprocessor. Since the cache memory is on the CPU chip, the speed of cache memory access is improved over that of **off-chip** cache memory. The capacity of on-chip cache memory varies from 8 kb to around 32 kb at the moment, while **off-chip** cache memory may range from x00 kb to a few megabytes; for example, Digital's Alpha 21064 microprocessor provides 16 kb on-chip cache memory and supports up to 16 Mb off-chip cache memory. On the other hand, all modern microprocessors do not provide on-chip cache memory, for example, Hewlett-Packard's PA7100 microprocessor provides 3 Mb off-chip cache memory, instead of utilizing on-chip cache memory.

Computers may use separate memories to store instructions and data and such an architecture is called a **Harvard architecture** because this idea emerged from machines built at Harvard University. Instructions and data may be stored in the same cache memory which is referred to as a **unified cache** memory. Alternatively, separate caches for instructions and data may be maintained along the lines of the Harvard architecture. The advantage of the Harvard architecture is that instructions and data can be fetched simultaneously, in parallel, since they will be connected to the other CPU components by separate buses. Cache memory is essential for processors employing pipelining and superscalar designs, to provide instructions and data at the high rate required by these designs.

7.5 CISC and RISC machines

In the current and previous chapter we have described the architecture of computers in general, although our description is best suited to microprocessor-based systems. We have described the instruction set, how instructions are executed and how they are retrieved from memory. In this chapter, we have described mechanisms for improving the performance of computers, such as pipelining and using cache memory. In the 1980s a new approach to the design of microprocessors was developed with the introduction of what has become known as a RISC (Reduced Instruction Set Computer) architecture, in contrast to the dominant machine architecture of the time, now referred to as a CISC (Complex Instruction Set Computer) architecture. CISC machines still dominate computer sales and include Digital VAXs, PCs using Intel's 8086 family of microprocessors, as well as systems based on Motorola's 68000 processors. RISC processors are widely used in workstations, such as Sun's SuperSparc machines, Digital's Alpha-based machines and Hewlett Packard's PA7100-based machines, and in Apple's PowerMac series, which is based on the PowerPC microprocessor.

There is no precise definition of what constitutes a RISC architecture. Instead of attempting such a definition, the following is a list of a number of features common to most RISC architectures:

- smaller number of instructions than used in CISC instruction sets;
- simpler instruction format to that of CISC instructions;
- instructions all of same length as opposed to variable length CISC instructions;
- load/store architecture;
- fewer and simpler addressing modes than available on CISC processors;
- execute one instruction per clock cycle (in general);
- larger number of registers than is available on CISC processors.

RISC machines use all of the techniques for increasing processor speed described in this chapter, such as pipelining, cache memory and multiple functional units (superscalar architecture). In fact, it is argued that the simpler fixed-length instructions are more suited to pipelined execution.

One of the underlying motivations behind RISC architectures was the realization in the 1980s that the machine code generated by compilers only uses a limited number of the instructions of any machine's (CISC at the time) instruction set. In addition, only a small number of addressing modes are used in compiler-generated code. This led to the notion of designing machines with the fewer, but frequently used, instructions and addressing modes that compilers used. Analysis of compiler-generated code reveals that the most frequently used instructions are those for data movement (some form of `move` instruction). Next in line come the comparison and branch instructions followed by procedure call instructions. Near the end of the list come arithmetic and logical instructions, making up only a few per cent of instruction counts. The RISC philosophy is to optimize frequently executed instructions. So, while CISC processors may have upwards from 200 instructions and between 10 and 20 different addressing modes, RISC processors typically have less than 100 instructions and only a few addressing modes. This allows RISC instructions to be encoded in a simple format. RISC instructions are also of fixed length which makes them very suitable for pipelining purposes, whereas most CISC processors use variable-length instructions. A variable-length instruction makes better use of storage as an instruction can be the precise length required from one byte to many bytes. However, this compact encoding of instructions makes for a more complex processor control unit, which has to decode the variable-length instructions.

In the case of a RISC processor, because the instructions are of a simpler fixed length format with simpler addressing modes, a hard-wired control unit can be used to process the instructions very quickly. CISC control units are typically micro-programmed, which is one of the reasons why a large number of instructions can be provided in the first place. With a micro-programmed control unit, the designer can easily add new instructions by creating appropriate micro-programs for the instructions. In this way, designers created a large variety of instructions in an effort to make processors more effective. The idea was that the compiler could choose a single instruction designed to carry out a complex operation, as opposed to using a sequence of simpler instructions. As an example, consider the C statement:

```
a = b + c ;
```

This could be translated to a single CISC instruction as:

```
add  a, b, c
```

whereas a typical RISC version might look like:

```
load   r1, b        ; r1 = b
load   r2, c        ; r2 = c
add    r1, r2       ; r1 = r1 + r2
store  c, r1        ; c = r1
```

The CISC version is much simpler for people to write and understand, but it is much more complex from a hardware standpoint, requiring that two operands (b and c) be fetched from memory, summed and the result stored in memory. Thus, the single CISC instruction requires that a number of hardware steps be carried out. The RISC version for the same operation is made up of four simple instructions. In the RISC case, each instruction requires that only one hardware operation be carried out. The RISC code fragment also illustrates the **load/store** architecture design, whereby memory operands must be explicitly loaded into registers before they can be processed by arithmetic or logical instructions. Thus, all arithmetic and logical instructions operate on register operands and the results must be explicitly stored in memory if required. An advantage of the load/store architecture is that, because RISC machines have more registers available, an operand may be kept in a register for a longer period of time than on a machine which has only a few registers. So, once an operand has been loaded into a register from memory, it is possible that it will be used a number of times, which means that only a single load operation may be required to provide repeated access to the memory operand. CISC machines, on the other hand, have fewer registers and will probably require more memory operand fetches.

While it is obvious that the RISC code above uses more instructions, it can be more efficient for a number of reasons. First, the instructions, because they are simpler, can be executed in a single clock cycle. Second, they are very suitable for a pipelined architecture, which, as mentioned earlier, increases execution efficiency. On the other hand, the CISC version can be coded to occupy fewer bytes of storage, so a CISC program will tend to take up less RAM storage than a RISC program. In the early years of computing and right up until the 1980s, RAM was an expensive resource and every effort was made to use it efficiently. CISC instruction encoding schemes took account of this and were designed to give a very compact encoding of programs. However, since the 1980s, RAM has become much cheaper and is available in much larger quantities. This means that compact instruction encoding is no longer as important as it was and designers now strive to make program execution faster, even though more memory may be required to store programs.

An important point about CISC micro-programmed control units is that they allow designers to change the underlying hardware (taking advantage of technology improvements) without impacting on the end-user; only the micro-programs need be changed. So a manufacturer can introduce a new processor with extra capabilities and new instructions to take advantage of these capabilities, while still providing the instruction set of a previous processor. This allows computer manufacturers to produce new and more powerful systems that are compatible with earlier systems used by customers. The success of the IBM 360/370 series is but one example of the importance of maintaining upward compatibility between different members of a computing family. Intel and Motorola provide similar upward compatibility with their 8086 and 68000 microprocessor series (all CISC machines). The importance of upward compatibility should not be underestimated. So, while new design techniques may be attractive and older designs may have serious limitations, the presence of a customer base for a particular machine X is always a strong influence for retaining X's design. Users will typically have large quantities of data (often accumulated over years) stored in a form supported by the machine's software. If these users are to contemplate changing machine for a higher-performance model, then they have to be satisfied that they can take their software and its associated data to the new machine. Compatibility, in essence, means that this is possible with little effort.

There is much debate about the relative merits of CISC and RISC architectures, the so-called RISC/CISC controversy. Many of the features mentioned above (pipelining, single cycle instruction execution, cache memory and so on) are also available on CISC machines. The debate can be highly technical and detailed as well as very confusing. It is certainly not abundantly clear if either architectural approach is greatly superior to the other. Given developments in chip technology that allow the design of complex processors (such as the Pentium – a CISC architecture – which employs features associated with RISC machines), perhaps the future points to the development of microprocessors combining the best of both the RISC and CISC worlds. Another possibility is that RISC processors, such as the PowerPC, using software that **emulates** the 80*x*86 CISC architecture, will gain widespread usage. Emulation is an old computer technique for allowing a new machine to replace an older one, by emulating the instruction set of the older machine. The emulated instructions will not run as quickly as the new machine's native instructions, but the important point is that they allow customers to take to the new machine the software they wish to use. The loss in performance resulting from emulation may be compensated by the high speed of modern RISC machines. For example, a RISC processor capable of executing 100 million instructions per second, could suffer a threefold degradation in speed and still operate at very acceptable speeds when compared to standard PC speeds. The PowerPC goal is that PC users can use all of their PC software, in addition to being able to use, say, Macintosh software and Unix software, on the same machine. This concept is certainly attractive to users; what remains to be seen is how well the concept is implemented and marketed, as well as the reaction of competitors in the market.

One point is clear for the moment and that is that CISC machines are not going to vanish in the foreseeable future. Tredennick (1993) in a very interesting article makes the point that CISC machines (dominating the PC market of 30 million units per year) have a very strong marketing advantage over RISC machines (which dominate the workstation market of 0.5 million workstations per year), given the relative sizes of the markets they dominate. In addition, there are many competing RISC CPU manufacturers for the relatively small workstation market, while there are only a few CISC CPU manufacturers (dominated by Intel and Motorola) for the larger PC market. [Tredennick also makes the interesting point that the vast majority of processors (around 1.8 billion in 1993) are 4-bit and 8-bit processors and they are not used in end-user computers but in embedded control systems such as in domestic appliances and cars.] Tredennick argues that it will be difficult for RISC manufacturers to recover development costs and make significant profits from the small workstation market and that a move to the larger PC market is difficult, given the huge customer base for current PC hardware and software technology. Stallings (1990) provides a very interesting collection of papers dealing with many aspects of RISC machines.

7.6 Measuring computer performance

So far in this chapter, we have mentioned the term **performance** a number of times. We have not actually defined what we meant by performance, but assumed that if we can increase the rate at which instructions may be executed and the rate at which data may be obtained from memory, then the performance of the computer will improve. In this section we wish to discuss the notion of computer performance. In particular, we want to look at how we can compare the performance of different computer *systems*. It is important to consider the performance of a computer *system* as a whole, including both the hardware and software and not just to consider the performance of the components of the system in isolation. It is very important to understand that measuring computer performance is a very difficult problem. There are a number of criteria that can be used for measuring the performance of a computer system and it is a non-trivial matter as to how to weigh up the relative importance of these criteria when comparing two computer systems. In addition, it is not easy to obtain totally objective information about different manufacturers' machines or to get the information in a form that makes it easy to use for comparison purposes.

Before looking at the performance of computer systems, let us consider the notion of performance by looking at a different area such as the automobile industry. How is the performance of cars measured? First, there is no one overall measure of performance. A number of performance criteria are used such as the following: fuel consumption; engine size; top speed; rate of acceleration; passenger capacity; comfort features; safety features; maintenance cost; warranty.

A prospective customer must weigh up the criteria that are important for their particular needs. But the buyer must beware! For example, take fuel consumption as an important metric. The actual fuel consumed depends on the driving conditions, the passenger and luggage load and the way the car is driven. So, someone spending a lot of time in rush-hour traffic will use more fuel than the typical rural driver. On the other hand, a rural driver may like travelling at high speeds, which also means a higher rate of fuel consumption. The rate of fuel consumption quoted by a salesman may be the optimal one, obtained under ideal driving conditions, at a slow speed. Such a rate is likely to vary considerably from that obtained under real driving conditions. Thus, the quoted fuel consumption figures may not be an accurate guide to the real consumption obtained under the conditions relevant to a particular customer. Similar caveats apply to other performance measures such as acceleration, top speed and maintenance costs.

A similar list of criteria may be constructed for almost anything you wish to buy: a computer system, a lawn mower or a new house. At the time of writing, I am purchasing a new lawn mower and I am amazed by the number of features that distinguish different machines. The task facing a prospective buyer is to weigh up the criteria that are important for their needs and to buy the model that best matches these criteria. This may often come down to a subjective decision since the following scenario may present itself. You are making a choice between Machines 1, 2, 3 and 4 and your criteria are A, B, C, D and E. The result of your evaluation of the machines is given in Table 7.4.

Table 7.4 Evaluation: making a decision.

	A	B	C	D	E
Machine 1	Good	Good	Good	Medium	Bad
Machine 2	Medium	Good	Good	Fair	Medium
Machine 3	Medium	Medium	Medium	Medium	Good
Machine 4	Good	Good	Good	Good	Good

You find Machine 1 satisfies A, B and C very well, it reasonably satisfies D and does not satisfy E. Machine 2 satisfies B and C very well, reasonably satisfies A and E, but barely satisfies D. Machine 3 satisfies E very well and all other criteria reasonably well. Finally, Machine 4 satisfies all criteria very well. Which machine do you choose? Machine 4 seems an obvious choice but is five times more expensive than any of the other machines and, although you can afford it, you may wonder if you can get by with a cheaper machine. In that case, it depends on how much weight you attach to the different criteria. If E represents safety, then Machine 1 might be ruled out and, if safety is the most important criterion, then Machine 3 would be a strong candidate. If criteria B and C are very important, then Machine 2 may be a strong candidate. The point being made is that frequently there is no obvious choice and the decision comes down to how much weight is attached to the respective criteria.

One of the common points about buying any piece of equipment, be it a car, lawn mower, dishwasher or computer system, is that the sales people typically quote the optimal performance features of the product they are selling. It is the customer's responsibility to relate this information to their specific requirements. This is not a criticism of sales people, who, after all, are employed to sell their products! One popular and very useful way of evaluating equipment is to test it on a trial basis. This gives you the opportunity to see it operate under the actual conditions of your environment. This is an ideal way of comparing different machines. However, it may not always be feasible to do this. A car salesman may be happy to let you take a test drive, but is unlikely to allow you to take the car home for a week! The next best approach is to see the equipment in use, in as similar as possible environment to your own and to get feedback from its users.

When it comes to evaluating computer system performance, everything we have said above applies. For home computers, it may be possible to borrow a friend's machine to evaluate it. But when it comes to larger computer systems, it is more difficult to get an opportunity to have a 'trial run'. Installing the software you require may be a time-consuming and complex task, which may prohibit the possibility of a trial run. However, unless you are involved in very specialist areas, it should be possible to see the prospective system in operation in a similar environment to your own. This can provide you with invaluable performance information.

7.6.1 Computer performance metrics

There are a number of ways of measuring the performance of a computer system or, indeed, that of the components that make up a computer system. One common measure is processor speed. The question of how to measure processor speed is not as simple as it appears. One simple measure is the number of instructions that can be executed per second, expressed in millions of instructions per second or **MIPS**. So, a given processor may have a processor speed of 5 MIPS, that is, it can execute five million instructions per second. But, wait, all instructions do not take the same amount of execution time. An instruction to clear a register may take one clock cycle. A multiplication instruction might take more than ten clock cycles. Obviously a processor which is capable of executing five million multiplication instructions per second is faster than one which is capable of executing five million clear register instructions per second, but the MIPS rate is the same! The way to compute the MIPS rate more usefully is to calculate the average time the processor takes to execute its instructions, weighted by the frequency with which each instruction is used. However, the frequency of instruction usage depends on the software being used. So, for example, word-processing software would not require much use of a multiplication instruction, whereas spreadsheet software would be more likely to use many multiplication instructions. When we compare the MIPS rate of two different machines, we must ensure that they are counting the same type of instructions. Another problem with the MIPS metric is that the amount of work an individual instruction carries out varies from processor to processor. For example, a single VAX `add` instruction is capable of adding two 32-bit memory variables and storing the result in a third memory variable, whereas a machine such as the 8086 requires three instructions (an `add` and two `mov` instructions) to accomplish the same task. Naively counting the number of `add` instructions that can be executed per second on these two machine will not give a true picture of either machine's performance.

We must also remember to take account of the processor word size when comparing instruction counts. A 32-bit processor is a more powerful machine than a 16-bit processor with the same MIPS rate, since it can operate on 32-bit operands as opposed to 16-bit operands. Similarly, a 64-bit processor will be more powerful than a 32-bit processor with the same MIPS rating. Computer manufacturers are likely to quote the optimal MIPS rate referred to as the **peak** MIPS rate in much the same way as car manufacturers quote optimal fuel consumption rates. Early PCs operated at speeds of about 0.3 MIPS, while a Pentium-powered PC operates from 100 MIPS upwards.

Another metric that is similar to the MIPS rate is the **FLOPS** or floating-point operations per second rate, which is expressed in megaFLOPS (MFLOPS) and gigaFLOPS (GFLOPS). This metric is particularly used for machines targeted at the scientific/engineering community, where much applications software requires large amounts of floating-point arithmetic. The idea is to count operations as opposed to instructions, since it might be assumed that a given program will carry out a specific number of floating-point operations on different machines, although the number of instructions executed on the machines may differ. A problem with the FLOPS metric is that different machines provide different floating-point operations, and indeed some floating-point operations are executed more quickly than others (compare addition and division). Like the MIPS metric, the FLOPS metric needs to be approached with caution.

The MIPS and MFLOPS metrics are concerned with processor speed. The processor is a crucial component of a computer system when it comes to performance measurement but it is not the only one and, in fact, it may not be the determining factor of the performance of a system. Other components are the memory and I/O devices, whose performances are also crucial to the overall system performance. For example, a database application may require searching for information among millions of records stored on hard disk. The dominant performance metric for such an application is the speed of disk I/O operations. In such an application, the CPU spends most of its time waiting for disk I/O operations to complete. If we use a faster processor without increasing the speed of the disk I/O operations, then the overall improvement in performance will be negligible.

I/O performance may be measured in terms of the number of megabytes that can be transferred per second (I/O bandwidth). This can be deceptive, as the maximum transfer rate quoted may not be achieved in practice. Take disk I/O; if the information required is stored on different tracks, then the seek time to move the head to the required tracks will slow I/O down considerably, whereas, if the information is on the same track, it can be transferred much more quickly. Another measure is the number of I/O operations that can be completed per second, which can take account of the fact that the information may not be conveniently available on disk.

Memory performance is often measured in terms of its access time, that is, the time taken to complete a memory write or read operation, which is in the 20 to 100 ns range. The amount of memory present is also a very important factor in system performance. The larger the amount of memory present, the lower the likelihood that page faults will occur in a virtual-memory system.

Overall system performance is determined by the performance of the processor, memory and I/O devices as well as the operating system and applications software performance. One measure of system performance that takes account of the processor, memory and I/O performance is the number of **transactions** per second (**TPS**) that the system can cope with. A transaction may be defined, for example, as the amount of work required to retrieve a customer record from disk, update the record and write it back to disk, as modelled on a typical bank transaction.

Another way of measuring computer system performance is to compare it to a known computer system such as a Digital VAX. One such unit is the **VUP** or VAX unit of performance based on the performance of a specific VAX configuration. So, a system whose performance is evaluated to be 10 VUPs would be expected to be better than one with a performance of 5 VUPs.

System performance can also be evaluated by writing **benchmark** programs and running the same benchmark program on a series of machines. A benchmark program is one written to measure some aspect of a computer's performance. For example, it might consist of a loop to carry out one million floating-point additions or a loop to carry out a million random read and write operations on a disk file. The time taken to execute the benchmark program gives a measure of the computer system's performance. By constructing a number of such programs for the different aspects of a systems performance, a suite of benchmarks may be developed that allows different computer systems to be compared. Benchmark programs are also used to test the performance of systems software such as compilers. The size of the executable file produced by the compiler and the efficiency of the machine code are two metrics that are used to compare compilers. Another system performance measure is the **SPECmark** which is obtained in a similar fashion to the use of benchmark programs, except that, instead of using contrived benchmark programs, a suite of ten real world application programs are used (these include a compiler application, a nuclear reactor simulation and a quantum chemistry application). SPECmarks are used by companies such as Sun and Hewlett Packard to measure the performance of their workstations.

One difficulty about using benchmarks and SPECmarks to evaluate system performance is that you are dependent on a compiler to translate the programs into efficient machine code for the computer under evaluation. However, compilers are not all equally efficient and, particularly with the advent of new processor features such as multiple functional units capable of parallel operation, compiler writers have a complex task in designing good so-called **optimizing** compilers. The code produced by a poor quality compiler can run significantly slower and use more memory than code produced by a good compiler. A computer manufacturer may have benchmark programs optimized for a particular machine so that the machine's performance is apparently superior to another machine running the same benchmark programs which have not, however, been optimized for the second machine! *Caveat emptor* ('Let the buyer beware').

In addition to the effects of the compiler, the operating system will also influence the performance of a computer system. In the case where two computer systems running different operating systems are being evaluated, care must be taken to ensure that both operating systems are properly configured. For example, a good machine with an efficient operating system may perform poorly as a result of having insufficient memory allocated to user programs, in comparison to a less powerful machine which has been expertly tuned to run its programs.

Other non-performance issues that arise when comparing computer systems are the actual cost of the system and its reliability, together with the availability of hardware and software support. Computer systems *fail* as a result of either hardware or software problems, or both. It is fundamentally important to take account of computing failures, from the moment of evaluating a new system right through to its day to day operation. There is no point in having the most sophisticated computer system in the world if, *when* it fails, you cannot get it operational again in a short period of time.

In summary, evaluating computer system performance is fraught with difficulties and the use of apparently simple metrics such as MIPS and MFLOPS can be quite misleading. The reality is that there is no easy alternative to that of running real world application programs (preferably the ones you wish to use) and choosing the system which best matches the performance criteria that you have laid down.

7.7 From silicon to CPUs!

One of the most fundamental components in the manufacture of electronic devices, such as a CPU or memory, is a **switch**. Computers are constructed from thousands to millions of switches connected together. In modern computers, components called **transistors** act as electronic switches. A brief look at the history of computing reveals a movement from mechanical to electromechanical to electronic to solid state electronic components being used as switches to construct more and more powerful computers as illustrated in Figure 7.6.

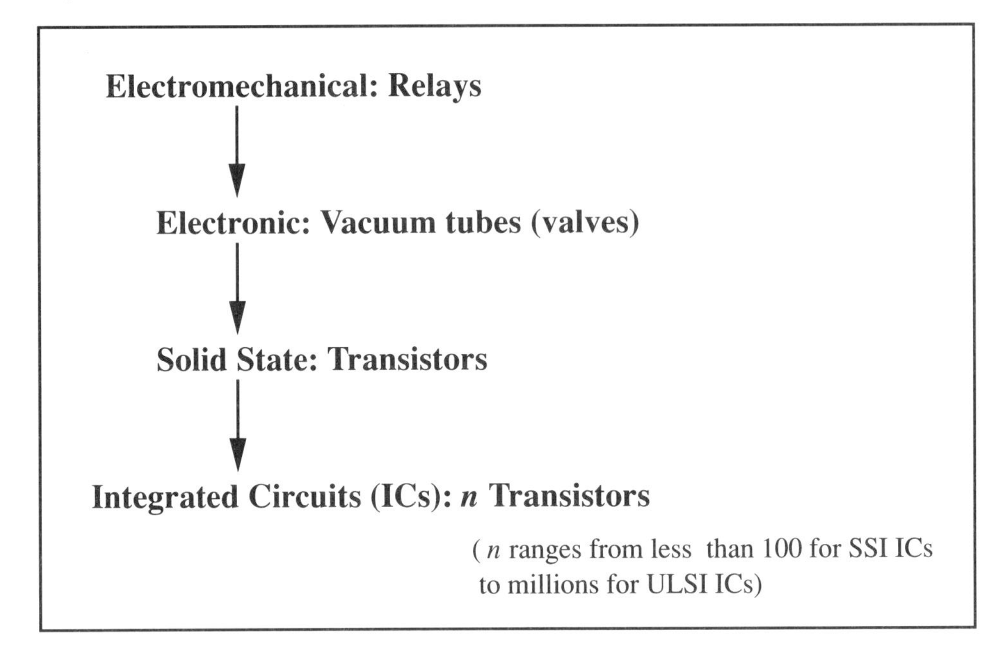

Figure 7.6 Evolution of switching technology.

Transistors are fundamental components in the construction of computers. In crude terms, they act as electronic switches, that is, they allow information to pass or not to pass under certain conditions. The invention of the transistor, at Bell Labs in 1948, revolutionized the development of computers. Transistors were much smaller, more rugged, cheaper to make and far more reliable than the valves which they replaced. The development of **integrated circuits** (ICs) allowed the construction of a number of transistors on a single piece of silicon (the material out of which ICs are made). ICs are also called **silicon chips**, or simply **chips**. The number of transistors on a chip is determined by its level of integration. Early chips had only a few transistors and used small-scale integration (**SSI**). As technology developed, medium-scale integration (**MSI**) allowed hundreds of transistors per chip, large-scale integration (**LSI**) allowed thousands of transistors per chip, very large scale integration (**VLSI**) allowed hundreds of thousands of transistors per chip. Today, millions of transistors are available per chip; for example, Intel's Pentium microprocessor consists of an IC with in excess of three million transistors. This level of integration is called ultra large scale integration (**ULSI**). In 1965, Gordon Moore (Chairman of Intel at the time) predicted that the complexity of integrated circuits would double every two years (this has become known as **Moore's Law**). This prediction has proved very reliable to date and it seems likely that it will remain so over the next ten years.

7.7.1 *Logic circuits*

Transistors are the fundamental components from which are constructed **logic circuits**. These logic circuits are in turn the basic building blocks of the CPU. They include devices called **gates** and **flip-flops**. (A single gate may use up to six transistors.) Gates and flip-flops are used to construct more complex circuits such as **adders**, **decoders**, **registers** and **counters**. These circuits in turn are used to build **ALUs** and **control units**, in other words CPUs, as illustrated in Figure 7.7. By way of analogy, houses are made up of rooms, rooms are made up of walls, walls are made up of bricks and bricks are made up of sand and cement. If by analogy, houses correspond to CPUs, then the sand and cement correspond to transistors. In one sense this analogy is quite appropriate since transistors are developed on silicon chips and silicon is the essential element of sand!

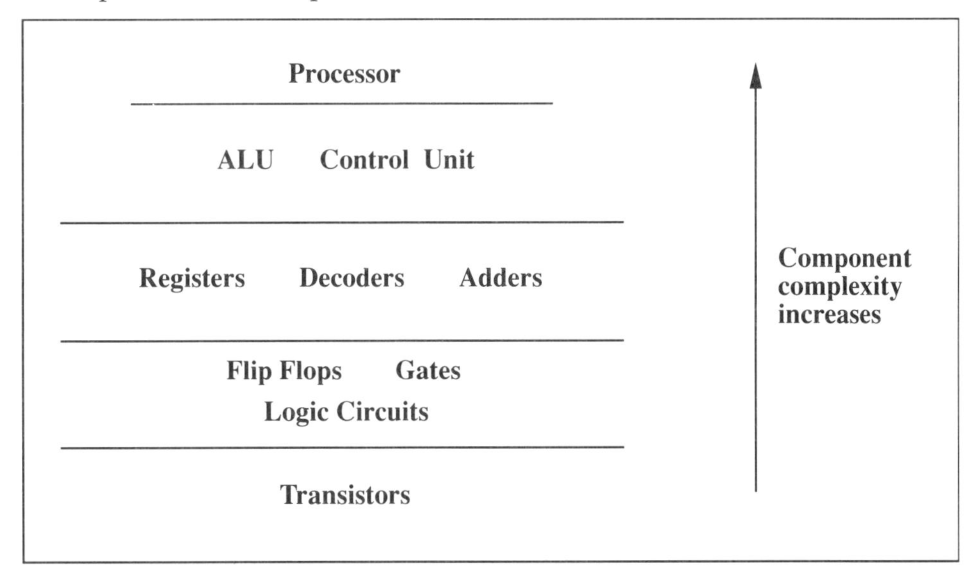

Figure 7.7 From transistors to processors.

Different names are used for the basic logic circuits and these include **binary** circuits, **digital** circuits, **Boolean** circuits and **gates**. They are called logic circuits because they perform the logic operations (such as `AND` and `OR`). There are a number of types of logic gates such as `and`, `or`, `xor`, `nand` and `nor` gates. The term **gate** refers to the fact that they act like gates, letting some signals through and blocking others, depending on their inputs. The term **Boolean** comes from George Boole, the originator of Boolean algebra.

Logic circuits fall into two classes: sequential logic circuits and combinatorial logic circuits. Combinatorial circuits are those where the output is at all times a function of the current inputs to the circuits (*no* feedback is allowed from the outputs to the inputs). **Decoders** and **adders** are important examples of such circuits, used in the construction of digital systems such as CPUs. Sequential circuits are those where the outputs depend on **past** inputs as well as **current** inputs (they allow feedback). They are sequential in that the output depends on the sequence leading to the present situation. As a consequence, such circuits exhibit **memory**, that is, they can retain information. The **flip-flop** is one of the best known sequential circuits. There are a number of types of flip-flop such as the R-S flip-flop, J-K flip-flop and **D-type** flip-flop. **Registers** can be constructed from D-type flip-flops and so D-type flip-flops are commonly used in computers. Memory may also be implemented using flip-flops, as may be **shift registers** and **counters**, which are also important computer components.

In summary, gates and flip-flops, which are constructed out of transistors, are the basic building blocks of computers.

7.7.2 Chip fabrication

Silicon chips have a surface area of similar dimensions to a thumb nail (or smaller) and are three-dimensional structures composed of microscopically thin layers (perhaps as many as 20) of insulating and conducting material on top of the silicon. The manufacturing process is extremely complex and expensive. Silicon is a **semiconductor**, which means that it can be altered to act as either a conductor allowing electricity to flow or as an insulator preventing the flow of electricity. Silicon is first processed into circular wafers and these are then used in the fabrication of chips. The silicon wafer goes through a long and complex process which results in the circuitry for a semiconductor device such as a microprocessor or RAM being developed on the wafer. It should be noted that each wafer contains from several to hundreds of the particular device being produced. Figure 7.8 illustrates an 8 inch silicon wafer containing microprocessor chips.

The individual chips are obtained by cutting them out of the wafer with a high-precision diamond saw. Before this process, the wafer goes through a 'wafer sort' facility which is an electrical test of each chip on the wafer to ensure it is working correctly. Malfunctioning chips are marked with ink so that they may be discarded. The percentage of functioning chips is referred to as the **yield** of the wafer. Yields vary substantially depending on the complexity of the device being produced, the feature size used and other factors. While manufacturers are slow to release actual figures, yields as low as 50% are reported and it is accepted that 80–90% yields are very good. A high chip-failure rate should not be surprising, given the complexity of the production task and the sub-micron feature size. A single short circuit, caused by two wires touching in a chip with a million-plus transistors, is enough to cause chip failure!

The **feature size** refers, in simple terms, to the size of a transistor or to the width of the wires connecting transistors on the chip. One micron or μm (one thousandth of a millimetre) is a common feature size and state of the art chips are using **sub-micron** feature sizes from 0.8 to 0.3 μm. Intel are producing 80486 and Pentium chips using 0.8 μm process technology at the time of writing while 0.6 μm technology will be in use for these microprocessors

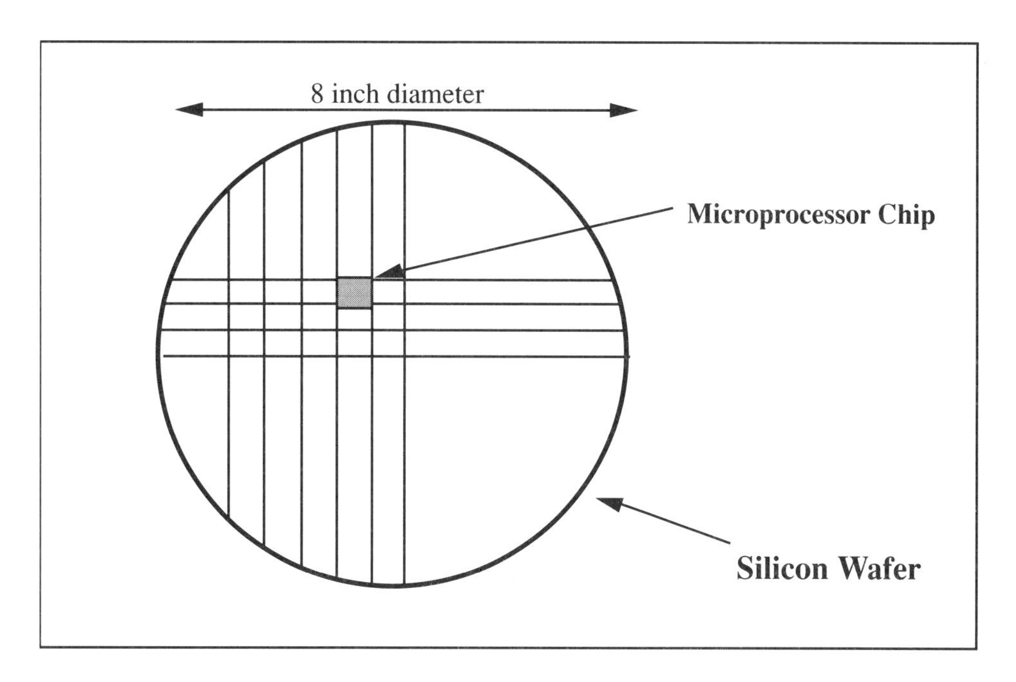

Figure 7.8 A single silicon wafer can contain a large number of microprocessors.

before this text is published. The smaller the feature size, the more transistors there are available on a given chip area. This allows more microprocessors to be obtained from a single silicon wafer. It also means that a given microprocessor will be smaller, run faster and use less power than its predecessor with a larger feature size. Since more of these smaller chips can be obtained from a single wafer, each chip will cost less, which is one of the reasons for cheaper processor chips. (Market forces are another powerful reason!) In addition, reduced feature size makes it possible to make more complex microprocessors, such as the Pentium, which uses in excess of three million transistors, and its planned successor (code-named the P6) will use around 5.5 million transistors. An obvious way to increase the number of transistors on a chip is to increase the area of silicon used for each chip (the **die size**), but this can lead to problems. Assume that a fixed number of faults occur randomly on the silicon wafer illustrated in Figure 7.8. A single fault will render an individual chip useless. The larger the die size for the individual chip, the greater the waste in terms of area of silicon when a fault arises on a chip. For example, if a wafer were to contain 40 chips and ten faults occur randomly, then up to 10 of the 40 chips may be useless, giving up to 25% wastage. On the other hand, if there are 200 chips on the wafer, we would only have 5% wastage with 10 faults. Hence, there is a trade-off between die size and yield, a larger die size leading to a decrease in yield.

When the chips have been extracted from the silicon wafer (they are now called **dies**), they are **packaged**. They are first connected to a set of leads that enable the chip to communicate with other devices. Then the chip is encased in plastic or ceramic material, which protects it from contamination. Three common forms of packaging are used. DIP (Dual In-line Packaging) is a familiar form where up to 64 metal leads or pins protrude from each side of the chip. These pins allow the chip to be inserted into holes on a printed circuit board (PCB). However, because of the increasing complexity of chips, more pins are required than DIP can easily support. Another form of packaging is PGA (Pin Grid Array) packaging. Here, the metal pins (up to several hundred) protrude from layers inside the packaging and plug into sockets on PCBs. Another form of packaging is called SMT (Surface Mount Technology) where the metal leads are on all four sides of the chip and are soldered directly to the conductors on the surface of a PCB. These chips can be mounted on both sides of the same PCB and SMT can accommodate chips requiring more than 200 leads.

Different types of chip technologies such as **MOS** (Metal Oxide Semiconductor) – for example, CMOS (Complementary MOS) and nMOS (Negative channel MOS) – and **bipolar** technologies, such as TTL (Transistor Transistor Logic) and ECL (Emitter Coupled Logic), have been developed that govern such things as the speed of operation and power consumption of a chip. MOS technology allows a high level of integration, but not as high a speed of operation as bipolar technology, which provides for very high operating speeds. On the other hand, bipolar chips are very expensive and consume larger amounts of power than, say, CMOS chips. ECL chips tend to be used in supercomputers, where speed of operation is a critical factor. In modern microprocessor designs, both technologies may in fact be used on the same chip, giving rise to BiCMOS chips. The speed-critical parts of the microprocessor can be implemented in bipolar technology, while the less speed-critical parts can be implemented in the slower CMOS technology.

One way that the performance of an architecture can be improved, without any changes to the instruction set architecture or organization, is to use a faster chip technology.

The advances in chip design are to a large extent due to the development of CAD (Computer Aided Design) tools that allow designers to create new chip designs and simulate how they will work, as well as to test them for design errors. It would be impossible to design state-of-the-art microprocessors without such software.

7.8 Summary

A number of techniques for improving processor performance, such as **pipelining**, **superscalar** architectures and the use of **cache** memory, have been described in this chapter. This was followed by a discussion of **RISC** and **CISC** architectures and their relative merits. The complex area of computer performance was then tackled, outlining such metrics as MIPS, MFLOPS and SPECmarks and the problems associated with them. Finally, a brief introduction to the world of semiconductor technology and chip fabrication was presented.

Exercises

7.1 Explain the concept of pipelining and define flow-through time and throughput.

7.2 What would be the throughput and flow-through time of a pipeline, made up of five stages, where the stages 1 to 5 take the following units of time to complete: 1, 2, 1, 3, 2?

7.3 Why are branch instructions a problem for pipelining? What other problems arise with pipelining?

7.4 What prevents the parallel execution of every pair of instructions in a superscalar machine with multiple functional units? Explain how instruction re-ordering can alleviate this problem.

7.5 What is cache memory and why is it so important? What is the average memory access time for a machine with a cache hit rate of 95%, where the cache access time is 10 ns and the memory access time is 80 ns?

7.6 Compare a typical RISC processor with a CISC processor using a table with headings such as: instruction length, addressing modes, instruction set size, clock cycles per second.

7.7 Why is measuring computer performance so difficult? What are the problems associated with using MIPS, FLOPS, benchmarks and SPECmarks as performance metrics?

7.9 Reading list

7.9.1 Textbooks

Anderson, J.A. (1994) *Foundations of Computer Technology*, Chapman & Hall, London.
Baron, R.J. and Higbie L. (1992) *Computer Architecture*, Addison-Wesley, Reading, MA.
Brink, J. and Spillman, R. (1987) *Computer Architecture and VAX Assembly Language Programming*, Benjamin Cummings, Menlo Park, CA.
Decegama, A.L. (1989) *The Technology of Parallel Processing*, Prentice-Hall, Englewood Cliffs, NJ.
Feldman, J.M. and Retter C.T. (1994) *Computer Architecture, a Designer's Text Based on a Generic RISC*, McGraw-Hill, New York.
Hennessy, J.L and Patterson, D.A. (1990) *Computer Architecture, a Quantitative Approach*, Morgan Kaufmann, San Mateo, CA.
Horvath, R. (1992) *Introduction to Microprocessors using the MC6809 or the MC68000*, McGraw-Hill, New York.
Hwang, K. and Briggs F.A. (1984) *Computer Architecture and Parallel Processing*, McGraw-Hill, New York.
Mead, C. and Conway L. (1980) *Introduction to VLSI*, Addison Wesley, Reading, MA.
Quinn, M.J. (1994) *Parallel Computing*, McGraw-Hill, New York.
Rafiquzzaman, M. and Chandra R. (1988) *Modern Computer Architecture*, West Publishing Co., St. Paul, MN.
Stallings, W. (1990) *Reduced Instruction Set Computers*, IEEE Computer Society Press, Los Alamitos, CA.
Stone, H.S. (1990) *High-Performance Computer Architecture*, Addison Wesley, Reading, MA.

7.9.2 Journal articles

Burger, R.M. and Holton, W.C. (1992) Reshaping the Microchip, *Byte*, February, **17**(2), 137–48.
Geppert, L. (1993) The New Contenders, *IEEE Spectrum*, **30**(12), 20–25.

Halfhill, T.R. (1994) 80x86 Wars, *Byte*, June, **19**(6), 74–88.
Halfhill, T.R. (1994) Emulation: RISC's Secret Weapon, *Byte*, April, **19**(4), 119–130.
Hardenberg, H.W. (1994) CPU Performance: Where are we headed?, *Dr. Dobbs Journal*, **19**(1), 30–38.
Marshall, T. (1992) Support Your Local CPU, *Byte*, February, **17**(2), 151–160.
Ryan, B. (1992) Built for Speed, *Byte*, February, **17**(2), 123–35.
Tredennick, N. (1993) Computer Science and the Microprocessor, *Dr. Dobbs Journal*, **18**(6), 18–32.
The Opening of FAB 10, short information booklet (1994), Intel Corporation, Leixlip, Ireland.

7.9.3 *Videos*

A very informative collection of videos is available from University Video Communications, PO Box 5129, Stanford, CA 94309 USA. They are organized as a series titled 'The Distinguished Lecture Series' and the following deal with some of the topics described in this and the following chapter.

Bell, C.G. (1993) Tracking the Teraflop.
Crawford, J., Alpert, D. and Fu, B. (1993) An Overview of Intel's Pentium Processor.
Newton, A.R. (1991) Introduction to Design Automation for Electronic Systems.
Patterson, D. (1993) Terabytes >> Teraflops.
Sites, D. and Meyer D. (1992) Alpha Architecture.
Watanabe, T. (1992) Toward the Ultra High-Speed Computing System.

7.9.4 *Internet: World Wide Web*

Details of Intel's P6 are available from: HTTP://www.intel.com.

8
Case studies

In this chapter we examine the architecture of the Intel 80*x*86 and Motorola 680*x*0 families of (CISC) microprocessors. In addition we look at the architecture of two RISC-based microprocessors, the IBM/Motorola PowerPC and Digital's Alpha 21064 microprocessor. Table 8.1 summarizes some of the features of the microprocessors described. Simplified block diagrams, which in some cases are really not much more than extended programming models of the microprocessors, are presented. The bus systems shown in all diagrams are not accurate representations of the actual bus systems used, but rather indicate the type of bus structure that must be present. These simplifications have been made in an effort to give the reader a feel for the microprocessors in question, without getting lost in a myriad of low-level details.

Table 8.1 Well known microprocessors.

Manufacturer	Processor	Word Size	Memory	Transistors	Year
Intel	4004	4-bit	4kb	2000	1971
	8080	8-bit	64kb	6000	1973
	8086	16-bit	1Mb	29000	1978
	80286	16-bit	16Mb	134000	1983
	80386	32-bit	4Gb	275000	1986
	80486	32-bit	4Gb	1.2 million	1989
	Pentium	32-bit	4Gb	3.1 million	1993
Motorola	6800	8-bit	64kb		1974
	68000	32-bit	16Mb	68000	1979
	68020	32-bit	4Gb	200000	1984
	68040	32-bit	4Gb	1.2 million	1989
	68060	32-bit	4Gb	2 million	1993
IBM/Motorola	PowerPC 601	32-bit	4Gb	2.8 million	1993
Digital	Alpha 20164	64-bit	16Gb	1.6 million	1992

8.1 The Intel 80x86 family of microprocessors

The abbreviations 80x86 and x86 are used to describe the 8086, 80186/286/386/486 and Pentium microprocessors.

8.1.1 The 8086

The first commercial microprocessor was the Intel 4004 introduced in 1971. It was designed for use in a calculator, not a computer. The 4004 was a 4-bit processor constructed on a chip having over a mere 2000 transistors. It was capable of executing 60 000 instructions per second with a clock rate of 0.7 MHz. It could address up to 4 kb of memory. In 1972, Intel introduced the 8-bit 8008 microprocessor, which could address up to 16 kb of memory. Another 8-bit microprocessor, the 8080, was launched by Intel in 1974 and this was very successful commercially. The 8080 could execute of the order of 500 000 instructions per second. A number of other companies also produced 8-bit microprocessors and these included the Motorola 6800 and the Zilog Z80 microprocessors.

The 16-bit Intel 8086 microprocessor was introduced in 1978. The 8086 can address up to 1 Mb of memory and has a clock speed of 5 MHz. The 8086 can execute up to 2.5 million instructions per second. It was initially constructed on a chip having about 29 000 transistors with a feature size of 3 μm. A simplified version of the architecture of the 8086 is shown in Figure 8.1. Intel also launched the 8088 microprocessor, which is almost identical to the 8086 except that it uses an 8-bit data bus. This means that it has to carry out two memory read operations to fetch 16 bits from memory as opposed to one memory read for the 8086 which uses a 16-bit data bus. The 8088 was used by IBM in the original

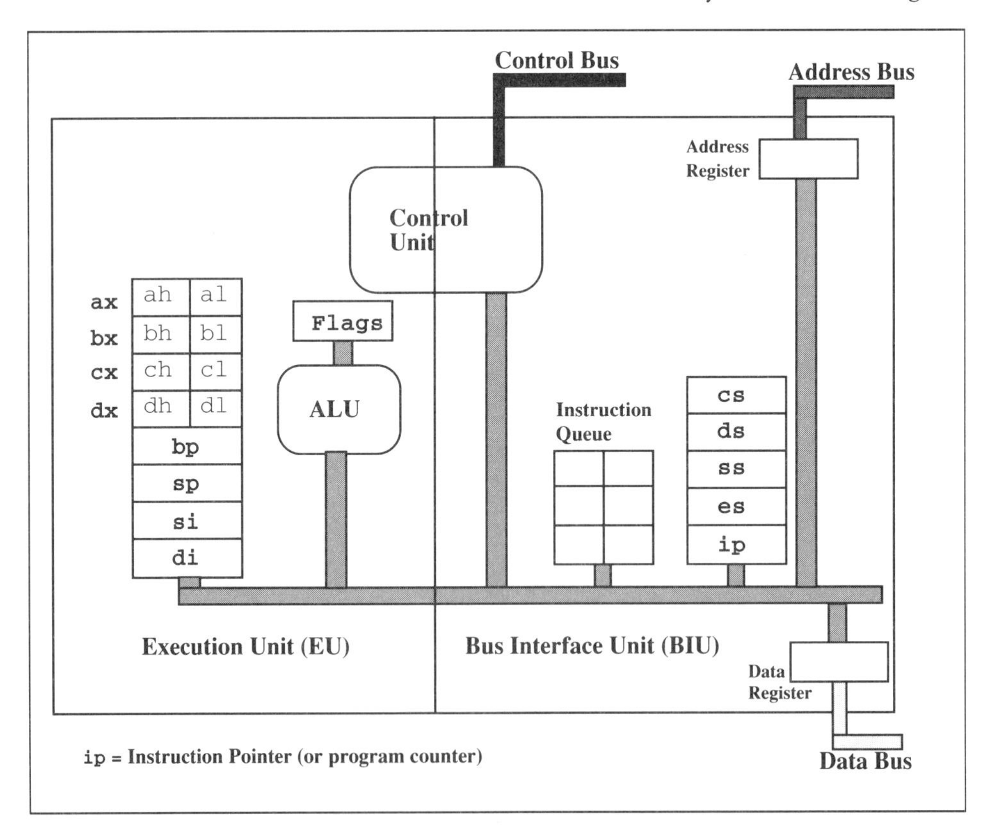

Figure 8.1 The 8086 microprocessor.

IBM PC. Because of its 8-bit external data bus, it could be used with the I/O devices which were widely available for the 8-bit microprocessors.

As can be seen from Figure 8.1 the 8086 microprocessor consists of two units, the **execution unit** (EU) and the **bus interface unit** (BIU). These are independent units, capable of operating in parallel, so that while the EU executes an instruction, the BIU fetches the next instruction. This overlap of instruction execution and instruction fetch is a form of pipelining, as described in Chapter 7. The BIU pre-fetches instructions into the instruction queue, which can store up to 6 bytes. The EU retrieves instructions from the instruction queue and rarely has to wait for an instruction to be fetched from memory. This is because while an instruction is being executed, if the BIU is idle and there is space in the instruction queue, the BIU will fetch instructions and store them in the instruction queue so that they are ready for the EU.

The 8086 architecture does not neatly map on to the simple architectural diagrams we have used in the text to date and the reader should note that the depiction of the control unit as straddling the EU and BIU is not accurate, but is intended to illustrate that there is control logic in both units.

Aside: The term **datapath** is used to refer to the ALU and registers (general purpose registers and `PC`, `SP`, `MAR` and `MDR`) as well as the buses linking these components together. It is responsible for carrying out operations, under direction from the control unit.

The 8086 provides more registers, which can contain 16-bits, and instructions than its 8-bit predecessors. For example, it provides multiply and divide instructions which were not available on the Intel 8-bit machines. It also provides more addressing modes. The 8086 provides 14 registers, which are usually classified as **data** registers (`ax`, `bx`, `cx`, `dx`), **pointer/index** registers (`sp`, `bp`, `si`, `di`) and segment registers (`cs`, `ds`, `ss`, `es`). In addition, there is the program counter called the **instruction pointer** (`ip`) and the status register called the **flags** register. The data registers may each be treated as a 16-bit register or as two 8-bit registers, so that `ax` is a 16-bit register while `ah` and `al` are 8-bit registers. The data, pointer and flags registers are located in the EU. The segment registers and the program counter are located in the BIU. The segment registers play a fundamental role in addressing memory. The address bus is 20 bits wide because a 20-bit address is required to access 1 Mb of memory (2^{20} = 1 Mb). However, the 8086 registers are 16-bit registers, so they cannot store a 20-bit address, which means that two registers must be used when accessing memory. One register (a segment register) is used to hold a base address of some location in memory. Another register, such as the program counter or the `bx` register holds what is referred to as an **offset** address. This offset address is added to the base address to obtain the actual or **effective address** of the location in memory to be accessed. The resulting address is stored in the address register, which must be large enough to accommodate it.

In fact, the 8086 scheme is a little more complicated than described here, because the scheme just outlined would only allow up to 128 kb of memory to be addressed since each 16-bit register is only capable of addressing up to 64 kb of memory. The 8086 segment register actually stores what is called a **paragraph number**, which must be multiplied by 16 to get the actual base address. Put another way, the 8086 treats memory as being logically divided into a number of 16-byte paragraphs. If the first paragraph (number 0 in the segment register) begins with memory address 0, then the second paragraph (number 1 in the segment register) begins at location 16 and the third begins at memory location 32 and so on. Thus, to compute the effective address in memory of an operand, the relevant segment register contents are multiplied by 16 and the offset address is added to this result. (Multiplying by 16 is the same as shifting the segment register contents four bits to the left, or appending four 0s to the right hand side of the 16-bit contents, which produces a 20-bit result.) Using this technique, any location in the 1 Mb address space can be accessed. This address calculation is carried out by a dedicated ALU in the BIU, not shown in Figure 8.1. One advantage of this **segmented** memory management scheme is that it allows programs to be easily relocated (moved to a different area) in memory. All that is required in computing the addresses required for the relocated program is to change the contents of the segment register to the base address of the new location.

There are four segment registers. The code segment register `cs` is used to access the instructions of a program in conjunction with the `ip` register. The stack segment register `ss` is used to access the stack in conjunction with the `sp` or `bp` registers. The data and extra segment registers `ds` and `es` are used in conjunction with the `bx`, `si` and `di` registers for accessing data operands.

The 8086 provides 12 different addressing modes and has in excess of 100 instructions in the instruction set.

8.1.2 The 80286/386/486

Intel developed the 8086 microprocessor to provide the 80186, which is an 8 MHz version of the 8086, with some extra instructions. Then came the **80286** with the clock initially operating at 8 MHz but more importantly with an increased address space of 16 Mb. The 80286 also provides additional memory management instructions. The 80286 is capable of executing up to four million instructions per second and is constructed on a chip with more than 130 000 transistors. The 80286 was used by IBM in the IBM AT computer. Versions of the 80286 can run at clock speeds of up to 25 MHz.

The 80386

The next major development in the 80x86 family was the introduction of the 80386 microprocessor in 1986. The 80386 is a full **32-bit microprocessor** and represents a major advance over its 16-bit predecessors. It provides 32-bit data and address buses. A 32-bit address allows up to 4 Gb (four billion bytes) of memory to be used. Different versions of the 80386 are available, such as the 80386SX which uses a 16-bit data bus and a 24-bit address bus (can address up to 16 Mb). The 80386SX can use the widespread range of I/O devices designed for 16-bit data buses as used by the 8086-based machines. This reduces the cost of an 80386SX-based PC. The 80386 also includes memory management hardware, which makes the allocation of memory more efficient. This is particularly important for the operating system software. It operates at speeds from 12.5 to 33 MHz and is constructed on a chip of 275 000 transistors. The 80386 uses instruction pipelining to increase its performance. The instruction set is the same as for the 8086/80286, with the addition of some instructions for memory management and other functions.

The 80386 provides for operations on 8-bit (byte), 16-bit (word) and 32-bit (double word) sized operands. The register set of the 80386, as illustrated in Figure 8.2, is an extended version of that of the 8086, in that the register size is now 32 bits, with the exception of the segment registers which remain as 16-bit registers. In addition, the 80386 provides two additional 16-bit segment registers, `fs` and `gs` which act as data segment registers, like `ds` and `es`. This means that there are four data segment registers, allowing the programmer to use the different data segments for different types of data. The 32-bit registers have the same names as the 8086 16-bit counterparts, except they all begin with the letter `e`: `eax`, `ebx` and so on. They can be accessed as 16-bit registers by omitting the initial `e`, so that 8086/80286 programs can be run without modification on the 80386; they are source code compatible. The 80386 also provides binary compatibility with its predecessors the 8086/80286, so that 8086/80286 object programs can also be executed on the 80386. This compatibility between the different processors in the 80x86 family is an important factor in the success of the architecture.

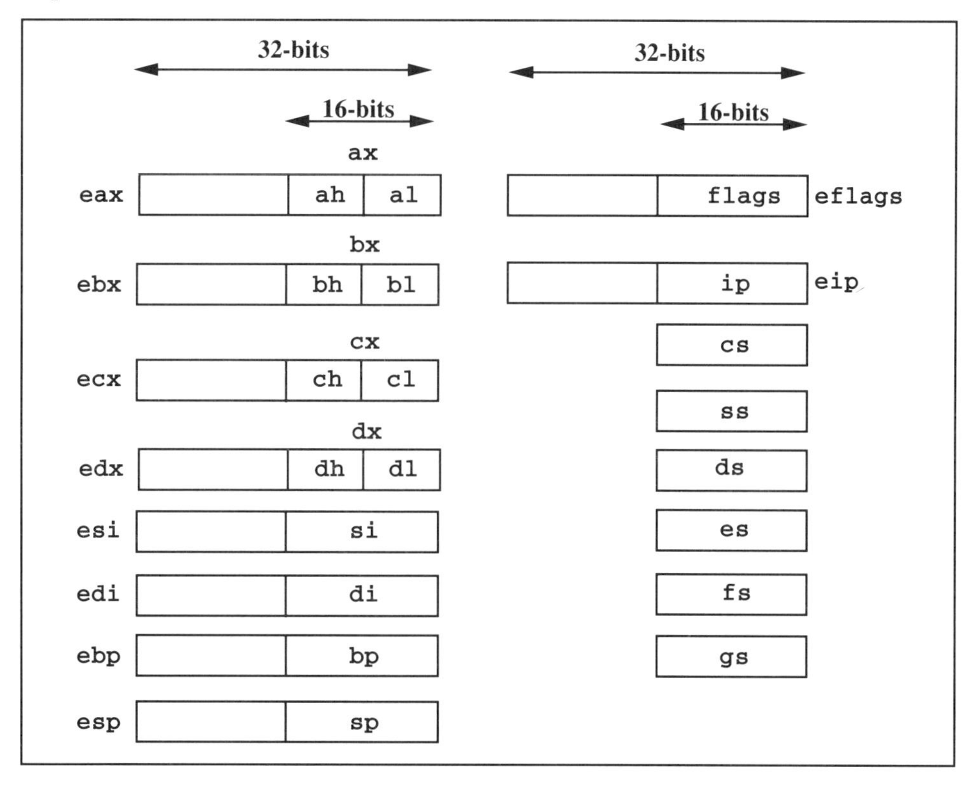

Figure 8.2 The 80386 register set.

The `eflags` and `eip` registers are the 32-bit equivalents of the `flags` and `ip` registers. The `eflags` register contains the same flags as the 8086 with some additional ones for memory management and other functions.

The 80386 processor can execute instructions in different modes, such as real and protected. Real mode is used to execute 8086 programs while protected mode is the normal mode of the 80386.

The 8086 architecture provides two functional units, the execution unit (EU) and the bus interface unit (BIU), which operate in parallel. The 80386 extends this by providing six functional units that can operate in parallel. The EU and BIU are still present, but with modified roles. There is a pre-fetch unit, which pre-fetches instructions and stores them in a 16-byte instruction queue when the BIU is free. There is a decoding unit, which decodes instructions and passes them to the EU. There are two units for handling memory address generation, the segmentation and paging units. The paging unit is used for virtual addressing, if it is being used. Figure 8.3 illustrates, in block diagram form, the six units making up the 80386 microprocessor.

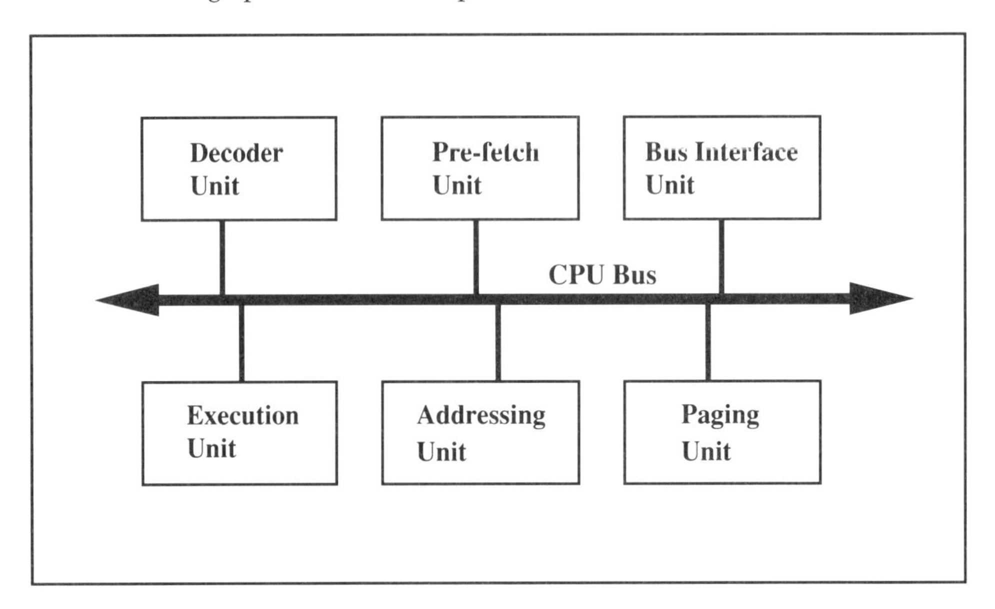

Figure 8.3 Functional units of the 80386.

The 80486

The 80486 microprocessor is an enhanced version of the 80386 which includes an FPU for supporting floating-point arithmetic and an 8 kb unified cache memory system, on the microprocessor chip. It is designed such that commonly executed instructions take only a single clock cycle and it is constructed on a chip with in excess of one million transistors. It gives a significant increase in performance over the 80386. This performance is due largely to the ability to carry out certain instructions in a single cycle and the presence of on-chip cache to reduce the time taken to fetch instructions and data.

The 80486 is fully compatible with the earlier 80x86 microprocessors. It is available operating at clock speeds such as 33MHz and 66MHz and is of the order of 50% faster than an 80386 operating at the same clock speed. The 80486DX2 is a version of the 80486, which internally runs at twice the clock speed of the rest of the system components. For example, a 66 MHz 80486DX2 operates with a CPU clock rate of 66 MHz, but it interfaces with the rest of the system (for example memory) at a clock rate of 33 MHz. This allows this CPU to give better performance while still using slower (and cheaper) system components.

8.1.3 The Pentium

The Pentium is the latest Intel microprocessor constructed on a chip with in excess of three million transistors. It is named Pentium (from the Greek for five) because a numeric name such as 586 cannot be trademarked and thus Intel's competitors could also make processors called 586s to rival Intel, as they have done with previous processors, such as the 386. The Pentium provides two 8 kb on-chip caches, one for data and one for instructions. It is capable of executing in excess of 100 million instructions per second (100 MIPS) when operating at a 66 MHz clock speed. One way of looking at the Pentium architecture is to view it as a combination of two 80486 processors and, as such, the Pentium is an example of a superscalar architecture. This means that it allows for the concurrent execution of instructions; in other words, it provides multiple functional units in the form of two integer ALUs and an FPU. When possible, two instructions are executed in parallel. The Pentium supports two pipelines for the integer ALUs called the **U** and **V** pipelines. The Pentium integer pipelines are similar to the 80486 pipeline and have five stages: fetch, decode1, decode2, execute and write back. The fetch and decode1 stages can operate on two instructions in parallel before issuing them to the U and V pipelines respectively, where the remaining stages can be carried out concurrently by the separate ALUs. As mentioned in Chapter 7, not all instructions can be carried out in parallel because of various dependencies that arise. So, for example, a second instruction will not be issued to the V pipe if the first instruction (issued to the U pipe) is a jump instruction. Similarly, if one of the operands in the second instruction is the destination operand of the first instruction, the second instruction will not be issued in parallel with the first instruction.

The FPU is also pipelined, unlike the 80486 FPU, and consists of eight stages. This means that under ideal conditions, a sequence of floating-point operations can be executed at a rate of one instruction per cycle. Integer instructions cannot be carried out in parallel with floating-point instructions which enables the FPU to use the full capacity of the internal bus to handle 64-bit floating-point numbers. In addition, the FPU provides hardware support for certain floating-point operations. These features combined with the larger data cache make the Pentium up to five times faster for floating-point operations than the 80486.

In order to keep the ALUs and FPU busy, high speed instruction and data caches are used. Cache hit rates of in excess of 95% for the instruction cache and from less than 90 to 95% for the data cache are reported. In addition, the bus interface unit uses a 64-bit data bus so that 8 bytes can be transferred between the CPU and memory. Similarly, 64-bit (double precision) floating-point numbers can be transferred to the FPU on the internal bus linking the FPU to the data cache. Figure 8.4 illustrates the micro-architecture (internal architecture of the CPU) of the Pentium. The register file referred to in Figure 8.4 is the name given to the collection of CPU registers.

One of the Pentium's important enhancements over the 80486 is the use of **branch prediction logic** to avoid unnecessary flushing of the pipeline when

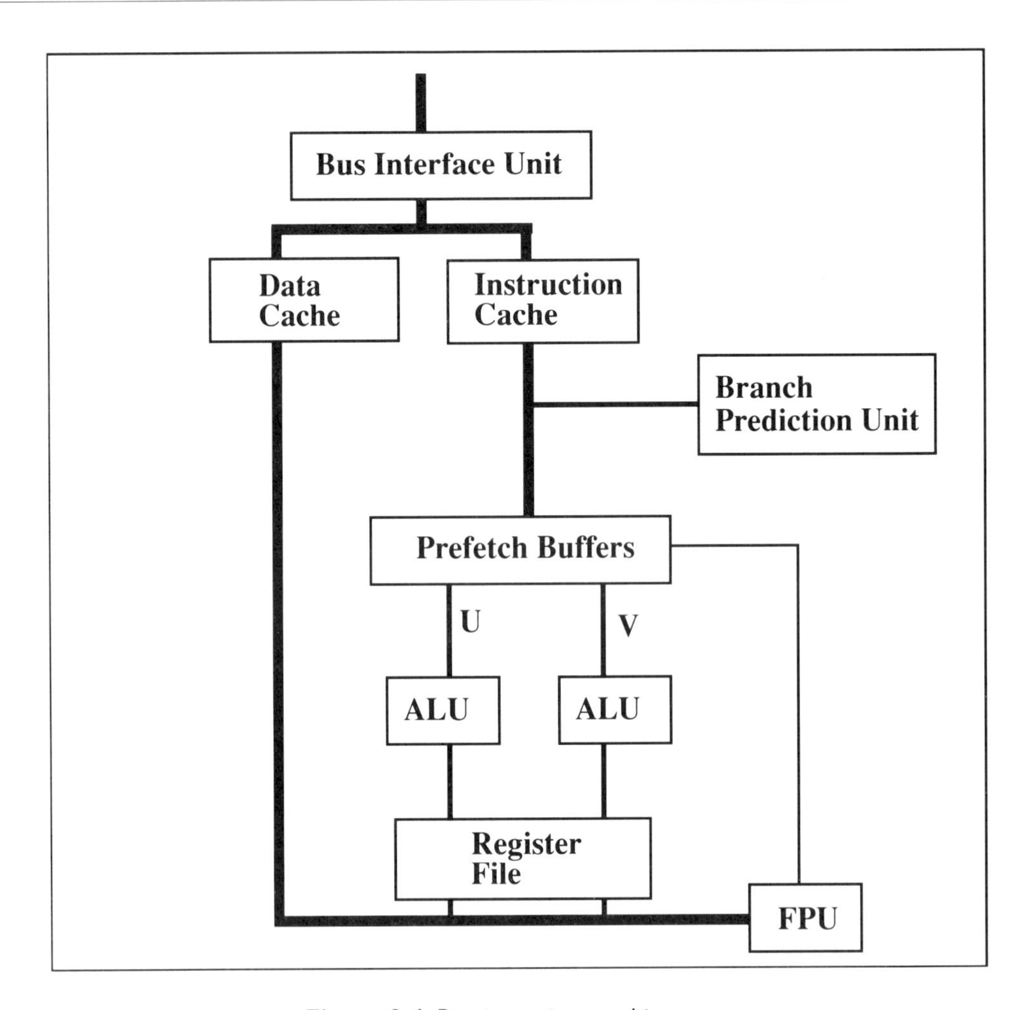

Figure 8.4 Pentium micro-architecture.

handling branch instructions. Successful prediction rates of 80–85% are reported. In the event of an incorrect prediction, the pipeline is flushed with a penalty of four or five cycles. Another issue for a superscalar processor is the control of updating a single status register by concurrent instructions. In the case of the Pentium special logic is provided to allow the `flags` register to be updated by two instructions that are being executed in parallel. This logic operates in such a fashion that it appears as if the `flags` register is updated sequentially, even though two instructions affecting the `flags` register can execute in parallel.

The Pentium retains binary code compatibility with the rest of the 80x86 family which means that an 8086, 80286, 80386 or 80486 program can be executed on the Pentium. However, it should be noted that the user will not notice a very significant gain in performance between a program compiled for and running on the 80486 and the same program running on the Pentium, unless the program is recompiled by a Pentium-aware compiler. In order for software to take advantage of the features of the Pentium processor, an appropriate optimizing compiler for the Pentium must be used. If you simply transfer executable programs from a 80486 (or one of its predecessors), then that code will not be able to take advantage of the Pentium's advanced features and so the performance gain will be disappointing.

Intel is already developing successors to the Pentium, code-named the P6 and P7. These will be constructed on chips boasting from five million transistors upwards. Higher clock speeds, larger cache memories and more functional units to increase the degree of parallelism are likely to be features of the new designs.

8.2 Motorola 6800 and M68000 family of microprocessors

Motorola is also a major microprocessor manufacturer with its flagship M68000 family of microprocessors driving the Apple Macintosh range of computers among others, although Apple are in the process of switching from the M680*x*0 to the IBM/Motorola PowerPC microprocessor for the Macintosh family. In this section, we firstly look at Motorola's 8-bit 6800 microprocessor before describing the M68000 family (which is referred to by the abbreviation M680*x*0), made up of the 68000, 68010, 68020, 68030, 68040 and 68060 microprocessors.

8.2.1 The M6800

The M6800 is an 8-bit processor launched by Motorola in 1974. Figure 8.5 is a simplified illustration of the architecture to the M6800.

The M6800 uses an 8-bit data bus and a 16-bit address bus, which allows it to address up to 64 kb of memory. The M6800 programming model has six registers, two of the most important for programming purposes being the accumulator registers `A` and `B`. These are 8-bit registers. In addition, it provides a 16-bit index register `ix` for memory addressing purposes. The `pc` and `sp` registers are also 16-bit registers, but the three 16-bit registers are accessed internally as being composed of two 8-bit registers. The `CCR` (Condition Codes Register) is the 8-bit status register of the M6800.

8.2.2 The M68000

The M68000 was launched in 1979 and is constructed on a chip of somewhat less than 70 000 transistors. The M68000 is a 32-bit processor, sometimes described as a 16/32-bit processor since internally it uses 32-bit registers while it uses a 16-bit data bus to communicate with memory and other devices. The M68000 uses a 24-bit address bus, which allows it to support up to 16 Mb of memory. It operates at clock speeds from 4 to 12 MHz and others, depending on the version. It provides 14 different addressing modes, some of which are quite sophisticated, such as indirect addressing with post-increment where the indirect address is automatically incremented after it has been used to compute the effective address of a memory operand. The M68000 bus unit pre-fetches instructions while the address and data buses are not being used during execution of an instruction. A 4 byte pre-fetch queue is maintained to store these pre-fetched instructions. Figure 8.6 illustrates the basic architecture of the M68000.

The M68000 microprocessor has a total of 17 general purpose registers. Each of them can contain a 32-bit binary number. Eight of the registers are referred to

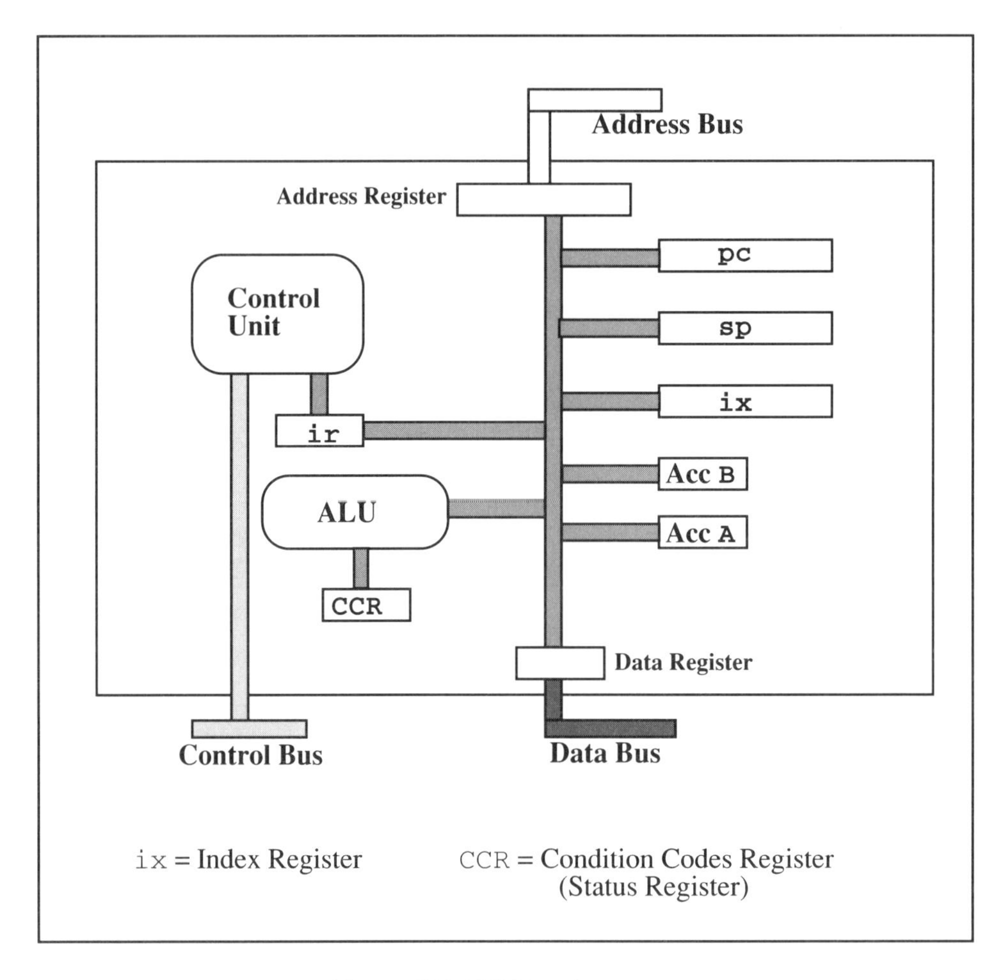

Figure 8.5 M6800 architecture.

as **data** registers. They are the `d0`, `d1`, `d2`, `d3`, `d4`, `d5`, `d6` and `d7` registers. These eight registers are general purpose registers, so they can be used by the programmer for data manipulation. An important feature of the M68000 data registers is that they can each be accessed as a single 32-bit register, as a 16-bit register or as an 8-bit register. To specify how a register is to be treated, each M68000 instruction has a suffix indicating the size of the operand to be used by the instruction. The suffix `.b` is used for byte-sized operands, the suffix `.w` is used for word-sized operands (16 bits) and the suffix `.l` for long word-sized operands (32 bits).

Another seven registers are referred to as **address** registers; they are the `a0`, `a1`, `a2`, `a3`, `a4`, `a5` and `a6` registers. These registers are used to contain the addresses of memory locations, typically for indirect addressing purposes, but they can also act as general purpose registers. The registers `a7` and `a7'` are used as **stack pointer** registers. In addition there are two other registers: the **program counter** register, `pc` and the **status** register, `sr`. The `pc` register is a 32-bit register, while the `sr` register is a 16-bit register. The low-order byte of the status register is called the **condition code register (ccr)** or **user byte** and is

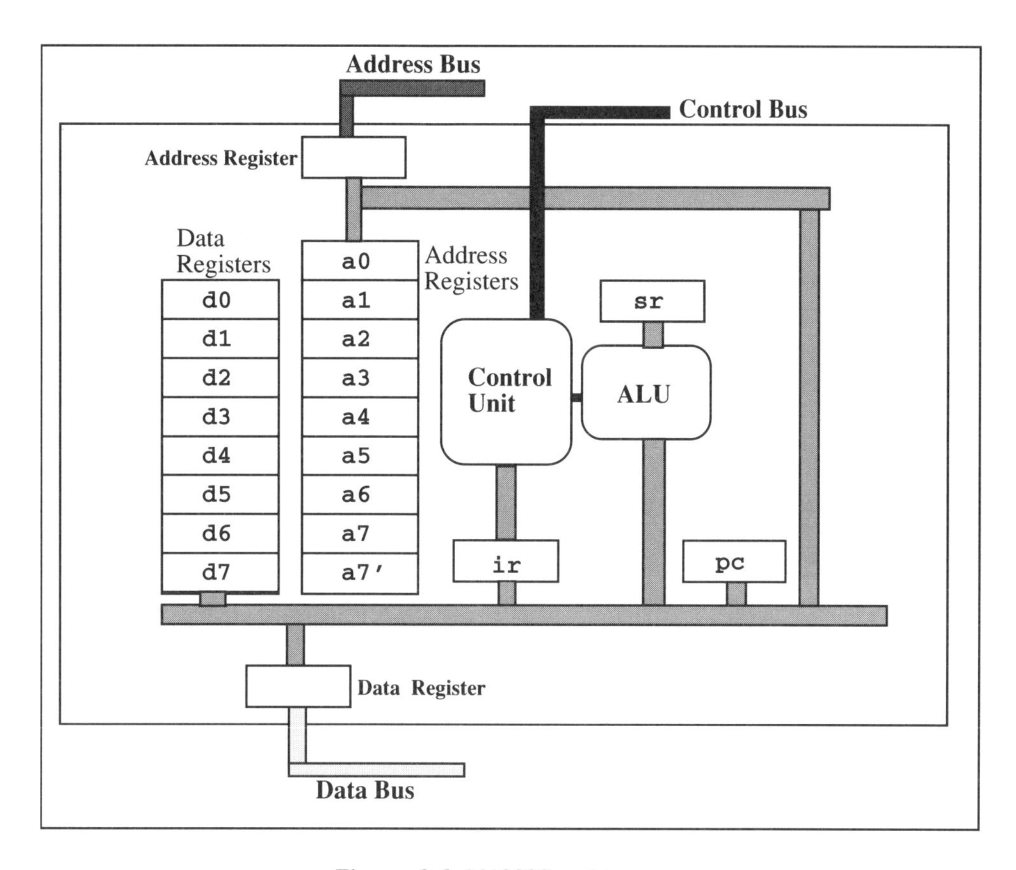

Figure 8.6 M68000 architecture.

really a collection of bits called flags. The status flags are used to record status information resulting from the execution of arithmetic and logical instructions. For example, the zero flag (Z-flag) is set to 1 if the result of an arithmetic operation is zero. The high-order byte of the status register is called the **system byte** which contains information about interrupts and the **mode** of the processor.

The M68000 can operate in two modes called **supervisor mode** and **user mode**. This feature is very useful for implementing operating systems. The idea is that there are certain privileged instructions that can only be executed when the processor is in the supervisor mode or, put another way, all instructions can be executed while the processor is in supervisor mode. The operating system will carry out many of its functions while executing in supervisor mode. The user mode is used for running user programs and these programs cannot execute any of the M68000 privileged instructions. This is also the reason for the two stack pointer registers `a7` and `a7'`. The `a7` stack pointer is the user stack pointer (USP), used when the processor is in user mode and the `a7'` stack pointer is the supervisor stack pointer (SSP), used when the processor is in supervisor mode. There is a flag in the system byte of the status register called the **S-flag** which determines the mode of the processor. Setting the S-flag to `1` causes the processor to operate in supervisor mode, while clearing the S-flag causes the processor to operate in user mode. When the M68000 is powered up, it operates in supervisor mode and then executes the operating system software which will execute in supervisor mode. The operating system software can then switch to user mode (using a privileged instruction) in order to run user programs. These programs cannot execute any privileged instructions. To switch back to supervisor mode, a software interrupt or **trap** can be used. This means that a user program can invoke the operating system (using a system call which will in turn use a trap to switch to supervisor mode) to carry out some task on its behalf. The net effect of all of this is that user programs cannot access resources (by error or design) without doing so in a controlled manner via the operating system.

Two interesting instructions provided by the M68000 are the `movem` (move multiple) instruction and the `dbcc` (test condition decrement and branch) instruction. The `movem` instruction allows the programmer to specify that the contents of a list of registers be moved to memory, for example to save them on the stack. The programmer can specify the particular registers to be moved. The `dbcc` instruction is used for loops and allows the programmer to test a condition, decrement a count register and branch depending on the outcome of the test. This is similar to the 8086 `loop` instruction, except that it is far more general in that the programmer can use any register and specify any of a range of conditions (for example, if positive, if negative or if zero). The condition is specified by replacing `cc` appropriately, for example with `eq` for equality, `gt` for greater than and so on. This is a good example of a CISC instruction.

Other versions of the M68000 include the M68008, M68010 and M68012. The M68008 is a less powerful version of the M68000 using an 8-bit data bus and a 20-bit address which allows it support 1 Mb of memory. The M68010 is similar to the M68000 and differs in that it provides hardware support for **virtual memory** and additional, more efficient, instructions for looping. Its data and address buses are the same as those of the M68000. The M68012 is the same as the 68010 except it provides a 31-bit address bus which allows it to support up to 2 Gb of memory (2^{31} bits = 2 Gb). The architecture of the M68000 forms the basis for the later members of the M680x0 family, the M68020, M68030, M68040 and M68060 microprocessors.

8.2.3 The M68020/30/40/60 microprocessors

The M68020 is a true 32-bit processor providing a 32-bit data bus as well as a 32-bit address bus which enables it to support up 4 Gb of memory. The M68020 provides all the features of the M68012, such as virtual memory. It is constructed on a chip containing 200 000 transistors and is capable of executing 2 to 3 million instructions per second when operating at 16 MHz. It can be operated at up to 24 MHz. In addition the M68020 provides an on-chip instruction cache capable of storing 256 bytes (or up to 100 instructions, depending on the size of the individual instructions), which speeds up its performance. The multiply and divide instructions handle 32-bit operands as opposed to the 16-bit operands of the earlier members of the M680x0 family. It has no hardware floating-point facilities, so the MC6881 floating-point co-processor may be used for such operations.

The M68030

This is an improved version of the M68020 and is constructed on a chip containing around 300 000 transistors. It provides an on-chip data cache of 256 bytes in addition to the 256 byte instruction cache. Instructions and data can be obtained from the respective caches in parallel. It also provides an FPU as well as memory management facilities. The on-chip memory-management unit increases the performance of the virtual memory system, while the FPU enhances the performance when carrying out floating-point operations. Current versions can operate at speeds of up to 50 MHz.

The M68040

The M68040 enhances the performance of the M68030 by providing much larger cache memories, a 4 kb data cache and a 4 kb instruction cache. It is a pipelined processor utilizing a six-stage instruction pipeline to increase its performance. The M68040 is constructed on a 1.2 million transistor chip and initially operated at 25 MHz. It outperforms the M68030 by a factor of three to ten and is capable of executing up to 20 million instructions per second.

The M68060

This is the most recently released member of the M680x0 family (there is no M68050) constructed on a two million transistor chip. This is a superscalar processor with two integer execution pipelines in addition to an FPU and a branch cache. It is capable, under the right conditions, of executing two instructions in parallel. It is available in 50 and 66 MHz versions and is significantly faster than the 68040 processor.

8.3 RISC microprocessors

There are a number of RISC microprocessors available at the moment, such as the IBM/Motorola PowerPC, Digital's Alpha 21064, Hewlett Packard's PA7100, Sun Microsystems/Texas Instruments SuperSparc, MIPS technologies R4000, Intel's i860, Motorola's 88000 and IBM's RS/6000. In this section we briefly review Digital's Alpha 21064 and the IBM/Motorola PowerPC 601.

8.3.1 The IBM/Motorola PowerPC 601

This is the first of a family of PowerPC microprocessors introduced in 1993 and it is now used in computers available from IBM, as well as in Apple's PowerMacs. It resulted from co-operation between Apple, IBM and Motorola to develop a high performance RISC architecture which they hoped would form the basis for another generation of powerful, low-cost computers. The PowerPC architecture is derived from IBM's POWER (**P**erformance **O**ptimized **W**ith **E**nhanced **R**ISC) architecture, used in IBM's RS/6000 machines. The PowerPC 601 can execute software already developed for the POWER architecture such as that used on RS/6000 machines. Other members of the PowerPC family that are being developed include the PowerPC 603, 604 and 620. The software architecture proposed for the PowerPC family is called the PowerOpen Environment, which has as its major aim the ability to allow users to choose whatever operating system and interface they wish to use from a number of available options. The idea is that a user could, for example, run Unix, Apple Macintosh or Windows software on their PowerPC workstation, in different windows, at the same time. One goal of the PowerOpen Environment is that software from any vendor that complies with PowerOpen standards will run on any PowerPC-based hardware. The PowerPC architecture is a full 64-bit architecture, but it has a 32-bit subset which permits the implementation of both 32-bit and 64-bit processors. The architecture is defined so that a 64-bit processor has a 32-bit mode which enables it to run 32-bit PowerPC software.

The PowerPC 601 is a 32-bit processor constructed on a chip containing 2.8 million transistors and operates at 80MHz. It provides 32 general purpose registers, 32 floating-point registers as well as a unified 32K on-chip cache (other PowerPC family members use separate caches for instructions and data). It has a superscalar architecture, illustrated in Figure 8.7, with three execution units (FPU, IU (Integer Unit) and BPU (Branch Processing Unit)) and can issue up to three instructions per cycle. The PowerPC has an instruction unit which is responsible for issuing instructions to the three execution units. The instruction

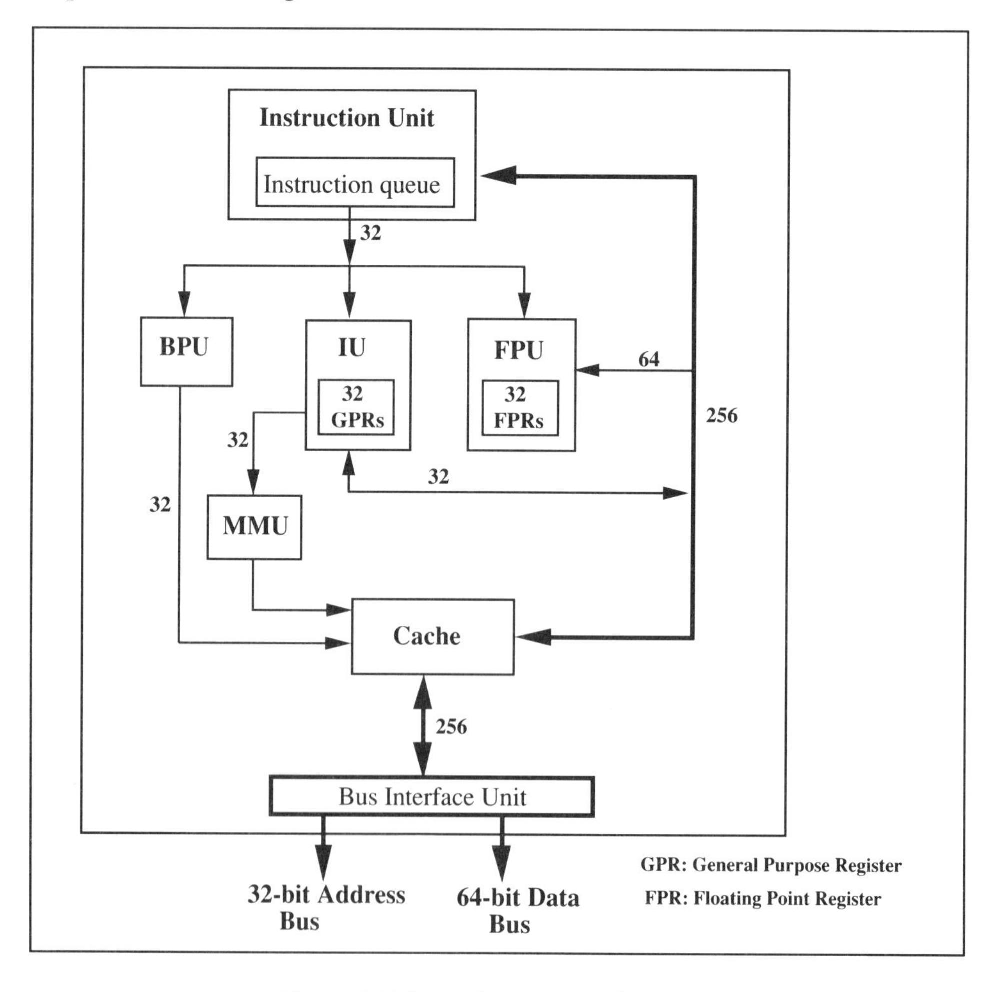

Figure 8.7 PowerPC micro-architecture.

unit maintains a queue of up to eight instructions, which it tries to keep full at all times using a 256-bit internal bus to the cache. The 256-bit bus allows it to fetch up to eight instructions at a time from the cache. The instruction unit issues instructions from the instruction queue to one of the three appropriate execution units and, given the right mix of instructions, can issue three instructions at a time. The instruction unit is also capable of computing the address of the next instruction to be fetched to the instruction queue. The BPU (logically part of the instruction unit) uses static branch prediction to guess whether a branch is taken or not, so that backward branches are predicted to be taken and forward branches are predicted not to be taken. If a branch is predicted to be taken, then instructions are pre-fetched from the branch target address. While this is happening, the actual branch condition is being evaluated and if the prediction was correct, the instruction queue will contain the correct instructions and the branch instruction will cause no delay in the pipelined execution of instructions. If the prediction was incorrect, then the effect of the pre-fetching must be undone, by flushing the pipeline and fetching the correct instructions.

The three execution units are pipelined, with the BPU consisting of a three-stage pipeline, the FPU consisting of a six-stage pipeline and the IU consisting of a four-stage pipeline. The IU handles integer arithmetic and bit manipulation as well as the load/store operations for accessing operands in memory. The 32 general purpose registers are logically part of the IU and exhibit two important features for boosting performance. First, they are **dual ported**, which means that two operations can be carried out on the registers at the same time. Second, they provide **feed fowarding**, which means that when a result is being written back to a register in the write back stage of the pipeline, it is also available to the execution stage of the next instruction in the pipeline. Thus, if the next instruction needs to access a register being updated by the previous instruction, it does not have to wait until that instruction writes its result to the register. This speeds up the pipeline by eliminating the delay that would normally arise under these circumstances. The FPU registers are also dual ported to allow two accesses in one cycle, but they do not support feed forwarding. The FPU is linked to the cache by a 64-bit bus.

Another feature of the PowerPC instruction unit is that it can issue instructions **out of order**. For example, if the queue contains two integer instructions followed by a floating-point instruction, then the first integer instruction can be issued to the IU, and the floating-point instruction can also be issued to the FPU, even though it is not the next instruction in the queue, provided there are no dependencies between the instructions. The same applies to branch instructions. This allows the instruction unit to increase the number of instructions that can be executed in parallel.

8.3.2 The Digital Alpha 21064

The Alpha 21064 microprocessor is a 64-bit microprocessor, the first of a family of microprocessors based on Digital's Alpha AXP 64-bit architecture and was introduced in 1992. The Alpha architecture supports 64-bit registers, a 64-bit address bus and a 128-bit data bus. A 64-bit address space is four billion times the 4 Gb address space of a 32-bit microprocessor. However, implementations of the architecture can implement a smaller version of the address bus. The Alpha 21064 uses a 34-bit address bus and is thus capable of supporting up to 16 Gb of memory. The architecture is a load/store one and all computation takes place on operands stored in registers.

The Alpha 21064 is constructed on a chip containing under 1.7 million transistors and operates at 200 MHz. It provides separate on-chip data and instruction caches, each of size 8 kb, as well as providing support for optional off-chip cache of up to 16 Mb. There are 32 general purpose and 32 floating-point registers available, one of each being a dedicated (hardwired) zero register, so that it always contains zero. It is a superscalar processor with four execution units and is capable of issuing two instructions per clock cycle. Figure 8.8 illustrates the Alpha micro-architecture in a simplified form.

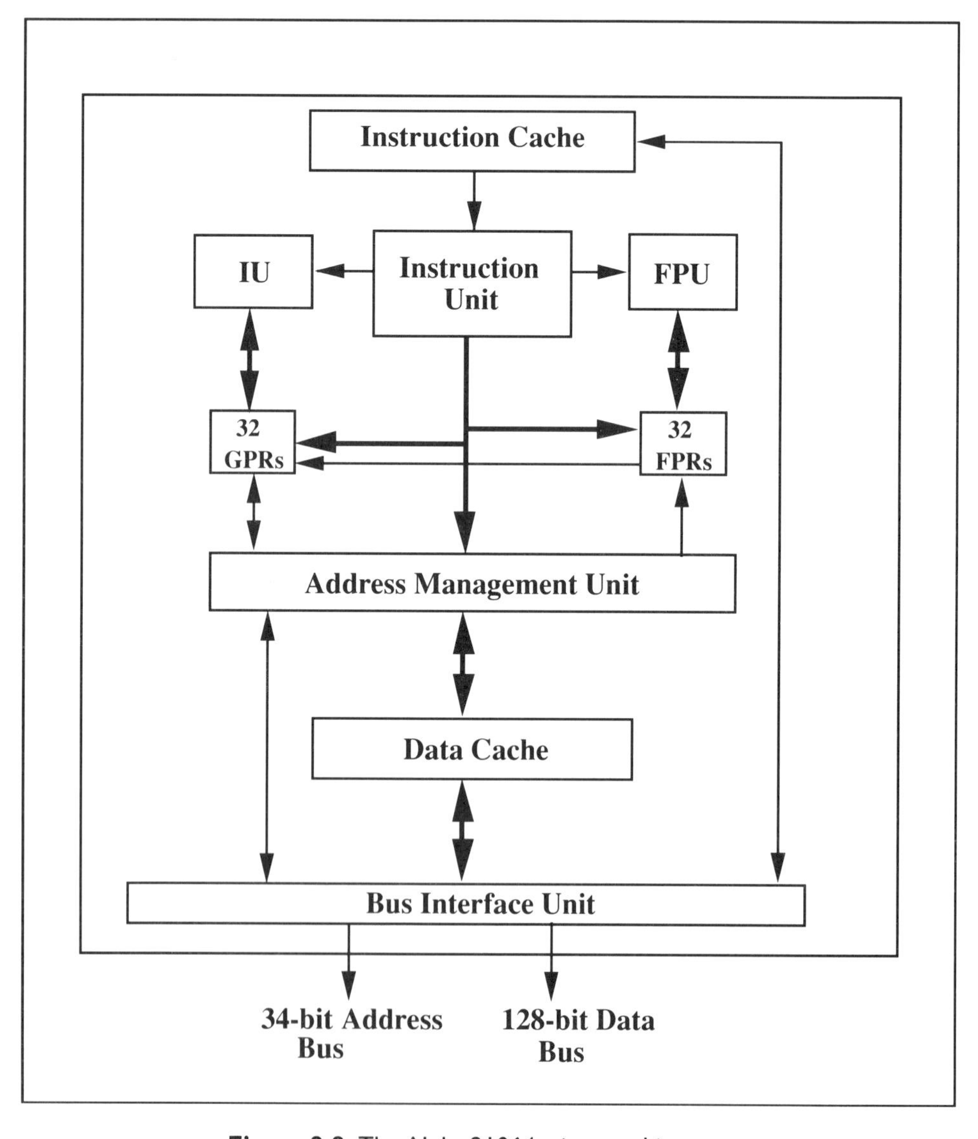

Figure 8.8 The Alpha 21064 micro-architecture.

The instruction unit is capable of extracting two instructions per cycle from the instruction cache. It is responsible for fetching, decoding and scheduling instructions for execution, that is, issuing the instructions to the integer unit or floating-point unit as appropriate. There are some restrictions on the dual issue of instructions, in other words, what instructions can be executed in parallel by the IU and FPU, but most combinations of instructions can be issued in parallel. To ease the multiple issue of instructions, the architecture avoids having a single status register, which can become a bottleneck if two or more instructions wish to access it simultaneously. (The Pentium provides special logic to allow for two instructions to update its status register.) Similarly, the use of special registers for particular instructions is avoided. For example, in many microprocessors (such as the 8086) a specific register is dedicated to holding an operand for a multiplication or division instruction. However, this means that two such instructions could not be issued simultaneously as they would require concurrent access to the dedicated register.

The IU is responsible for arithmetic and logical operations and the FPU handles floating-point arithmetic. The address management unit is responsible for dealing with memory addresses and handles load/store instructions. It allows the dual issue of a load/store instruction and arithmetic instructions. The address management unit contains an adder to calculate addresses so that the IU does not have to carry out such computations; thus, the address management unit can operate in parallel with the IU. All of the units are pipelined, with a seven-stage pipeline being used for integer instructions and a ten-stage pipeline for floating-point instructions.

The Alpha uses branch prediction to improve the performance of handling branch instructions. A combination of static and dynamic branch prediction is used. Static branch prediction adopts the policy that backward branches are predicted to be taken and forward branches are predicted not to be taken. In addition, some history information is noted to record whether the branch was actually taken or not. Future execution of the same instruction can make use of the history information to predict dynamically whether the branch should or should not be taken. In addition, the Alpha instruction set includes conditional move instructions which allow the value of an operand to be tested and the contents of a register to be moved on the basis of the test. These instructions reduce the number of branch instructions required in an Alpha program.

An interesting feature of the Alpha architecture is the provision of a **Privileged Architecture Library** (**PAL**), which is a set of subroutines designed to support the implementation of operating systems. PAL subroutines (called PALcode) handle such issues as resource management, context switching and interrupt mechanisms. This idea is similar to the use of BIOS subroutines on Intel 80x86 machines. The Alpha instruction set provides `Call__Pal` instructions to interface with these subroutines. Each operating system can have its own set of PAL subroutines and this greatly facilitates Alpha's support for operating systems such as VMS and Unix.

To facilitate migration of software from different Digital platforms, such as VAXs and MIPS-based workstations, to Alpha-based machines, a mechanism known as **binary translation** is used. Binary translation involves the translation of an executable program (binary program) from, for example, a VAX instruction set to an equivalent Alpha program. This required the implementation of an appropriate runtime system (software) on the Alpha. A binary translator is similar to a cross compiler, except that it translates from machine code for one machine to machine code for another machine, as opposed to translating from a high-level language program on one machine to a machine code program for another machine. The Alpha does *not* use a compatibility mode like that used for handling the migration of PDP11 programs to VAX machines.

8.4 Co-processors

Many computer systems use co-processors to carry out certain operations in parallel with the processor. Floating-point co-processors (also called maths co-processors or floating-point accelerators) are very often used to speed up floating-point operations. A floating-point co-processor is a specialized device designed to handle floating-point operations, such as adding and multiplying floating-point numbers. Co-processors are also used for carrying out memory management, I/O and graphics operations. Intel provided the 8087 as a maths co-processor for the 8086 microprocessor and the 8089 as an I/O co-processor. The 80287 maths co-processor was developed for the 80286 microprocessor. Motorola provides the 68881 floating-point co-processor for the M68000 family of microprocessors. A faster version called the 68882 is available for the higher-performance members of the M68000 family. As can be seen from the case studies, the more advanced microprocessors now include on-chip floating-point processors as well as on-chip memory management units.

8.5 System bus

The system bus links the microprocessor to the I/O and storage devices. A number of proprietary and standard bus systems have been developed. The advantage of a standard bus system is that different hardware manufacturers can produce a variety of devices for interfacing with machines using the standard bus system. Digital used the Unibus bus in the PDP11 family of minicomputers and allowed other manufacturers to produce devices, such as disks, that could use the Unibus. Such an open standard means that competing manufacturers are likely to use lower prices to attract customers. The **SCSI** (Small Computer Systems Interface) is also an open **I/O bus** standard. The SCSI bus is widely used in workstations and is also supported by the Apple Macintosh. The bus used in IBM PCs became a *de facto* standard known as the **ISA** (Industry Standard Architecture) bus and is used in machines based on the 8086/80286 and more powerful processors. It provides a 16-bit data bus and a 24-bit address bus. The **EISA** (Extended ISA) bus is used in many 80386/486 compatible systems and is a 32-bit bus. It is also compatible with devices designed for the ISA bus. IBM introduced the **MCA** (MicroChannel Architecture) 32-bit bus for IBM machines and this is not compatible with the EISA bus. There are also **PCI** and **VL** buses, which provide a higher performance than ISA, EISA and MCA buses. Motorola developed the **VME** bus which can handle both 16 and 32-bit processors. The **NuBus** is a 32-bit bus which is used in Apple Macintosh computers.

8.6 Summary

In this chapter we have reviewed the two most widely used (in computers) families of microprocessors, namely the Intel 80x86 and the Motorola 680x0 families. In addition, we have looked at two exciting RISC-based microprocessors which are generating a lot of interest at the time of writing (1994). Finally, we have mentioned a number of co-processors and bus systems that are in widespread use.

Exercises

8.1 Describe the trends in architecture design that can be observed by comparing successive members of the 80*x*86 and 680*x*0 families.

8.2 What are the common micro-architecture features of the PowerPC 601, Alpha 21064 and Pentium microprocessors? What are the major differences?

8.3 Why is branch prediction important? Find out more about branch prediction from the reading list and compare static with dynamic prediction mechanisms.

8.4 Find out what rules govern the issue of multiple instructions in the Pentium, PowerPC and Alpha 21064. Which microprocessor is the most flexible and which is the most restrictive in terms of allowing multiple issue of instructions?

8.5 Illustrate, in the form of a block diagram, the major features of a high-performance microprocessor, based on the architecture of the Pentium, the PowerPC and the Alpha 21064.

8.6 Compare the reasons for using separate data and instruction caches in the Pentium and Alpha 21064 with those for using a unified cache like that in the PowerPC 601.

8.7 Why is pipelining important? Find out more about the pipelining stages used in the Pentium, PowerPC and Alpha 21064. What have the pipelines in common and where do they differ?

8.8 Compare any three superscalar microprocessors in terms of the number and functionality of the multiple execution units provided.

8.9 Draw up a table to compare a CISC processor, such as the Pentium, with two or more RISC machines, using such headings as clock speed, cache size and type, number of pipeline stages, number of functional units and so on.

8.7 Reading list

Anderson, J.A. (1994) *Foundations of Computer Technology*, Chapman & Hall, London.
Brey, B.B. (1994) *8086/8088, 80286, 80386, and 80486 Assembly Language Programming*, Merrill (MacMillan), New York.
Geppert, L., (1993) The New Contenders, *IEEE Spectrum*, December, **30**(12), 20–25.
Rafiquzzaman, M. (1992) *Microprocessors: Theory and Applications*, Prentice Hall, Englewood Cliffs, NJ.
Stallings, W. (1990) *Reduced Instruction Set Computers*, IEEE Computer Society Press, Los Alamitos, CA.
Subbarao, W.V. (1991) *16/32-Bit Microprocessors: 68000/68010/68020, Software, Hardware and Design Applications*, Macmillan, New York.

8.7.1 PowerPC

Burgess, B., Ullah, N., Van Overen, P. and Ogden, D. (1994) The PowerPC 603 Microprocessor, *CACM*, **37**(6), 34–42.
Becker, M.C., Allen, M.S., Moore, C.R., Muhich, J.S. and Tuttle D.P. (1993) The PowerPC 601 Microprocessor; *IEEE Micro*, **13**(5), 54–68.
Diefendorff, K. (1994) History of the PowerPC Architecture, *CACM*, **37**(6), 28–33.
Diefendorff K., Oehler, R., and Hochsprung R. (1994) Evolution of the PowerPC Architecture; *IEEE Micro*, **14**(2), 34–49.
Ryan, R. (1993) RISC Drives the PowerPC; *Byte*, August, **18**(9), 79–90.
Thompson, T. (1993) PowerPC Performs for Less; *Byte*, August, **18**(9), 56–74.

8.7.2 IBM RS/6000

Oehler, R.R and Blasgen, M.W.(1991) IBM RISC System/6000: Architecture and Performance; *IEEE Micro*, **11**(3), 14–17.

8.7.3 Motorola 88000

Alsup, M. (1990) Motorola's 88000 Family Architecture; *IEEE Micro*, **10**(3), 48–66.

8.7.4 Intel Pentium

Alpert, D. and Avnon, D. (1993) Architecture of the Pentium Microprocessor; *IEEE Micro*, **13**(3), 11–21.
Crawford, J., Alpert, D. and Fu, B. (1993) An Overview of Intel's Pentium Processor, video from University Video Communications, PO Box 5129, Stanford, CA 94309, USA.

8.7.5 Intel i860

Kohn, L. and Margulis N. (1989) Introducing the Intel i860 64-bit Microprocessor; *IEEE Micro*, **9**(4), 15–30.

8.7.6 MIPS R4000

Mirapuri, S., Woodacre, M. and Vasseghi, N. (1992) The MIPS R4000 Processor, *IEEE Micro*, **12**(2), 10–22.

8.7.7 Hewlett Packard PA7100

Asprey, T., Averill, G.S., DeLano, E., Mason, R., Weiner, B., and Yetter J. (1993) Performance Features of the PA7100 Microprocessor; *IEEE Micro*, **13**(3), 22–35.

8.7.8 *Digital Alpha*

McLellan, E. (1993) The Alpha AXP Architecture and 21064 Processor; *IEEE Micro*, **13**(3), 36–47.

Sites, D and Meyer, D. (1992) Alpha Architecture, video from University Video Communications, PO Box 5129, Stanford, CA 94309, USA.

8.7.9 *Bus standards*

Richardson, W. (1994) Popular Card Slot Standards, *Information Alley*, 31st October, Volume I, Issue 14. This is available from Apple on the Internet: ftp.austin.apple.com:Apple.Support.Area/The.Information.Alley.

Appendix A
Units of measurement in computing

Table A.1 summarizes the units of measurement we encounter in describing the world of computers. The processing speed of a computer is enormous compared with the speed at which humans operate. When dealing with units of time, the familiar units of seconds, minutes, hours and so on, are much too large for describing the time it takes a computer to carry out some of its basic actions. We use sub-multiples of a second such as the millisecond (1 ms = 1/1000 or 10^{-3}s), microsecond (1 μs = 1/1000 000 or 10^{-6}s), nanosecond (1 ns = 1/1000 million or 10^{-9}s) and picosecond (1 ps = 1 /million millions, or 10^{-12}s) when measuring the time it takes the processor to carry out its tasks.

Computers are also capable of storing huge amounts of information. The fundamental unit of storage is the byte (also called character). Since this is a small amount of information, we group bytes into larger units so that we can easily refer to thousands, millions or billions of them. (The term billion is used to mean 1000 millions in computing measurements but in other circumstances it can also mean – at least in European usage – 1 million millions.) When counting bytes we deal in powers of 2 such as 2^{10}, which is called a kilobyte (**kb**), 2^{20} called a megabyte (**Mb**), 2^{30} called a gigabyte (**Gb**) and 2^{40} called a terabyte (**Tb**).

A crucial component of a computer system is a clock, the frequency of which is important in determining a computer's processing speed. Frequency is measured in units call hertz (Hz) where 1 Hz equals one cycle per second and one million hertz is one megahertz (MHz). This unit is very small when we consider that modern computers operate with clock frequencies of up to 100 MHz. A basic PC now operates from typically 25 MHz upwards.

Table A.1 Units of measurement in computing.

	Unit	2^{10}	2^{20}	2^{30}	2^{40}
Storage	byte (b)	kilobyte (kb)	megabyte (Mb)	gigabyte (Gb)	terabyte (Tb)
Speed	bits per sec (bps)	kilo (kbps)	mega (Mbps)	giga (Gbps)	tera (Tbps)
	Unit	10^{-3}	10^{-6}	10^{-9}	10^{-12}
Time	second (s)	millisecond (ms)	microsecond (Mμs)	nanosecond (ns)	picosecond (ps)
	Unit	10^{3}	10^{6}	10^{9}	10^{12}
Frequency	hertz (Hz)	kiloherz (kHz)	megaherz (MHz)	gigaherz (GHz)	teraherz (THz)

Appendix B
Information representation

In order to understand what happens inside a computer we must understand how a computer represents information internally. For example, the text you are reading is stored on a computer disk. It was entered into a computer system using a word processing program. Inside the computer's memory and on the disk this text (and all other information) can be thought of as being represented by a very long sequence of ones and zeros, that is, in **binary form.** It appears as text only on a computer's monitor or on printed output. A computer monitor's hardware receives binary information and transforms it to the symbols that are displayed. Similarly, a printer's hardware converts binary information to the text (or graphic) that is printed. Inside the CPU and the computer's memory, information is actually stored and transmitted in electrical form, while on disk it is stored in magnetic form. A particular electrical signal represents a one (`1`) and another signal represents a zero (`0`). Similarly, a specific magnetic orientation represents `1` and another orientation `0`. A group of these binary digits (bits) can be considered to form a binary code and information is encoded as a sequence of individual units, each of which corresponds to a distinct binary code.

Fundamental principle: All information is represented by binary codes in a computer system.

B.1 Classifying information

From a computing perspective, we can broadly classify the information we wish to store as either *numeric* or *textual*. Numeric information refers to information with which we may wish to do arithmetic, numbers such as 23, 404, 3.14159, 0.96 and so on. Numbers without a decimal point are called **integers** and those that have a decimal point are called **reals.** Computer scientists often refer to real numbers as **floating-point** numbers. It is important to note that different techniques are used to represent integers and reals inside a computer system. Textual information is made up of individual characters (`a`, `b`, `c`, ..., `A`, `B`, `C`, ..., `-`, `+`, `;`, `"`, `&`, `%`, `#`, `'`, `£`, `0`, `1`, `2`, ..., `9` and so on). Examples include a person's name, address, phone number, an essay, the information on the page you are reading. The term **alphanumeric** refers to text containing both alphabetic characters and numbers such as an address, say, *London W12.* Fortunately international standards for information representation have been developed to make life easier for computer manufacturers and users. This means that we can easily transfer information from one make of computer to another. One such standard is the **ASCII** (American Standard Code for Information Interchange) standard. This standard is used for representing textual information and is described later.

B.2 Representing numbers

B.2.1 *Integers*

We are so familiar with the decimal number system that we might think that everything that uses numbers would, by default, use the decimal system. However, computers, as we have said, use a number system called **binary**, which involves only two digits: 0 and 1. In the decimal system, we represent numbers using ten digits based on powers of 10. For example, the number 2376 may also be written as:

$$2*10^3 + 3*10^2 + 7*10^1 + 6*10^0$$

More formally, we say that the digits in a positive decimal number are weighted by increasing powers of 10. We say that they use the **base** 10. To illustrate this further, we could write the above number in the following form:

weighting:	10^3	10^2	10^1	10^0
digits	2	3	7	6
decimal 2376 =	$2*10^3$ +	$3*10^2$+	$7*10^1$+	$6*10^0$

The left-most digit, 2 in this example, is called the **most significant** digit. The right-most digit, 6 in this example, is called the **least significant** digit. The digits on the left-hand side are called the **high-order** digits (higher powers of 10) and the digits on the right-hand side are called the **low-order** digits (lower powers of 10). The above system can be used to write numbers in any base m as follows, assuming we are dealing with a four-digit number:

weighting:	m^3	m^2	m^1	m^0
digits	d_3	d_2	d_1	d_0
$base_m\ d_3d_2d_1d_0$=	d_3*m^3 +	d_2*m^2 +	d_1*m^1 +	d_0*m^0

We refer to the digits making up a number by their position, starting from the right-hand side with position 0 (note that we count from zero). As we have seen earlier, when the base is 10, we replace m by 10. In the binary number system the base is **2** so we can write the 8-bit binary number 0101 1100 (In this text, we usually insert a space after every four bits when writing a binary number to make it easier to read. Spaces should not be inserted when using a binary number in a program.) as:

weighting:	2^7	2^6	2^5	2^4	2^3	2^2	2^1	2^0
bits	0	1	0	1	1	1	0	0

$$01011100 = 0*2^7+1*2^6+0*2^5+1*2^4+1*2^3+1*2^2+0*2^1+0*2^0$$
$$= 0 + 64_{10} + 0 + 16_{10} + 8_{10} + 4_{10} + 0 + 0$$
$$= 92_{10}$$

The left-most bit is called the **most significant bit** (**MSB**). The left-most bits in a binary number are referred to as the **high-order** bits. The right-most bit in a binary number is called the **least significant bit** (**LSB**). The rightmost bits in a binary number are referred to as the **low-order** bits. In the case of a 16-bit number, we use the above scheme with the powers of 2 ranging from 0 to 15, with a 32-bit number, the powers of 2 range from 0 to 31.

Exercises

B.1 Convert the following binary numbers to decimal:

(i)	0000 1000	(ii)	0000 1001	(iii)	0000 0111
(iv)	0100 0001	(v)	0111 1111	(vi)	0110 0001

Converting from decimal to binary

To convert from any number base to another, you repeatedly divide the number to be converted by the new base and the remainder of the division at each stage becomes a digit in the new base until the result of the division is 0. So to convert decimal 35 to binary we do the following:

	Remainder
35 / 2	1
17 / 2	1
8 / 2	0
4 / 2	0
2 / 2	0
1 / 2	1
0	

The result is read *upwards* giving $35_{10} = 100011_2$. The number 100011_2 is an unsigned binary number. We can convert any positive decimal number to binary with the above method. Signed numbers are represented differently, as described later.

Short cuts

To convert to binary any decimal number which is a power of 2, you simply write 1 followed by the number of zeros, which is given by the power of 2. For example, 32 is 2^5, so we write it as 1 followed by 5 zeros, 10000; 128 is 2^7 so we write it as 1 followed by 7 zeros, 100 0000. Another thing worth remembering is that the largest binary number that can be stored in a given number of bits is made up of all 1s. An easy way to convert this to decimal is to note that this value is one less than 2 to the power of the number of bits. For example, if we are using 4-bit numbers, the largest value we can represent is 1111 which is $2^4 - 1 = 15$; with a 6-bit number the largest value we can represent is 11 1111, the decimal equivalent is $2^6 - 1 = 63$. The same techniques apply to decimal numbers, so that the largest value that a three-digit decimal number can represent is $999 = 10^3 - 1$.

Exercises

B.2 Convert the following decimal numbers to binary, writing them as 8-bit binary numbers. You may pad with 0s on the left hand side to make up 8 bits when necessary:

(i) 3 (ii) 15 (iii) 16
(iv) 63 (v) 64 (vi) 255

Hexadecimal numbers

One difficulty with binary numbers is that they tend to be composed of long sequences of bits and so it is easy to err in working with them. Thus, in writing them down we might arrange them in groups of three or four. A 16-bit binary number such as 0110100011001010 could be written as 0110 1000 1100 1010, which is easier to read. However, it is still tedious to work with such numbers. For this reason we use other number systems. Because 10 is not an exact power of 2, it is not as convenient for working with binary numbers as a system using a base which is a power of 2. Two commonly used computer number systems are the **hexadecimal** (**base 16**) and **octal** (**base 8**) systems. It is easier to convert a binary number to hexadecimal or octal (and vice versa) than it is to convert a binary number to decimal.

With the hexadecimal system, we require 16 distinct digits (representing the numbers 0 to 15). Using the number digits alone only gives us ten digits, so we use letters as well. The decimal numbers 0 to 15 are represented by the hexadecimal digits 0 to 9 and the letters A to F. The hexadecimal digits correspond to their decimal equivalents. The letter A represents 10, B represents 11, C represents 12, D represents 13, E represents 14 and F represents 15. Hexadecimal numbers are weighted in powers of 16, so the number 2FA can be converted to decimal as follows:

weighting:		16^2	16^1	16^0
digits		2	F	A
2FA	=	$2 * 16^2 +$	$F * 16^1 +$	$A * 16^0$
	=	$2 * 16^2 +$	$15 * 16^1 +$	$10 * 16^0$
	=	256 + 240 + 10		
	=	506_{10}		

A hexadecimal digit is represented by **four bits** (since $2^4 = 16$ and we require 16 bit patterns for 16 digits). Thus, all 32-bit numbers can be written as eight-digit hexadecimal numbers, 16-bit binary numbers can be written as four-digit hexadecimal numbers and 8-bit binary numbers can be represented by two-digit hexadecimal numbers. This is the major advantage of using hexadecimal numbers, since computers tend almost always to use 32-bit, 16-bit or 8-bit numbers to represent information. So, if we wish to write down the contents of a processor register which can store 16 bits, we can write it as a four-digit hexadecimal number. If we were to use decimal, we would have to write it as a number between 0 and 65 536 and this is not nearly so convenient or useful.

To convert a binary number to hexadecimal, you break the number into groups of four bits from the right-hand side. Then you convert each group of four bits into its equivalent hexadecimal digit. This process gives you the hexadecimal equivalent of the original binary number. If there are fewer than four bits in the leftmost group, you still convert them to their hexadecimal equivalent (pad on the left with 0s). For example, the 16-bit binary number 0110100011001010 can be divided into the groups: 0110 1000 1100 1010. These are converted to the hexadecimal digits 68CA. Assembly language programmers make extensive use of the hexadecimal numbering system, so it is important to be familiar with it. For example, the letter A is represented inside a computer by the binary code 0100 0001, which can be written in hexadecimal as 41. To convert from hexadecimal to binary, we simply convert each hexadecimal digit to its 4-bit equivalent, padding with 0s on the left, if necessary to make up the 4 bits. For example, hexadecimal digit 4 is written as 0100 in binary, hexadecimal digit 1 is written as 0001 in binary and thus hexadecimal number 41 is 0100 0001 in binary.

When we write a number, we must indicate its base so that we know which number we are referring to. For example, the number 10 in binary represents two; in decimal it represents ten and in hexadecimal it represents sixteen. There are two common methods for indicating the base when writing a number in an assembly language program. One method (used in 8086 programs) is to add a character to the end of the number to indicate the base, H for hexadecimal, D for decimal and B for binary. Thus, we can easily distinguish between the numbers 10H, 10D and 10B. Lowercase letters may also be used. The second method (used in M68000 programs) is to begin the number with a character which indicates the base. For example, hexadecimal numbers may be written so as to begin with the $ character and binary numbers written so as to begin with the % character. Using this notation, the number $10 represents the hexadecimal number 10 and %10 represents the binary number 10. The absence of a leading character indicates a decimal number in an M68000 program. Table B.1 displays the numbers 1 to 15 in the binary, hexadecimal and decimal bases.

Table B.1 Representing numbers in binary, hexadecimal and decimal bases.

Binary	Hexadecimal	Decimal
0000	0	0
0001	1	1
0010	2	2
0011	3	3
0100	4	4
0101	5	5
0110	6	6
0111	7	7
1000	8	8
1001	9	9
1010	A	10
1011	B	11
1100	C	12
1101	D	13
1110	E	14
1111	F	15

Exercises

B.3 Convert the following:

(a) From hexadecimal to 16-bit binary numbers : `1B87h`, `AF33h`, `713Ch`, `80EFh`.

(b) From binary to hexadecimal: `1111 1100 1000 0111` and `1010 1110 1001 1100`.

Negative numbers

So far the only numbers we have looked at were **unsigned** numbers. It is important to be able to represent both unsigned and **signed** numbers, both positive and negative numbers. This raises the question of how to represent negative numbers. In our everyday representation of negative numbers, we use a **minus sign** '–' (hyphen on a keyboard) to indicate that a number is negative. Inside a computer we must represent the sign in binary, since all information is stored in binary form. There are a number of methods for representing negative numbers, two of which are the **signed magnitude** and **two's complement** representations.

Signed-magnitude numbers

In a signed-magnitude number, the most significant bit is used as a **sign** bit to indicate whether the number is positive or negative. Thus for an 8-bit number, the most significant bit, bit number `7`, acts as the sign bit. The value `1` is used to indicate a **negative** number and the value `0` indicates a **positive** number. The remaining bits are used to represent the **magnitude** of the number.

Example B.1

The numbers `45` and `-45` are represented in signed magnitude as:

```
+45  =  00101101B
-45  =  10101101B
```

If we are not interested in negative numbers, we can represent numbers ranging from `0` to `255` using 8 bits. Such numbers are called **unsigned** numbers. Using signed magnitude the range that can be represented using 8 bits is from `-127` to `+127` and we should note that `0` is represented twice (as `1000 0000B` and `0000 0000B`, that is, as a positive and negative zero). This dual representation of zero causes problems when we wish to compare a variable with `0`. In addition, the hardware to do arithmetic using signed-magnitude numbers is complex and slow when compared with using the two's complement representation of signed numbers. As a result, the signed magnitude representation is rarely used in computers.

Complementary number representation

We are used to the concept of a sign and a magnitude when dealing with decimal numbers. A positive sign is implicit (if not written) and negative numbers are written by preceding the positive number by a minus sign. The idea of a complementary number system is that each number has a unique representation. Two's complement is a complementary number system used in computers and is the most commonly used method for representing signed numbers.

Two's complement numbers

We still use a sign bit as an indicator of the sign of the number. In the case of positive numbers, the representation is identical to that of signed magnitude, so that the sign bit is 0 and the remaining bits represent the positive number. In the case of negative numbers, the sign bit is 1 but the bits to the right of the sign bit do not *directly* indicate the magnitude of the number. The number -1 for example is represented by 1111 if we use 4-bit two's complement numbers while 1111 would represent the number -7 using a signed magnitude representation. Figure B.1 shows the range of numbers that can be represented using a 4-bit two's complement representation.

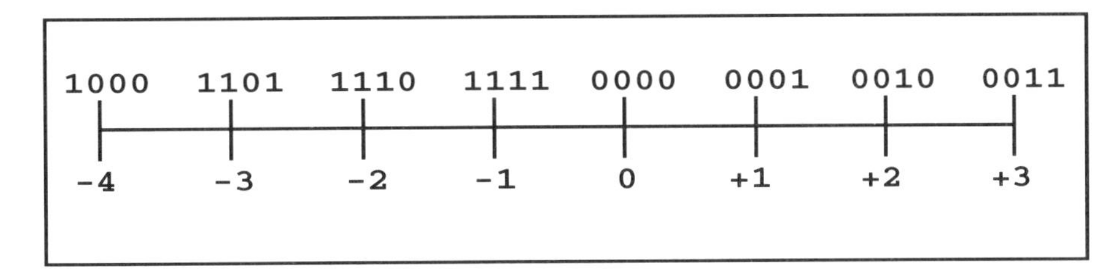

Figure B.1 Four-bit two's complement numbers with their decimal equivalents.

In terms of digit weightings we can interpret two's complement numbers as using a negative weight for the most significant bit. In the case of a 4-bit two's complement number, the sign bit can be interpreted as having a weight of $-2^3 = -8$ and the remaining bits have their usual positive weightings. In the case of an 8-bit two's complement number, the sign bit has a weight of $-2^7 = -128$. Thus the weightings of an 8-bit two's complement number may be written as:

Bit position:	7	6	5	4	3	2	1	0
Weighting:	-2^7	2^6	2^5	2^4	2^3	2^2	2^1	2^0
Signed equivalent:	-128	+64	+32	+16	+8	+4	+2	+1

The two's complement number 1000 0000 (-128) is the largest negative number that can be represented using 8 bits. The two's complement number 0111 1111 (127) is the largest positive number that can be represented using 8 bits. In other words a total of 256 numbers can be represented using 8-bit two's complement numbers, ranging from -128 to 127. There is only one representation for zero. Table B.2 lists the decimal equivalents of some 8-bit, two's complement and unsigned binary numbers.

Table B.2 Some 8-bit unsigned and two's complement numbers.

Bit pattern	Unsigned	Two's complement
0000 0000	0	0
0000 0001	1	1
0000 0010	2	2
0111 1110	126	126
0111 1111	127	127
1000 0000	128	-128
1000 0001	129	-127
1111 1110	254	-2
1111 1111	255	-1

To convert a two's complement number such as 1000 0001 to decimal, we can use the weightings given above to compute the decimal equivalent, in this case, -128 + 1 = -127. However, there is an easier method for carrying out two's complement conversions. To convert a binary number such as 0110 0011 (99_{10}) to its negative two's complement form, we carry out two operations. First, we complement the number by changing all the one bits to zeros and the zero bits to ones (this is called the **one's complement** representation of the number). This step is also described as **flipping** the bits. The one's complement of 0110 0011 is 1001 1100. The second step in converting to two's complement is to add 1 to the one's complement representation. The one's complement was 1001 1100, so the two's complement of this number is 1001 1100 + 0000 0001 giving 1001 1101 (-99_{10}). In summary, to convert any unsigned binary number to its two's complement form, we flip the bits of the number and add 1.
In addition, to convert a two's complement number to its positive form, we carry out the same steps: we flip the bits and add one. For example, converting 1001 1101 from two's complement yields 0110 0010 + 1 which gives 0110 0011 (99_{10}) and, because the sign bit was 1, we know that the original number represented -99_{10}.

Example B.2

Convert -89_{10} to two's complement:

	89_{10}	=	01011001
One's complement	89_{10}	=	10100110
Add one			+1
Two's complement	-89_{10}	=	10100111

Two's complement conversion rule

To negate a number to two's complement: Flip the bits and add 1.

A nice property of two's complement numbers is that we can add them together without concern for the sign. For example adding +89 to -89 is carried out as:

	01011001_2	89_{10}
+	10100111_2	-89_{10}
	00000000_2	0_{10}

This means that to subtract one number from another number, we just negate the number to be subtracted and then add the two numbers. This operation is performed whether the number to be subtracted is positive or negative. This means that using two's complement numbers, the processor can add and subtract using the same hardware circuit and a separate circuit for subtraction is not required. This simplifies the design of the ALU and is one of the reasons why two's complement is the most commonly used method for representing negative numbers in microprocessors.

Number range and overflow

The range of numbers (called the number range) that can be stored in a given number of bits is important. Given an 8-bit number, we can represent unsigned numbers in the range 0 to 255 ($2^8 - 1$) and two's complement numbers in the range -128 to +127 (-2^7 to 2^7). Given a 16-bit number, we can represent unsigned numbers in the range 0 to 65 535 ($2^{16} - 1$) and two's complement numbers in the range -32 768 to 32 767 (-2^{15} to $2^{15} - 1$). In general given an n-bit number, we can represent unsigned numbers in the range 0 to $2^n - 1$ and two's complement numbers in the range -2^{n-1} to $2^{n-1} - 1$.

When we wish to know the maximum amount of memory that a processor can access, we look at the number of bits that the processor uses to represent a memory address. This determines the maximum memory address that can be accessed. For example, a processor that uses 16-bit addresses will be able to access up to 65 536 memory locations (64 kb), with addresses from 0 to 65 535. A 20-bit address allows up to 2^{20} (1 Mb) memory locations to be accessed, a 24-bit address allows up to 16 Mb (2^{24}bytes) of RAM to be accessed, a 32-bit address allows up to 4Gb (2^{32}bytes) of RAM to be accessed.

What happens if we attempt to store a larger unsigned value than 255 (or a more negative signed value than -128) in an 8-bit register? For example, if we attempt the calculation 70 + 75 using 8-bit two's complement numbers, the result of 145 (1001 0001B) is a **negative number** in two's complement! This situation, when it arises, is called **overflow**. It occurs when we attempt to represent a number outside the range of numbers that can be stored in a particular register or memory variable. Overflow is detected by the hardware of the CPU and its occurrence is recorded in the CPU's status register. This register uses a flag called the overflow flag or O-flag to record the occurrence of an overflow. This allows the programmer to test for this condition in an assembly language program and deal with it appropriately. The 8086 provides the jo/jno instructions to branch (or not to branch) if overflow occurs. Figure B.2 illustrates the relationship between number range and overflow for 8-bit two's complement numbers.

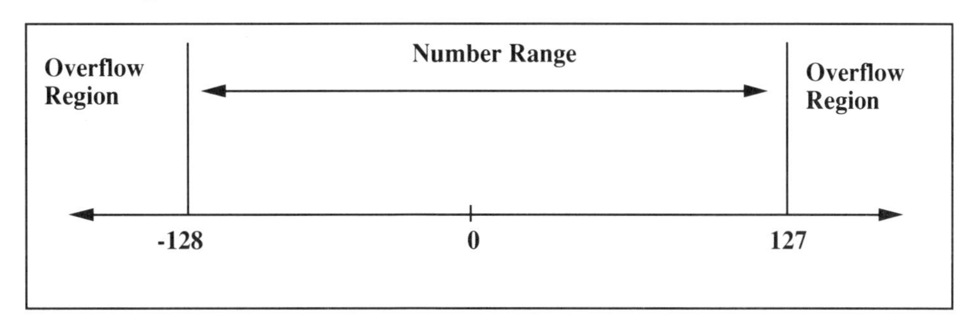

Figure B.2 Number range and overflow regions for 8-bit two's complement numbers.

Note: In our programs we may use two's complement numbers or unsigned binary numbers. However, this raises a very important question, how can we tell by looking at a number whether it is a two's complement number or an unsigned number. Does 1111 1111B represent the decimal number 255 or the number -1? The answer is that we *cannot* tell, by looking at a number, how it should be interpreted. It is the responsibility of the programmer to use the number correctly. It is important to remember that you can never tell how any byte (word or long word) is to be interpreted by looking at its value alone. It could represent a signed or unsigned number, an ASCII code, a machine code instruction and so on. The context (in which the information stored in the byte is used) will determine how it is to be interpreted. Assembly languages provide separate conditional jump instructions for handling comparisons involving unsigned or signed numbers. It is the programmer's responsibility to use the correct instructions.

Exercises

B.4 Convert the decimal numbers -64, -127, -15, -16, -1, +32 and +8 to 8-bit signed-magnitude and two's complement numbers.

B.5 What is the range of unsigned numbers that can be represented by 20-bit, 24-bit and 32-bit numbers?

B.6 What is the range of numbers that can be represented using 32-bit two's complement numbers?

B.7 What problem arises in representing zero in signed magnitude and one's complement?

B.8 What is overflow and how might it occur?

B.2.2 Floating-point numbers

So far we have described how to represent integers in a computer system, which is sufficient for the purposes of this text. We now briefly introduce methods for representing real numbers. A different representation is required for real (usually called floating-point) numbers. We sometimes write such numbers in scientific notation so that the number 562.42 can be written as 0.56242×10^3. We can express any floating-point number as: $\pm m \times r^{exp}$ where m is the **mantissa,** r is the **radix** and exp is the **exponent**. For decimal numbers the radix is 10 and for binary numbers the radix is 2. Since we use binary numbers in a computer system, we do not have to store the radix explicitly when representing floating-point numbers. This means that we only need to store the mantissa and the exponent of the number to be represented. Thus, for the number $0.110\ 11011 \times 2^3$ only the values 11011011 and the exponent 3 (converted to binary) need to be stored. The binary point and radix are implicit.

A floating-point number is **normalized** if the most significant digit of the mantissa is **non-zero**, as in the above example. Any floating-point number can be normalized by adjusting the exponent appropriately. For example, 0.0001011 is normalized to 0.1011×2^{-3}. To represent 0 as a floating-point number, both the mantissa and the exponent are represented as zero.

There are various standards (IEEE, ANSI and others) that define how the mantissa and exponent of a floating-point number should be stored. Most standards use a 32-bit format for storing single precision floating-point numbers and a 64-bit format for storing double precision floating-point numbers. A *possible* format for a 32-bit floating-point number is the following, which uses a sign bit, 23 bits to represent the mantissa and the remaining eight bits to represent the exponent. The mantissa could be represented using either signed magnitude or two's complement. The exponent could be in two's complement (but another form called **excess notation** is also used). Thus a 32-bit floating-point number could be represented as in Figure B.3(a), where S is the sign bit. Using this format, the number 0.1101 1011 × 2^3 could be stored as shown in Figure B.3(b).

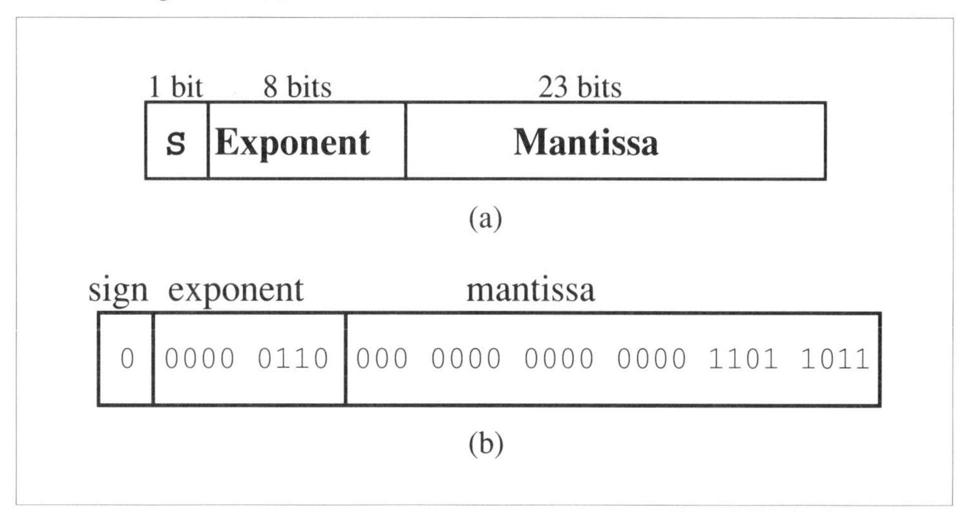

Figure B.3 Storing floating-point numbers.

B.2.3 *Binary coded decimal (BCD) numbers*

This form of number representation allows us to represent numbers in their decimal form, in that each digit of the decimal number is translated to binary and the binary representations of the digits making up the decimal number are stored. This makes I/O operations for BCD numbers easier than if we represent decimal numbers as pure binary numbers, as described earlier. For example, when we read a number like 254 from the keyboard, we convert it to binary if we wish to do arithmetic with it. This involves converting the 2 to its binary form, multiplying it by 100, converting the 5 to its binary form, multiplying it by 10 and adding it to the previous number (giving 250) and finally reading the 4, converting it to its binary form and adding it to the previous sum giving the number 254. The **BCD** method of representing numbers is used to get around this problem. Each digit is simply encoded into its equivalent 4-bit form and each digit is stored separately, instead of storing the binary equivalent of the whole number. Thus 254D would be stored as

```
0000 0010 0000 0101 0000 0100
        2         5         4
```

in BCD form, using eight bits per digit (**unpacked**) as opposed to representing it as

```
1111 1110
```

in unsigned binary form. The above BCD number can be **packed** so as to store two digits per byte:

```
0000 0010 0101 0100
  0    2    5    4
```

The 8086 provides special instructions that allow addition, subtraction, multiplication and division to be carried out on BCD numbers.

B.3 Representing characters: ASCII codes

ASCII codes are used to represent characters in a computer system. Each character we wish to use must be assigned a unique **binary code** or number to distinguish it from all other characters. There are over 100 characters to be represented, when we count the upper-case letters (`A` to `Z`), the lower-case letters (`a` to `z`), the digits (`0` to `9`), the punctuation (`, ; . " ? !`) and other characters. Using ASCII codes, the letter `A` is represented by the binary code `1000001`, the letter `B` by `1000010` and so on. Because it is awkward to write these codes in binary form, we usually convert them to their **decimal** (or **hexadecimal**, base 16) equivalents. So the letter `A` may be represented by code `65` in decimal and `B` by code `66`. Inside the computer they are always represented as binary numbers.

The standard ASCII code uses seven bits, so that each character is represented by seven bits. As we have seen, the letter **A** is represented by the seven bits `1000001`. Because standard ASCII codes use seven bits, a total of 128 different characters may be represented ($2^7 = 128$, the number of combinations of seven bits). There are codes for the upper-case letters, lower-case letters, digits, punctuation and other symbols (`, ; : " ? ' ! *&%$#+-<>/ [ ] { } \ ~ ( )` and so on). In addition, there are ASCII codes for a number of special characters called **control characters.** Control characters are used to control devices attached to the computer and to control communications between the computer and these devices. For example, one such character causes your computer to beep: the **Bel** character (ASCII code `7`). The **Line-feed** (ASCII code `10`) character causes a print head or screen cursor to go onto a new line. The **Carriage Return** (ASCII code `13`) character causes the print head or screen cursor to go to the start of a line. The **Form-feed** (ASCII code `12`) character causes a printer to skip to the top of the next page. Other control characters are used to control communication between devices and the computer. Table B.3 is a list of some commonly used ASCII codes and the full list of ASCII characters is given in Table B.4. Remember, inside the computer it is the binary form of the ASCII code that is used. The decimal and hexadecimal values are useful for people to refer to a particular ASCII code.

Table B.3 Some commonly used ASCII codes.

Char	Binary	Hex	Decimal	Char	Binary	Hex	Decimal
NUL	000 0000	00	0	A	100 0001	41	65
BEL	000 0111	07	7	B	100 0010	42	66
LF	000 1010	0A	10	C	100 0011	43	67
FF	000 1100	0C	12	D	100 0100	44	68
CR	000 1011	0D	13	E	100 0101	45	69
SP	010 0000	20	32	F	100 0110	46	70
				G	100 0111	47	71
				H	100 1000	48	72
*	010 1010	2A	42	Y	101 1001	59	89
+	010 1011	2B	43	Z	101 1010	5A	90
,	010 1100	2C	44	[	101 1011	5B	91
-	010 1101	2D	45	Ø	101 1100	5C	92
.	010 1110	2E	46				
/	010 1111	2F	47	a	110 0001	61	97
0	011 0000	30	48	b	110 0010	62	98
1	011 0001	31	49	c	110 0011	63	99
2	011 0010	32	50	d	110 0100	64	100
3	011 0011	33	51	e	110 0101	65	101
4	011 0100	34	52	f	110 0110	66	102
5	011 0101	35	53	g	110 0111	67	103
6	011 0110	36	54	h	110 1000	68	104
7	011 0111	37	55				
8	011 1000	38	56	y	111 1001	79	121
9	011 1001	39	57	z	111 1010	7A	122

Table B.4 Standard ASCII codes

Char	Binary	Hex	Decimal	Char	Binary	Hex	Decimal
NUL	000 0000	00	0	SP	010 0000	20	32
SOH	000 0001	01	1	!	010 0001	21	33
STX	000 0010	02	2	"	010 0010	22	34
ETX	000 0011	03	3	#	010 0011	23	35
EOT	000 0100	04	4	$	010 0100	24	36
ENQ	000 0101	05	5	%	010 0101	25	37
ACK	000 0110	06	6	&	010 0110	26	38
BEL	000 0111	07	7	'	010 0111	27	39
BS	000 1000	08	8	(	010 1000	28	40
HT	000 1001	09	9	)	010 1001	29	41
LF	000 1010	0A	10	*	010 1010	2A	42
VT	000 1011	0B	11	+	010 1011	2B	43
FF	000 1100	0C	12	,	010 1100	2C	44
CR	000 1011	0D	13	-	010 1101	2D	45
SO	000 1110	0E	14	.	010 1110	2E	46
SI	000 1111	0F	15	/	010 1111	2F	47
DLE	001 0000	10	16	0	011 0000	30	48
DC1	001 0001	11	17	1	011 0001	31	49
DC2	001 0010	12	18	2	011 0010	32	50
DC3	001 0011	13	19	3	011 0011	33	51
DC4	001 0100	14	20	4	011 0100	34	52
NAK	001 0101	15	21	5	011 0101	35	53

SYN	001 0110	16	22	6	011 0110	36	54
ETB	001 0111	17	23	7	011 0111	37	55
CAN	001 1000	18	24	8	011 1000	38	56
EM	001 1001	19	25	9	011 1001	39	57
SUB	001 1010	1A	26	:	011 1010	3A	58
ESC	001 1011	1B	27	;	011 1011	3B	59
FS	001 1100	1C	28	<	011 1100	3C	60
GS	001 1101	1D	29	=	011 1101	3D	61
RS	001 1110	1E	30	>	011 1110	3E	62
US	001 1111	1F	31	?	011 1111	3F	63
@	100 0000	40	64	`	110 0000	60	96
A	100 0001	41	65	a	110 0001	61	97
B	100 0010	42	66	b	110 0010	62	98
C	100 0011	43	67	c	110 0011	63	99
D	100 0100	44	68	d	110 0100	64	100
E	100 0101	45	69	e	110 0101	65	101
F	100 0110	46	70	f	110 0110	66	102
G	100 0111	47	71	g	110 0111	67	103
H	100 1000	48	72	h	110 1000	68	104
I	100 1001	49	73	i	110 1001	69	105
J	100 1010	4A	74	j	110 1010	6A	106
K	100 1011	4B	75	k	110 1011	6B	107
L	100 1100	4C	76	l	110 1100	6C	108
M	100 1101	4D	77	m	110 1101	6D	109
N	100 1110	4E	78	n	110 1110	6E	110
O	100 1111	4F	79	o	110 1111	6F	111
P	101 0000	50	80	p	111 0000	70	112
Q	101 0001	51	81	q	111 0001	71	113
R	101 0010	52	82	r	111 0010	72	114
S	101 0011	53	83	s	111 0011	73	115
T	101 0100	54	84	t	111 0100	74	116
U	101 0101	55	85	u	111 0101	75	117
V	101 0110	56	86	v	111 0110	76	118
W	101 0111	57	87	w	111 0111	77	119
X	101 1000	58	88	x	111 1000	78	120
Y	101 1001	59	89	y	111 1001	79	121
Z	101 1010	5A	90	z	111 1010	7A	122
[	101 1011	5B	91	{	111 1011	7B	123
Ø	101 1100	5C	92	Ø	111 1100	7C	124
]	101 1101	5D	93	}	111 1101	7D	125
^	101 1110	5E	94	~	111 1110	7E	126
_	101 1111	5F	95	DEL	111 1111	7F	127

A non-standard 8-bit version of the ASCII codes is also used, which means that 256 characters may be represented. This allows Greek letters, card suits, line drawing and graphic characters to be represented. The 8-bit version is usually referred to as extended ASCII. When standard 7-bit ASCII codes are used, the eighth bit is available for other uses. One such use is as a **parity** bit. A parity bit is used for error detection. When data is transmitted over long distances, perhaps using telephone lines, there is a possibility that the data will be corrupted due to electrical noise. This means that a bit may be flipped and a 1 bit gets changed to a 0 bit or vice versa. A parity bit can give some protection to allow you detect that such corruption has occurred. There are two parity schemes called **even parity** and **odd parity**. In an even parity scheme, the parity bit is used to ensure that the code for each character contains an **even number of**

1s. Thus, the parity bit would be set to 0 in the case of the letter A, whose ASCII code is 100 0001 and the character would be transmitted as 0100 0001. The parity bit would be set to 1 in the case of the letter B whose ASCII code is 100 0011 in order to make the number of 1s even and the character would be transmitted as 1100 0011. In an odd parity scheme, the parity bit is used in the same fashion, except that it is set to 0 or 1 in order to make the number of 1s transmitted **odd**. Thus , with an odd parity scheme, A would be transmitted as 1100 0001 and B as 0100 0011.

When using parity bits, the receiver of a character can detect a single bit error, by computing the parity bit for the other seven data bits and comparing it with the **actual** parity bit transmitted. If they are not the same, then an error has occurred. Parity checking cannot detect the corruption of a number of bits in the same byte, but this is relatively rare. Other methods may be used to detect such errors and they are studied in the field of data communications. The 8086 has conditional jump instructions for testing parity (jpo to jump on odd parity and jpe to jump on even parity).

ASCII is not the only such standard for representing information. IBM mainframe computers use **EBCDIC** (Extended Binary Coded Decimal Interchange Code) codes, which are 8-bit codes, different from those used in the ASCII standard. In addition, work is in progress to provide a 16-bit standard code (referred to as **Unicode**) for representing characters. The problem with ASCII codes is that a maximum of 256 characters can be represented. While this is fine for handling text in the English language, it is useless for handling other languages such as Chinese or Japanese where there are literally thousands of individual characters making up the language alphabet. A 16-bit code allows in excess of 65 000 characters to be represented and so is sufficient for the alphabet of almost any language.

Exercises

B.9 Look up the ASCII codes for the digits 0 to 9. What do you notice about the rightmost (low-order) four bits and the leftmost (high-order) 4 bits of each code?

B.10 What is the numeric difference between the ASCII codes for *any* upper-case letter (say A) and the corresponding lower-case letter (a)?

B.4 Summary

In this appendix we have described how information is represented inside a computer system. We have described how signed and unsigned numbers can be represented and we also discussed the use of ASCII codes for representing characters. Table B.4 is a full listing of the ASCII codes.

B.5 Reading List

Megarry, J. (1985) *Inside Information: Computers, Communications and People*, BBC, London.
See also the lists for Chapters 2 and 5.

Appendix C
M68000 assembly language programming

In Part I, 8086 assembly language programming was introduced. In this chapter, we build upon the concepts and programs developed in Part 1, to describe M68000 assembly language programming. Some of the same examples presented in Chapters 3 and 4 are used. We begin by looking at the M68000 register set.

C.1 M68000 CPU registers

The M68000 microprocessor has a total of 16 general purpose registers. Each register can contain a 32-bit quantity as opposed to the 16-bit registers used by the 8086 processor. Eight of the registers are referred to as **data** registers. They are called `d0`, `d1`, `d2`, `d3`, `d4`, `d5`, `d6` and `d7`. These eight registers are general purpose registers and thus they can be used by the programmer for data manipulation. Another eight are referred to as **address** registers; they are called `a0`, `a1`, `a2`, `a3`, `a4`, `a5`, `a6` and `a7`. These registers are used to contain the addresses of memory locations typically for indirect addressing purposes. In addition there are two other registers: the **program counter** register `pc` and the **status** register `sr`. The `pc` register is a 32-bit register while the `sr` register is a 16-bit register. The `pc` is equivalent to the 8086 `ip` register and is used to contain the address of the next instruction to be executed. The M68000 processor only uses 24 bits of the program counter for addresses, which means that up to 16 Mb (2^{24} bytes) of memory can be addressed. The `sr` register is used for the same purposes as the 8086 `flags` register. It is treated as two registers, corresponding to its low- and high-order bytes. The low-order byte of the status register is called the **condition code register (ccr)** or **user byte** and is used in a similar fashion to the `flags` register of the 8086 processor. The status flags are used to record status information resulting from the execution of arithmetic and logical instructions. The high-order byte of the status register is called the **system byte** and contains information about interrupts and the mode of the processor. The M68000 uses address register `a7` to act as the stack pointer register; this is also called the `sp` register.

An important feature of the M68000 registers is that they can be accessed as single 32-bit registers, as single 16-bit registers or as single 8-bit registers. To specify how a register is to be treated, M68000 instructions use a suffix indicating the size of the operand to be operated on by the instruction. So, there may be three forms of an instruction, one for accessing byte-sized operands (8 bits), one for word-sized operands (16 bits) and one for long word-sized operands (32 bits). For example, to assign register d0 the decimal value 15 (1111 in binary) we can write:

```
move.b  #15,  d0   ; low-order byte of d0 = 00001111
move.w  #15,  d0   ; low-order word of d0 = 0000 0000 0000
                   ; 1111
move.l  #15,  d0   ; d0 = 0000 0000 0000 0000 0000 0000 0000
                   ; 1111
```

C.1.1 M68000 notation

- The suffix .b indicates a byte-sized operand, .w indicates a word-sized operand and .l indicates a long-word or 32-bit operand. Note that the move instruction is spelt with an e, unlike its equivalent 8086 mov instruction.
- Instructions may be written in either upper- or lower-case letters.
- Constants (immediate operands) *must* be preceded by the # symbol. For example, a character constant 'x' is written as #'x' in an M68000 instruction. In the above instructions, #15 is the decimal constant 15. If the # symbol is omitted, the value is assumed to be a memory address.
- The source operand is the *first* operand of an instruction and the destination operand is the *second* operand. This is the opposite order to that used by 8086 instructions.
- Hexadecimal numbers are written preceded by a $ symbol, so that $f represents hexadecimal number f. Binary numbers are preceded by a % symbol, so that %00001111 represents binary number 00001111. Decimal numbers require no prefix. For example, the last move instruction above could also be written as:

```
move.l  #$f,  d0             ; d0 = $f
move.l  #%00001111,  d0      ; d0 = $f
```

In the following sections we look at M68000 instructions for data manipulation, arithmetic operations and transfer of control instructions. We also look at mechanisms for carrying out I/O operations.

C.2 Data manipulation: move instruction

The move instruction allows us to transfer data between registers or between memory and registers. The general format of the move instruction is:

```
move.s  source, destination
```

where the .s indicates the suffix (b, w, l) used for specifying byte, word or long word operands. Note again that the source and destination operands are specified in the opposite order to that of 8086 instructions.

Example C.1

Some examples of the move instruction:

```
move.b  #2, d0        ; d0 = 2 (decimal)
move.l  d0, d1        ; d1 = d0
move.l  d2, x         ; x = d2      (x is a memory variable)
move.b  y, d3         ; d3 = y      (y is a memory variable)
move.b  #'a', d4      ; d4 = 'a'
move.w  #$ffff, d0    ; d0 = $ffff
move.b  x, y          ; y = x (low-order byte of x)
```

The last move instruction illustrates that you can transfer the contents of one memory variable to another on the M68000, an operation that is not allowed on the 8086. You should note that there is an important difference between the following move instructions:

```
move.b  #'?', d0              ; d0 = '?' (ASCII code $3f)
move.w  #'?', d0
move.l  #'?', d0
```

In the first case, only the low-order byte of the d0 register gets changed, the rest of the d0 register remains unchanged. In the second case, the low-order word (16 bits) of the register gets changed and the high-order word remains unchanged. In the third case, the entire register is modified. This is illustrated in Figure C.1.

Note: In this appendix, register contents are represented by hexadecimal numbers. This allows us to represent the 32 bits contained in a register by 8 hexadecimal digits (each hexadecimal digit represents 4 bits).

The M68000 provides the clr instruction to clear an operand, that is, to set all bits of the operand to 0. This is a common operation and the clr instruction is a more efficient instruction than the equivalent move instruction. The M68000 also provides the exg instruction to swap the contents of two registers:

Example C.2

Using the clr and exg instructions:

```
clr.l  d0        ; clears entire d0 register
clr.w  d1        ; clears low-order word of d1
clr.b  d3        ; clears low-order byte of d3
clr.w x          ; clears low-order word of x memory
                 ; variable
exg  d0, d1      ; swap d0 with d1
exg  a0, a3      ; swap a3 with a0
```

C.3 Arithmetic instructions

These instructions carry out the normal arithmetic operations.

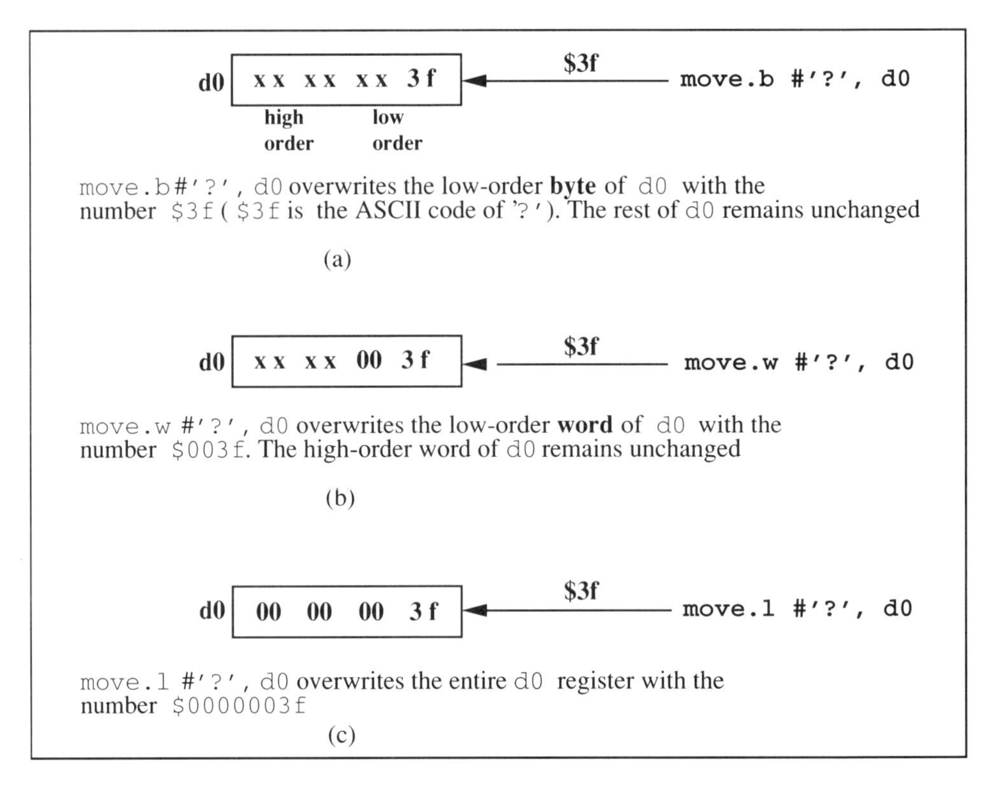

Figure C.1 Moving (a) bytes, (b) words and (c) long words.

Example C.3

Some arithmetic instructions:

```
    move.b  #5, d0   ; d0 = 5
    addi.b  #3, d0   ; d0 = d0 + 3    (d0 now contains 8)
    subi.b  #6, d0   ; d0 = d0 - 6    (d0 now contains 2 )
    move.b  #8, d1   ; d1 = 8
    add.b   d1, d0   ; d0 = d0 + d1   (d0 now contains 10 )
    sub.b   d1, d0   ; d0 = d0 - d1   (d0 now contains 2 )

; The following are examples of word-sized addition and
subtraction.
    move.w #0, sum  ; sum = 0       (sum is a memory variable)
    add.w  d0, sum  ; sum = sum + d0 (sum now contains 2)
    sub.w  sum, d1  ; d1 = d1 - sum  (d1 now contains 6)
```

The `add` instruction adds the source operand (first one) to the destination operand (second one), leaving the result in the destination operand. When the source operand is a constant, we use the `addi` instruction where the `i` indicates an immediate operand (the constant). The same suffixes as used with `move` as are used with `add` and all similar M68000 instructions.

The `sub` instruction subtracts the source operand from the destination operand, leaving the result in the destination operand. The subi instruction is used when the source operand is a constant. As we can see, the source operand may be a constant, register or (memory) variable. The destination operand must be register or a memory variable. You may *not* operate on two memory variables in a single arithmetic instruction (the same applies to the 8086). Thus to add variable x to variable y, you must write something similar to:

```
move.l    x, d0     ; d0 = x
add.l     d0, y     ; y = y + d0
```

The M68000 provides the muls, mulu, divs and divu instructions for multiplication and division. The muls instruction is used to carry out multiplication for signed numbers and mulu is used for unsigned numbers.

Example C.4

Multiply d1 (containing 9) by d0 (containing 7), storing the result in d1. Then multiply the result by 10.

```
move.w  #7, d0
move.w  #9, d1
muls.w  d0, d1      ; d1 = d1* d0 = 63
muls.w  #10, d1     ; d1 = d1 * 10 = 630
```

Here we use muls for signed multiplication. Unsigned multiplication is carried out in the same fashion with the mulu instruction. Both muls and mulu take word-sized operands and produce long-word results.

The divs and divu instructions carry out division in a similar fashion. In the case of division, the destination operand (long word) is divided by the source operand (word), with divs being used for signed division and divu for unsigned division. The result of the division is stored in the low-order word of the destination and the remainder is stored in the high-order word of the destination operand.

Example C.5

Divide d1 (containing 1235) by d2 (containing 10) and divide the result by 2:

```
move.l  #1235, d1
move.w  #10, d2
divu    d2, d1      ; low-order word of d1 = d1/10
                    ; high-order word of d1 = d1 mod 10
divu    #2, d1      ; divide d1 by 2
```

Unlike the 8086 multiplication and division instructions, which can only be used with specific registers, the M68000 instructions can be used with any data register.

Exercises

C.1. Write instructions to:

(a) Load the character '?' into register d0.
(b) Load the space character into register d1.
(c) Load 26 (decimal) into register d3.
(d) Copy the contents of d0 to d4 and d5.

C.2. What errors are present in the following instructions:

```
move.l  d1, #3
move.b  #1000, d2
mov.b   d3, d4,
addi.b  d0, #2
addi.b  #3 d4
```

C.3. Write instructions to evaluate the arithmetic expression 5 + (6 - 2) leaving the result in d0 using (a) one register, (b) two registers, (c) three registers.

C.4. Write instructions to compute the value of the expressions
(a) 6 + (10 * 12)
(b) 4 * (60 / 20)

C.4 Input and output (I/O) in M68000 assembly language programs

Unlike the 8086 family of microprocessors, which are almost always associated with the MS-DOS operating system, the M68000 is used in a number of different makes of computer, each having its own operating system. So an M68000-based machine may be running the Unix operating system or that of the Apple Macintosh or that of the Commodore Amiga. Each operating system provides its own range of I/O sub-programs, in much the same way as there is an extensive library of sub-programs available to the C programmer. In this text, we use the Apple Macintosh for developing M68000 programs and an M68000 programming environment called MAS (Macintosh Assembly System – see reading list for details). This is an excellent environment for learning how to write M68000 programs. The system comes with a library of I/O sub-programs which may be used in M68000 programs. In this text we use four of these sub-programs, namely `getchar` to read a character from the keyboard, `putchar` to display a character on the screen, `putstr` to display a string and `stop` to terminate a program. We then build up our own collection of sub-programs, as in Chapters 3 and 4, to read and display strings and numbers. Initially, we consider character I/O with the keyboard and screen.

C.4.1 *Character output*

The task here is to display a single character on the screen. There are two elements to displaying a character. First the character is stored in a specific register and second a sub-program is invoked to display the contents of this register.

Example C.6

Write a code fragment to display the character 'a' on the screen:

```
move.w  #'a', d0   ; d0 = 'a' for output
jsr     putchar    ; display character in d0
```

The putchar sub-program is part of the MAS I/O library and is invoked using the M68000 jsr (jump to sub-routine) instruction. The jsr instruction is the equivalent of the 8086 call instruction. The parameter passed to putchar must be stored in the low-order word of the d0 register.

C.4.2 Character input

The mechanism for reading a character is similar to that used for displaying one. A specific sub-program is invoked and it stores the character in a specific register, in this case the d0 register is used with the getchar sub-program.

Example C.7

Write a code fragment to read a character from the keyboard:

```
jsr    getchar     ; keyboard input sub-program
                   ; read character into d0
```

C.4.3 A complete program

We are now in a position to write some M68000 programs. In this text, as we have said, we use the MAS 2.0 system for assembling and linking M68000 assembly language programs. MAS program files have names terminating with .a. We will call our first program io1.a; it displays the letter 'x' on the screen. MAS provides a menu of commands for assembling, running and debugging programs and these are described in the MAS documentation.

Example C.8

A complete program to display the letter 'x' on the screen:

```
; io1.a: displays the character 'x' on the screen
; Author:  Joe Carthy
; Date:    June 1994

           xref   getchar, putchar, stop

start:
           move.w  #'x', d0   ; d0 = 'x' for output
           jsr     putchar

           jsr     stop
           end
```

We write our M68000 programs using the same style as the 8086 programs of

Part I, beginning with three comment lines. The following line contains the `xref` assembler directive. This tells the assembler that there are sub-programs called `putchar`, `getchar` and `stop`, which have been defined elsewhere. This means that we can call these sub-programs without worrying about their definition. In this case they are part of the `MAS` library, in a similar fashion to the way we use `getchar()` and `putchar()` in our C programs. The `stop` sub-program is used to terminate execution of the program and return to the `MAS` environment. The `end` directive signals the last line of the program. Since our programs will start and finish using the same format, we use a template file as suggested for 8086 programs. When we wish to write a new program, we copy this template program to a new file, say for example, `io2.a` (using the `MAS` Save As option from the `MAS` File menu). You then edit the new program, `io2.a` in this case, and enter your code in the appropriate place.

Example C.9

The following template could be used for our first programs:

```
; <filename goes here>.a:
; Author:
; Date:

          xref  getchar, putchar, stop

start:
;         < your code goes here >

          end
```

To write a new program, we enter our code in the appropriate place as indicated above.

Example C.10

Write a program to read a character from the keyboard and display it on the screen (based on Examples C.7 and C.8):

```
; io2.a: read a character and display it
; Author:   Joe Carthy
; Date:     June 1994

          xref  getchar, putchar, stop

start:
          jsr   getchar   ; read character into d0
          jsr   putchar   ; display character in d0

          jsr   stop      ; terminate program

          end
```

Note: Just as in C, when reading characters, you must press the Return key before a character (or string) is actually read. (The character input sub-program we used in our 8086 programs reads a character as soon as it is entered, you do not have to press the Return key.) Assuming you enter the letter 'b' at the keyboard when you execute the program, the output will appear as follows:

```
b
b
```

We rewrite this program to produce the following output:

```
?b
b
```

In this version, we display a prompt, read the character and then output the Return character to display the blank line on the Macintosh. Return (ASCII 13D) is the control character to bring the cursor to the start of a line and is used by the Macintosh to start a new line. On a different system, the Line-feed character may also have to be output, as is the case with 8086 assembly language programs for MS-DOS.

Example C.11

Displaying a newline character:

```
; io3.a:    prompt user with ? , read character and display
;           new line followed by the character entered.
; Author:   Joe Carthy
; Date:     June 1994

        xref  getchar, putchar, stop

start:

        move.w  #'?', d0    ; display ?
        jsr     putchar

        move.w  #' ', d0    ; display ' '
        jsr     putchar
        jsr     getchar     ; read character
        move.w  d0, d1      ; save it in d1

        move.w  #13, d0     ; display newline
        jsr     putchar

        move.w  d1, d0      ; display character entered by
                            ; user
        jsr     putchar

        jsr     stop        ; terminate program

end
```

In this example we must save the character entered (we use the `d1` register) so that we can use `d0` to display the newline character.

Exercises

C.5 Modify the program presented in Example C.11 to display a hyphen as part of the prompt (`?-`) so that you get the following output:

```
?- B
B
```

C.6 Write a program to display the word `MAS`.

C.7 Write a program to display the letter `'a'`, followed by two blank lines followed by the letter `'b'`.

C.8 Write a program to read two characters and display them:

```
ab
ab
```

C.9 Write a program to read two characters and display them on separate lines:

```
ab
a
b
```

C.10 Write a program to read two characters and display them on separate lines in reverse order:

```
ab
b
a
```

C.4.4 Strings

In M68000 assembly language, strings are defined using the `dc.b` (define constant byte) directive, in a similar fashion to using the `db` directive in an 8086 program. The following three definitions are equivalent ways of defining the string `'abc'`:

```
string1  dc.b  97, 98, 99       ; individual ASCII codes
string2  dc.b  'a', 'b', 'c'    ; individual characters
string3  dc.b  'abc'            ; string constant
```

You can combine the above methods to define a string such as:

```
message    dc.b  'Hello world', 13, 0
```

The string message contains 'Hello world' followed by Return (ASCII 13), followed by the Null (ASCII 0) character. We will use this kind of definition quite often because there is a MAS library sub-program called putstr for displaying strings, which expects the string to be terminated by the Null character. Later we define our own string output sub-program called put_str which uses the same convention for terminating strings. Uninitialized string variables may be defined by using the ds.b directive. For example, the following code fragment defines a string called buffer, which may contain up to 100 characters and a string called colour which may contain up to 70 characters.

```
buffer  ds.b  100   ; buffer may contain up to 100
                    ; characters
colour  ds.b  70   ; colour may contain up to 70 characters
```

Displaying a string

The following example shows how the string 'Hello world' followed by the Return character can be displayed using the putstr sub-program. This sub-program must know where the string is stored in memory, that is, it needs to know the address of the string to be displayed. The required address must be stored in the a0 register for putstr to operate. The a0 register is one of the address registers provided by the M68000 for handling memory addresses. The M68000 lea (load effective address) instruction is used to store the address of a variable in a register.

Example C.12

Displaying a string using the MAS putstr sub-program:

```
; io8.a: Display the message 'Hello World', 13, 0
; Author:  Joe Carthy
; Date:    June 1994

     xref  putstr, stop

CR         equ  13

start:
           lea   message, a0   ; a0 = address of message
           jsr   putstr        ; display message

           jsr   stop          ; terminate program

           data
message    dc.b    'hello world', CR, 0
                               ; note the terminating 0

end
```

The instruction:

```
lea   message, a0
```

loads the address of the string message into the a0 register. The putstr sub-program uses this address to indirectly access the string, in this case to display the string on the screen.

The above example uses the equ directive to define the constant CR to represent the ASCII code of Return. Note that you must include the # symbol with the constant name when using the constant in an instruction. This is to indicate that the constant represents an immediate value, as shown in the following:

```
move.w  #CR, d0
```

Note: In Example C .12, we also used the data directive. This is required when memory variables are used in a program. In this example we define the variables after the code of the program but before the end directive. We could declare variables elsewhere in M68000 programs, for example before the code of the program, in which case we must ensure that the code starts on a word boundary. This means that the first instruction following the data must start on an even numbered byte, even if the string (or whatever data are being defined) takes up an odd number of bytes. To ensure that this is the case, the even directive may be used. This directive forces the following instruction to be stored on an even word boundary. To distinguish between data and instructions we use the code directive to indicate where the instructions begin in a program. Example C.13 illustrates the use of these directives:

Example C.13

Using the data, code and even directives.

```
; io9.a: Display the message 'Hello World', 13, 0
; Author:  Joe Carthy
; Date:    June 1994


     xref    stop,
putstr

CR          equ   13

            data
message     dc.b  'hello world', CR, 0
            even

            code
start:
            lea          message, a0
```

```
        jsr         putstr

        jsr         stop    ; terminate program

        end
```

As a further example of what we have learned to date, the following program reads an upper-case letter entered by the user and displays its lower-case equivalent.

Example C.14

Converting an upper-case letter to lower case.

```
; char.a: character conversion: upper to lowercase
        xref getchar, putchar, putstr, stop
CR      equ     13

        data
msg1    dc.b  'Enter an uppercase letter: ', 0
result  dc.b  CR, 'The lowercase equivalent is: ', 0
        even

        code
;                  main program
start:
        lea   msg1, a0
        jsr   putstr
        jsr   getchar           ; read uppercase letter

        add   #32, d0           ; convert to lowercase

        lea   result, a0
        jsr   putstr            ; display result message

        jsr   putchar           ; display lowercase letter

        jsr   stop              ; terminate program
        end
```

Executing this program produces as output:

```
Enter an uppercase letter: G
The lowercase equivalent is: g
```

Exercises

C.11 Modify the above program to convert a lower-case letter to upper case.

C.12 Write a program to convert a single digit number such as 5 to its character equivalent `'5'` and display the character.

C.5 Control flow instructions: sub-programs

In M68000 assembly language the instruction `jsr` (jump to sub-program) is used to invoke a sub-program and the instruction `rts` (return from sub-program) is used to return from a sub-program. These are equivalent to the 8086 `call` and `ret` instructions. The M68000 also provides the `bsr` (branch to sub-program) instruction to invoke a sub-program. The difference between `bsr` and `jsr` is that the `bsr` instruction uses relative addressing to transfer control to a sub-program. This means that it adds a specified number of bytes to the current program counter value to access the sub-program. This in turn means that a program using the `bsr` instruction can be relocated in memory (moved to another memory region) without having to change the `bsr` instruction. On the other hand, the `jsr` instruction uses absolute addressing, which means that it transfers control to a fixed address (that of the sub-program). If we relocate the sub-program, then a new address must be generated for the `jsr` instruction.

The `jsr` instruction can transfer control to a sub-program that is anywhere in memory. The `bsr` instruction comes in two forms: `bsr.s` (short) and `bsr` (sometimes written as `bsr.l` – long). The `bsr.s` instruction uses an 8-bit field to record the relative address and so can transfer control to sub-programs that are within 128 bytes of the instruction. The `bsr.l` instruction uses a 16-bit relative address and thus can transfer control to sub-programs that are within 64 kb of the `bsr` instruction. So far we have used the `jsr` instruction to invoke sub-programs that come with the `MAS` system. We can use the `bsr` instruction for the sub-programs we define ourselves. These are stored with our main program and they are close enough to the `bsr` instruction for it to operate. In general, it is recommended practice to use the `bsr` instruction if possible, as it means that your program can be relocated in memory without difficulty. In addition, it takes less memory space to encode the `bsr` instruction than it does to encode the `jsr` instruction. The `rts` instruction terminates a sub-program regardless of how it is called.

Example C.15

Rewrite the program presented in Example C.11 using a sub-program called `put_nl` to display the blank line. We use the `bsr` instruction to call the `put_nl` sub-program:

```
; io10.a: Prompt for character input and display character
; entered
; Author:  Joe Carthy
; Date:    June 1994

         xref  getchar, putchar, stop

start:

         move.w  #'?', d0   ; display ?
         jsr     putchar
```

```
        move.w  #' ', d0    ; display ' '
        jsr     putchar

        jsr     getchar     ; read character
        move.w  d0, d1      ; save it in d1

        bsr     put_nl      ; display newline

        move.w  d1, d0      ; display character entered
        jsr     putchar

        jsr     stop        ; terminate program

; Sub-program definitions:

put_nl:                     ; display newline
       move.w  #13, d0
       jsr     putchar
       rts

end
```

C.5.1 *Using the stack to save registers*

The stack, as introduced in Chapter 2, is typically used to save the value of registers in sub-programs and to restore them before returning from the sub-program. It is also used to save the return address for sub-programs. We can save registers by pushing their values onto the stack at the start of a sub-program and retrieving (popping) the register values from the stack at the end of the sub-program. The M68000 (unlike the 8086 processor) does not provide separate instructions to push a value onto the stack or to pop a value from the stack. Instead it uses the `move` instruction to carry out both operations.

To push a value onto the stack, the `move` instruction accesses the stack indirectly via the stack pointer register `sp` (`a7` is also used as a synonym for `sp`). Before storing a value on the stack the `sp` register is decremented (by 4), so that `sp` points to the next free location on the stack and then a value is stored on the stack at that location. This can be carried out in a single M68000 instruction:

```
move.l    d0, -(sp)       ; push d0 onto stack
```

The notation `-(sp)` requires explanation. The brackets are used by the M68000 to indicate **indirect addressing**, in this case to access the location pointed at by `sp`. The minus sign before the brackets signifies that the operand in brackets is to be decremented *before* using its value. This is called the indirect with **pre-decrement** addressing mode. It could also be carried out using two separate instructions, one to decrement the stack pointer and the other to move the `d0` register contents to the location pointed to by the stack pointer.

A similar `move` instruction is used to pop values from the stack. In this case, the stack pointer must be incremented *after* retrieving a value from the stack. This is achieved by the following move instruction:

```
move.l    (sp)+, d0        ; pop d0 from stack
```

The notation (sp)+ is called the indirect with **post-increment** addressing mode. This means that the value of sp is incremented (by 4) after its value has been used to retrieve the last element pushed on the stack.

Example C.16

Rewrite the put__nl sub-program presented in the last example, to save the value of d0 and to restore it appropriately, before the sub-program returns. This version of put__nl is therefore safer, in that register d0 does not get changed without the programmer realizing it:

```
put__nl:                          ; display newline
          move.l  d0, -(sp)       ; push d0 onto stack
          move.w  #CR, d0
          jsr     putchar         ; display character in d0
          move.l  (sp)+, d0       ; pop d0 from stack
         rts
```

The above example illustrates how a single value may be pushed onto or popped off the stack. The M68000 provides the facility to push (or pop) several items onto the stack in a single instruction. This is very useful if we wish to save a number of registers, say all the data registers, on the stack. The movem (move multiple) instruction is used for transferring the contents of a number of registers to memory or vice versa. It is typically used for accessing the stack to save and restore registers:

```
movem.l  d0-d7, -(sp)   ; push registers d0 to d7
movem.l  a0-a4, -(sp)   ; push registers a0 to a4
movem.l  (sp)+, a0-a4   ; pop registers a0 to a4
movem.l  (sp)+, d0-d7   ; pop registers d0 to d7
```

The list of registers to be used may be specified to range from a starting register to a finishing register, as in the above examples, using a hyphen between the starting and finishing register, so that d4 - d6 specifies registers d4 to d6. Alternatively, individual registers may be specified by using a / to separate the register names:

```
movem.l  d0/d4/a0/a2, -(sp)   ; push registers d0, d4, a0
                              ; and a2
movem.l  (sp)+, d0/d4/a0/a2   ; pop registers d0, d4, a0
                              ; and a2
```

Finally both a range of registers and individual registers may be specified by using both the - and / symbols:

```
movem.l  d0-d4/d7/a1, -(sp)   ; push d0 to d4, d7 and a1
movem.l  (sp)+, d0-d4/d7/a1   ; pop d0 to d4, d7 and a1
```

C.6 Control flow: jump (branch) instructions

C.6.1 Unconditional jump instructions

The M68000 provides two unconditional jump (branch) instructions, the `bra` and `jmp` instructions. Both instructions take a single operand, which specifies where control is to be transferred to. Using the `jmp` instruction, control may be transferred to *any* location in your program. The operand used with the `jmp` instruction is the address of the location to which we wish to transfer control. The `bra` instruction uses relative addressing and so we are restricted in the distance (the number of instructions from the `bra` instruction) to which we can transfer control. This situation is the same as that described for the `jsr` and `bsr` instructions. There are also two forms of the `bra` instruction: `bra.s` and `bra.l`, which can branch the same distances as the `bsr.s` and `bsr.l` instructions.

The reason for using the `bra` instruction is that it is faster and occupies less storage when translated to machine code than the `jmp` instruction. The `bra.s` instruction for example only occupies two bytes when translated to machine code. In addition, the `bra` instruction, since it uses relative addressing, leads to code that can be relocated anywhere in memory, while the `jmp` instruction, because it uses absolute addressing, leads to code that is not relocatable. We will use the `bra` instruction for unconditional jumps in this text. When using this instruction, the assembler will generate an error message if the distance to be jumped is too great.

Example C.17

This example illustrates the use of the `bra.s` instruction to implement an endless loop:

```
again:  jsr   getchar   ; read a character into d0
        jsr   putchar   ; display character in d0
        bra.s again     ; jump to again
```

This is an example of a backward jump as control is transferred to an earlier place in the program. The code fragment causes the instructions between the label `again` and `bra.s` to be repeated endlessly.

Example C.18

The following code fragment illustrates a forward jump as control is transferred to a later place in the program:

```
        jsr   getchar    ; read a character into d0
        jsr   putchar    ; display character in d0
        bra.l finish     ; jump to finish assuming its far
                         ; away

          <do other things>  ; Never gets done !!!

finish:
```

In this case the code between the `bra.l` instruction and the label `finish` will not be executed, because the `bra.l` instruction causes control to skip over it.

C.6.2 *Conditional branch instructions*

The M68000 provides a similar collection of conditional branch instructions to those of the 8086 processor. For example, the `beq` and `bne` instructions are equivalent to the 8086 `je` and `jne` instructions. The M68000 also provides a `cmp` instruction, for comparing operands.

Example C.19

Using the `cmp` and `beq` instructions:

```
          move.w  #2, d0   ; d0 := 2
          cmp.w   d1, d0   ; (d1 == d0) ?
          beq     next1    ; branch if result is 0 i.e. d1 ==
                           ; d0
          addi.w  #1, d0   ; d0 = d0 + 1, if d1 != d0

next1:
          addi.w  #1, d1
```

The `cmpi` instruction is used if one of the operands is a constant, for example

```
cmpi  #4, d1
beq   label          ; branch if d1 == 4
```

The M68000 also provides the `tst` instruction to compare an operand with 0. For example to compare the `d1` register with `0` we can write:

```
tst.l d1              ; compare d1 with 0
beq   equals_zero     ; branch to equals_zero if d1 == 0
```

The `tst` and `cmp` instructions can be used with byte, word or long word operands.

Table C.1 lists the branch-on-condition instructions, specifying where relevant which ones are concerned with signed and unsigned numbers.

Table C.1 M68000 conditional branch instructions.

Name(s)	Branch if	Signed/Unsigned
`beq`	equal/zero	either
bne	not equal/not zero	either
`bhi`	greater than	unsigned
`bhs/bcc`	greater or equal	unsigned
`blo/bcs`	less than	unsigned
`bls`	less than or equal	unsigned

bgt	greater than	signed
bge	greater or equal	signed
blt	less than	signed
ble	less than or equal	signed
bvs	overflow occurs	
bvc	overflow does not occur	
bcs	carry occurs	
bcc	carry clear	
bmi	negative result	
bpl	positive result	

C.6.3 *Implementation of* `if-then` *and* `if-then-else` *control structures*

These two control structures are implemented in M68000 assembly language in the same manner as in 8086 assembly language. As an example, the following program allows the user to guess a letter that the program 'knows'. If the user guesses correctly, the program congratulates them, otherwise the program displays its disappointment!

Example C.20

Implementing `if-then-else` in M68000 assembly language.

```
; guess.a: Guessing game program. User is asked to guess
; which letter the program 'knows'
; Author:  Joe Carthy
; Date:    June 1994

               xref putstr, getchar, stop
CR             equ     13
               code
start:
               lea     prompt, a0
               jsr     putstr
               jsr     getchar       ; read character
               cmpi.b  #'a', d0      ; d0 = 'a' ?
               bne     wrong_guess   ; no, goto
                                     ; wrong_guess
                 lea   yes_msg, a0   ; if action
                 jsr   putstr        ; display correct
                                     ; message
               bra.s   end_else1
wrong_guess:                         ; else action
               lea     no_msg, a0
               jsr     putstr        ; display wrong
                                     ; guess message
end_else1:
               jsr  stop             ; terminate program
```

```
                 data
prompt           dc.b  'Guessing game: Enter a letter (a to
                       z): ', 0
yes_msg          dc.b  CR, 'You guessed correctly !!', 0
no_msg           dc.b  CR, 'Sorry incorrect guess', 0
                 end
```

Example C.21

As another example of implementing the `if-then` control structure, this program converts an upper-case letter to lower case, first testing that the letter entered was an upper-case letter. The C and 8086 versions are presented in Chapter 3, Example 3.30.

```
; char3.a: character conversion: uppercase to lowercase

          xref putstr, getchar, putchar, stop
CR        equ     13
start:

          lea     msg1, a0
          jsr     putstr
          jsr     getchar          ; read uppercase letter
          cmpi.b  #'A', d0
          blt     invalid          ; if d0 < 'A' goto invalid
          cmpi.b  #'Z', d0
          bgt     invalid          ; if d0 > 'Z' goto invalid
                                   ; otherwise its valid
          addi.b  #32, d0          ; convert to lowercase

          lea     result, a0
          jsr     putstr           ; display result message
          jsr     putchar          ; display lowercase
                                   ; letter
          jmp     finish           ; we are now finished

invalid:  lea     bad_msg, a0      ; not an uppercase letter
          jsr     putstr           ; display bad_msg
          jsr     putchar          ; display character
                                   ; entered

finish:
          jsr     stop             ; terminate program

          data

msg1      dc.b    'Enter an uppercase letter: ', 0
result    dc.b    CR, 'The lowercase equivalent is: ', 0
bad_msg   dc.b    CR, 'Not an uppercase letter: ', 0

          end
```

This program produces as output, assuming the digit 8 is entered:

```
Enter an uppercase letter: 8
Not an uppercase letter: 8
```

This program produces as output, assuming the digit K is entered:

```
Enter an uppercase letter: K
The lowercase equivalent is: k
```

Exercises

C.13 Write a program to read a digit and display an error message if a non-digit character is entered.

C.14 In the code fragments below, where will execution continue from when `<branch-on-condition>` is replaced by (a) `beq lab1` ; (b) `bgt lab1`; (c) `ble lab1`; (d) `blt lab1`?

```
(i)  move.l  #10, d0
     cmpi.l  #9, d0
     branch-on-condition
     ; rest of program
     ...........
     ...........
lab1:
```

```
(ii) move.w  #0, d1
     cmpi.w  #0, d1
     <branch-on-condition>
     ; rest of program
     ...........
     ...........
lab1:
```

C.15 Write programs to test that a character read from the keyboard is:
(a) a valid lower-case letter (`'a'` <= character <= `'z'`)
(b) either an upper-case or lower-case letter (`'A'` <= character <= `'Z'` OR `'a'` <= character <= `'z'`)
(c) is not a lower-case letter, that is character < 'a' or character > 'z'.
The programs should display appropriate messages to prompt for input and indicate whether the character satisfied the relevant test.

C.6.4 *Loops*

Loops in M68000 may also be implemented in the same fashion as their 8086 equivalents.

Example C.22

Write a code fragment to display 60 stars (*).

```
            move.b   #1, d1        ; d1 = 1
            move.w   #'*', d0      ; d0 = '*'

disp_char:
            cmpi.b   #60, d1       ; while d1 <= 60
            bgt      end_disp      ; if d1 > 60 goto
                                   ; end_disp
             jsr     putchar       ; display '*'
             addi.b  #1, d1        ; d1 = d1 + 1
            bra.s    disp_char     ; repeat loop test

end_disp:
```

The M68000 also provides the dbra (also called dbf) instruction, which is similar to the 8086 loop instruction. This instruction allows you to implement a deterministic loop, one where you know in advance how many times the loop body instructions are to be executed. The dbra has the following general format:

dbra data_register, start_loop

Unlike the 8086 loop instruction (which always uses register cx), we can use any register with the dbra instruction to contain the number of loop iterations, so that data-register can be any of the data registers (a word-sized value is used). The label start_loop indicates the first instruction of the loop body. The dbra instruction decrements the data register by 1 and if the result is -1, the loop terminates. Otherwise, if the result is not -1 dbra branches to start_loop. Since it tests for -1 as the value to terminate the loop, an initial value of n for the data register will cause n+1 loop iterations, so that, if the data register has value 4, then the loop will repeat five times with the data register having the values 4, 3, 2, 1, 0 in the loop body. Thus, to repeat a loop n times the initial value used for the data register should be $n - 1$, so that, to repeat the loop body four times the data register should be initialized to 3.

Example C.23

Using the dbra instruction to implement a loop to display 60 stars:

```
            move.w  #'*', d0        ; d1 := '*'
            move.w  #59, d1         ; d1 := 59
disp_char:
                                    ; for d1 = 59 to 0
            jsr     putchar         ; display '*'
            dbra    d1, disp_char
```

The general format for using the dbra instruction to implement a for-loop is given below, where dn represents one of the data registers:

```
                 move.w      count, dn ; count = no. of times to
                                       ; repeat loop
start__loop:                           ; use any label name
                  <loop body           ; while dn > -1
                        instructions>

                 dbra dn, start__loop  ; goto start__loop if dn
                                       ; != -1
```

The loop body will always be executed at least once, since the `dbra` instruction tests the value of the data register after executing the loop body. If the data register is initialized to –1, the `dbra` instruction will repeat the loop body 65 536 times, in the same way as the 8086 loop instruction operates if the `cx` register is initially 0. The basic point being made is that the loop will not behave as might be expected if the data register is incorrectly initialized to a negative number.

Note: The `dbra` instruction is one of a family of instructions referred to as `dbcc` where `cc` refers to one of the branching conditions such as `gt`, `lt`, `ge`, `le` and so on. Every `dbcc` instruction combines testing a condition, decrementing a register and branching depending on the outcome of the test.

Exercises:

C.16 Modify the guessing game program to allow the user to have as many guesses as they wish. The user is asked to enter `'y'` to continue after each guess.

C.17 Modify the guessing game program to allow the user three guesses, terminating if any guess is correct.

C.18 Modify the guessing game program to allow users to guess as many or as few times as they wish, terminating if any guess is correct.

C.19 Modify the guessing game program to loop until a correct guess is made.

C.7 More about I/O

C.7.1 Numbers

Sub-programs (written in C and 8086 assembly language) to read and display numbers and strings were presented in Chapter 3. We are now in a position to implement these sub-programs in M68000 assembly language. First, we rewrite the `getn` and `putn` sub-programs. The `getn` sub-program reads a number from the keyboard and returns it. The `putn` sub-program displays the number in the `d0` register. We maintain our convention of using the `d0` register to pass a parameter to or from I/O sub-programs.

Example C.24

M68000 `getn` and `putn` sub-programs based on C equivalents from Examples 1.22 and 1.24 in Chapter 1.

Sub-program getn

```
getn: ; read a number from the keyboard
      ; returns value in d0 register
      ;                                        C variables
      ; d3 records sign of number              variable sign
      ; d1 stores each digit                   variable digit
      ; d2 stores the number read in so far    variable n
      ; d0 stores each character read in.      variable c

      movem.l d1-d3, -(sp)      ; save registers d1 to d3
      clr.l   d1                ; initialise digit to 0
      clr.l   d2                ; initialise number to 0
      move.l  #1, d3            ; record sign, 1 for
                                ; positive

jsr
getchar
; read first character
      cmpi.b  #'-', d0          ; is it negative
      bne     newline           ; if not goto newline
      neg.l   d3                ; else record sign as
                                ; negative
      jsr     getchar           ; get next digit
newline:
      cmpi.w  #13, d0           ; if (d0 == CR)
      beq     fin__read         ; then goto fin__read
      subi.w  #'0', d0          ; otherwise convert to
                                ; digit
      move.w  d0, d2            ; d2 = first digit
      jsr     getchar           ; get next character
read__loop:
      cmpi.b  #13, d0           ; if (d0 == CR)
      beq     fin__read         ; then goto fin__read
      subi.w  #'0', d0          ; otherwise convert to
                                ; digit
      move.w  d0, d1            ; d1 = digit
      muls.w  #10, d2           ; d2 = d2 * 10
      add.w   d1, d2            ; n = n + digit
      jsr     getchar           ; read next digit
      bra.s   read__loop
fin__read:
      move.w  d2, d0            ; number is returned in d0.w
      tst     d3                ; test sign
      bgt     fin__getn         ; if positive then finish
      neg.w   d0                ; otherwise negate d0.w
fin__getn:
      movem.l (sp)+, d1-d3      ; restore registers
      rts
```

Sub-program putn

```
putn:                           ; display number in d0.w
        movem.l d0-d2, -(sp)    ; save registers

        move.l  #0, -(sp)       ; stack sentinel
        move.l  d0, d1          ; move number to d1

        tst.w   d1              ; test if d1 is positive
        bge     calc_digits     ; number is positive
        neg.w   d1              ; otherwise d1 = -d1, i.e. d1
                                ; is now positive
        move.w  #'-', d0        ; display - sign
        jsr     putchar
calc_digits:
        divu.w  #10, d1         ; d1.w = d1 / 10; rem in high-
                                ; order word
        move.l  d1, d2          ; save d1 in d2
        swap    d1              ; get remainder in d1.w
        addi.b  #'0', d1        ; convert remainder to digit
        move.l  d1, -(sp)       ; save digit on stack
        clr.l   d1              ; clear all of d1
        move.w  d2, d1          ; restore result of division
                                ; to d1.w
        tst.w   d1              ; d1.w == 0: finished ?
        bne.s   calc_digits     ; if not, compute next digit
                                ; all digits now on stack,
                                ; display them
disp_loop:
        move.l  (sp)+, d0       ; get last digit from stack
        tst.w   d0              ; is it sentinel
        beq     end_disp_loop   ; if yes, we are finished
        jsr     putchar         ; otherwise display digit
        bra.s   disp_loop
end_disp_loop:
        movem.l (sp)+, d0-d2    ; restore registers from
                                ; stack
        rts
```

Example C.25

This program reads two numbers, sums them and displays the result. The C version is presented as Example 1.5 in Chapter 1.

```
; calc.a:   Read and sum two numbers. Display result.
; Author:   Joe Carthy
; Date:     June 1994
            xref    putstr, getchar, putchar, stop
start:
            lea     prompt1, a0
            jsr     putstr          ; display prompt1
```

```
        bsr     getn            ; read first number
        move.w  d0, num1
        lea     prompt2, a0
        jsr     putstr          ; display prompt2
        bsr     getn            ; read second number
        move.w  d0, num2
        move.w  num1, d0        ; d0 = num1
        add.w   num2, d0        ; d0 = d0 + num2
        lea     result, a0
        jsr     putstr          ; display result message
        bsr     putn            ; display sum stored in d0
        jsr     stop

; Insert sub-programs putn and getn here.
        data
prompt1 dc.b  'Enter first number: ', 0
prompt2 dc.b  'Enter second number: ', 0
result  dc.b  'The sum is ', 0
        even
num1    ds.w  1
num2    ds.w  1

        end
```

We used memory variables `num1` and `num2` in the above program for illustration purposes, although we could have used registers to store the numbers.

Exercises

C.20 Write a program that reads characters from the keyboard and counts the number of characters entered. The program stops reading characters when the Return character (ASCII `13`) is entered. It should display the number of characters entered.

C.21 Write a program to sum the integers `1` to `99` and display the result using `putn`.

C.22 Write a program to read numbers and sum them. It should continue reading until `0` is entered. It should then display on a new line the sum of all numbers entered. The C version was presented in Chapter 1, Example 1.11.

C.23 Write a program to read in a list of numbers terminated by `0`, as in Exercise C.22, and display the largest number in the list.

C.7.2 *String I/O sub-programs:* `get_str` *and* `put_str`

In Chapter 3 we developed the two sub-programs `get_str` and `put_str` to read and display strings. We used indirect addressing to access the strings. We now present the M68000 versions of these sub-programs. In M68000 assembly language we use the notation `(a0)` to denote the value pointed to by register `a0`, that is, for indirect addressing. This allows us to indirectly access a memory variable using its address, in this case stored in `a0`. We can use any of the address registers for indirect addressing. We use the `lea` instruction to load the address of a string (or any memory variable) into an address register. We adopt the convention of using `a0` as the register for storing the address of the string to be manipulated by the `get_str` and `put_str` sub-programs in our M68000 programs. The M68000 versions closely resemble their 8086 counterparts.

Example C.26

Reading a string: `get_str`

```
get_str:                    ; read string terminated by CR into
                            ; array whose address is in a0

            move.l  d0, -(sp)   ; save d0

get_loop:   jsr     getchar     ; read character
            move.b  d0, (a0)    ; In C: str[i] = d0

            cmpi.b  #CR, d0     ; d0 == CR ?
            beq     get_fin     ; if d0 == CR goto get_fin

             adda.l #1, a0      ; In C, i = i+1

            bra.s   get_loop    ; repeat loop
get_fin:    move.b  #0, (a0)    ; terminate string with 0

            move.l  (sp)+, d0   ; restore d0

            rts
```

The get_str sub-program reads characters one at a time until the user enters Return. Assume the user enters the characters `'abc'` followed by Return. Initially, `a0` points to the first element in the array and we copy the first character entered, `'a'`, into this element. We then test if Return was entered and if not we increment `a0` and read the next character. We continue in this manner until Return is entered.

Note: We use special instructions to operate on address registers. The `adda` instruction is used to increment an address register, for example

```
adda.l #1, a0
```

We use the `suba` instruction to subtract from an address register, the `movea` instruction to move data into an address register and the `cmpa` instruction to compare address registers.

When we increment the address register, it points to the next element of the string. We continue reading characters and storing them in the string, incrementing the address register as we do so, until Return is entered. When Return is entered, it is also stored in the string, in this case in the fourth element of the string. However, when the loop terminates, the Null character is then stored as the fourth element of the array, overwriting the Return character. This terminates the string with Null, so that we can display it using put_str if we wish.

The sub-program behaves sensibly if the user enters Return as the first character. In this event, having stored the Return character in the first element of the array, we branch to get_fin where we store Null in the first element, thus overwriting the Return character. Thus an empty string is returned if the user enters Return as the first character, which is how this situation is handled by the C library function gets.

The put_str sub-program is implemented in a similar manner. It displays the string whose address is stored in a0.

Example C.27

Displaying a string: put_str:

```
put_str:                    ; display string terminated by 0
                            ; whose address is in a0

            move.l  d0, -(sp)   ; save d0

            move.b  (a0)+, d0   ; In C: str[i] = d0; i = i+1

put_loop:   tst.b   d0          ; d0 == 0 ?
            beq     put_fin     ; while d0 != 0
            jsr     putchar     ; display character in d0
            move.b  (a0)+, d0   ; In C: d0 = str[i], i = i + 1
            jmp put_loop        ; repeat loop test
put_fin:
            move.l  (sp)+, d0   ; restore d0
            rts
```

The instruction move.b (a0)+, d0 uses **post-increment** indirect addressing in the same fashion as popping an element from the stack. It copies the bytes pointed to by a0 in d0 and then increments a0 by 1. This could also be written using two instructions:

```
move.b   (a0), d0
adda.l   #1, a0
```

but the post-increment form is usually used. The put_str sub-program saves d0 on the stack and copies the first character of the string to d0. It then tests if d0 equals the Null character and if so, the sub-program restores d0 from the stack and terminates. Otherwise, it displays the character in d0, copies the next character into d0 and loops back to test if d0 is equal to Null. It continues in this fashion until the Null character at the end of the string is encountered. Note, if the first character of the string is Null, then put_str produces no output.

We can now write programs which read and display strings using our own string I/O sub-programs. As an example we implement the program to prompt a user to enter a colour, display a message followed by the colour entered by the user (the C version is presented in Chapter 1, Example 1.2 and the 8086 version is presented as Example 3.42 of Chapter 3).

Example C.28

Using get_str and put_str:

```
; colour.a:   Prompt for a colour, display a message
;             followed by the colour entered.
; Author:     Joe Carthy
; Date:       March 1994

              xref putchar, getchar, stop

CR            equ   13

start:
              lea   prompt, a0
              bsr   put_str       ; display prompt
              lea   colour, a0
              bsr   get_str       ; read colour
              lea   msg2, a0
              bsr   put_str       ; display msg2
              lea   colour, a0
              bsr   put_str       ; display colour entered
              jsr   stop

; <insert definitions of get_str and put_str here>
              data
prompt        dc.b  'Enter your favourite colour: ', 0
msg2          dc.b  CR, 'Yuk ! I
                    hate ', 0
colour        ds.b  80
              even
              end
```

This program produces as output:

```
Enter your favourite colour: yellow
Yuk ! I hate yellow
```

Exercises

C.24 Modify the guessing game program to use the put_str sub-program.

C.25 Write a program to read a string using `get_str` and count the number of characters in the string. The program should display the number of characters entered using `putn`.

C.26 Write a program to read a string and display a message indicating whether or not the string is a palindrome.

C.8 Bit manipulation

C.8.1 The logical instructions: `and, or, eor, not`

The M68000 `eor` operation is the equivalent of the 8086 `xor` instruction. The M68000 logical instructions operate in the same fashion as their 8086 equivalents and we illustrate their use in the following example.

Example C.29

Using the logical instructions.

```
                              ; lowercase to uppercase conversion
move.b   #'b', d0             ; d0 = 'b' (= 98 or $62)         01100010
and.b    #$0df, d0            ; mask =                         11011111
                              ; d0 now = 'B' (= 66 or $42)     01000010

                              ; uppercase to lowercase conversion
move.b   #'A', d0             ; d0 = 'A' =          0100 0001
or.b     #$20, d0             ; or d0 with          0010 0000
                              ; gives d0 = 'a':     0110 0001

move.b   #$67, d0             ; d0 =                0011 0111
eor.i    #$08, d0             ; eor it with         0100 0011
                              ; d0 is $34           0111 0100

move.b   #$33, d0             ; d0 =                00110011
not.b    d0                   ; d0 is               11001100
```

Exercises

C.27 Specify the instructions and masks you would use to
(a) set bits 2, 3 and 4 of the `d0` register
(b) clear bits 4 and 7 of the `d1` register

C.28 How would `d0` be affected by the following instructions?:
(a) `and.b #$00f, d0`
(b) `and.b #$0f0, d0`
(c) `or.b #$00f, d0`
(d) `or.b #$0f0, d0`

C.8.2 Testing bits: the `btst` *instruction*

We can test bits using the `and` instruction, as explained in Chapter 4, or we can use the `btst` instruction (similar to the 8086 `test` instruction).

Example C.30

Test if bit 1 of `d0` is clear, using `btst` instruction:

```
btst.l  #%00000010, d0   ; mask has bit 1 set
beq     bit1_clear       ; goto to bit1_clear if bit 1 = 0
                         ; if its 1 we end up here
```

Here `d0` remains unchanged after the `btst` instruction. You can only test a *single* bit with the `btst` instruction. If the destination operand is a register, then it *must* be treated as a **long word** operand. If it is a memory variable then it must be treated as a **byte** operand. The M68000 also provides single instructions to test and set, test and clear, and test and change single bits.

Exercises

C.29 Write instructions to test:
- (a) if bit `15` of `d2` is set;
- (b) if bit `7` of `d0` is clear;
- (c) if bits `2` and `4` of `d1` are clear;
- (d) if any of bits `1`, `2` and `3` of `d3` are set.

C.8.3 Shifting bits

The M68000 shift and rotate instructions operate in a similar fashion to their 8086 equivalents. With all the shift and rotate instructions, the destination operand contains the value to be manipulated and the source operand specifies the number of bits to shift or rotate. If the destination operand is a register, it may be treated as a byte-, word- or long-word-sized operand. The source operand may be a constant in the range 1 to 8 or a data register containing a value in the range 0 to 63. If the destination operand is a memory variable, then it is treated as a word-sized operand and the shift or rotate is by one bit only – no source operand is used.

The `asl` (arithmetic shift left) instruction is used to shift bits to the left. There is also a `lsl` (logical shift left) instruction, which has the same effect on the destination operand as the `asl` instruction.

Example C.31

Register `d0` containing `0000 0100 (4)` can be multiplied by `2` as follows:

```
move.b  #4, d0   ; d0 =                 0000 0100
asl.b   #1, d0   ; shift left 1 bit
                 ; d0 now contains      0000 1000
```

We use the `asr` (arithmetic shift right) instruction for right shifts if we wish to preserve the sign bit, otherwise we can use the logical shift right instruction `lsr`. It is obviously important to use the `asr` instruction when dealing with signed numbers.

Example C.32

Dividing `d0` (which contains 12) by 2 using the `asr` instruction:

```
move.b  #12, d0   ; d0 =                 0000 1100
asr.b   #1, d0    ; divide by 2
                  ; d0 now contains 6    0000 0110
```

Exercises:

C.30 Using bit shifts multiply d0 by 8 and d1 by 32.

C.31 Using bit shifts, divide d2 by 4 and d4 by 16.

C.8.4 Rotate instructions

The rol (rotate left) instruction rotates bits so that the left-most bit is initially moved into bit zero. The ror (rotate right) instruction rotates bits so that bit 0 is initially moved into the right-most position.

Example C.33

Use the ror instruction to swap the 4 high-order bits with the 4 low-order bits of d0 (treated as a byte-sized operand), that is, rotate d0 4 bits to the right (or to the left):

```
move.b  #%0010 1111, d0   ; d0 =             0110 1111
ror.b   #4, d0            ; d0 now contains 1111 0010
```

Displaying binary and hexadecimal numbers

We can illustrate the use of some of the bit manipulation instructions in developing sub-programs to display binary and hexadecimal numbers. The sub-program put_bin displays the contents of the d0 register as a 32-bit number. The sub-program put_hex displays the contents of d0 as an eight-digit hexadecimal number. We first present the put_bin sub-program, including it as part of a complete program which sets all the bits of d0 and displays d0 using put_bin. It then clears the low-order word of d0 using the and instruction with an appropriate mask and again displays d0 using put_bin.

Example C.34

The put_bin sub-program:

```
; putbin.a : Demonstrates the use of bit manipulation
;            instructions to display d0 as 32-bit binary
;            number

             xref getchar, putchar, putstr, stop

; main program

start:
             lea     s1, a0
```

```
            jsr      putstr
            move.l   #$0fffffff, d0 ; set all bits in d0.l
            bsr      put__bin       ; display d0 in
                                    ; binary
            lea      s2, a0         ; display after
                                    ; message
            jsr      putstr
            andi.l   #$0ffff0000, d0 ; clear 16 low-order
                                    ; bits

            bsr      put__bin       ; display d0 in
                                    ; binary
            jsr      stop           ; terminate program

; sub-programs

put__bin:                           ; Display d0 in
                                    ; binary
            movem.l d0-d2, -(sp)    ; save registers d1
                                    ; and d2
            move.l   d0, d1
            move.b   #31, d2        ; counter for loop
check:
            btst     #31, d1        ; test if bit 31 set
                                    ; is set in d1
            bne      display__1     ; if it's not set,
                                    ; display a 1

            move.b   #'0', d0       ; otherwise display
                                    ; a 0
            bra.s    rest
display__1:
            move.b   #'1', d0       ; display '1'

rest:       jsr      putchar        ; display bit
            lsl.l    #1, d1         ; shift d1 one bit to
                                    ; left
            dbra     d2, check      ; repeat for all 32
                                    ; bits

            movem.l (sp)+, d0-d2    ; restore registers
                                    ; d1 and d2

            rts

            data
s1          dc.b  13, 'd0 before ', 0
s2          dc.b  13, 'd0 after ', 0

  end
```

In this example, we use the btst instruction to test each bit of the d0 register. The d2 register contains the loop count, in this case 31, for the dbra instruction. (Remember, the dbra instruction terminates on -1, so we use a loop count of $n - 1$ for a loop to be repeated n times.) The sub-program loops so that the d1 register is shifted left one bit each time around the loop. We use the btst instruction to test the most significant bit, bit 31, and display a one or zero appropriately. (Remember bits are numbered from 0 to 31 in a long word.) Since d1 is then shifted left one bit, the original bit numbered 30 is moved to position 31 and is tested. This procedure is repeated so that all the bits get tested. We start at bit number 31, as we wish to display the bits in that order. This program is very useful for demonstrating the effects of the bit manipulation instructions.

Another method of testing each bit in d1 would be to use the d2 register in the btst instruction:

```
btst      d2, d1
```

Since d2 is initialized to 31, the first time around the loop, bit 31 would be tested. Each time around the loop d2 is decremented by the dbra instruction. So, on the second iteration bit number 30 would be tested, then bit number 29 and so on until bit 0 is tested and the loop terminates. The lsl instruction would not be required if we used this method of testing the bits in d1.

We now present the sub-program put_hex which displays the contents of d0 as an 8-digit hexadecimal number. It operates in the same fashion as putn, which displays a decimal number except it repeatedly divides the value to be displayed by 16 to generate the hexadecimal digits. The digits to be displayed are stored on the stack and after 8 digits have been generated they are popped from the stack and displayed. Because d0 is a 32-bit register, we know that we need to generate exactly 8 hexadecimal digits.

Example C.35

Sub-program put_hex: displays d0 in hexadecimal form:

```
put_hex:                           ; display d0 in
                                   ; hexadecimal
      movem.l d0-d4, -(sp)         ; save registers d1 and d2

      move.l  d0, d1
      move.l  #$00000000f, d3      ; mask to clear all but bits
                                   ; 0 to 3
      move.l  #7, d2               ; counter for loop

gethx:                             ; repeat 8 times: rotate
                                   ; left 4 bits
                                   ; and display digit
      rol.l   #4, d1               ; rotate left 4 bits
      move.l  d1, d4               ; save d1
      and.l   d3, d1               ; mask out bits 4 to 31
```

```
        cmpi.b  #10, d1          ; if (d1>10) display one of
                                 ; a to f
        bhs     displetter
        addi.b  #'0', d1         ; else convert to ASCII
                                 ; and display digit
        move.b  d1, d0
        jsr     putchar          ; display digit
        bra.s   next             ; process next digit
displetter:                      ; digit values 10-15 map
                                 ; onto a-f
                                 ; the digit value + 'a'-10
                                 ; gives the
                                 ; correct ASCII code
        addi.w  #87, d1
        move.b  d1, d0
        jsr     putchar          ; display the letter

next:
        move.l  d4, d1
        dbra    d2, gethx

        move.b  #'h', d0         ; display h for hex
        jsr     putchar

        movem.l (sp)+, d0-d4     ; restore registers
        rts
```

Values in the range 10 to 15 must be displayed as hexadecimal digits a to f. This is carried out by adding the constant 'a'-10 (87) to the digit value. For example, value 11 + 87 gives 98 which is the ASCII code for 'b', the hexadecimal digit for 11.

Example C.36

This example illustrates the use of put_bin and put_hex, to show the effects of the and instruction being used to clear the 16 low-order bits of d0.

```
; puthex.a :  Demonstrates the use of bit manipulation
;             instructions to display d0 as 32-bit number
;             and 8 digit hex number

    xref  getchar, putchar, putstr, stop

; main program

start:
        lea     s1, a0             ; display before message
        jsr     putstr
        move.l  #$0fffffff, d0     ; set all bits in d0
        bsr     put_bin            ; display d0 in binary
```

```
        bsr     put_tab           ; display a tab
        bsr     put_hex           ; display d0 in hex

        lea     s2, a0            ; display after message
        jsr     putstr

        andi.l  #$0ffff0000, d0   ; clear 16 low-order
                                  ; bits

        bsr     put_bin           ; display d0 in binary
        bsr     put_tab           ; display a tab
        bsr     put_hex           ; display d0 in hex

        jsr     stop              ; terminate program

; Insert put_bin and put_hex sub-programs inserted here

put_tab:                          ; display a tab
        move.l  d0, -(sp)
        move.b  #9, d0            ; ASCII code for tab is 9
        jsr     putchar
        move.l  (sp)+, d0
        rts

        data
s1      dc.b  13, 'd0 before ', 0
s2      dc.b  13, 'd0 after ', 0

  end
```

Executing this program produces as output:

```
d0 before: 11111111111111111111111111111111  ffffffffh
d0 after:  11111111111111110000000000000000  ffff0000h
```

C.9 Summary

In this appendix we have presented the basic features of M68000 assembly language programming. We described how character I/O can be carried out using MAS sub-programs and looked at the various unconditional and conditional branch instructions used in control structures such as loops. We then developed sub-programs for string and numeric I/O based on those presented in Chapter 2. Finally, we described the instructions provided for bit manipulation and gave some examples of their usage.

This concludes our introduction to M68000 assembly language programming. We have described the commonly used instructions and programming techniques used for the M68000 processor. You should now be in a position to write some useful M68000 assembly language programs.

C.10 Reading list

Bramer, B. and Bramer, S. (1991) *MC68000 Assembly Language Programming*, Edward Arnold, London.

Clements, A. (1992) *Microprocessor Systems Design, 68000 Hardware, Software and Interfacing*, PWS-Kent, Boston, MA.

Ford, W. and Topp, W. (1989) *Assembly Language and Systems Programming for the M68000 Family*, D.C. Heath., Lexington, MA. [The Macintosh Assembly System (MAS) is referenced in this text and further information is available from D.C. Heath and Company, Lexington, MA, or Toronto.]

Stenström, Per, (1992) *68000 Microcomputer Organization and Programming*, Prentice Hall, London.

Subbarao, W.V. (1991) *16/32-Bit Microprocessors: 68000/68010/68020, Software, Hardware and Design Applications*, Macmillan, New York.

Appendix D
Intel 8086 instruction encoding

Instruction encoding is quite complicated and in this appendix we take a very brief look at how some 8086 instructions are encoded. We can group 8086 instructions into those that take a single operand and those that take two operands. Each instruction is encoded using a particular bit pattern (encoding pattern).

D.1 Single operand instructions

These include `inc`, `dec`, `mul`, `div` and `not`. They all require a single operand. The operand may be a literal (immediate value), register or memory value, depending on the instruction. As an example, take the `inc` instruction – there are two ways to encode it in machine code. One is used when the operand is one of the 16-bit registers. In this case the instruction is encoded using 8 bits. The leftmost five bits are used to represent the `inc` instruction opcode, `01000`, when the operand is a 16-bit register. The register is specified by the rightmost three bits. This allows us to specify one of the eight registers `ax`, `cx`, `dx`, `bx`, `sp`, `bp`, `si` and `di`. The registers are represented by the numbers `0` to `7` where `ax` is represented by `0` and `di` by `7`. So an `inc` instruction, using a 16-bit register, is encoded as `01000 REG` where the bits `REG` represent the binary code of the 16-bit register. For example `inc cx` is encoded as `01000 001` (`41h`) since `cx` is represented by the number `001` (`1h`).

The other way of encoding the `inc` instruction is more general and occupies 16 bits. In this case, `inc` is encoded using a 10-bit opcode `1111 111 000`, which is split into two parts. The first seven bits of the opcode are stored in the first byte of the instruction and the remaining 3 bits of the opcode are stored in the second byte. The instruction can be represented as `1111 111w mm 000 r/m` where `w`, `mm` and `r/m` represent three additional fields. The `w` field specifies the width of the operand (`w=0` for an 8-bit operand and `w=1` for a 16-bit (word) operand). The 2-bit `mm` field is called the `mod` field and specifies whether the operand is in a register (`mm = 11`) or in memory (`mm != 11`). If the operand is in a register, then the `r/m` field specifies the register.

For example, the instruction `inc dh` is encoded as `1111111 0 11 000 110` where the opcode for `inc` is `1111 111 000`. Register `dh` is encoded as `110` and so `r/m` has the value `110`. The `mod` field has the value `11` to indicate a register operand and the `w` field has the value 0 to indicate an 8-bit operand.

If the operand is in memory, its 16-bit offset address follows the first 16 bits of the instruction. For example the instruction `inc memvar` is encoded as follows:

```
1111111 0 00 000 110   0000 0000 0000 0100
opcode  w mm     r/m<address of memvar>
```

where `memvar` is a byte variable (w=0) with an address of `0004H`. The combination of the `mod` field value of `00` and the `r/m` field value of `110` specifies that direct memory addressing is being used and that the 16-bit address of `memvar` forms the second 16 bits of the instruction.

D.2 Two-operand instructions

Instructions such as `mov`, `add`, `cmp` and `test` take two operands. The general format of a two-operand instruction, such as the `add` instruction (`add` has opcode `000000`), is given by:

```
000000 dw mm REG r/m
```

The `REG` field specifies a register. If there is only one register, the `d` field denotes whether the `REG` field specifies the source operand (`d=0`) or the destination operand (`d=1`). If there are two registers, the REG field specifies the destination operand and the `r/m` field specifies the source operand. For example, `add bl, dh` is encoded as:

```
000000  10  11  011  110
opcode  dw  mm  REG  r/m
```

where `bl` is encoded as `011` and `dh` is encoded as `110`. The value `0` in the `w` field indicates 8-bit operands and the `mod` field value of `11` indicates that the `r/m` field specifies a register code.

The instruction `add memvar, dx` is encoded as:

```
000000 01  00  010 110  0000 0000 0000 0010
opcode dw  mm  REG r/m   address of memvar
```

where the address of `memvar` is `0002h`. It is a word variable because the `w` field is `1`. The `d` field is `0`, indicating that the REG field specifies the source operand (`dx`). The combination of the `mod` value of `00` and the `r/m` value of `110` indicates that direct memory addressing is being used and that the next two bytes contain the offset address of the memory variable.

If an immediate operand is used in an instruction, it is encoded in the third and fourth bytes if there is a register operand, otherwise in the case of a memory operand, the immediate value is encoded in the two bytes following the memory operand.

Note that two-operand instructions have only one `w` field and so both operands must be the same size (either 8 or 16 bits for the 8086).

D.3 Reading list

Morneau, P. (1992) *PC Assembly Language: An Introduction to Computer Systems*, West Publishing Co., St. Paul, MN.

See also the other references in the Reading Lists in Chapters 2 and 5.

Appendix E
Selected solutions to exercises

In this appendix we present possible solutions to some of the exercises from Chapters 2, 3, 4, 6 and Appendix 3. For convenience, we repeat each question, before outlining the solution.

Exercise 2.1

Translate the following C code fragment to assembly language, (a) using C-like variables and (b) using registers to do the assignments:

```
int i, k ,d;
char c;
char colour[80];

i = 10 ;
k = i + 4;

c = '5';
d = c - '0'
```

Solution:

```
i        dw     ?
k
dw
?
d        dw     ?
c        db     ?
colour   db 80  dup(?)

mov  i, 10    ; i = 10
add  i, 4     ; i = i + 4
mov  ax, i    ; ax = i
mov  k, ax    ; .k = ax

mov  c, '5'
sub  c, '0'   ; c = c - '0'
mov  bx, c    ; bx = c
mov  d, bx    ; d = bx
```

Exercise 2.2

Write a code fragment to sum the sequence 2, 4, 6, 8, ..., 18, 20, 22, 24. The result should be stored in a variable called sum.

Solution:

```
          mov  sum, 0
          mov  cx, 2          ; loop counter
while1:   cmp  cx, 26
          je   finished
               add  sum, cx   ; sum = sum + cx
               add  cx, 2     ; cx = cx + 2
          jmp  while1
finished:                    ; sum now contains the result
```

Exercise 2.3

Translate the following C code fragment to assembly language. It tests if the variable c contains a digit in character form and converts it to its numeric form if it does. (It could be written more elegantly in C!)

```
if ( c < '0' )        /* c is not a digit */
   goto fin ;
if ( c > '9' )        /* c is not a digit */
   goto fin ;
d = c - '0' ;         /* c must be a digit
fin:
```

Solution:

```
cmp  c, '0'
jb   not_digit   ; if al < '0' then don't convert
cmp  c, '9'
ja   not_digit   ; if al > '9' then don't convert
                 ; otherwise it must be between 0 and 9
mov  al, c       ; copy c to al
sub  al, '0'     ; convert to character
mov  d, al       ; d = al
not_digit:
```

Exercise 2.7

Write a code fragment to count the number of occurrences of the letter 'e' in the string "Hello everyone" using (a) indirect addressing and (b) indexing to access the elements of the string. Show the definition of the string variable.

Solution (a): Indirect Addressing

```
message         db      'Hello everyone', 0
.......
........
          mov   bx, offset message       ; store address of
                                         ; message in bx
          mov   cx, 0                    ; set count to 0

start:
          cmp   byte ptr [bx], 0         ; is this end of
                                         ; string?
          je    fin                      ; if yes goto fin
                cmp byte ptr [bx], 'e'   ; is this character
                                         ; an 'e'
                jne   not_e              ; if not don't count
                                         ; it
                inc   cx                 ; count the 'e'
not_e:          inc   bx                 ; bx points to next
                                         ; character
          jmp start
                     ; cx now contains the number of 'e's in
                     ; message
fin:
```

Solution (b): Indexing

```
message         db    'Hello everyone', 0
.......
........
          mov   si, 0                    ; index of 1st
                                         ; character of
                                           message
          mov   cx, 0                    ; set count to 0
start:
          cmp   message[si], 0           ; is this end of
                                         ; string?
          je    fin                      ; if yes goto fin
                cmp message[si], 'e'     ; is this character
                                         ; an 'e'
                jne   not_e              ; if not don't count
                                         ; it
                inc   cx                 ; count the 'e'
not_e:          inc   si                 ; increment index to
                                         ; next element
          jmp start
                     ; cx now contains the number of 'e's in
                     ; message
fin:
```

Exercise 3.1

Write instructions to:	Solution
Load the character `'?'` into register `bx`	`mov bx, '?'`
Load the space character into register `cx`	`mov cx, ' '`
Load `26` (decimal) into register `ax`	`mov ax, 26`
Copy the contents of `ax` to `bx` and `dx`	`mov bx, ax` `mov dx, ax`

Exercise 3.2

What errors are present in the following instructions (solution follows each one):

```
mov  ax  3d     ; Comma missing after ax
mov  23,  ax    ; Destination operand must be register or variable
mov  cx, ch     ; Cannot move 8-bit register to 16-bit register
move ax, 1h     ; Spelling error – no e in mov
add  2, cx      ; Destination operand must be register or variable
add  3, 6       ; Destination operand must be register or variable
inc  ax, 2      ; Only one operand required by inc
```

Exercise 3.3

Write instructions to evaluate the arithmetic expression `5 + (6 - 2)` leaving the result in `ax` using (a) one register, (b) two registers and (c) three registers.

Solution:

```
(a)  mov ax, 6     (b)  mov ax, 6     (c)  mov ax, 6
     sub ax, 2          mov bx, 2          mov bx, 2
     add ax, 5          sub ax, bx         mov cx, 5
                        add ax, 5          sub ax, bx
                                           add ax, cx
```

Exercise 3.8

Write a program to display the message `'Ding! Ding! Ding!'` and output ASCII code `7D` three times. (ASCII code `7D` is the Bel character. It causes your machine to beep!)

Solution:

```
;ding.asm:   display message and ring bell 3 times
             .model small
             .stack 100h
             .data
message      db    'Ding! Ding! Ding!',7,7,7, 13, 10, '$'
             .code
start:
             mov      ax, @data
             mov      ds, ax
```

```
mov     dx, offset message
mov     ah, 9
int     21h
mov     ax, 4c00h
int     21h
end     start
```

Exercise 3.12

Write a program to convert a single digit number such as 5 to its character equivalent '5' and display the character.

Solution: Relevant code fragment:

```
mov    bl, 5
add    bl, 48   ; ASCII code of '0' is 48
mov    dl, bl   ; display '5' = 5 + 48 = 53
call   putc
```

Exercise 3.15

Write programs to test that, where a character is read from the keyboard, control is transferred to label `ok_here` if the character is:

(a) a valid <= lower-case letter (`'a'` <= character <= `'z'`)
(b) either an upper-case or lower-case letter (`'A'` <= character <= `'Z'` OR `'a'` <= character <= `'z'`)
(c) is not a lower-case letter (character < `'a'` OR character > `'z'`)

The programs should display appropriate messages to prompt for input and indicate whether the character satisfied the relevant test.
Solution: Relevant tests:

```
(a)           call    getc
              cmp     al, 'a'
              jb      not_ok       ; not lowercase
              cmp     al, 'z'
              ja      not_ok       ; not lowercase
ok_here:      .....
              ......
not_ok:

(b)           call    getc
              cmp     al, 'a'
              jb      test_upper   ; it might be
                                   ; uppercase
              cmp     al, 'z'
              ja      not_ok       ; not lowercase
              jmp     ok_here      ; lowercase

test_upper:   cmp     al, 'A'
```

```
                jb      not_ok          ; not uppercase
                cmp     al, 'Z'
                ja      not_ok          ; not uppercase
                                        ; otherwise its
                                        ; uppercase
ok_here:        .....
                ......
not_ok:

(c)             call    getc
                cmp     al, 'a'
                jb      ok_here         ; not lowercase
                cmp     al, 'z'
                ja      ok_here         ; not lowercase
not_ok:                                 ; its lowercase

ok_here:                                ; its not lowercase
```

Exercise 3.19

Modify the guessing game program, to loop until a correct guess is made.

```
; ex3_19.asm Exercise 3.19: Guessing game terminating
; only on a correct guess.

           .model small
           .stack 100h

CR         equ    13d
LF         equ    10d

           .data
prompt     db     CR, LF, "Guessing game: Enter a letter
                  (A to Z): $"
yes_msg    db     CR, LF, "You guessed correctly !! $"
no_msg     db     CR, LF, "Sorry incorrect guess, try
                  again ! $"

           .code
start:
           mov    ax, @data
           mov    ds, ax
loop1:     mov    ax, offset prompt
           call   puts                 ; prompt for input
guess:
           call   getc                 ; read character
           cmp    al, 'A'
           jne    is_not_an_a
           mov    ax, offset yes_msg   ; if correct guess
```

```
                call    puts                    ; display correct
                                                ; guess message
jmp finish
is_not_an_A:
                mov     ax, offset no_msg
                call    puts                    ; display wrong
                                                ; guess message
                jmp     guess                   ; try again!
finish:         mov     ax, 4c00h
                int     21h

;       <User defined subprograms go here>
                end     start
```

Exercise 3.22

Write a program to read numbers and sum them. It should continue reading until 0 is entered. It should then display on a new line the sum of all numbers entered. The C version was presented in Chapter 1, Example 1.11.

```
; ex3_22.asm: Exercise 3.22: Sum list of numbers
; terminated by 0 ; and display the result
                .model small
                . stack 256
CR              equ     13d
LF              equ     10d
                .data
prompt1         db      CR, LF, 'Enter a number: $'
response        db      CR, LF, 'The sum of the numbers is: $'
num             dw      ?

                .code
start:
                mov     ax, @data
                mov     ds, ax
                mov     bx, 0                   ; bx contains sum
                sum:
                mov     ax, offset prompt1
                call    puts
                call    getn
                mov     num, ax

                cmp     num, 0d
                je      finish
                add     bx, num
                jmp     sum

finish:         mov     ax, offset response
                call    puts
                mov     ax, bx
```

```
            call    putn

            mov     ax, 4c00h
            int     21h
;       <definitions of getn, putn, puts, getc, putc go here>
            end start
```

Exercise 4.1

Specify the instructions and masks you would use to (solution follows each one):

(a) set bits 2, 3 and 4 of the `ax` register `or ax, 001Ch`
(b) clear bits 4 and 7 of the `bx` register `and ax, 006Fh`

Exercise 4.2

How would `al` be affected by the following instructions (solution follows each one):

(a) `and al, 00fh` ; Clears bits 4, 5, 6 and 7
(b) `and al, 0f0h` ; Clears bits 0, 1, 2 and 3
(c) `or al, 00fh` ; Sets bits 0, 1, 2 and 3
(d) `or al, 0f0h` ; Sets bits 4, 5, 6 and 7

Exercise 4.4

Check a code fragment to transfer control to label `L`, using a conditional jump instruction combined with the `test` instruction (solution follows each one):

(a) if bit 15 of `ax` is set
```
test ax, 8000h
jnz  L
```
(b) if bit 7 of `al` is clear
```
test al, 80h
jz   L
```
(c) if bits 2 and 4 of `cx` are clear
```
test cx, 0014h
jz   L
```
(d) if any of bits 1, 2 and 3 of `bx` are set
```
test bx, 0Eh
jnz  L
```
(e) if bit 5 of `al` is set
```
test al, 10h
jnz  L
```
(f) if bit 5 of `bl` is clear
```
test bl, 10h
jz   L
```

Exercise 4.11

Rewrite `putc` to take its parameter from the stack and show how it would be called.

Solution:

```
putc:
        mov  bp, sp
```

```
        mov  dx, [bp+2]   ;copy character from stack to dl
        mov ah, 2h
        int 21h
       ret 2
```

To call putc

```
mov  al, 'x'
push  ax
call putc
```

Exercise 7.2

What would be the throughput and flow-through time of a pipeline, made up of five stages where the stages 1 to 5 take the following units of time to complete: 1, 2, 1, 3, 2?

Solution:

Flowthrough time: 9
Throughput: 3

Exercise 7.5

What is the average memory access time for a machine with a cache hit rate of 95%, where the cache access time is 10ns and the memory access time is 80ns?
Solution:

Average access time = (0.95 * 10) + (0.05 * 80) = 9.5 + 4 = 13.5 ns

Exercise C.1

Write instructions to (solution follows each one):

(a)	Load the character `'?'` into register `d0`	`move.b #'?', d0`
(b)	Load the space character into register `d1`	`move.b #' ', d1`
(c)	Load `26` (decimal) into register `d3`	`move.b #26, d3`
(d)	Copy the contents of `d0` to `d4` and `d5`	`move.l d0, d4` `move.l d0, d5`

Exercise C.2

What errors are present in the following instructions (solution follows each one):

```
move.l    d1, #3       ; destination cannot be a constant
move.b    #1000, d2    ; 1000 too big for a byte
mov.b     d3, d4       ; spelling, missing 'e'
addi.b    d0, #2       ; destination cannot be a constant
addi.b    #3, d4       ; missing comma
```

Exercise C.9

Write a program to read two characters and display them on separate lines:

```
ab
a
b
```

Solution:

```
        xref  getchar, putchar, stop
start:
        jsr     getchar  ; read 1st character
        move.w  d0, d1   ; save it in d1
        jsr     getchar  ; read 2nd character
        move.w  d0, d2   ; savc it in d2
        move.w  d1, d0   ; display 1st character
        jsr     putchar
        move.w  #13, d0  ; display newline
        jsr     putchar
        move.w  d2, d0   ; display 2nd character
        jsr     putchar
        jsr     stop     ; terminate program
        end
```

Exercise C.17

Modify the guessing game program to allow the user three guesses, terminating if any guess is correct.

Solution:

```
        xref putstr, getchar, stop
CR      equ     13
        code
start:
        move.b      #0, d1        ; number of
                                  ; attempts
begin:
        lea         prompt, a0
        jsr         putstr
        jsr         getchar       ; read character
        cmpi.b      #'a', d0      ; d0 = 'a' ?
        beq         correct       ; yes, goto correct
                                  ; else action
        lea         no_msg, a0
        jsr         putstr        ; display wrong
                                  ; message
        addi.b      #1, d1        ; count attempt
        cmpi.b      #3, d1        ; only 3 tries
                                  ; allowed
```

```
         beq      sorry
         jsr      getchar      ; read Return
                               ; character
         jmp      begin        ; try again

correct: lea      yes_msg, a0
         jsr      putstr       ; display correct
         jmp      finish

sorry:   lea      guess_3, a0
         jsr   putstr          ; display 3 guesses
                               ; message
finish:  jsr   stop            ; terminate program

         data
prompt   dc.b  CR, 'Guessing game: Enter a letter (a to
               z): ', 0
yes_msg  dc.b  CR, 'You guessed correctly !!', 0
no_msg   dc.b  CR, 'Sorry incorrect guess. Try again ',
               0
guess_3  dc.b  CR, 'Sorry only 3 guesses allowed', 0
         end
```

Note: When reading characters using the MAS environment, the Return character is left in the input buffer and it must be removed by reading it. In other words after reading in a user's guess, after which the user presses Return, we must arrange to read the Return. This is the purpose of the `jsr getchar` in bold print above. This is the same situation that we encountered with the `scanf()` function in Example 1.8 in Chapter 1.

Appendix F
Sample program disk

A PC floppy disk which accompanies this volume contains all the example programs presented in this text. It also includes sample solutions to a number of the exercises.

The programs are organized in three directories:

- C__PROGS, which contains all the C programs and solutions to selected C exercises.
- X86__PROG, which contains the 8086 programs and solutions to selected 8086 exercises.
- 680__PROG, which contains the 68000 programs and solutions to selected 68000 exercises.

F.1 Accessing C and 8086 programs

To access the files in the C__PROGS directory or the X86__PROGS directory the disk should be inserted into the disk drive A (or B). Then you change to the appropriate directory using the MS-DOS cd command:

```
      > cd a:\c__progs
or
      > cd a:\x86__progs
```

You may access the files on the floppy disk or alternatively you may wish to copy them to your hard disk. You may copy one or all of the programs to your hard drive using a command such as:

```
      A> copy *.* c:\asmprogs\*.*
```

This command copies all the programs from the floppy disk directory you selected earlier to a directory called c:\asmprogs which has been created **already** by an md command:

```
      > md c:\asmprogs
```

Finally, you use your C environment to access the C programs, or masm and link to assemble and link the 8086 programs.

F.2 Accessing 68000 programs

The `680__PROG` directory was created on an Apple Macintosh and copied to the disk using a Macintosh utility called PC Exchange. This folder can be accessed from a Macintosh using the Macintosh's Apple File Exchange software or a utility like PC Exchange.

The 68000 programs were developed using the MAS system which is referenced in Appendix C. To run one of them, you need to use the MAS system and open the appropriate project file (`.p` extension) using the `Open Project` option under the `Project` menu. You then use the `Run Project` option from the `Project` menu. You may be asked to locate one of the library files (for example, Maslib.io). These files are stored in a folder called `Library` in the MAS folder on your Macintosh.

Index